GENDER INEQUALITY

Feminist Theories and Politics

Third Edition

Judith Lorber

Brooklyn College and Graduate School, CUNY

Roxbury Publishing Company
Los Angeles, California

Library of Congress Cataloging-in-Publication Data

Lorber, Judith
Gender inequality : feminist theories and politics / Judith Lorber.—3rd ed.
  p. cm.
  Includes bibliographical references.
  ISBN 1-931719-52-7
  1. Sex discrimination against women. 2. Sex role. 3. Women—Social conditions.
    4. Equality. 5. Feminist theory. I. Title.

HQ1237.L67 2005
305.42'01—dc22

2004051098
CIP

Publisher: Claude Teweles
Managing Editor: Dawn VanDercreek
Production Editor: Nina M. Hickey
Copy Editor: Virginia Hoffman
Proofreader: Christy Graunke
Typography: Jeremiah Lenihan
Cover Design: Marnie Deacon Kenney

Printed on acid-free paper in the United States of America. This book meets the standards for recycling of the Environmental Protection Agency.

ISBN 1-931719-52-7

ROXBURY PUBLISHING COMPANY
P.O. Box 491044
Los Angeles, California 90049-9044
Voice: (310) 473-3312 • Fax: (310) 473-4490
Email: roxbury@roxbury.net
Website: www.roxbury.net

In Memory of Zina Segre
May 8, 1933–April 27, 1997

"Her wounds came from the
same source as her power."
—Adrienne Rich

Table of Contents

Preface

Is feminism dead, or has it gone mainstream? Are we into a third wave or still in the second wave? What did feminism accomplish in the past 40 years? What still needs to be done about persistent gender inequality?

Gender Inequality: Feminist Theories and Politics presents the variety of feminist theories developed to explain the sources of gender inequality, and how the various theories have diverged and converged in the second wave of feminism as a political movement. My intent is to describe feminism's significant contributions to redressing gender inequality in order to give credit for its enormous accomplishments in the last 40 years, to document ongoing political activism, and to indicate the work still to be done.

The Third Edition continues the main perspectives of the first two editions—laying out the sources of gender inequality, as seen by a variety of feminisms, and the politics to redress gender inequality. For the older feminisms, this edition separates marxist and socialist feminisms to show their different development and contributions to feminist theory and activism. It also discusses the influence of the earlier theories on current feminist research and politics; therefore, in many of the sections I have paired a classic with a contemporary version of the feminism.

Along with the focus on the continuities in theory and politics of the earlier second-wave feminisms, this edition expands the discussion of recent developments in the later second-wave feminisms, particularly those that have led into what is now being called *third-wave feminism*. Multicultural feminism, feminist studies of men, social construction feminism, and post-modern feminism are sometimes included under the rubric of "third wave." Because third-wave feminists see their movement as different from the second wave, I have included a separate section on third-wave feminism. The book ends with a consideration of whether we need a new conceptualization of gender inequality, and new guidelines for feminist research and politics.

In the Second Edition, I added a section on feminist body politics. The biology-versus-culture controversy was, in fact, the starting point of

ix

the current feminist movement, with feminists arguing that women (and men) as social beings are not born, but made. Today, the debate is much more complicated. Biology has become a shorthand term for genes, hormones, the body, the brain, and long-standing evolutionary adaptation. Culture is more than childhood learning and adult reinforcement. It involves the constant production and maintenance of the attributes, attitudes, emotions, and behavior patterns that a society associates with and deems appropriate for boys and girls, women and men. Biology and culture are conceptualized today by most feminists not as antithetical, but as reciprocal elements in individual development and in social patterns—intertwining and looping back on each other.

The burgeoning research and theoretical developments in gender and the body are so significant and varied that I have taken them out of this book and put them into a separate text with readings—*Gendered Bodies: Feminist Perspectives from Birth to Death,* to be published by Roxbury in 2006 and co-edited with Lisa Jean Moore.

Some sections of this text have been adapted from my books *Paradoxes of Gender* (New Haven, CT: Yale University Press, 1994), and *Breaking the Bowls: Degendering and Feminist Change* (New York: W. W. Norton, 2005).

I have given presentations from the First and Second Editions throughout the United States and in Israel and Germany. The input I received from students and faculty at all these presentations was enormously helpful in shaping this edition, as were the comments by the reviewers of the book manuscripts. Throughout, the discussions and critiques of Maren Carden, Carolle Charles, Susan Farrell, Eileen Moran, and Barbara Katz Rothman—my multi-feminist writing group—have made my thinking clearer. I particularly thank Susan Farrell for her information on women ethicists and feminist religions.

I also thank Claude Teweles for getting me started on this book, Carla Max-Ryan for her work and patience during the writing and production of the First Edition, and Phong Ho and Nina M. Hickey for their work on this edition.

—*Judith Lorber*
New York City

Part I

The Variety of Feminisms and Their Contributions to Gender Equality

Feminism is a social movement whose basic goal is equality between women and men. In many times and places in the past, people have insisted that women and men have similar capabilities and have tried to better the social position of all women, as well as the positions of disadvantaged men. As an organized movement, however, feminism rose in the nineteenth century in Europe and America in response to the great inequalities between the legal statuses of women and men citizens of Western industrialized countries.

A Brief History of Organized Feminism

The *first-wave* feminists of the nineteenth and early twentieth centuries fought for rights we take for granted today. It is hard to believe these rights were among those once denied to women of every social class, racial category, ethnicity, and religion—the right to vote (suffrage), to own property and capital, to inherit, to keep money earned, to go to college, to become a professionally certified physician, to argue cases in court, and to serve on a jury.

The theory of equality that feminists of the nineteenth century used in their fight for women's rights came out of liberal political philosophy, which said that all men should be equal under the law, that no one should have special privileges or rights. Of course, when the United States of America was founded, that concept of equality excluded enslaved men and indentured menservants because they were not free citizens, as well as all women, no matter what their social status, because they were not really free either. Their legal status was the same as that of children—economically dependent and borrowing their social status from their father or husband. In Ibsen's famous play *A Doll's House,* Nora forged her dead father's signature because she could not legally sign her own name to the loan she needed to save her sick husband's life.

First-wave feminism's goal was to get equal legal rights for women, especially the vote, or suffrage. (Feminists were often called *suffragists.*) In the United States, women did not get the right to vote until 1919. Many European countries also gave women the right to vote after World War I, in repayment for their war efforts. French women, however, did not get suffrage until after World War II, when a grateful Charles de Gaulle enfranchised them for their work in the underground fight against the Nazis and the collaborationist government of occupied France.

The Russian revolution of the early twentieth century gave women equal rights, even though the Bolsheviks criticized the individualism of "bourgeois feminism." Their emphasis was on work in the collective economy, with prenatal care and child care provided by the state so women could be both workers and mothers.

Suffrage was the main goal of women's liberation in the first wave of feminism in Western countries, but rights concerning property, earnings, and higher education—many of which were granted by the end of the nineteenth century—gave women a chance for economic independence. These rights were vital for raising married women's status from childlike dependence on a husband and for giving widows and single women some way of living on their own instead of as a poor relation in their father's or brother's or son's household. Liberated women in the first part of the twentieth century included independent factory girls who worked all day and went dancing at night, and middle- and upper-class educated women who had "Boston marriages" (were housemates for life).

There was another branch of nineteenth-century feminism that did not focus on equal rights but on a woman's right to "own" her body and to plan her pregnancies. A twentieth-century feminist struggle that was as hard fought in Western countries as that for suffrage was the fight for legal means of contraception that could be controlled by the woman. Women could not be free to be good mothers and wives, especially if they were poor, if they had one child after another. But doctors were forbidden to fit women with diaphragms or cervical caps (the precursors of the coil and the pill). In the United States, even mailing information across state lines was illegal. The widespread use of contraception by married women was feared by traditionalists, who saw the downfall of the family. Feminists feared that men would sexually exploit unmarried women who were protected against pregnancy. For women themselves, the positive outcome of this long battle for legalized woman-controlled contraception has been both greater sexual freedom before marriage and planned parenthood after marriage.

As is evident from this brief overview, the first-wave feminist movement had many of the theoretical and political differences of the feminist movement that succeeded it. The question of differences between women and men, and whether they should be treated *equally* because they are essentially the same or *equitably* because they are essentially different, is still under debate. The question of where feminist politics should put the most effort—the public sphere (work and government) or the private sphere (family and sexuality)—is also still with us.

Feminism's Second Wave

The current feminist movement is called the *second wave*. A post-World War II movement, it began with the publication in France in 1949 of Simone de Beauvoir's *The Second Sex*. This sweeping account of the historical and current status of women in the Western World argues that men set the standards and values and that women are the Other, those who lack the qualities the dominants exhibit. Men are the actors, women the reactors. Men thus are the first sex, women always the second sex. Men's dominance and women's subordination is not a biological phenomenon, de Beauvoir insisted, but a social creation:

> One is not born, but rather becomes, a woman. . . ; it is civilization as a whole that produces this creature . . . which is described as feminine. (1953, 267)

Although *The Second Sex* was widely read, the second wave of feminism did not take shape as an organized political movement until the 1960s, when young people were publicly criticizing many aspects of Western society. In the years since, feminism has made many contributions to social change by focusing attention on the continued ways women are more socially disadvantaged than men, by analyzing the sexual oppressions women suffer, and by proposing interpersonal as well as political and legal solutions. However, the feminist view of what makes women and men unequal is less unified today than in first-wave feminism, and there is a myriad of feminist solutions to gender inequality. If feminist voices seem to be much more fragmented than they were in the nineteenth century, it is the result of a deeper understanding of the sources of gender inequality. It is also the contradictory effect of uneven success. Feminists who are now members of corporations, academia, or government, who are lawyers or doctors or respected artists and writers, are well aware of the limitations of their positions, given glass ceilings and sexual harassment. But their viewpoint is different from that of the more radical antiestablishment feminist critics, who decry institutionalized sexual oppression and pervasive devaluation of women.

Although much of the feminist movement of the twentieth century has happened in industrialized countries, there have also been vital and important struggles for resources for girls and women in African and South and Central American countries. As countries of Africa, Asia, and Central and South America broke free of colonial control after World War II and set up independent governments, they, too, gave their women citizens the right to vote. Thanks to strong women's movements, many of the new states wrote equal rights for women into their constitutions, and some even mandated guaranteed political representation. Rwanda, a new democracy, in 2004 had 48.8 percent women in the lower house and 30 percent in the upper house. In contrast, the United States had 60 women (14.5 percent) in the House of Representatives and 14 women (out of 100) in the Senate.

At the other end of the political scale, in some Muslim countries, women still cannot vote, leave the country without their husband's permission, or get licenses to drive cars. In the Middle East, women and men have struggled to reconcile the rights of women with the traditional precepts of Islam and Judaism. In Asia, the problems of poverty and overpopulation, even though they more often adversely affect women and girls, need remedies that affect everyone. Women's political movements in these countries may not be called "feminist," but they are gender-based battles nevertheless.

Further from the mainstream are feminisms that challenge "what everyone knows" about sex, sexuality, and gender—the duality and oppositeness of female and male, homosexual and heterosexual, women and men. They argue that there are many sexes, sexualities, and genders, and many ways to express masculinity and femininity. Some of these feminist theories are now being called the feminist *third wave.* If these ideas seem farfetched or outlandish, remember that at the beginning of the second wave, when feminists used "he or she" for the generic "he," "Ms." instead of "Miss" or "Mrs.," and "full-time worker in the home" for "housewife," they were called radical troublemakers. Social change does not come without confrontation, and it is important to know what feminists who are not heard in the mass media are saying about gender inequality and how it can be eradicated.

Gender Inequality

The goal of feminism as a political movement is to make women and men more equal, legally, socially, and culturally. *Gender inequality* takes many different forms, depending on the economic structure and social organization of a particular society and on the culture of any particular group within that society. Although we speak of *gender* inequality, it is usually women who are disadvantaged relative to similarly situated men.

Women often receive lower pay for the same or comparable work, and they are frequently blocked in their chances for advancement, especially to top positions. There is usually an imbalance in the amount of housework and child care a wife does compared to her husband, even when both spend the same amount of time in paid work outside the home. When women professionals are matched with men of comparable productiveness, men still get greater recognition for their work and move up career ladders faster. On an overall basis, gender inequality means that work most often done by women, such as teaching small children and nursing, is paid less than work most often done by men, such as construction and mining.

Gender inequality can also take the form of girls getting less education than boys of the same social class. Nearly two-thirds of the world's illiterates are women, but in Western societies, the gender gap in education is closing at all levels of schooling. In many countries, men get priority over women in the distribution of health care services. Contraceptive use has risen in industrial countries, but in developing countries, complications in childbirth are still a leading cause of death for young women. AIDS takes an even more terrible toll on women than men globally, since women's risk of becoming infected with HIV during unprotected sex is two to four times higher than in men. In May 2004, the World Health Organization reported that by the end of 2003 about 40 million people were living with HIV/AIDS, and that more than half were women. Sexual politics influence the transmission of HIV/AIDS. Many women with HIV/AIDS have been infected through early sexual exploitation, or by husbands who have multiple sexual partners but who refuse to use condoms.

Sexual exploitation and violence against women are also part of gender inequality in many other ways. In wars and national uprisings, women of one racial ethnic group are often raped by the men of the opposing racial ethnic group as a deliberate weapon of shaming and humiliation. Domestically, women are vulnerable to beatings, rape, and murder—often by their husbands or boyfriends, and especially when they try to leave an abusive relationship. The bodies of girls and women are used in sex work—pornography and prostitution. They are on display in movies, television, and advertising in Western cultures. In some African and Middle Eastern cultures their genitals are ritually cut and their bodies are covered from head to toe in the name of chastity. They may be forced to bear children they do not want or to have abortions or be sterilized against their will. In some countries with overpopulation, infant girls are much more often abandoned in orphanages than infant boys. In other countries, if the sex of the fetus can be determined, it is girls who are aborted.

Gender inequality can also disadvantage men. In many countries, only men serve in the armed forces, and in most countries, only men

are sent into direct combat. It is mostly men who do the more dangerous work, such as firefighting and policing. Although women have
fought in wars and are entering police forces and fire departments, the
gender arrangements of most societies assume that women will do the
work of bearing and caring for children while men will do the work of
protecting and supporting them economically.

This gendered division of labor is rooted in the survival of small
groups living at subsistence level, where babies are breastfed and food is
obtained for older children and adults by foraging and hunting. The
child-carers (mostly women) gathered fruits and vegetables and hunted
small animals, while babies were carried in slings and older children
were helpers. Those not caring for children (mostly men, but also
unmarried women) could travel farther in tracking large animals—more
dangerous work. Hunters who came back with meat and hides were
highly praised, but if the hunt was unsuccessful, they still had something
to eat when they returned to the home camp, thanks to the child-mind-
ers' more reliable foraging.

Most women in industrial and postindustrial societies do not spend
their lives having and caring for babies, and most women throughout
the world do paid and unpaid work to supply their families with food,
clothing, and shelter, even while they are taking care of children. The
modern forms of gender inequality are not a complementary exchange
of responsibilities but an elaborate system within which, it was esti-
mated by a United Nations report in 1980, women do two-thirds of
the world's work, receive 10 percent of the world's income, and own 1
percent of the world's property. The gender gap in paid work is nar-
rowing, but women still do most of the domestic work and child care,
and at the same time do agricultural labor, run small businesses, and do
a great deal of home-based paid work, all of which is low-waged labor.

The major social and cultural institutions support this system of gender inequality. Religions legitimate the social arrangements that produce
inequality, justifying them as right and proper. Laws support the status
quo and also often make it impossible to redress the outcomes—to prose-
cute husbands for beating their wives, or boyfriends for raping their girl-
friends. In the arts, women's productions are so often ignored that they are
virtually invisible, leading Virginia Woolf to conclude that Anonymous
must have been a woman. Sciences have been accused of asking biased

questions and ignoring findings that do not support conventional beliefs about sex differences.

Except for the Scandinavian countries, which have the greatest participation of women in government and the most gender-equal laws and state policies, most governments are run by socially dominant men, and their policies reflect their interests. In every period of change, including those of revolutionary upheaval, men's interests, not women's, have prevailed, and many men, but few women, have benefited from progressive social policies. Equality and justice for all usually means for men only. Women have never had their revolution because the structure of gender as a social institution has never been seriously challenged. Therefore, all men benefit from the "patriarchal dividend"—women's unpaid work maintaining homes and bringing up children; women's low-paid work servicing hospitals, schools, and myriad other workplaces; and women's emotional nurturing and caretaking.

The main point recent feminisms have stressed about gender inequality is that it is not an individual matter, but is deeply ingrained in the structure of societies. Gender inequality is built into the organization of marriage and families, work and the economy, politics, religions, the arts and other cultural productions, and the very language we speak. Making women and men equal, therefore, necessitates social and not individual solutions. These solutions have been framed as feminist politics. They emerge from feminist theories about what produces gender inequality.

Feminist Theories

The foregoing portrait of a gender-unequal world is a summation of the work of generations of feminist researchers and scholars. Feminist theories were developed to explain the reasons for this pervasive gender inequality. Feminists are not satisfied with the explanation that it is natural, God-given, or necessary because women get pregnant and give birth and men do not. With deeper probing into the pervasiveness of gender inequality, feminists have produced more complex views about gender, sex, and sexuality. Although there is considerable overlap among them, it is useful to separate the concepts of gender, sex, and sexuality in order to illustrate how gendering modifies bodies and sexual behavior. This book uses the following definitions and vocabulary:

Gender: a social status, a legal designation, and a personal identity. Through the social processes of gendering, gender divisions and their accompanying norms and role expectations are built into the major social institutions of society, such as the economy, the family, the state, culture, religion, and the law—the gendered social order. *Woman* and *man* are used when referring to gender.

Sex: a complex interplay of genes, hormones, environment, and behavior, with loop-back effects between bodies and society. *Male, female,* and *intersex* are used when referring to sex.

Sexuality: lustful desire, emotional involvement, and fantasy, as enacted in a variety of long- and short-term intimate relationships. *Homosexuality, heterosexuality,* and *bisexuality* are used when referring to sexuality.

Recent feminist theories have analyzed the complex interplay of sex, sexuality, and gender. These theories speak of genders, sexes, and sexualities. The two "opposites" in each case—women and men, female and male, homosexual and heterosexual—have become multiple. Since recent research has shown that female and male physiology is produced and maintained by both female and male hormones, the new theories argue that sex is more of a continuum than a sharp dichotomy. Similarly, studies of sexual orientation have shown that neither homosexuality nor heterosexuality is always fixed for life, and that bisexuality, in feelings and in sexual relationships, is widespread.

The phenomenon of *transgendering* further complicates the interplay of sex, sexuality, and gender. Transgendering includes *transvestism*—living in a gender that is different from that assigned at birth but not surgically altering the body—and *transsexuality*—surgical and hormonal transformation of bodies to change genders. The goal of many transgendered people is to "pass" as a "normal" gendered person, a goal that is necessary for solving problems of daily life, but not one that disrupts the gendered social order. Radical gender-benders, who sometimes call themselves "queers," do not claim identity with men or women, heterosexuals or homosexuals. Queers openly subvert binary gender and sexual categories through their deliberate mixtures of clothing, makeup, jewelry, hair styles, behavior, names, and use of language. By not constructing gender and sexuality in expected ways, they make visible, in Judith Butler's term, the *performativity* on which the whole gender order depends. They parody and play with gender, transgressing gender norms, expectations, and behavior.

Many feminist social scientists now prefer to speak of genders, since men's and women's social statuses, personal identities, and life chances are intricately tied up with their racial, ethnic, and religious groups, their social class, their family background, and their place of residence. Nonetheless, these widely differing groups of people have to fit into two and only two socially recognized genders in Western societies—"men" and "women." The members of these two major status categories are supposed to be different from each other, and the members of the same category are supposed to have essential similarities. Work and family roles, as well as practically all other aspects of social life, are built on these two major divisions of people. This gendering produces the *gendered social order.* Gender inequality is built into the structure of the gendered social order because the two statuses—women and men—are treated differently and have significantly different life chances. How and why these social processes have come about and continue to operate is the subject of feminist theories. What to do about them is the aim of feminist politics.

Feminist Politics

Feminist politics does not refer only to the arena of government or the law; it can be confrontational protests, such as Take Back the Night marches, or work through organizations with a broad base, such as the National Organization of Women (NOW) and the National Organization for Men Against Sexism (NOMAS). It can be service centers, such as battered women's shelters, and service activities, such as gender-sensitivity and antirape sessions for college men.

Neighborhood or grassroots feminist activism tends to be woman-focused and concerned with local problems, while transnational non-governmental organizations (NGOs) and national and international governing bodies and agencies are loci for diversity-based political action. Some feminists have despaired as women's movements break up over racial ethnic, religious, and national identity politics. The "borderlands" view offers the possibility of new perspectives and new politics based on panethnic, cross-racial, and transgendered affiliations and coalitions.

Changing language and media presentations to remove sexist put-downs that denigrate men as well as women is also feminist politics. Other remedies for redressing gender inequality, such as creating culture and knowledge from a woman's point of view, may not look political, but to feminists, they are deeply political because their intent is to change the way people look at the world.

Feminism and the Gendered Social Order

Second-wave feminism's major theoretical accomplishment has been to make visible the structure, practices, and inequities of the gendered social order. It took gender beyond individual attributes and identities and showed that gender, like social class and racial categories, is imposed on rather than developed from individuals. Gendering divides the social world into two complementary but unequal sets of people—"women" and "men." This binary division confers a legal, social, and personal status that overrides individual differences and intertwines with other major social statuses—racial categorization, ethnic grouping, economic class, age, religion, and sexual orientation. Although we act out gender norms and expectations constantly in our interactions with others, gender's thrust is *structural* in that it orders the processes and practices of a society's major sectors—work, family, politics, law, education, medicine, the military, religions, and culture. Gender is a system of power in that it privileges some groups of people and disadvantages others in conjunction with other systems of power (racial categories, ethnicity, social class, and sexual orientation).

Gender operates at one and the same time to give individuals status and identities and to shape their everyday behavior, and also as a significant factor in face-to-face relationships and organizational practices. Each level supports and maintains the others, but—and this is the crucial aspect of gender—the effects of gender work from the top down. Gendered norms and expectations pattern the practices of people in workplaces, in families, groups, and intimate relationships, and in creating individual identities and self-assessments. Peoples' gender conformity supports gendered practices; peoples' gender diversity and deviance challenge it.

The gendered social order, however, is very resistant to individual challenge. Its power is such that people act in gendered ways based on their position within the gender structure without reflection or question. We "do gender" and participate in its construction once we have learned to take our place as a member of a gendered social order. Our gendered practices construct and maintain the gendered social order. Our practices also change it. As the social order changes, and as we participate in different social institutions and organizations throughout our lives, our gendered behavior changes.

Politically, the major types of feminism have confronted the gendered social order differently.

- **Gender reform feminisms** (liberal, marxist, socialist, postcolonial)—want to purge the gendered social order of practices that discriminate against women.
- **Gender resistance feminisms** (radical, lesbian, psychoanalytic, standpoint)—want women's voices and perspectives to reshape the gendered social order.
- **Gender rebellion feminisms** (multicultural, feminist studies of men, social construction, postmodern, third-wave)—want to take apart the gendered social order by multiplying genders or doing away with them entirely.

Types of Feminisms

In this book, current feminisms are categorized according to their *theory* or *theories of gender inequality*—what they consider the main reason for women having a lesser social status and fewer advantages than men of similar education, class background, religion, racial category, and ethnic group. From these theories follow the feminism's proposed solutions or remedies—its *politics*.

Gender reform feminisms have made visible the pervasiveness of discriminatory practices, both formal and informal, in the work world and in the distribution of economic resources and family responsibilities. The

1960s and 1970s brought dissatisfaction with conventional ideas about women and men, their bodies, sexualities, psyches, and behavior. The beliefs prevalent at that time about women and men tended to stress differences between them and to denigrate women in comparison with men, who were seen as stronger, smarter, and generally more capable than women—except for taking care of children. Mothering was women's strength and responsibility, and so women were seen as mothers before, during, and after they were anything else. The extent of the work women did—in the family, in kinship networks, as volunteers and as "off-the-books" workers, and in family enterprises—was virtually invisible and uncounted in national economic statistics.

Gender reform feminists locate the source of gender inequality in women's and men's status in the social order, arguing that it is structural and not the outcome of personal attributes, individual choices, or unequal interpersonal relationships. The structural sources are women's relegation to low-paid work and a devaluation of the work women do, overwhelming responsibilities for child care and home maintenance, and unequal access to education, health care, and political power. These inequalities, reform feminists argue, are built into national and international social structures, and so have to be redressed structurally. An overall strategy for political action to reform the unequal gendered social structure is *gender balance.* The goal of gender balance is to attain equality or parity in numbers of women and men throughout society, in their domestic responsibilities, and in their access to work and business opportunities, positions of authority, political power, education, and health care. Affirmative action in workplaces and universities and mandated quotas to increase the number of women in government are common gender-balancing policies.

Gender reform feminisms want women to be valued as much as men and to be free to live their lives according to their *human* potential. People should be able to work, parent, produce culture and science, govern, and otherwise engage in social life as they choose, whether they are women or men. Gender balance helps to achieve the goal of equal participation of women and men in all walks of life and equal recognition and reward for the work they do.

Gender resistance feminisms identified more oppressive sources of gender inequality in the exploitation of women's bodies, sexuality, and emotions. They argue that this exploitation and women's intellectual and cultural productions are repressed by a "phallocentric" or male-centered Western culture. Women's "voices"—their perspectives, their knowledge, and their view of the world around them—are unheard. The emphasis on listening to women's voices is known as *standpoint theory.*

Gender resistance feminists claim that the gender order cannot be made equal through gender balance because men's dominance is too strong. Gender equality, they argue, ends up with women becoming like men, rather than bringing a new perspective to bear on the problems of the world—a perspective based on women's experience. By examining the gender order from the standpoint of women, they make visible the hidden relationships among organizations, institutions, and daily practices that allow men to control women's lives. They call it *patriarchy,* a concept referring to men's family domination introduced by marxist feminism and expanded by radical feminism to encompass the entire gender order.

In the 1970s and 1980s, gender resistance feminisms developed an important theoretical insight—the power of *gender ideology,* the values and beliefs that justify the gendered social order. Gender resistance feminisms argue that gender inequality has been legitimated by major religions that say men's dominance is a reflection of God's will, by sciences that claim that dominance is a result of genetic or hormonal differences, and by legal systems that deny women full citizenship status. The mass media, sports, and pornography encourage the excesses of men's power—violence, rape, and sexual exploitation.

Some feminists feel that men's oppression of women is so universal that the best way to resist is to form a woman-centered society and create a woman-oriented culture, ethics, and even religion. This strategy is called *cultural feminism.* It is not really a separate feminism but a trend within radical and lesbian feminism. Other gender resistance feminists say that the systemic violence against women and exploitation of women's sexuality needs continued political engagement with the larger society, at the same time as woman-only spaces are created for refuge and recreation. All the gender resistance feminisms stress the importance of countering the negative evaluations of women by valorizing their nurturance, emotional supportiveness, and mothering capacities, by encouraging pride in women's bodies, and by teaching women how to protect themselves against sexual violence.

The gender-resistant feminists focus on *standpoint*—the view of the world from where you are located physically, mentally, emotionally, and socially—is a major theoretical contribution and springboard for action. Although women's voices were the original source of standpoint theory, the concept has been successfully used by women and men of diverse classes, racial ethnic groups, nations, and cultures.

Gender rebellion feminisms trace the connections among gender, racial category, ethnicity, religion, social class, and sexual orientation to show how people become advantaged or disadvantaged in complex stratification systems. The gendered social order, they argue, sets men against men as well as men against women. Men and women of the same racial and ethnic group or in the same economic stratum have much in common with each other, more than men may have with men or women with women in other groups. Sexual orientation also divides groups of women and men, with gay men and lesbian women splitting off and forming their own communities. But gays and lesbians together also form homosexual-rights coalitions and work together in AIDS service organizations.

Feminist studies of men bring a critical men's perspective to feminism. Women feminists have written about men and masculinity, both in relationship to women and separately; studies of men by feminist men adds an additional dimension. These studies follow in the footsteps of working-class social research and politics, and expand their political arena to include gay men. In conjunction with the radical feminist fight against rape and pornography, feminist men have gone directly to men in college workshops, seminars, and conferences to make them aware of how their behavior can be so harmful to women. Their condemnation of the price paid for the rewards of professional sports and the physical and sexual violence they foster is another part of feminist men's political agenda.

Gender rebellion feminisms attack the gender order directly by multiplying gender categories and undermining the boundaries between women and men, female and male, heterosexual and homosexual. Since the 1980s, feminist *deconstruction* of the categories of sex, sexuality, and gender has shown how their taken-for-grantedness maintains the gender order. By questioning the dualities of male and female, heterosexual and homosexual, masculine and feminine, man and woman, gender rebellion feminisms undermine the legitimacy of favoring one group over its opposite. Thus, according to gender rebellion feminism, both personal identities and the identity politics of groups are constantly shifting. There is room in life for individual and social change, for new kinds of relationships, and for new ways of organizing work and family.

Continuities in Second-Wave Feminism

Gender reform feminisms laid the theoretical groundwork for second-wave feminism by making visible the structural underpinnings of the gendered social order. Their politics of gender balance are practical and perhaps the best way to redress gender inequality at the present time. The fight for equal legal status and political representation for women and men, and for autonomy for women in making procreative, sexual, and marital choices, still has not been won in most countries of the world. Gender segregation in the workplace and lower pay for women's work is pervasive in all kinds of economies. The global economy exploits poor women and men as cheap labor, and economic restructuring in industrializing and postindustrial economies has reduced social-service benefits to mothers and children. These economic problems are another arena for feminist gender politics.

Although the politics of gender reform feminisms spill over into the politics for every disadvantaged person, the battles of gender resistance feminisms are for women alone. Fighting to protect women's bodies against unwanted pregnancies and sterilizations, abortions of female fetuses, genital mutilation, rape, beatings, and murder has been an enormous and never-ending struggle. The sexual integrity of women and girls needs protection from forced prostitution, exploitative sex work in pornographic productions and nightclubs, and loveless marriages. Both lesbians and gay men need to be able to live free of discrimination and violent attacks, but many lesbian women also want their own physical space and cultural communities, where they can live free of sexual harassment and men's domination, nourish their loves and friendships, and produce books, music, art, and drama that reflect their different ways of thinking and feeling. Standpoint feminists argue that women's experiences and distinctive outlooks on life have to be included in the production of knowledge, especially in science and social science research. It is not enough to just add women subjects to research designs; questions have to be asked from a critical feminist perspective, data have to include women's voices, and analysis has to reflect the points of view of those who have been marginalized and silenced.

Picking up on the importance of social position and distinctive standpoints, gender rebellion feminisms exploded the categories of women and men into all sorts of multiples. Multicultural, multiracial, and multiethnic feminisms are part of a powerful political movement to redress past and present legal and social discrimination of disadvantaged groups in so many societies, and to preserve their cultures.

Feminist studies of men have analyzed the racial ethnic and social class aspects of masculinity and the interplay of power and privilege, powerlessness and violence. They have described the hierarchies of men in a society and the ways that less advantaged men retain patriarchal control over women in their status group.

Social construction, postmodern, and third-wave feminisms have just begun to translate their destabilization of the gender order into politics or praxis. Degendering needs to be translated into everyday interaction, which could be revolutionary enough. But to fulfill their political potential, the gender rebellion feminisms need to spell out what precisely has to be done in all the institutions and organizations of a society—family, workplace, government, the arts, religion, law, and so on—to ensure equal participation and opportunity for every person in every group. Gender rebellion feminists have said that there are multiple voices in this world; now they have to figure out how to ensure that every voice can be heard in the production of knowledge and culture and in the power systems of their societies.

Organization of the Book

The focus of this book is the continuities, discontinuities, and convergences in recent feminist theories and politics. I will be combining ideas from different feminist writers, and usually I will not be talking about any specific writers, except for the excerpted authors. A list of suggested readings can be found at the end of each chapter.

Because I am not examining the ideas of particular feminists but speaking of ideas that have emerged from many theorists, I will usually talk of feminisms rather than feminists. Any feminist may incorporate ideas and politics from several feminisms, and many feminists have shifted their views over the years. I myself was originally a liberal feminist, then a socialist feminist, and now consider myself to be primarily a gender rebellion feminist.

What I am looking at first are *feminist theories* about why women and men are unequal, and second, *feminist politics,* the activities and strategies for remedying gender inequality. Feminist theories and feminist politics are the result of personal experiences shared among friends and in consciousness-raising groups. They are developed in classes and conferences on all kinds of topics. They are refined in journals and books. And they are translated into political action through large and small feminist organizations, in marches and voting booths, in the marble halls of the United Nations, and in grassroots efforts in urban racial ethnic ghettos and developing countries of Africa, South and Central America, and Asia.

In Parts Two through Four, the theories and politics of *gender reform, gender resistance,* and *gender rebellion feminisms* are first described in a general way, followed by more detailed descriptions of the feminisms within the larger grouping. Except for third-wave feminism, each discussion of a particular feminism begins with an outline of its attribution of the main causes of gender inequality, its politics, and its contributions to social change. Third-wave feminism begins with a comparison with second-wave feminism. The discussion of each type of feminism includes two excerpts from feminist theorists who use that viewpoint, one more theoretical, the other more focused on current politics. Each chapter ends with a discussion of the feminism's theoretical and political limitations.

In the final section, "Do We Need a New Feminism?" I present my own ideas about fruitful theoretical and political directions for feminism.

Suggested Readings—Overviews and History

Bem, Sandra Lipsitz. 1993. *The Lenses of Gender: Transforming the Debate on Sexual Inequality.* New Haven, CT: Yale University Press.

Bernard, Jessie. 1981. *The Female World.* New York: Free Press.

Butler, Judith. 1990. *Gender Trouble: Feminism and the Subversion of Identity.* (10th Anniversary Edition, 1999). New York: Routledge.

———. 1993. *Bodies That Matter: On the Discursive Limits of "Sex."* New York: Routledge.

———. 2004. *Undoing Gender.* New York: Routledge.

Chafetz, Janet Saltzman. 1990. *Gender Equity: An Integrated Theory of Stability and Change.* Thousand Oaks, CA: Sage.

Chafetz, Janet Saltzman, and Anthony Gary Dworkin. 1986. *Female Revolt: Women's Movements in World and Historical Perspective.* Totowa, NJ: Rowman & Allanheld.

Clough, Patricia Ticineto. 1994. *Feminist Thought: Desire, Power, and Academic Discourse.* Cambridge, MA: Blackwell.

Collins, Patricia Hill. [1990] 2000. *Black Feminist Thought: Knowledge, Consciousness, and the Politics of Empowerment,* 2nd ed. New York: Routledge.

Connell, R. W. 1987. *Gender and Power.* Stanford, CA: Stanford University Press.

———. 1995. *Masculinities.* Berkeley: University of California Press.

Cott, Nancy F. 1987. *The Grounding of Modern Feminism.* New Haven, CT: Yale University Press.

de Beauvoir, Simone. [1949] 1953. *The Second Sex.* Translated by H. M. Parshley. New York: Knopf.

De Lauretis, Teresa. 1987. *Technologies of Gender.* Bloomington: Indiana University Press.

Epstein, Cynthia Fuchs. 1988. *Deceptive Distinctions: Sex, Gender and the Social Order.* New Haven, CT: Yale University Press.

Evans, Judith. 1995. *Feminist Theory Today: An Introduction to Second-Wave Feminism.* Thousand Oaks, CA: Sage.

Evans, Sara M. 2002. "Re-viewing the Second Wave." *Feminist Studies* 28:259–267.

Fausto-Sterling, Anne. 2000. *Sexing the Body: Gender Politics and the Construction of Sexuality.* New York: Basic Books.

Ferree, Myra Marx, Judith Lorber, and Beth B. Hess, eds. 1999. *Revisioning Gender.* Thousand Oaks, CA: Sage.

Firestone, Shulamith. 1970. *The Dialectic of Sex: The Case for Feminist Revolution.* New York: William Morrow.

Ginzberg, Lori D. 2002. "Re-viewing the First Wave." *Feminist Studies* 28:419–434.

Gordon, Linda. 1990. *Woman's Body, Woman's Right: Birth Control in America.* Rev. ed. Baltimore, MD: Penguin.

Harrison, Wendy Cealey, and John Hood-Williams. 2002. *Beyond Sex and Gender.* Thousand Oaks, CA: Sage.

hooks, bell. [1984] 2000. *Feminist Theory: From Margin to Center.* Boston: South End Press.

Hrdy, Sarah Blaffer. 1999. *Mother Nature: A History of Mothers, Infants, and Natural Selection.* New York: Pantheon.

Hull, Gloria T., Patricia Bell Scott, and Barbara Smith, eds. 1982. *All the Women Are White, All the Blacks Are Men, But Some of Us Are Brave: Black Women's Studies.* New York: Feminist Press.

Jackson, Robert Max. 1998. *Destined for Equality: The Inevitable Rise of Women's Status.* Cambridge, MA: Harvard University Press.

Jaggar, Alison M. 1983. *Feminist Politics and Human Nature.* Totowa, NJ: Rowman & Allanheld.

Joseph, Gloria I., and Jill Lewis, eds. 1981. *Common Differences: Conflicts in Black and White Feminist Perspectives.* Garden City, NY: Doubleday Anchor.

Kessler, Suzanne J., and Wendy McKenna. 1978. *Gender: An Ethnomethodological Approach.* Chicago: University of Chicago Press.

Kraditor, Aileen S. 1981. *The Ideas of the Woman Suffrage Movement/1890–1920.* New York: W. W. Norton.

Lerner, Gerda. 1986. *The Creation of Patriarchy.* New York: Oxford University Press.

Lorber, Judith. 1994. *Paradoxes of Gender.* New Haven, CT: Yale University Press.

———. 2005. *Breaking the Bowls: Degendering and Feminist Change.* New York: W. W. Norton.

Marks, Elaine, and Isabelle de Courtivron, eds. 1981. *New French Feminisms.* New York: Schocken.

McCann, Carole R., and Seung-Kyung Kim, eds. 2002. *Feminist Theory Reader: Local and Global Perspectives.* New York: Routledge.

Mernissi, Fatima. 1987. *Beyond the Veil: Male-Female Dynamics in Muslim Society.* Bloomington: Indiana University Press.

Millett, Kate. 1970. *Sexual Politics.* Garden City, NY: Doubleday.

Moi, Toril. 1985. *Sexual/Textual Politics: Feminist Literary Theory.* New York: Methuen.

Oakley, Ann. 2002. *Gender on Planet Earth.* New York: The New Press.

Richards, Amy, and Jennifer Baumgardner. 2000. *Manifesta: Young Women, Feminism, and the Future.* New York: Farrar, Straus, and Giroux.

Riley, Denise. 1988. *Am I That Name? Feminism and the Category of Women in History.* Minneapolis: University of Minnesota Press.

Rossi, Alice S., ed. 1973. *The Feminist Papers: From Adams to de Beauvoir.* New York: Columbia University Press.

Rowbotham, Sheila. 1973. *Women's Consciousness, Man's World.* New York: Penguin.

————. 1974. *Women, Resistance and Revolution: A History of Women and Revolution in the Modern World.* New York: Vintage.

————. 1976. *Hidden from History: Rediscovering Women in History from the 17th Century to the Present.* New York: Vintage.

————. 1989. *The Past Is Before Us: Feminism in Action Since the 1960s.* Boston: Beacon Press.

Sanday, Peggy Reeves. 1981. *Female Power and Male Dominance: On the Origins of Sexual Inequality.* Cambridge, UK: Cambridge University Press.

Scott, Joan Wallach. 1988. *Gender and the Politics of History.* New York: Columbia University Press.

Showalter, Elaine, ed. 1985. *The New Feminist Criticism: Essays on Women, Literature, and Theory.* New York: Pantheon.

Smith, Barbara. [1983] 2000. *Home Girls: A Black Feminist Anthology.* New York: Kitchen Table, Women of Color Press.

Snitow, Ann, Christine Stansell, and Sharon Thompson, eds. 1983. *Powers of Desire: The Politics of Sexuality.* New York: Monthly Review Press.

Stites, Richard. [1978] 1990. *The Women's Liberation Movement in Russia: Feminism, Nihilism, and Bolshevism, 1860–1930.* Princeton, NJ: Princeton University Press.

Thompson, Becky. 2002. "Multiracial Feminism: Recasting the Chronology of Second Wave Feminism." *Feminist Studies* 28:337–355.

Tong, Rosemarie. 1989. *Feminist Thought: A Comprehensive Introduction.* Boulder, CO: Westview Press.

Warhol, Robyn R., and Diane Price Herndl, eds. 1991. *Feminisms: An Anthology of Literary Theory and Criticism.* New Brunswick, NJ: Rutgers University Press.

Whittle, Stephen. 2002. *Respect and Equality: Transsexual and Transgender Rights.* London: Cavendish Publishing.

Wing, Adrien Katherine, ed. 2000. *Global Critical Race Feminism: An International Reader.* New York: New York University Press.

Woolf, Virginia. 1929 [1957]. *A Room of One's Own.* New York: Harcourt, Brace & World. ✦

Part II

Gender Reform Feminisms

The feminisms of the 1960s and 1970s were the beginning of the *second wave* of feminism. Like the first wave of feminism, which sought equal rights as citizens for women in Western societies, liberal feminism's roots are in eighteenth and nineteenth century political philosophies that developed the idea of individual rights. Liberal feminism asks why women's rights are not part of these individual human rights. Marxist feminism's base is Marx's nineteenth-century analysis of capitalism and the division of labor. Marxist feminism argues that women's place in the capitalist division of labor is invisible. Socialist feminism inserts gender into twentieth-century debates over class and racial ethnic relations and inequities. Post-colonial feminism uses twentieth-century ideas of national development and economic globalization and examines their effects on women.

From the beginning of the second wave, the goal of gender reform feminism has been *gender equality*—legally treating women and men alike, even while granting that they are biologically different. Gender reform feminisms argue that society uses and exaggerates sex differences, especially in the socialization of children. Their main argument about socialization is that it creates personality and attitude differences in boys and girls to prepare them to live different lives—men as power brokers, bosses, laborers, soldiers, assertive husbands, and authoritative fathers; women as helpers, clerical workers, teachers, nurses, dedicated mothers, and compliant wives. Gender reform feminisms are critical of the exploitation of women's labor and emotions in the service of marriage and argue that the gender division of labor makes women dependent on a waged husband or state support. Their main solution has been the encouragement of women's entry into the labor force or, in developing countries, support for women's land ownership and small businesses. These solutions give women economic independence, but do not address the problem of the "second shift," women's continued responsibility for the maintenance of the household and husband and children. Given the unequal distribution of domestic work, mothers who work outside the home constantly juggle work and family. With their time binds and relegation to lower-paying jobs, gender equality is an elusive goal. Racial ethnic inequalities further undermine the goal of equality for women of disadvantaged groups.

Gender reform feminisms see men as advantaged in the sphere of paid work, in that they usually have better jobs and are paid more than women. Theoretically, men's work should allow them to support a wife and children, but throughout the world and throughout history, women have taken care of children and also produced food, clothing, and other material necessities as part of their work for their family. When the industrial revolution moved the production of commodities outside of the home into the factory, not only men, but women and children, went out to work for wages. The men who could support their families completely were the factory owners and those who had inherited wealth, and their wives were expected to be hostesses and supervisors of the household servants. By the middle of the twentieth century, working-class women were still juggling family work and paid work to supplement the family income, and middle-class, college-educated women were languishing in the suburbs, feeling useless once their children were in school. In the last 25 years, these women have stayed in or re-entered the labor force, often in high-pressured professional and managerial occupations. The workplace, however, has not altered to meet the needs of "working families"—households where parents are economic providers and child carers at the same time. It is this historically intertwined structure of work and family and women's roles within it that gender reform feminisms tackle.

From an international perspective, the goal of gender equality in developing countries is for the education of girls, maternal and child health care, and economic resources for women who contribute heavily to the support of their families. However, feminist gender politics of equality may run into opposition from traditional cultural values and practices that give men power over their daughters and wives. The women's own solution to this dilemma is community organizing around their family roles, another form of feminism.

Gender reform feminisms' politics are based in concepts of equality, domestic and economic exploitation of women's labor, and the global economy. Feminist ideas are current in national and international political activities that are not necessarily called feminism but do have the goal of advancing the status of women, placing their needs into policy agendas, and recognizing that "women's rights are human rights." ✦

Chapter One

Liberal Feminism

Sources of Gender Inequality

- Gendered socialization of children.
- Women's primary responsibility for child care and household maintenance.
- Division of work into women's jobs and men's jobs.
- Devaluation and low pay for women's jobs.
- Restricted entry into top positions (*glass ceiling*).
- Limitations on reproductive choice.

Politics

- Gender-neutral child-rearing and education.
- Bringing women into occupations and professions dominated by men and breaking through the glass ceiling to positions of authority (*affirmative action*).
- Bringing more women into politics through equal-representation rules and financial support.
- Promoting gender mainstreaming in policies ensuring attention to women's needs.
- Sharing parenting and subsidizing child care.
- Legal, accessible, and affordable reproductive services.

Contributions

- Making language, children's books, and education more gender-neutral.
- Making formal and informal gender discrimination visible and countering its effects by mentoring and networking in multicultural women's professional and occupational associations.
- Working with civil rights organizations to frame affirmative action guidelines and to bring lawsuits for women and disadvantaged men.
- Getting more women elected and appointed to government positions.
- Encouraging employers and governments to provide workplace child care and paid parental leave.
- Getting abortion legalized and reproductive rights recognized as human rights.

In the 1960s and 1970s, the feminist focus in the United States was on women as individuals and the narrowness of their lives. Liberal feminism's complaint that women were confined to a main "job" of wife-mother, with anything else they did having to take a backseat to child care and housework, was the theme of Betty Friedan's best-selling book *The Feminine Mystique.* Women who wanted careers or who were ambitious to make a mark in the arts or in politics were suspect unless they were also "good" wives and mothers (especially mothers). Another problem that kept women down was men's devaluation of them as not too bright, clothes-conscious, and overly emotional. Of course, these impressions were exactly what a woman was taught to convey to a man if she wanted to get a husband.

Liberal feminism claims that gender differences are not based in biology and therefore that women and men are not all that different: Their common humanity supersedes their procreative differences. If women and men are not so different, then they should not be treated differently under the law. Women should have the same legal rights as men and the same educational and work opportunities. Liberal feminism accepts and works with the gender system, with the goal of purging it of its discriminatory effects on women. Today this goal is termed *undoing gender*. A parallel current goal is *mainstreaming gender*—ensuring that government or organizational policies address women's needs.

The early appeals of liberal feminism were open and straightforward—stop calling a wife "the little woman," use Ms. instead of Mrs. or Miss, recognize women's past achievements and current capabilities in many fields, let women do the kind of work they want to do outside the home, share some of the housework and child care, legalize abortion. It does not sound very earthshaking today because so many of these goals have been achieved, including the routine use of "he and she" in public discourse. Women have entered every field, from mining to space travel. Women in the police force and the military are no longer an oddity, and women in high positions, including leaders of countries, are no longer a rarity.

Other liberal feminist goals are still being debated. One is the question of whether men can be as good at parenting as women. Liberal feminism argues that gendered characteristics, such as women's parenting abilities, may seem biological but are really social products. Their proof that mothering skills are learned and not inborn, for example, is that men learn them, too, when they end up with the responsibility for raising children alone. But when there is a woman around, the assumption is that she is better at child care than any man, and so women end up doing most of the physically and emotionally intensive work of bringing up children. Mothers' primary responsibility for child care undermines the accomplishment of gender equality in paid jobs, since employers assume that mothers cannot be as committed to their work as fathers or childless women.

A second continuing problem is that families, teachers, picture books, school books, and the mass media still encourage boys to be "masculine" and girls to be "feminine," even when they show adult women and men acting in more gender-neutral ways. Gender inequality is built into this socialization because supposedly masculine characteristics, such as assertiveness, are more highly valued than supposedly feminine characteristics, such as emotional supportiveness. Liberal feminism promotes nonsexist socialization and education of children as well as media presentations of men and women in nontraditional roles, especially men as caring and competent fathers. These areas still need constant monitoring—computer software programs for girls feature sexy Barbie dolls and kissing skills, while boys' computer games feature violent adventure fantasies.

Successes and failures in the workplace. The workplace is an arena where liberal feminism has made important contributions, but where women are still a long way from gender equality. Thanks to feminist pressure, more and more women have entered fields formerly dominated by men, such as the sciences, and women in positions of authority are not the big news they once were. However, sexist patterns of hiring and promotion still produce workplaces where men and women work at different jobs and where most of the top positions are held by men. Liberal feminism has developed theories to explain the persistence of the *gender segregation* of jobs (men work with men and women work with women) and the *gender stratification* of organizational hierarchies (the top of the pyramid is invariably almost all men).

The theory of *gendered job queues* argues that the best jobs are kept for men of the dominant racial ethnic group. When a job no longer pays well or has deteriorating working conditions, dominant men leave for other work, and men of disadvantaged racial ethnic groups and all women can move into them. Occupations stay segregated, but who does the job changes. Some jobs have shifted from men's work to women's work within a decade. A typical case is a bank teller in the United States.

Disadvantaged groups of workers continue to get lower pay and have poorer working conditions than the dominant group because the new crop of "best jobs" again goes to the most advantaged group of workers. Thus, in the United States, White men monopolize the most lucrative financial and computer jobs.

The strategy of *affirmative action* was developed to redress the gender, racial category, and ethnic imbalance in workplaces, schools, and job-training programs. Affirmative action programs develop a diversified pool of qualified people by encouraging men to train for such jobs as nurse, elementary school teacher, and secretary, and women to go into fields like engineering, construction, and police work. Employers are legally mandated to hire enough workers of different racial categories and genders to achieve a reasonable balance in their workforce. The law also requires employers to pay the workers the same and to give them an equal chance to advance in their careers.

With regard to gender, this change in numbers of women in a workplace was supposed to have a psychological effect on both men and women. Earlier theories had argued that women were not aggressive about competing with men on the job or at school because they feared that success would make them so disliked that they would never have a social life. Rosabeth Moss Kanter, a sociologist and management researcher, said that it was token status as the lone woman among men, visible and vulnerable, that created women's fears. The *Kanter hypothesis* predicted that as workplaces became more gender-balanced, men would become more accepting of women colleagues, and women would have other women to bond with instead of having to go it alone as the single token woman. The following excerpt from her influential book, *Men and Women of the Corporation,* lays out Moss Kanter's hypothesis about the effect of numbers of women on the culture and social structure of a workplace.

Numbers: Minorities and Majorities

Rosabeth Moss Kanter
Professor of Business Administration,
Harvard University Business School

Yet questions of how many and how few confound any statements about the organizational behavior of special kinds of people. For example, certain popular conclusions and research findings about male-female relations or role potentials may turn critically on the issue of proportions. One study of mock jury deliberations found that men played proactive, task-oriented leadership roles, whereas women in the same groups tended to take reactive, emotional, and nurturant postures—supposed proof that traditional stereotypes reflect behavior realities. But, strikingly, *men far outnumbered women in all of the groups studied.* Perhaps it was the women's scarcity that pushed them into classical positions and the men's numerical superiority that encouraged them to assert task superiority. Similarly, the early kibbutzim, collective villages in Israel that theoretically espoused equality of the sexes but were unable to fully implement it, could push women into traditional service positions because there were *more than twice as many men as women*. Again, relative numbers interfered with a fair test of what men or women can "naturally" do, as it did in the case of the relatively few women in the upper levels of Indsco (the company in this example). Indeed, recently Marcia Guttentag has found sex ratios in the population in general to be so important that they predict a large number of behavioral phenomena, from the degree of power women and men feel to the ways they cope with the economic and sexual aspects of their lives.

To understand the dramas of the many and the few in the organization requires a theory and a vocabulary. Four group types can be identified on the basis of different proportional representations of kinds of people. . . . *Uniform* groups have only one kind of person, one significant social type. The group may develop its own differentiations, of course, but groups called uniform can be considered homogeneous with respect to salient external master statuses such as sex, race, or ethnicity. Uniform groups have a typological ratio of 100:0. *Skewed* groups are those in which there is a large preponderance of one type over another, up to a ratio of perhaps 85:15. The numerically dominant types also control the group and its culture in enough ways to be labeled "dominants." The few of another type in a skewed group can appropriately be called "tokens," for . . . they are often treated as representatives of their category, as symbols rather than individuals. If the absolute size of the skewed group is small, tokens can also be solos, the only one of their kind present; but even if there are two tokens in a skewed group, it is difficult for them to generate an alliance that can become powerful in the group. . . . Next, *tilted* groups begin to move toward less extreme distributions and less exaggerated effects. In this situation, with ratios of perhaps 65:35, dominants are just a "majority" and tokens become a "minority." Minority members have potential allies among each other, can form coalitions, and can affect the culture of the group. They begin to become individuals differentiated from each other as well as a type differentiated from the majority. Finally, at about 60:40 and down to 50:50, the group becomes *balanced*. Culture and interaction reflect this balance. Majority and minority turn into potential subgroups that may or may not generate actual type-based identifications. Outcomes for individuals in such a balanced peer group, regardless of type, will depend more on other structural and personal factors, including formation of subgroups or differentiated roles and abilities.

It is the characteristics of the second type, the skewed group, that underlay the behavior and treatment of professional and managerial women observed at Indsco. If the ratio of women to men in various parts of the organization begins to shift, as affirmative action and new hiring and promotion policies promised, forms of relationships and peer culture should also change. But as of the mid-1970s, the dynamics of tokenism predominated in Indsco's . . . ranks, and women and men were in the positions of token and dominant. Tokenism, like low opportunity and low power, set in motion self-perpetuating cycles that served to reinforce the low numbers of women and, in the absence of external intervention, to keep women in the position of token.

The recognition that a token or two did not make for a truly diversified workplace provided the impetus for affirmative action. The goal is not perfect balance but a workplace where different kinds of people are fully integrated and respected colleagues. The Kanter hypothesis predicted a positive attitude change when a formerly imbalanced workplace becomes more gender-balanced. However, later research found that as more women enter an organization, there is often a backlash in the form of increasing sexual harassment and denigration of women's capabilities—a defense against what is felt to be the encroachment of women on men's territory. Men's stonewalling is particularly likely when women are competing with them for jobs on the fast track up the career ladder.

Another contradiction to the Kanter hypothesis is that men who are tokens in women-dominated occupations, such as nursing, tend to be pushed into administrative jobs. This phenomenon became known as the *glass escalator,* a contrast to the *glass ceiling* that keeps women from the top jobs in occupations dominated by men.

Gatekeeping and the glass ceiling. The concept of *gatekeeping* explains how most women are kept from getting to the top in occupations and professions dominated by men. Gatekeeping used to keep women out of those fields entirely. Now gatekeeping keeps women out of the line for promotion to top positions. The ways that most people move up in their careers are through *networking* (finding out about job and promotion opportunities through word-of-mouth and being recommended by someone already there) and *mentoring* (being coached by a protective senior to understand the informal norms of the workplace). Becoming part of a network and getting a mentor are made much easier if you become a *protégé* of a senior colleague.

In professions and in managerial positions, where jobs pay the best, have the most prestige, and command the most authority, few senior men take on women as their *protégés*. As a result, there has been a *glass ceiling* on the advancement of women in every field they have entered in the last 25 years. The concept of the glass ceiling assumes that women have the motivation, ambition, and capacity for positions of power and prestige, but hidden barriers keep them from reaching the top. They can see their way to their goal, but they bump their heads on a ceiling that is both invisible and impenetrable. Similar processes of informal discrimination hinder the careers of men of disadvantaged groups as well; women of color have had to face both racism and sexism.

Despite the glass ceiling, the efforts of liberal feminism to make women equal to men in the workplace in Western societies have succeeded. Women now receive the higher education and professional training needed to enter medicine and law. Women have formed professional associations and unions by occupation, and also by racial ethnic groups, to enhance the networking and mentoring so useful in getting jobs and then getting promoted. Although men in work and other organizations still bypass women for promotion (and the organizations are getting successfully sued for such behavior), the liberal feminist goal of workplace gender equality is a major accomplishment. But this accomplishment is foundering for mothers.

Work-family balance. Liberal feminism has always claimed that women and motherhood are not synonymous. Its proponents argue that the assumption that mothers have prime responsibility for child care and cannot therefore be responsible workers builds gender discrimination into the workplace. Childless women can be treated as men workers are. For them and for fathers, employers demand that work comes before family. For professions and politics, so-called "greedy occupations," the pressure to put the job first is even more intense. Mothers are bounced between two powerful cultural commitments—their children and their work.

When workplaces do not accommodate to family needs and fathers do not share child care, mothers pay a price in lowered wages, reduced lifetime earnings, and minimal pensions because of part-time and interrupted work. When they want to return to full-time work or get off the "mommy track," they are discriminated against in hiring and promotions. Thus, mothers bear most of the economic and occupational cost of parenting, even though everyone in a society benefits from good child care.

Many European countries and Israel have policies of maternal leave and subsidized child care that encourage women with small children to stay in the paid workforce, but because they have the organizational and emotional responsibility for their families, they are discouraged from competing with men for high-level, better-paid, full-time positions. Some countries subsidize mothers and children but do not provide child care; that policy encourages women to stay out of the paid workforce. Countries like the United States, which subsidize neither mothers nor child care, make the "juggling act" between parenting and earning a living the responsibility of individual families.

The other part of the balance, the workplace, has felt less governmental and social pressure to adjust to 25 years of married mothers' staying on the job. In much of the literature on dual-career and two-job families, liberal feminism has suggested that an obvious way to accommodate workers' family responsibilities is to expand the use of *flextime*. Flextime offers employees a choice of what hours and what days of the week to work. But it has to guarantee equal benefits, such as health insurance, advancement opportunities, and seniority tracks. Family-friendly workplaces have for a long time provided flextime, parental leaves, on-site child care, and referral services for care of children and the elderly. But they have not offered them without penalties in advancement or the stigmatization of part-time work. Formal policies and informal practices need to reflect awareness of the whole lives of every worker if the transformation in families is to be met with transformation in the workplace.

The following excerpt from *The Time Bind* by Jerry Jacobs and Kathleen Gerson, two sociologists who have separately contributed excellent research to gender, work, and family issues, lays out the crucial issues in balancing work and family and how the problems might be remedied.

Integrating Family and Work in the 21st Century

Jerry A. Jacobs
Professor of Sociology, University of Pennsylvania

Kathleen Gerson
Professor of Sociology, New York University

Efforts to achieve gender equality, like policies that call for government regulation or spending, continue to evoke deep ambivalence and considerable opposition. Several decades ago, when women's movement into paid work began to elicit popular notice, criticism often focused on the costs women bore as they moved away from domestically centered lives. Some even argued, in Sylvia Ann Hewlett's words, that these changes meant a "lesser life" for women.[1] Several decades later, this argument appears far less tenable. As women have established themselves across an array of jobs and occupations, most have welcomed their increased economic and social autonomy. Women continue to face obstacles at work and in the home, but the solutions to these problems can be found in creating more equal opportunities, not in confining women to domesticity.

The more common focus of contemporary critiques of women's equality has moved from adults to children. According to this argument, women's workplace commitments may appeal to adults, but they pose dangers for the young. The concern over "neglected" or "latchkey" children has insidious overtones, implying maternal indifference and fueling a moral panic over the transformation in women's lives. While it is appropriate and important to focus on the ways our society is not meeting the needs of children, it is equally important to disentangle these concerns from parental, and especially maternal, blame. The dangers to children rest not with their mothers' work commitments, but rather with the paucity of supports—at the workplace and in our communities—for employed parents and their children.

Rather than causing harm, the paid employment of mothers tends to enhance children's well-being in a number of ways. Most obviously, women's employment provides economic resources to their families; whether they live in a two-income or a single-parent home, children depend on their mothers' earnings. Equal economic opportunity for women thus protects children from poverty and improves their life chances.

Children tend to recognize the benefits of having an employed mother, as well as the challenges posed by long hours and inflexible work settings. Most children support their working parents and believe employed mothers are making crucial contributions to their welfare (Galinsky 1999; Gerson 2001). They report emotional and social benefits as well. Both daughters and sons tend to see employed mothers as uplifting models for women and dual-income partnerships as attractive models for marriage (Barnett and Rivers 1996; Gerson 2002). And when the focus is on direct, "quality" time devoted to children, employed mothers appear to spend almost as much time with their children as do nonemployed mothers (Bianchi 2000).

While children appreciate the resources their parents' jobs provide, they also recognize the toll that long days and unsatisfying work can take on mothers and fathers alike. What children need, then, are flexible, family-friendly workplaces for their parents as well as family-supportive communities for children and adolescents (Glass 2000). Rather than focusing on maternal employment as a social problem, we need to attend to the ways that workplaces and communities can better accommodate this fundamental transformation in family life.

Concerns over replacing full-time maternal care with other forms of child rearing are also based on the dubious, but persisting, belief that biological mothers are uniformly and universally superior to all other caretakers. It is hard to imagine any other form of work for which such a claim could be made or taken seriously. Mothers are an enormously large and varied group, with differing interests, desires, and talents. It makes little sense to assume that they are all equally and uniquely prepared to be their child's only or best caretaker. Instead, children benefit from having a range of committed, concerned caretakers—including fathers, other relatives, and paid professionals. They also benefit from having parents who are satisfied with their choices, whether that means working or staying home.[2]

The expansion of opportunities for professional women in the United States and other countries has fueled a demand for paid caretakers, especially in the absence of widely available, high-quality, publicly sponsored child care. Conservatives, uneasy with women's march into the workplace, have consistently raised concerns about the propriety of relying on paid caretakers to help rear children. Recently, however, some feminists have joined the chorus of critics who worry about this strategy, especially when these caretakers are drawn from the ranks of immigrants from poorer countries. Some worry that the expanded market for paid caretaking encourages working parents—especially full-time employed mothers—to participate in a new form of international colonialism. From this perspective, affluent families in rich countries are extracting caregiving and even love from poorer immigrants, who may leave their own children behind (Ehrenreich and Hochschild 2002).

In a society that fails to accord appropriate social or economic value to the care of children, all child-care workers (like all involved parents) face disadvantage and discrimination. Immigrants and other women who work as caretakers in private households may, indeed, be even more vulnerable than others who care for children in public settings, especially if they do not speak English and can count on few friends or relatives for support. Like their American-born counterparts, immigrant domestic workers may not be paid fairly or regularly and may be physically or emotionally abused; unlike their American peers, they may be threatened with deportation if they complain. And the problems facing private domestic workers, whether or not they are immigrants, are especially prone to invisibility because the isolation of these workers limits their options for organizing as a group or informing others of their plight.

The deficiencies and dangers of an inadequate child-care system should not, however, be laid at the feet of employed mothers, who confront equally perplexing obstacles. Such an approach pits women against each other, making it seem that the economic independence of middle-class women comes at the expense of poor, immigrant women and their children. By framing paid caretaking as the "commodification" of care, this perspective adds to the critique facing all women who hold paid jobs, whether in public workplaces or private homes. As important, the focus on private child care obscures the more widespread trend toward greater reliance on child-care centers, where the conditions of work and the rights of workers are more visible. . . .

The policies we suggest represent only a few of the myriad of possible approaches to address the dilemmas created by work and family change. Effective policies, whatever their form, can only emerge from a national debate that extends beyond cultural critiques and a framework of parental blame to reconsider workplace organization, community support, and the structure of opportunities confronting workers and their families.

The time balance people are able to strike in their lives matters, but the picture is not a simple one of overwork. For the "overworked Americans," job flexibility and genuine formal and informal support for family life matter as much as, and possibly more than, actual hours. For the underworked, who are concentrated in the less rewarded jobs, security and opportunity are paramount for their own welfare and that of their children.

One facet of change, however, spans occupation and class: the emergence of women as a large and committed group of workers. They need and have a right to expect the same opportunities afforded men, and their families depend on their ability to gain these opportunities. There are significant points of convergence between women and men in their commitment to work and their desire for family supports. However, women workers, especially those putting in long days at the workplace, do not enjoy the same level of support as do their male counterparts. Principles of justice as well as the new realities of families suggest that gender equity needs to be integral to any policy initiatives aimed at easing the conflicts between family and work.

At the broadest level, our discovery of multiple and intertwined time divides suggests that reform efforts should uphold two important principles: equality of opportunity for women and men, and generous support for all involved parents regardless of gender or class position. We cannot afford to build work-family policies on old, outdated stereotypes, in which women are seen as less committed to work than men. Yet we can also not afford to build our policies on new stereotypes, in which working mothers and, to a lesser extent, fathers are depicted as avoiding their families and neglecting their children.

These images place all too many workers in a difficult bind, in which work commitment is defined as family neglect and family involvement is defined as a lack of work commitment. These are inaccurate images that result in untenable choices. If our findings are a guide, what workers need most is flexible, satisfying, and economically rewarding work in a supportive setting that offers them a way to integrate work and family life. With these supports, contemporary workers and the generations to follow will be able to bridge the time divides they face.

Notes

1. See Hewlett 1986. Sylvia Hewlett's recent book, *Creating a Life* (2002), focuses on the relatively high rates of childlessness among highly accomplished professional women, using this development as a cautionary tale about the costs of success for women. The real story here, however, is not women's ticking biological clock, but rather the lack of change in the time demands and "career clocks" of highly rewarded jobs to accommodate the needs of working women.

2. Recent research shows that the absolute amount of time spent with children is less important than the amount of support and sensitivity parents provide. A. C. Crouter and colleagues (1999), for example, report that children's willingness to share information with their parents matters more than parental monitoring of their time. These researchers also find that when mothers work, fathers become more knowledgeable about, and involved in, their children's care.

References

Barnett, Rosalind C., and Caryl Rivers. 1996. *She Works/He Works: How Two-Income Families Are Happier, Healthier, and Better-Off.* San Francisco: HarperCollins.

Bianchi, Suzanne M. 2000. "Maternal Employment and Time With Children: Dramatic Change or Surprising Continuity?" *Demography* 37 (4):401–414.

Ehrenreich, Barbara, and Arlie R. Hochschild, eds. 2002. *Global Woman: Nannies, Maids, and Sex Workers in the New Economy.* New York: Metropolitan Books.

Galinsky, Ellen, Stacy S. Kim, and James T. Bond. 2001. *Feeling Overworked: When Work Becomes Too Much.* New York: Families and Work Institute.

Gerson, Kathleen. 2001. "Children of the Gender Revolution: Some Theoretical Questions and Findings From the Field," 446–461 in Victor W. Marshall, Walter R. Heinz, Helga Krueger, and Anil Verma, eds., *Restructuring Work and the Life Course.* Toronto: University of Toronto Press.

———. 2002. "Moral Dilemmas, Moral Strategies, and the Transformation of Gender: Lessons From Two Generations of Work and Family Change," *Gender and Society,* 16 (1) (February):8–28.

Glass, Jennifer. 2000. "Toward a Kinder, Gentler Workplace: Envisioning the Integration of Family and Work." *Contemporary Sociology* 29:129–143.

Hewlett, Sylvia A. 1986. *A Lesser Life: The Myth of Women's Liberation in America.* New York. Morrow.

———. 2002. *Creating a Life: Professional Women and the Quest for Children.* New York: Miramax.

As long as work-family balance is the burden of individual families or mothers alone, there will continue to be gender inequality in the family and in the workplace. Few men feel they can afford, economically and psychologically, to jeopardize their financial support of their families. Similarly, few mothers feel they can live with the burden of guilt over splitting their time between their job and their children in the light of the continuing moral imperative to be a good (i.e., intensive) mother.

Critique. There is an internal theoretical contradiction in liberal feminism that centers on the question of whether women and men have to be the same to be equal. The campaign to bring up children in a gender-neutral way has meant encouraging a mixture of existing masculine and feminine characteristics and traits, so that boys and girls will be similar in personalities and behavior. The corollary campaign to integrate women into all parts of public life, especially the workplace, and for men to share parenting and other family roles, means that women and men can be more interchangeable.

The logical outcome of liberal feminism is a degendered society, one not based on women and men as socially meaningful categories. But because of men's social domination, the actual thrust of both gender-neutrality and gender integration is often the continued predominance of masculine traits and values, such as devotion to a career, with the consequence that women are expected to act like men. For this reason, liberal feminism has been accused of denigrating *womanliness* (nurturance, empathy, care) and pregnancy and childbirth in their fight to advance the social status of women.

The goal of liberal feminism in the United States was embodied in the Equal Rights Amendment to the U.S. Constitution, which was never ratified. It said, "Equality of rights under the law shall not be denied or abridged by the United States or any state on account of sex." The negative response of the American public to the Equal Rights Amendment may have been a gut reaction to the revolutionary possibilities of an absolutely even-handed legal status for women and men. When laws speak of "pregnant persons," as did a Supreme Court decision equating pregnancy with disability or illness, many people, including some feminists, feel that degendering has gone too far. The feminists who fought for the legalization of abortion and still fight for women to control their procreative lives pushed liberal feminism to recognize that the battle for gender equality could not be confined to advancing women in the workplace.

Summary

The main contribution of liberal feminism has been to show how much modern society discriminates against women by insisting that women and men must be treated differently. Liberal feminist theory says that biological differences should be ignored in order to achieve gender equality. Women and men should be treated in a gender-neutral manner, especially under the law.

In the United States, liberal feminism has been successful in breaking down many barriers to women's entry into jobs and professions formerly dominated by men, in helping to equalize wage scales, and in legalizing abortion. But liberal feminism has not been able to overcome the prevailing belief that women and men are intrinsically different. Although gender differences can coexist with equitable or even-handed treatment, the way women are treated in modern society, especially in the workplace, still produces large gaps in salaries, job opportunities, and advancement. Liberal feminism early on recognized that the gendered structure of organizations and the uneven distribution of domestic work were the intertwined source of workplace inequality.

Politically, liberal feminism's focus has been on visible sources of gender discrimination, such as gendered job markets and inequitable wage scales, and with getting women into positions of authority in the professions, government, and cultural institutions. Liberal feminist politics takes important weapons of the civil rights movement—antidiscrimination legislation and affirmative action programs—and uses them to fight gender inequality, especially in the job market. Liberal feminism has been less successful in fighting the informal processes of discrimination and exclusion that have produced the glass ceiling that so many women face in their career advancement.

The great strides that women of the last generation have made have led many young people to think that feminism is passé. But the gender equality in the workplace and the home that liberal feminism achieved depends on good jobs, steady incomes, two-parent households, and family-friendly employers and colleagues. The Scandinavian countries have achieved gender equality through welfare-state benefits to all parents and children. They also have many more women in government and in policy-making positions than the rest of the Western world, and so are able to promote gender-sensitivity in many public arenas.

Most of the world's women, however, have very little economic security. Their social problems produce a level of gender inequality that needs quite different feminist theories and politics.

Suggested Readings in Liberal Feminism

Appelbaum, Eileen, Thomas Bailey, Peter Berg, and Arne L. Kalleberg. 2002. *Shared Work, Valued Care: New Norms for Organizing Market Work and Unpaid Care Work.* Washington, DC: Economic Policy Institute.

Bartlett, Katharine T., and Rosanne Kennedy, eds. 1991. *Feminist Legal Theory: Readings in Law and Gender.* Boulder, CO: Westview Press.

Bem, Sandra Lipsitz. 1998. *An Unconventional Family.* New Haven, CT: Yale University Press.

Blair-Loy, Mary. 2003. *Competing Devotions: Career and Family Among Women Executives.* Cambridge, MA: Harvard University Press.

Budig, Michelle J. 2002. "Male Advantage and the Gender Composition of Jobs: Who Rides the Glass Escalator?" *Social Problems* 49:258–277.

Cockburn, Cynthia. 1991. *In the Way of Women: Men's Resistance to Sex Equality in Organizations.* Ithaca, NY: ILR Press.

Collinson, David L., David Knights, and Margaret Collinson. 1990. *Managing to Discriminate.* New York: Routledge.

Coltrane, Scott. 1996. *Family Man: Fatherhood, Housework, and Gender Equity.* New York: Oxford University Press.

———. 1998. *Gender and Families.* Thousand Oaks, CA: Pine Forge Press.

Crittenden, Ann. 2001. *The Price of Motherhood: Why the Most Important Job in the World Is Still the Least Valued.* New York: Metropolitan Books.

Daniels, Arlene Kaplan. 1988. *Invisible Careers: Women Civic Leaders From the Volunteer World.* Chicago: University of Chicago Press.

Deutsch, Francine M. 1999. *Halving It All: How Equally Shared Parenting Works.* Cambridge, MA: Harvard University Press.

Dienhart, Anna. 1998. *Reshaping Fatherhood: The Social Construction of Shared Parenting.* Thousand Oaks, CA: Sage.

Ehrensaft, Diane. 1987. *Parenting Together: Men and Women Sharing the Care of Their Children.* Urbana: University of Illinois Press.

Eisenstein, Zillah. 1981. *The Radical Future of Liberal Feminism.* New York: Longman.

———. 1984. *Feminism and Sexual Equality: Crisis in Liberal America.* New York: Monthly Review Press.

———. 1988. *The Female Body and the Law.* Berkeley: University of California Press.

Epstein, Cynthia Fuchs. 1971. *Women's Place: Options and Limits in Professional Careers.* Berkeley: University of California Press.

———. 1981. *Women in Law.* New York: Basic Books.

Epstein, Cynthia Fuchs, and Arne L. Kalleberg, eds. 2004. *Rethinking Time and Work.* New York: Russell Sage Foundation.

Epstein, Cynthia Fuchs, Carroll Seron, Bonnie Oglensky, and Robert Sauté. 1999. *The Part-Time Paradox: Time Norms, Professional Lives, Family, and Gender.* New York: Routledge.

Fineman, Martha Albertson. 1995. *The Neutered Mother, the Sexual Family and Other Twentieth Century Tragedies.* New York: Routledge.

Folbre, Nancy. 1994. *Who Pays for the Kids? Gender and the Structures of Constraint.* New York: Routledge.

———. 2001. *The Invisible Heart: Economics and Family Values.* New York: The New Press.

Friedan, Betty. 1963. *The Feminine Mystique.* New York: W. W. Norton.

Garey, Anita. 1999. *Weaving Work and Motherhood.* Philadelphia: Temple University Press.

Gerson, Kathleen. 1993. *No Man's Land: Men's Changing Commitments to Family and Work.* New York: Basic Books.

Gherardi, Silvia. 1995. *Gender, Symbolism and Organizational Cultures.* Thousand Oaks, CA: Sage.

Greif, Geoffrey L. 1985. *Single Fathers.* Lexington, MA: Lexington Books.

Hertz, Rosanna, and Nancy L. Marshall, eds. 2001. *Working Families: The Transformation of the American Home.* Berkeley: University of California Press.

Hobson, Barbara, ed. 2002. *Making Men Into Fathers: Men, Masculinities and the Social Politics of Fatherhood.* Cambridge, UK: Cambridge University Press.

Hochschild, Arlie Russell [with Anne Machung]. 1989. *The Second Shift: Working Parents and the Revolution at Home.* New York: Viking.

———. 1997. *The Time Bind: When Work Becomes Home and Home Becomes Work.* New York: Metropolitan Books.

Jacobs, Jerry A. 1989. *Revolving Doors: Sex Segregation and Women's Careers.* Stanford, CA: Stanford University Press.

Jacobs, Jerry A., and Kathleen Gerson. 2004. *The Time Divide: Work, Family, and Gender Inequality.* Cambridge, MA: Harvard University Press.

Jacobs, Jerry A. and Janice Fanning Madden. 2004. "Mommies and Daddies on the Fast Track: Success of Parents in Demanding Professions." Special Issue: *Annals of the American Academy of Political and Social Science* 596 (November): 6–244.

Kanter, Rosabeth Moss. 1977. *Men and Women of the Corporation.* New York: Basic Books.

Komarovsky, Mirra. 1976. *Dilemmas of Masculinity: A Study of College Youth.* New York: W. W. Norton.

———. 1985. *Women in College: Shaping New Feminine Identities.* New York: Basic Books.

Lamb, Michael E., ed. 1987. *The Father's Role: Cross-cultural Perspectives.* Hillsdale, NJ: Lawrence Erlbaum.

Landry, Bart. 2000. *Black Working Wives: Pioneers of the American Family Revolution.* Berkeley: University of California Press.

Lewis, Susan, Dafna N. Izraeli, and Helen Hootsmans, eds. 1992. *Dual-Earner Families: International Perspectives.* Thousand Oaks, CA: Sage.

Lorber, Judith. 1984. *Women Physicians: Careers, Status, and Power.* London: Tavistock.

Luker, Kristin. 1984. *Abortion and the Politics of Motherhood.* Berkeley: University of California Press.

Martin, Patricia Yancey. 2001. " 'Mobilizing Masculinities': Women's Experiences of Men at Work." *Organization* 8:587–618.

Mathews, Donald G., and Jane Sherron De Hart. 1990. *Sex, Gender, and the Politics of ERA: A State and the Nation.* New York: Oxford University Press.

Moen, Phyllis, ed. 2003. *It's About Time: Couples and Careers.* Ithaca, NY: ILR Press.

Okin, Susan Moller. 1989. *Justice, Gender and the Family.* New York: Basic Books.

Petchesky, Rosalind Pollack. 1984. *Abortion and Woman's Choice: The State, Sexuality, and Reproductive Freedom.* Boston: Northeastern University Press.

Pitt-Catsouphes, Marcie, and Bradley K. Googins, eds. 1999. "The Evolving World of Work and Family: New Stakeholders, New Voices." Special Issue: *Annals of the American Academy of Political and Social Science* 562 (March):8–211.

Potuchek, Jean L. 1997. *Who Supports the Family? Gender and Breadwinning in Dual-Earner Marriages.* Stanford, CA: Stanford University Press.

Reskin, Barbara F., and Patricia A. Roos. 1990. *Job Queues, Gender Queues: Explaining Women's Inroads Into Male Occupations.* Philadelphia: Temple University Press.

Ridgeway, Celia. 1997. "Interaction and the Conservation of Gender Inequality: Considering Employment." *American Sociological Review* 62:218–235.

Risman, Barbara J. 1998. *Gender Vertigo: American Families in Transition.* New Haven, CT: Yale University Press.

Stacey, Judith. 1991. *Brave New Families: Stories of Domestic Upheaval in Late Twentieth-Century America.* New York: Basic Books.

———. 1996. *In the Name of the Family: Rethinking Family Values in the Postmodern Age.* Boston: Beacon Press.

Valian, Virginia. 1998. *Why So Slow? The Advancement of Women.* Cambridge, MA: MIT Press.

Wajcman, Judy. 1998. *Managing Like a Man: Women and Men in Corporate Management.* University Park: Pennsylvania State University Press.

Weisberg, D. Kelly, ed. 1993. *Feminist Legal Theory: Foundations.* Philadelphia: Temple University Press.

Weitzman, Lenore J. 1985. *The Divorce Revolution: The Unexpected Social and Economic Consequences for Women and Children in America.* New York: Free Press.

Williams, Christine L. 1992. "The Glass Escalator: Hidden Advantages for Men in the 'Female' Professions." *Social Problems* 39:253–267.

Williams, Joan. 2000. *Unbending Gender: Why Family and Work Conflict and What to Do About It.* New York: Oxford University Press. ✦

Chapter Two

Marxist Feminism

Sources of Gender Inequality

- Exploitation of women in unwaged work for the family.
- Use of women workers as a *reserve army of labor*—hired when the economy needs workers, fired when it does not.
- Low pay for women's jobs.

Politics

- Permanent waged work for women.
- Government-subsidized maternal and child health care, child care services, financial allowances for children, free education.
- Union organizing of women workers.

Contributions

- Recognition that women are subordinated as a class.
- Gender analysis of the exploitation of women as paid and unpaid workers in capitalist, communist, and socialist economies.
- Making visible the necessity and worth of women's unpaid work in the home to the functioning of the economy and to the social reproduction of future workers.
- Getting government-subsidized maternal and child services.

During the 1970s, marxist feminist theories identified the economic structure and the material aspects of life as the main source of gender inequality. These theories are grounded in historical materialism, which says that every major change in production—from hunting and gathering to farming to the industrial revolution—changes the social organization of work and family. In preindustrial societies, women's domestic labor not only maintained the home and brought up the children but also entailed getting or growing food, making cloth and sewing clothing, and other work that allowed the family to subsist. This work was done side by side with the men and children of the family. The industrial revolution of the nineteenth century brought a major change: the removal of production work from the home to factories, and the change from making household goods at home to their becoming mass-produced commodities. The means of production, then, were no longer owned by the worker but by capitalists, who hired workers at wages low enough to make a profit.

Marx's analysis of the social structure of capitalism was supposed to apply to people of any social characteristics. If you owned the means of production, you were a member of the capitalist class; if you sold your labor for a wage, you were a member of the proletariat. That should be true of women as well, except that until the end of the nineteenth century, married women in capitalist countries were not allowed to own property in their own name; any wages they earned and their profits from any businesses they ran belonged legally to their husband.

Although Marx and other nineteenth-century economic theorists recognized the exploitation of wives' domestic labor, it was marxist feminism that put housewives at the forefront of its analysis of the gendered structure of capitalism. Housewives are vital to capitalism, indeed to any industrial economy, because their unpaid work in the home maintains bosses and workers and reproduces the next generation of bosses and workers (and their wives). Furthermore, if a bourgeois husband falls on hard times, his wife can do genteel work in the home, such as dressmaking, to earn extra money, or can take a temporary or part-time white-collar job. And when a worker's wages fall below the level needed to feed his family, as it often does, his wife can go out to work for wages in a factory or shop or another person's home, or she can turn the home into a small factory and put everyone, sometimes including the children, to work.

Because the housewife's prime responsibility is *social reproduction,* maintaining a husband and children and teaching children how to be members of society, she becomes part of a *reserve army of labor,* encouraged to work when the economy needs more workers, fired when unemployment rises. She can also be paid minimal wages and not expect promotions. The housewife's unpaid labor in the home is supposedly for her family. But both her paid and unpaid labor have economic value. Marxist feminism argues that this exploitation of women's work, both in the home and in the marketplace, is the prime source of gender inequality.

Dual systems theory. Marxist feminism analyzes the ways in which two parallel systems—the economy (capitalism) and the family (patriarchy)—structure women's and men's lives. A man who works for wages is exploited by capitalism because he is never paid as much as the profits he produces. At home, however, he has someone to work for him—his wife. She cooks his food, washes his clothing, satisfies his sexual needs, and brings up his children. If he loses his job, or cannot earn enough to support his family, she will go out to work or take work into the home, but she will continue her domestic duties as well. She will be paid less than a man doing comparable work because her main job is supposed to be taking care of her husband and children, and she can be fired when she is no longer needed by her employer, even if she would like to continue to work and her family could use extra income. Women's exploitation as a class is dual: a source of cheap labor in the marketplace and a source of unpaid labor in the home.

Work in the marketplace and work in the home are inextricably intertwined. Because of women's low value in the workplace, few can support themselves and their children in capitalist economies, so marriage or a man's financial help is an economic necessity. A wife earns her husband's economic support by doing housework and taking care of their children. Her work in the home is not only necessary to the physical and emotional well-being of her husband and children, it is also vital to the economy. Women's housework and child care make it possible for men to go to work and children to go to school, where they learn to take their future place in society—as workers, bosses, or the wives of workers or bosses. Mothers reproduce the social values of their class by passing them on to their children, teaching future bosses to be independent and take initiative and future workers and wives to be docile and obey orders.

A paper that was given at a workshop conference on occupational seg-regation at Wellesley College in 1975 was the start for what came to be known as *dual systems theory* in marxist feminism—an analysis of patriar-chy and capitalism as twin systems of men's domination of women. The conference was mainstream and not at all marxist in its auspices—it was funded by the Carnegie Corporation and jointly sponsored by the Ameri-can Economics Association Committee on the Status of Women and the Wellesley Center for Research on Women in Higher Education and the Professions. Yet the seed of a countertheory to the liberal feminist view of gender inequality was planted there by Heidi Hartmann, an economist.

Capitalism and Patriarchy

Heidi Hartmann
*Director of the Institute for Women's Policy Research,
Washington, DC*

The present status of women in the labor market and the current arrange-ment of sex-segregated jobs is the result of a long process of interaction between patriarchy and capitalism. I have emphasized the actions of male workers throughout this process because I believe that emphasis to be cor-rect. Men will have to be forced to give up their favored positions in the divi-sion of labor—in the labor market and at home—both if women's subordi-nation is to end and if men are to begin to escape class oppression and exploitation. Capitalists have indeed used women as unskilled, underpaid labor to undercut male workers, yet this is only a case of the chickens com-ing home to roost—a case of men's cooptation by and support for patriar-chal society, with its hierarchy among men, being turned back on them-selves with a vengeance. Capitalism grew on top of patriarchy; patriarchal capitalism is stratified society par excellence. If nonruling-class men are to be free they will have to recognize their cooptation by patriarchal capitalism and relinquish their patriarchal benefits. If women are to be free, they must fight against both patriarchal power and capitalist organization of society.

Because both the sexual division of labor and male domination are so long standing, it will be very difficult to eradicate them and impossible to eradicate the latter without the former. The two are now so inextricably intertwined that it is necessary to eradicate the sexual division of labor itself in order to end male domination. Very basic changes at all levels of society and culture are required to liberate women. In this paper, I have argued that the maintenance of job segregation by sex is a key root of women's status, and I have relied on the operation of society-wide institutions to explain the maintenance of job segregation by sex. But the consequences of that division of labor go very deep, down to the level of the subconscious. The subconscious influences behavior patterns, which form the micro underpinnings (or complements) of social institutions and are in turn reinforced by those social institutions.

I believe we need to investigate these micro phenomena as well as the macro ones I have discussed in this paper. For example, it appears to be a very deeply ingrained behavioral rule that men cannot be subordinate to women of a similar social class. Manifestations of this rule have been noted in restaurants, where waitresses experience difficulty in giving orders to bartenders, unless the bartender can reorganize the situation to allow himself autonomy; among executives, where women executives are seen to be most successful if they have little contact with others at their level and manage small staffs; and among industrial workers, where female factory inspectors cannot successfully correct the work of male production workers. There is also a deeply ingrained fear of being identified with the other sex. As a general rule, men and women must never do anything which is not masculine or feminine (respectively). Male executives, for example, often exchange handshakes with male secretaries, a show of respect which probably works to help preserve their masculinity.

At the next deeper level, we must study the subconscious—both how these behavioral rules are internalized and how they grow out of personality structures. At this level, the formation of personality, there have been several attempts to study the production of gender, the socially imposed differentiation of humans based on biological sex differences. A materialist interpretation of reality, of course, suggests that gender production grows out of the extant division of labor between the sexes, and, in a dialectical process, reinforces that very division of labor itself. In my view, because of these deep ramifications of the sexual division of labor we will not eradicate sex-ordered task division until we eradicate the socially imposed gender differences between us and, therefore, the very sexual division of labor itself.

In attacking both patriarchy and capitalism we will have to find ways to change both society-wide institutions and our most deeply ingrained habits. It will be a long, hard struggle.

Wages for housework. Marxist feminism once proposed that all women should get paid for housework and child care; they should not do it for love alone. If wives were waged workers, they would be part of the gross national product and could get raises and vacations and sick leave. But there is a sense in which wives *are* paid for their work for the family; husbands supposedly are paid enough to maintain their families as well as themselves—they are supposed to get what is called a *family wage.* The problem is that when a husband "pays" his wife for work in the home, either directly or indirectly, she is an economic dependent with few financial resources, a dangerous situation should her husband get sick, die, or leave her. The marxist feminist solution, like that of liberal feminism, is that women, too, should have permanent, full-time jobs. They would have independent means to fall back on in case they got a divorce or became a widow—or they did not have to get married at all, since they would be economically independent. For a mother, this solution entails affordable and accessible child care services.

And what about people living in areas where neither women nor men can get jobs? Since the men in their communities are equally poor, women do not have an economic advantage in marrying. They have to rely on government support—what we call "welfare." In the United States, government welfare benefits go only to poor women (after a means test), and so these benefits—and the women who receive them—are singled out as deviant and stigmatized. In many industrialized countries, there is government financial support for all mothers, and benefits are much more extensive than in the United States. The benefits include prenatal care, paid maternity leave, maternal and child health services, cash allowances each month for each child, free education through college (including books), and child care services. Every mother in the Scandinavian and other European countries and Israel receives some or most of these benefits. These *welfare states* recognize that producing children is work and that mothers therefore deserve state support. Their governments do not distinguish among poor and middle-class or wealthy women, or among full-time employees, part-time workers, and full-time homemakers. These services make it possible for all women to be both mothers and economically independent.

Such state benefits were the norm in the former communist countries, but feminists there soon recognized that this solution to gender inequality only substitutes economic dependence on the state for dependence on a husband. Women are even more responsible for child care, since the benefits are usually for the mother and rarely for the father. (Even when it is offered to them, few fathers take advantage of paid child care leave.) Furthermore, when women take paid jobs, it is other women who still do the child care, as paid workers in the home or in a child care facility, or as unpaid "othermothers." The women who do paid domestic labor in people's homes are usually from disadvantaged social groups; under capitalism, their wages tend to be minimal, and they rarely get any sick leave or health insurance, but in socialist countries, they get what any other worker receives.

The following excerpt is by sociologist Myra Marx Ferree, who has done research on German feminism when the country was split between communist East German Democratic Republic (GDR) and capitalist West Germany (Federal Republic of Germany, FRG) and after the fall of the Berlin Wall in 1989. The contrast between women's lives in the two Germanies, their sense of themselves, and the feminist movements that emerged was a "natural experiment" in the effects of two economic systems, which Marx Ferree calls *public patriarchy* and *private patriarchy*. Marx Ferree notes that the condition of public patriarchy, or reliance on the state for economic support, is similar to that of African American women on welfare in the United States.

Public and Private Patriarchies

Myra Marx Ferree
Professor of Sociology and Women's Studies,
University of Wisconsin-Madison

The distinction between public and private patriarchy rests fundamentally on the role of the state as either supplanting or supporting the conventional authority and practical power of the individual male as household head. The state socialism of East Germany (German Democratic Republic, GDR) supplanted the individual male head and thus embodied principles of public patriarchy; the state policies undergirding the social market economy of West Germany (Federal Republic of Germany, FRG) are, in contrast, strongly oriented to sustaining private patriarchy. The issue defining this distinction is *not* whether the state is more or less influential in women's lives, but rather the nature of the effects that it strives for and accomplishes.

In the GDR, state policy tended to diminish the dependence of women on individual husbands and fathers, but it enhanced the dependence of women as mothers on the state (Ferree 1993; Bastian, Labsch, and Miller 1990). In the FRG, state policy instead followed the principle of subsidiarity and actively encouraged private dependencies. In particular, the state had a mandate to pre-serve "the family," which it defined primarily as the husband-wife relationship as a context in which children can be raised (Moeller 1993; Ostner 1994). Thus, overall, the nature of the state's role in public patriarchy was to emphasize the *direct* relationship of mothers to the state; the nature of the state's role in pri-vate patriarchy was to encourage wives' dependence on husbands and chil-dren's on parents. In turn, this means that in public patriarchy women experi-enced their oppression as *mothers* and as more directly connected to the activities of the state as patriarch; in private patriarchy, women experienced their oppression as *wives* and as more directly connected to their individual dependence on their spouses.

To make these abstractions more concrete, compare the nature of women's ordinary life experiences in the two systems. In the former GDR, approximately one-third of all babies were born out-of-wedlock, and virtu-ally all women were in the labor force and worked essentially full-time jobs, where they earned on average 40 percent of the family income. Out-of-home child care for children under three and kindergartens and after-school care for older children were universally available at low cost (which, incidentally, is an exception among socialist as well as nonsocialist countries). State subsidies for child care, rent, and other basic necessities reduced differences in the standards of living between single mothers and two-parent, two-income families. Divorce was easy to obtain; women were more often the ones who petitioned for divorce; and the divorce rate was the highest in the world.[1] Dependence on an individual husband appears to have been reduced to a minimum.

In the FRG, by contrast, 90 percent of babies were born within marriages. Living together was not uncommon, but when the baby arrived, so did mar-riage (87 percent of cohabiting relationships were childless compared to 18 percent of marriages). Having a child was structurally inconsistent with hold-ing a full-time job, given the short and irregular school hours and scarcity of child care for preschool children. There were child care places for less than 5 percent of the children under three years of age. This incompatibility forced women to choose between having a baby or having a job. Of women aged 30 to 50, only one-third had full-time jobs; on the other hand, fully 15 percent of women aged 40–50 remained childless. A majority of employed mothers interrupted their careers for at least six years; even mothers of older children (15 years and older) were less likely than nonmothers to be in the labor force at all, not even considering the reductions they faced in the hours they worked or the status of their jobs. Given their restricted labor force participation, it is not surprising that West German women provided on average only 18 percent of the family income and that the majority of employed women did not earn enough to support themselves independently, let alone raise a child. Tax subsidies such as income splitting further widened the gulf between the standard of living of two-parent families and single mothers; if a mother was confronted with the choice of keeping her job or keeping her marriage, the economic incentives strongly favored the latter.[2] Dependence on an individual husband was thus strongly institutionalized.

These differences are well-known. The way they play themselves out in feminist identity and analysis is less obvious. There are several distinct areas where I think the differences between public and private patriarchy, and thus the structurally different experiences of dependency and oppression, were expressed in the specifics of feminist consciousness and politics before unification and which still carry a residue into current interactions.

Feminist Identity and the Structures of Experience

The most central difference relevant for feminism may be how women's identities are shaped in relation to the dominant form of patriarchy in general and how patriarchy has been institutionalized in particular. In West Germany, there was a conceptual package invoked by the phrase "wife-mother": these two roles were inseparably bundled together. This conceptualization has not carried over easily to the eastern part of unified Germany where motherhood was not bound so structurally to wifehood. Thinking about mothers in the FRG shaded easily into imagining them only as wives; one needed to specify "single mother" and, in doing so, one invoked the image of mothers who were politically and culturally deviant as well as impoverished. In the East, the imagery of single mother was not so necessary: women were mothers and workers and they may or may not have chosen to be or stay married. Being unmarried and a mother was not an identity that carried a connotation of victimhood, deviance, or struggle.

The imagery of "woman" was more shaped by the wife role in the West; the "conventional" picture of womanhood was structured in terms of a woman's tenuous connection to the labor force, her need to attend to her appearance and to the care of the household, and to be sexually attractive to and able to depend on an individual man. Women's magazines instructed their readers in how they could achieve the current style of satisfying their husband's needs. Identity was expressed in "lifestyle," which for most women meant the nature of their consumer activities and personal appearances.

For East Germans, the conventional woman was not at the disposal of an individual man but instrumentalized by the state as patriarch. The image of woman was thus the "worker-mother" who contributed both reproductive and productive labor to a collectively male-defined state. The concept of worker-mother appears to have been as much a self-evident package as the West's concept of wife-mother; the ability to combine paid employment and motherhood was not questioned any more in the East than the ability to combine wife and mother roles was in the West. In both the conventional image and the self-understanding of GDR women, wifehood was much less salient than the role of worker. Not only did the GDR woman's constant work at home and in the labor force take precedence over her appearance or the appearance of her home in others' perceptions of her, but she identified her children and her job, not her spouse or her home, as her achievements. . . .

In reality, neither public nor private patriarchy constitutes liberation for women, but each tends to shift the focus of women's attention to different aspects of their oppression. In the context of private patriarchy, the family, sexuality, and marital relations are initially at the forefront of theorizing (Janssen-Jurreit 1976; Millett 1970; Friedan 1963). The initial feminist idea is that if relationships between men and women as individuals could be put on a different footing, it would lead to structural change and vice versa—the structural changes that are sought are those that would change the balance of power within familial relationships. Power relationships within the family are often problematized and are seen as "spilling over" into the rest of social organization. In fact, rejecting marriage and seeking full-time employment, in the context of private patriarchy, are ways for women to challenge the status quo—to struggle against the individualized dependency prescribed by gender norms and almost invisibly upheld by state policy.

In the context of public patriarchy, the role of public policy and the state is more immediately central and obvious. The male domination of political decision-making in all areas, the role of the state as the "guardian" who speaks for women rather than allowing them to speak for themselves, and the felt absence of collective political voice are all aspects of the sense of powerlessness that are directly evident in the experience of women's subordination by collective rather than by individual male power. Power relations within the family, if problematized at all, are seen as stemming from more fundamental policies and decisions taken at the public political level. Private relationships—whether lesbian or heterosexual—are experienced as irrelevant or secondary in comparison (e.g., Merkel et al. 1990; Kahlau 1990; Hampele 1991). The common theme of feminist critiques is that women are "instrumentalized" by the state and that such state power must be challenged.

Neither of these experientially grounded perceptions is wholly wrong. Both the family and the state are arenas in which women's power and self-determination are restricted and where efforts to reconstitute social relations along less patriarchal lines are essential to the feminist project. Both forms of patriarchal organization, however, tend to encourage a distinctively one-sided form of analysis, because each type of model "fits" and explains certain gut-level experiences of oppression better. What is particularly instructive, albeit painful, is the collision between these two understandings. . . .

What "feels true" as a collective self-representation has to resonate with each woman's experience of her own oppression to be accepted, and that feeling of authenticity varies based on the fundamental political structuring of personal experience. Given such different ways of structuring experience in public and private patriarchy, what "feels true" to a woman raised in one system will likely "feel alien" to a woman whose identity has been formed in the other. Because an authentic feminist politics has to "feel true," it cannot—and should not—aspire to universal priorities or any single dimension of "correctness." Although sustaining a view of feminism as intrinsically multiple in its analyses and emphases is difficult, such pluralism enriches and strengthens feminist practice. . . .

Public Patriarchy in African-American Women's Lives

One of the most interesting of these potential analogies is the way in which Black feminist thought has also attempted to come to terms with the greater significance of public patriarchy in African American women's lives than in the lives of White American women.[3] Using such an analogy should not be interpreted to suggest that African American women's experience with a racist state is in any way identical to East German women's experience in the GDR, but rather to indicate that some of the elements that define public patriarchy, especially the direct relation of mothers to the state, may be responsible for observed similarities in identity and perspective that would otherwise be very surprising. Thus, despite dramatic differences in economic opportunity, family poverty, and social devaluation, among many other things, there are some points where African American feminist thought touches closely on issues that women in eastern Germany have also been attempting to express (the best summary of the diverse insights from Black feminist thought is Collins [1990]). Such surprising commonalities need some explanation. One possibility is that they reflect some general characteristics of difference between public and private patriarchy.

First, there has been a tendency for feminists in eastern Germany to talk more positively about the family and to see a challenge for feminism in integrating men more fully into family life. In comparison to women under private patriarchy, they did not see men's exclusion from the family as offering a good in itself nor did they define single parenting as freedom from male oppression—but they were also not so willing to marry, unless men met their expectations for family participation (e.g., Rohnstock 1994). Men's relationship to children was something that women valued and that the state ignored and actively marginalized. These are experiences on which African American feminists have also had to insist and about which White feminists have been skeptical (Collins 1990).

The experience of family as a support system in opposition to the culture at large, of withdrawal into the family as a form of privacy from the state, is another theme that presents family in a positive light in African American feminist writing; it is also echoed in some of the descriptions of the role of the family in state socialism in East Germany and elsewhere (e.g., Einhorn 1993; Funk and Mueller 1993). Because private patriarchy has not been so dominant in the experience of Black women or women in East Germany, it may be easier for them to imagine bringing men more centrally into families, without conceding patriarchal authority to them, than it is for many White American women or West German feminists. It seems at least possible that political practices that simply exclude men, as if changing them were either irrelevant or impossible, do not make nearly as much sense from a vantage point of public patriarchy as they do for women whose experiences have been more shaped by domination by individual men.

Second, women's labor force participation is easy to connect to women's liberation in the context of private patriarchy since the extent of women's earnings are in practice directly related to their independence from individual husbands. This link is more problematic in public patriarchy, since women's labor is expected—even demanded—in the paid labor force as well as in unpaid domestic chores. For African American feminists and feminists in East Germany, paid employment has provided a self-evident part of their identity as well as a burden—but it is hard to confuse it with "emancipation." The conditions of their integration into the paid labor force (e.g., ongoing discrimination), rather than the fact of employment itself, tend to draw theoretical attention and need more explanation. . . .

Ultimately, however, the reality of such diversity in women's experiences—not just in their interpretations of them—demands a definition of feminism that encompasses difference. What is now so often expressed as "better" and "worse" versions of feminism in Germany should not be understood so much as matters of women being naive or antimale or careerist or statist—in other words, not as expressions of deficiencies of feminist analysis—but rather as reflections of the differences in the organization of patriarchy and of women's lives. Theorizing difference in this context takes on a new meaning and a new urgency.

NOTES

1. For details and statistics on the status of women in the GDR, see Einhorn (1993); Helwig and Nickel (1993); Maier (1992). For a history of policy that discusses its objectives and how it has secured these outcomes, see Penrose (1990).
2. For more extensive and detailed data on the status of women in the preunification Federal Republic of Germany, see Helwig and Nickel (1993); Maier (1992); Kolinsky (1989). For a history of policy that suggests how these outcomes were sought and institutionalized, see Moeller (1993) and Ostner (1994).
3. Black and White are used here as political terms and thus captitalized.

REFERENCES

Bastian, Katrin, Evi Labsch, and Sylvia Muller. 1990. "Zur situation von Frauen als Arbeitskraft in der Geschichte der DDR." Originally published in *Zaunreiterin* (Leipzig), reprinted in *Streit* 2:59–67.

Collins, Patricia Hill. 1990. *Black Feminist Thought.* Boston: Unwin Hyman.

Einhorn, Barbara. 1993. *Cinderella Goes to Market: Citizenship, Gender, and Women's Movements in East Central Europe.* New York: Verso.

Friedan, Betty. 1963. *The Feminine Mystique.* New York: Dell.

Funk, Nanette, and Magda Mueller, eds. 1993. *Gender Politics and Post-communism.* New York: Routledge.

Hampele, Anne. 1991. "Der unabhangige Frauenverband." pp. 221–282 in *Von der Illegalitat ins Parlament,* edited by Helmut Muller-Enbergs, Marianne Schulz, and Jan Wielgohs. Berlin: LinksDruck Verlag.

Helwig, Gisela, and Hildegard Maria Nickel, eds. 1993. *Frauen in Deutschland, 1945–1992.* Band 318, Studien zur Geschichte and Politik. Bonn: Bundeszentrale fur politische Bildung.

Janssen-Jurreit, Marielouise. 1976. *Sexismus.* München: Carl Hanser Verlag.

Kahlau, Cordula, ed. 1990. *Aufbruch! Frauenbewegung in der DDR.* Munich: Frauenoffensive.

Kolinsky, Eva. 1989. *Women in West Germany: Life, Work, and Politics.* Oxford: Berg.

Maier, Friederike. 1992. "Frauenerwerbstätigkeit in der DDR and BRD: Gemeinsamkeiten and Unterschiede." Pp. 23–35 in *Ein Deutschland-Zwei Patriarchate?,* edited by Gudrun-Axeli Knapp and Ursula Müller. Bielefeld: University of Bielefeld.

Merkel, Ina, Eva Schäfer, Sünne Andresen, Frigga Haug, Kornelia Hauser, Jutta Meyer-Siebart, Eva Stäbler, and Ellen Woll, eds. 1990. *Ohne Frauen ist kein Staat zu machen.* Hamburg: Argument Verlag.

Millett, Kate. 1970. *Sexual Politics.* Garden City, NY: Doubleday.

Moeller, Robert. 1993. *Protecting Motherhood: Women and the Family in the Politics of Postwar West Germany.* Berkeley: University of California Press.

Ostner, Ilona. 1994. "Back to the Fifties: Gender and Welfare in Unified Germany." *Social Politics: International Studies in Gender, State, and Society* 1, no. 1:32–59.

Penrose, Virginia. 1990. "Vierzig Jahre SED-Frauenpolitik: Ziele, Strategien, Ergebnisse." *IFG: Frauenforschung* 4:60–77.

Rohnstock, Katrin. 1994. *Stiefschwestern: Was Ost-Frauen and West-Frauen voneinander denken.* Frankfurt a/M: Fischer.

Gender consciousness. The marxist feminist critique of the family as the source of women's oppression includes an account of how women's social location of wife and mother shapes their view of the world. Building on Marx's concept of *class consciousness,* which says that capitalists and members of the proletariat have conflicting interests and therefore an entirely different outlook on life, marxist feminism explores the ways that a wife's work in the home shapes her consciousness to be different from that of her husband. His work is future-oriented, geared to making a product or a profit; hers is present-oriented, getting dinner on the table and the children dressed for school every day. His work is abstract, dealing with money or ideas or an object; her work is hands-on, directly involved with living people who have bodily and emotional needs. He is supposed to be cool and impersonal and rational on the job; her job as wife and mother demands sensitivity to interpersonal cues and an outpouring of affection. He works as an individual, even when he brings home his paycheck; she is first and foremost a family member.

In their ways of thinking and feeling, men and women are different kinds of people, not because their brains are wired differently but because their life experiences give them diverse consciousnesses. The marxist feminist insight into women's *class consciousness* was the basis of feminist standpoint theory and radical feminism's *consciousness raising,* a strategy for sharing personal experiences of oppression.

Critique. Marxist feminism has been the foundation of an influential economic theory of gender inequality that links the gendered division of labor in the family and in the workplace. The political solutions based on this theory, as carried out in the former communist countries and in democratic welfare states, improve women's material lives but fall far short of freeing women from men's control.

Marxist feminism shows that women are locked into a condition of lesser economic resources whether they are wives of workers or workers themselves. If they marry economically successful men, they become dependents, and if they marry poor men or do not marry at all, they and their children can starve. The welfare-state solution—benefits to all mothers—is rooted in this analysis. There is, however, a negative side to state payments for child care (the equivalent of wages for housework); they are important in giving mothers independent economic resources, but they can also keep women out of the paid marketplace or encourage part-time work. These policies thus have the latent function of keeping women a reserve army of cheap labor in capitalist, state-owned, and welfare-state economies.

Women's economic inequality in the family division of labor has been somewhat redressed in countries that give all mothers paid leave before and after the birth of a child and that provide affordable child care. But that solution puts the burden of children totally on the mother and encourages men to opt out of family responsibilities altogether. (To counteract that trend, feminists in the government of Sweden allocated a certain portion of paid child care leave to fathers specifically.)

Women in the former communist countries had what liberal feminism in capitalist economies always wanted for women—full-time jobs with state-supported maternity leave and child care services. But as marxist feminists recognize, the state can be as paternalistic as any husband. They argue that male-dominated government policies put the state's interests before those of women: When the economy needs workers, the state pays for child care leave; with a downturn in the economy, the state reduces the benefits. Similarly, when the state needs women to have more children, it cuts back on availability of abortions and contraceptive services. Thus, the marxist feminist solution to women's economic inequality—full-time jobs and state-provided maternal and child welfare benefits—does not change women's status as primarily wives and mothers and men's status as the primary breadwinners. The gendered social order has been reformed but not significantly changed.

Summary

Marxist feminist theory emphasizes the economic and psychological differences between women and men, and men's power over women that emerges from their different statuses in the gendered division of labor. Marxist feminist theory is based on the division between work in the family (primarily women's work) and work in paid production (primarily men's work). Women are exploited because they work at production *and* reproduction in the home, and frequently at low-paying jobs outside the home as well.

In state economies that provide maternal and child care benefits, a woman with children is better off materially, but she is not economically independent. Instead of the private patriarchy of economic dependence on a husband, women are subject to the public patriarchy of a paternalistic state, which is more interested in women as paid and unpaid workers and as child producers than in furthering gender equality in the home or in the workplace.

In all industrial economies, women and men have a different "class" consciousness because they do different work. Women have prime responsibility for child care, even though they may work full time outside the home. Thus, they live a significant part of their lives in a world of reciprocity and cooperation, personal responsibility and sharing, physical contact and affection, in contrast to the impersonal and abstract world of industrial production, the world of men's work. Men's work in the marketplace is rewarded according to time spent or product made. Women's work in the home is never-ending; rewards depend on personalized standards, and others come first. It is emotional as well as intellectual and physical labor. Just as the economic positions of capitalists and the proletariat shape their class consciousness, women's daily material and socioemotional labor differentiates their consciousness from that of men.

Suggested Readings in Marxist Feminism

Bannerji, Himani. 1995. *Thinking Through: Essays on Feminism, Marxism, and Anti-Racism.* Toronto: Women's Press.

Barrett, Michèle. 1988. *Women's Oppression Today: The Marxist/Feminist Encounter.* Rev. ed. London: Verso.

Brenner, Johanna. 2000. *Women and the Politics of Class.* New York: Monthly Review Press.

Collins, Jane L., and Martha E. Gimenez, eds. 1990. *Work Without Wages: Comparative Studies of Domestic Labor and Self-Employment.* Albany: State University of New York Press.

Coontz, Stephanie, and Peta Henderson. 1986. *Women's Work, Men's Property: The Origins of Gender and Class.* London: Verso.

Funk, Nanette, and Magda Mueller, eds. 1993. *Gender Politics and Post-Communism: Reflections from Eastern Europe and the Former Soviet Union.* New York: Routledge.

Glazer, Nona Y. 1993. *Women's Paid and Unpaid Labor: The Work Transfer in Retailing and Health Care.* Philadelphia: Temple University Press.

Hartsock, Nancy C. M. 1983. *Money, Sex, and Power: Toward a Feminist Historical Materialism.* New York: Longman.

Hennessy, Rosemary. 1993. *Materialist Feminism and the Politics of Discourse.* London: Routledge.

Holter, Harriet, ed. 1984. *Patriarchy in a Welfare Society.* Oslo, Norway: Universitetsforlaget.

Johnson, Kay Ann. 1983. *Women, the Family and Peasant Revolution in China.* Chicago: University of Chicago Press.

Milkman, Ruth. 1987. *Gender at Work.* Urbana: University of Illinois Press.

Redclift, Nanneke, and Enzo Mingione, eds. 1985. *Beyond Employment: Household, Gender and Subsistence.* Oxford: Basil Blackwell.

Rueschemeyer, Marilyn, ed. 1994. *Women in the Politics of Postcommunist Eastern Europe.* Armonk, NY: M. E. Sharpe.

Sainsbury, Diane, ed. 1994. *Gendering Welfare States.* Thousand Oaks, CA: Sage.

Sargent, Lydia, ed. 1981. *Women and Revolution: A Discussion of the Unhappy Marriage of Marxism and Feminism.* Boston: South End Press.

Sayers, Janet, Mary Evans, and Nanneke Redclift, eds. 1987. *Engels Revisited: New Feminist Essays.* London: Tavistock.

Sokoloff, Natalie J. 1980. *Between Money and Love: The Dialectics of Women's Home and Market Work.* New York: Praeger.

Stacey, Judith. 1983. *Patriarchy and Socialist Revolution in China.* Berkeley: University of California Press.

Tax, Meredith. 1980. *The Rising of the Women: Feminist Solidarity and Class Conflict, 1880–1917.* New York: Monthly Review Press.

Walby, Sylvia. 1986. *Patriarchy at Work: Patriarchal and Capitalist Relations in Employment.* Minneapolis: University of Minnesota Press.

———. 1990. *Theorizing Patriarchy.* Oxford: Basil Blackwell.

Weigand, Kate. 2001. *Red Feminism: American Communism and the Making of Women's Liberation.* Baltimore, MD: Johns Hopkins University Press. ✦

Chapter Three

Socialist Feminism

Sources of Gender Inequality

- The accumulation of advantages that gives men wider social power and the means to dominate women.
- Second-class citizenship—the result of the accumulation of women's disadvantages.
- Double and triple oppression of women in racial ethnic groups that suffer from economic and cultural discrimination.

Politics

- Redistribution of responsibilities in the family, equal sharing of family work.
- Degendered access to economic opportunities, upgrading women's jobs.
- Universal entitlements to education, child care, health care, income support.
- Access to governmental and nongovernmental political power for all.

Contributions

- Structural analysis of the status of women beyond the family and the economy.

- Making visible the combined effects of gender, class, and racial ethnic status.
- Concept of complex inequality to describe accumulated economic, cultural, and political disadvantages.

During the 1980s, socialist feminism expanded the ideas of marxist feminism beyond the family and the economy. Socialist feminism argues that gender inequality is not just the result of women's oppression as an unpaid worker for the family and as a low-paid worker in the economy. There are broader injustices from the effects of gender and class, gender and racial ethnic status, and all three combined. Work in the home is invisible as work, but it is often done for pay by women disadvantaged by racial ethnic and immigrant status. Gender discrimination devalues the status and income of women's jobs. Because most women in industrialized countries are housewives or have low-paying jobs, they are less likely to belong to unions and to hold political office. Women in groups disadvantaged by race, ethnicity, and immigrant status suffer double or triple discrimination, but the interests of the men of their groups are more likely to prevail in political conflicts. Women's interests, socialist feminism argues, are not represented in class, racial ethnic, or national politics. In short, women are second-class citizens.

Gender, class, and racial ethnic status. Gender blurs class distinctions in the workplace; work organizations and salary scales are not gender-neutral. Class relations of women bosses and the men who work for them differ substantially from the conventional gendered authority pattern. In most workplaces, women have authority over other women, not men. A job in a field where most of the workers are women has less status and pays less than a job where most of the workers are men, even if the jobs are comparable on credentials and responsibilities. Salaries are highest in jobs where men are the predominant workers, whether the worker is a woman or a man, and lowest in jobs where women are the predominant workers, again whether the worker is a man or a woman. Looked at from the perspective of the worker, men have the advantage no matter what the gender composition of the job or workplace. Men earn more than women in jobs where men are the majority, in jobs where women are the majority, and in gender-neutral jobs.

Gender also blurs the public and private dimensions of class. Women do domestic work and child care in other women's homes for pay. Jobs that call for nurturance and empathy, such as nursing and social work—emotion work—are typically women's jobs because these attributes are supposedly natural. Women do nursing and other caretaking as part of family work, but they also do it for pay, as trained professionals. Yet because this work is "doing what comes naturally" to women, it pays less.

A woman's class position, like that of a member of a disadvantaged racial ethnic group, is a mixed status—high in some respects, low in others. A single woman's occupation and income level are devalued by her gender. A married woman's class status is defined by her husband's occupation, income, and education. She may have a college education and he may not, but it is his social class that counts for the family. He may be a boss or an employee; in class terms, she is his subordinate in the home since he is considered the chief breadwinner. His salary is a "family wage," implicitly paid as well to his wife for her work in home and in the care of their children. But she may hire a woman to clean the house and another to care for her children. In that sense, she is an employer, in the "boss" class, especially if it is her income that goes to pay their salaries. If she is not employed, and her husband's income pays for the household help she has hired and directs, who is the boss?

Racial ethnic status often breaks up working-class, middle-class, and upper-class women and men into multiple tiers, but it sometimes reinforces class status. In the following excerpt from "The Social Construction and Institutionalization of Gender and Race: An Integrative Framework," which was written for *Revisioning Gender*, sociologist Evelyn Nakano Glenn describes the complexities of gender, class, and racial ethnic status among women doing reproductive labor in the home and in the public sphere and the consequences for citizenship.

Gender, Race, and Citizenship

Evelyn Nakano Glenn
Professor of Women's Studies, University of California, Berkeley

The Race and Gender Division of Private Reproductive Labor. From the late nineteenth century to the mid-twentieth century, poor and working-class women not only did reproductive labor in their own homes, they also performed it for middle-class families. The division between White women and women of color grew in the latter half of the nineteenth century, when the demand for household help and the number of women employed as servants expanded rapidly (Chaplin 1978). Rising standards of cleanliness, larger and more ornately furnished homes, the sentimentalization of the home as a "haven in a heartless world," and the new emphasis on childhood and mother's role in nurturing children all served to enlarge middle-class women's responsibilities for reproduction at a time when technology had done little to reduce the sheer physical drudgery of housework (Cowan 1983; Degler 1980; Strasser 1982).

By all accounts, middle-class women did not challenge the gender-based division of labor or the enlargement of their reproductive responsibilities. To the contrary, as readers and writers of literature, and as members and leaders of clubs, charitable organizations, associations, reform movements, religious revivals, and the cause of abolition, they helped to elaborate and refine the domestic code (Epstein 1981; Ryan 1981). Instead of questioning the inequitable gender division of labor, they sought to slough off the burdensome tasks onto more oppressed groups of women (see Kaplan 1987).

In the United States, the particular groups hired for private reproductive work varied by region. In the Northeast, European immigrant women, especially Irish, were the primary servant class. In regions with a substantial racial minority population, the servant caste consisted almost exclusively of women of color. In the early years of the twentieth century, 90 percent of non-agriculturally employed Black women in the South were servants or laundresses, constituting more than 80 percent of female servants (Katzman 1978:55). In cities of the Southwest, such as El Paso and Denver, where the main division was between Anglos and Mexicans, approximately half of all employed Mexican women were domestic or laundry workers (Deutsch 1987; Garcia 1981). In the San Francisco Bay Area and in Honolulu, where there were substantial numbers of Asian immigrants, a quarter to half of all employed Japanese women were private household workers (Glenn 1986; Lind 1951, table 1:74).

Women of color shouldered not only the burdens of household maintenance, but also those of family nurturing for White middle-class women. They did both the dirty, heavy manual labor of cleaning and laundering and the emotional work of caring for children. By performing the dirty work and time-consuming tasks, they freed their mistresses for supervisory tasks, for leisure and cultural activities, or, more rarely during this period, for careers. Ironically, then, many White women were able to fulfill White society's expectation of feminine domesticity only through the domestic labor of women of color.

For the domestic worker, the other side of doing reproductive labor for White families was not being able to perform reproductive labor for their own families. Unlike European immigrant domestics, who were mainly single young women, racial ethnic servants were usually wives and mothers (Stigler 1946; Watson 1937). Yet the code that sanctified White women's domesticity did not extend to them. In many cases, servants had to leave their own children in the care of relatives in order to "mother" their employers' children. A 6½-day workweek was typical. A Black children's nurse reported in 1912 that she worked 14 to 16 hours a day caring for her mistress' four children. Describing her existence as a "treadmill life," she said she was allowed to go home

> only once in every two weeks, every other Sunday afternoon—even then I'm not permitted to stay all night. I see my own children only when they happen to see me on the streets when I am out with the children [of her mistress], or when my children come to the "yard" to see me, which isn't often, because my white folks don't like to see their servants' children hanging around their premises. (quoted in Katzman 1982:179)

The dominant group ideology naturalized the mistress-servant relationship by portraying women of color as particularly suited for service. These racialized gender constructions ranged from the view of African American and Mexican American women as incapable of governing their own lives and requiring White supervision to the view of Asian women as naturally subservient and accustomed to a low standard of living. Although racial stereotypes undoubtedly preceded their entry into domestic work, household workers were also induced to enact the role of race-gender inferiors in daily interactions with employers. Domestic workers interviewed by Rollins (1985) and Romero (1992) described a variety of rituals that affirmed their subordination and dependence; for example, employers addressed the household workers by their first names and required them to enter by the back door, eat in the kitchen, wear uniforms, and accept with gratitude "gifts" of discarded clothing and leftover food.

The lack of respect for racial ethnic women's family roles stood in marked contrast to the situation of White middle-class women in the late nineteenth and early twentieth centuries, when the cult of domesticity defined White womanhood primarily in terms of wifehood and motherhood. While the domestic code constrained White women, it placed racial ethnic women in an untenable position. Forced to work outside the home, they were considered deviant according to the dominant gender ideology. On the one hand, they were denied the buffer of a protected private sphere; on the other, they were judged deficient as wives and mothers compared with White middle-class women who could devote themselves to domesticity full-time (Pascoe 1990). Women of color had to construct their own definitions of self-worth and womanhood outside the standards of the dominant culture. Their efforts to maintain kin ties, organize family celebrations, cook traditional foods, and keep households together were crucial to the survival of ethnic communities.

The Race and Gender Construction of Public Reproductive Labor. Due to the expansion of capital into new areas for profit making, the fragmentation of families and breakdown of extended kin and community ties, and the squeeze on women's time as they moved into the labor market, the post–World War II era saw the expansion of commodified services to replace the reproductive labor formerly performed in the home (Braverman 1974:276). Among the fastest-growing occupations in the economy in the 1980s and 1990s were lower-level service jobs in health care, food service, and personal services (U.S. Department of Labor 1993). Women constitute the main labor force in these occupations. Within this new realm of "public reproductive labor," we find a clear race-gender division of labor. Women of color are disproportionately assigned to do the dirty work, as nurse's aides in hospitals, kitchen workers in restaurants and cafeterias, maids in hotels, and cleaners in office buildings. In these same institutional settings, White women are disproportionately employed as supervisors, professionals, and administrative support staff. This division parallels the earlier division between the domestic servant and the housewife. And just as in the household, dirty work is considered menial and unskilled, and the women who do it are too; moreover, White women benefit by being able to do higher-level work.

With the shift of reproductive labor from the household to market, face-to-face race and gender hierarchies have been replaced by structural hierarchies. In institutional settings, race and gender stratification is built into organizational structures, including lines of authority, job descriptions, rules, and spatial and temporal segregation. Distance between higher and lower orders is ensured by structural segregation. Much routine service work is organized to be out of sight. It takes place behind institutional walls, where outsiders rarely penetrate (nursing homes, chronic care facilities), in back rooms (restaurant kitchens), or at night or other times when occupants are gone (office buildings and hotels). Although workers may appreciate this time and space segregation, which allows them some autonomy and freedom from demeaning interactions, it also makes them and their work invisible. In this situation, more privileged women do not have to acknowledge the workers or confront any contradiction between shared womanhood and inequality by race and class.

Implications. Both historically and in the contemporary United States, the racial construction of gendered labor has created divisions between White and racial ethnic women that go beyond differences in experience and standpoint. Their situations have been interdependent: The higher status and living standards of White women have depended on the subordination and lower standards of living of women of color. Moreover, White women have been able to meet more closely the hegemonic standards of womanhood because of the devaluation of the womanhood of racial ethnic women. This analysis suggests that if these special forms of exploitation were to cease, White women as well as men would give up certain privileges and benefits. Thus, social policies to improve the lot of racial ethnic women may entail loss of privilege or status for White women and may therefore engender resistance from them as well as from men.

The Race and Gender Construction of Citizenship

The second institutional domain that often has been looked at as either gendered or raced, but rarely as both, is the state. Because the topic of the state is vast, I will focus this discussion on one aspect, namely, the construction of who is a citizen and what rights and responsibilities go with that status.

Gender and Citizenship. The denial of first-class citizenship has been a central issue for feminist political theorists. Pateman (1988, 1989), Young (1989), and Okin (1979) have analyzed the conception of citizenship in Hobbes, Locke, Rousseau, and other canonical writings and have found that the "universal citizen" defined in these writings is male. Pateman (1988, 1989), for example, traces women's exclusion to the construction of a public/private binary and other oppositions in liberal political thought. The "public" and the "private" are constructed in opposition; the public is the realm of citizenship, rights, and generality, whereas sexuality, feeling, and specificity—and women—are relegated to the private. Citizenship thus is defined in opposition to womanhood.

Recently there has been a growing interest in social citizenship, a key concept in analyses of the modern welfare state (Marshall 1950). Some feminist critics have characterized the state as patriarchal in its provision of welfare, in that it both supports the male-headed household and exerts authority over women by regulating their conduct (e.g., Abramovitz 1996; Sapiro 1986). Other critics have pointed out that from the 1890s on, the United States institutionalized a two-tiered system of social rights (e.g., Gordon 1994; Michel 1996; Nelson 1990). The upper level, consisting of entitlements such as unemployment benefits, old-age insurance, and disability payments, disproportionately goes to men by virtue of their record of regular employment; the lower level, consisting of various forms of stigmatized "welfare," such as AFDC, is what women disproportionately are forced to turn to because of need.

Race and Citizenship. Historians and sociologists looking at race and citizenship have generally been animated by Myrdal's *An American Dilemma* (1944), the disjunction between a professed belief in equal rights existing alongside the denial of fundamental civil and political rights to major segments of the population. In his monumental study, *We the People and Others,* Ringer (1983) argues that this exclusion was not a "flaw," but an inherent feature of the American political system from its very inception. According to Ringer, the United States established a dual legal political system based on colonialist principles. The "people's domain," made up of those considered full members of the national community, "among whom principles of equality and democracy might prevail despite unequal distribution of wealth, power and privilege," exists alongside a second level of those excluded from the national community, "who become the objects of control and exploitation and who are subject to the repressive powers of the state without the basic protection of citizenship" (Ringer and Lawless 1989:86).

Horsman (1981) notes that republican discourse tied the idea of Whiteness to notions of independence and self-control necessary for self-governance. This conception emerged in concert with European and Anglo-American conquest and colonization of non-Western societies. Understanding non-European others as dependent and lacking the capacity for self-governance rationalized the extermination and forced removal of Native Americans, the enslavement of Blacks, and the takeover of land from Mexicans in the Southwest. Smith (1988) notes,

"From the revolution era on, many American leaders deliberately promoted the popular notion that Americans had a distinctive character, born of their freedom-loving Anglo-Saxon ancestors and heightened by the favorable conditions of the new world," that "set them above Blacks and truly Native Americans, and later Mexicans, Chinese, Filipinos, and others who were labeled unfit for self-government" (p. 233).

Citizenship as Raced and Gendered. The problem with looking at citizenship as only gendered or only raced is the familiar one: Women of color fall through the cracks. According to existing accounts, White women were not accorded full adult citizenship by dint of having their identities subsumed by their husbands and fathers. White women were "virtual citizens" because men were assumed to represent their wives' and children's interests along with their own. Men of color were deemed noncitizens by virtue of their being "unfree labor," "lacking the cultural traits of "freedom," and being "servile." The question remains: Where do women of color fit? In what follows, I attempt to synthesize the largely separate literatures on gendered citizenship and raced citizenship to trace the racialized gender construction of American citizenship. Although necessarily sketchy, this account may suggest some directions for future analyses.

At its most general level, *citizenship* refers to the status of being a full member of the community in which one lives (Hall and Held 1989). Citizenship in Western societies always has had a dual aspect as a system of equality and as a major axis of inequality. On the one hand, citizenship is defined as a universal status in which all who are included have identical rights and responsibilities, irrespective of their individual characteristics. This conception emerged out of the political and intellectual revolutions of the seventeenth and eighteenth centuries, as the older concept of society organized as a hierarchy of status, expressed by differential rights, gave way to the notion of a political order established through social contract. The concept of social contract implied free and equal status among those party to it. On the other hand, the process of defining membership and rights of citizenship entailed drawing boundaries that created "noncitizens." Rhetorically, the citizen was defined and gained meaning through its contrast with the "noncitizen" as one who lacked the essential qualities of a citizen. Materially, the autonomy and freedom of the citizen were made possible by the often involuntary labor of noncitizen wives, slaves, children, servants, and employees. . . .

References

Abramovitz, Mimi.1996. *Regulating the Lives of Women.* Rev ed. Boston: South End.

Braverman, Harry L. 1974. *Labor and Monopoly Capital.* New York: Monthly Review Press.

Chaplin, David. 1978. "Domestic Service and Industrialization." *Comparative Studies in Sociology* 1:97–127.

Cowan, Ruth Schwartz. 1983. *More Work for Mother.* New York: Basic Books.

Degler, Carl. 1980. *At Odds: Woman and the American Family from the Revolution to the Present.* New York: Oxford University Press.

Deutsch, Sarah. 1987. *No Separate Refuge: Culture, Class and Gender on an Anglo-Hispanic Frontier in the American Southwest, 1880–1920.* New York: Oxford University Press.

Epstein, Barbara. 1981. *The Politics of Domesticity: Women, Evangelism and Temperance in Nineteenth-Century America.* Middletown, CT: Wesleyan University Press.

Garcia, Mario. 1981. *Desert Immigrants: The Mexicans of El Paso, 1880–1920.* New Haven, CT: Yale University Press.

Glenn, Evelyn Nakano. 1986. *Issei, Nisei, Warbride: Three Generations of Japanese American Women in Domestic Service.* Philadelphia: Temple University Press.

Gordon, Linda. 1994. *Pitied but Not Entitled: Single Mothers and the History of Welfare 1890–1935.* New York: Free Press.

Hall, Stuart and David Held. 1989. "Citizens and Citizenship." Pp. 173–88 in *New Times,* edited by Stuart Hall and Jacques Martin. London: Lawrence & Wishart.

Horsman, Reginald. 1981. *Race and Manifest Destiny.* Cambridge, MA: Harvard University Press.

Kaplan, Elaine Bell. 1987. " 'I Don't Do No Windows': Competition between the Domestic Worker and the Housewife." In *Competition: A Feminist Taboo?* edited by Valerie Minor and Helen E. Longino. New York: Feminist Press.

Katzman, David. 1978. *Seven Days a Week: Women and Domestic Service in Industrializing America.* New York: Oxford University Press.

Lind, Andrew W. 1951. "The Changing Position of Domestic Service in Hawaii." *Social Process in Hawaii* 15:71–87.

Marshall, T. H. 1950. *Citizenship and Social Class and Other Essays.* Cambridge: Cambridge University Press.

Michel, Sonya. 1996. "A Tale of Two States." Presented at the Women's Studies Colloquium, University of California, Berkeley.

Myrdal, Gunnar (with R. Sterner and A. Rose). 1944. *An American Dilemma: The Negro Problem and Modern Democracy.* New York: Harper & Row.

Nelson, Barbara. 1990. "The Origins of the Two-Channel Welfare State: Workman's Compensation and Mothers' Aid." Pp. 123–51 in *Women, the State and Welfare,* edited by Linda Gordon. Madison: University of Wisconsin Press.

Okin, Susan. 1979. *Women in Western Political Thought.* Princeton, NJ: Princeton University Press.

Pascoe, Peggy. 1990. *Relations of Rescue.* New York: Oxford University Press.

Pateman, Carole. 1988. *The Sexual Contract.* Cambridge: Polity.

———. 1989. *The Disorder of Women.* Stanford, CA: Stanford University Press.

Ringer, Benjamin B. 1983. *We the People and Others: Duality and America's Treatment of Its Racial Minorities.* New York: Tavistock.

Ringer, Benjamin B. and Elinor Lawless. 1989. *Race, Ethnicity and Society.* New York: Routledge.

Rollins, Judith. 1985. *Between Women: Domestics and Their Employers.* Philadelphia: Temple University Press.

Romero, Mary. 1992. *Maid in the U.S.A.* New York: Routledge.

Ryan, Mary P. 1981. *Cradle of the Middle Class: The Family in Oneida County, New York, 1790–1865.* Cambridge: Cambridge University Press.

Sapiro, Virginia. 1986. "The Gender Basis of American Social Policy." *Political Science Quarterly* 101:221–38.

Smith, Rogers M. 1988. " 'One United People': Second-Class Female Citizenship and the American Quest for Community." *Yale Journal of Law and the Humanities* 1:229–93.

Stigler, George J. 1946. "Domestic Servants in the United States, 1900–1940." Occasional Paper 24, National Bureau of Economic Research, New York.

Strasser, Susan 1982. *Never Done: A History of American Housework.* New York: Pantheon.

U.S. Department of Labor, Bureau of Labor Statistics. 1993. *Occupational Outlook Quarterly* (Fall).

Watson, Amey. 1937. "Domestic Service." In *Encyclopedia of the Social Sciences.* New York: Macmillan.

Young, Iris Marion. 1989. "Polity and Group Difference: A Critique of the Ideal of Universal Citizenship." *Ethics* 99:250–74.

Complex inequality. Socialist feminism sees race and ethnicity, gender, and class as overlapping parts of a social structural, world-wide system of privilege and disadvantage. Each system is intertwined with the others. Although the term *intersectionality* would not be used widely until the 1990s, the concept of interlocked effects was an important contribution of socialist feminism. Social class, gender, and racial ethnic membership cannot be separated from each other, because each of those statuses affect others—a Black woman physician has a different status mix and social position than a White woman physician or a Black man physician. Furthermore, privilege (and disadvantage) on any one status enhances or brings down the others. Wealth is a social good in its own right, but it can also be used to buy a good education for one's children and political candidacy for one's husband. It is less likely to foster a woman's political ambitions. The accumulation of advantages gives people wider social power and the means to dominate those with fewer advantages. Their disadvantages also accumulate. The result is *complex inequality.*

The concept of *complex inequality* was originally used by political and social theorists to describe how economic success can be parlayed into political power, social position, and media attention—the "bold-face names." The problem is that it does not apply in the same way to women. Women are embedded into families in ways that men are not. Even if a woman can hire domestic help and child care, as a mother and wife in Western societies, she alone is responsible for the emotional, social, and physical well-being of her family. The demands of family on women are an additional aspect of complex inequality, with material and social penalties. Compared to men and childless women, mothers make less money, are more likely to be fired, achieve fewer positions of authority and prestige, and have much less chance to wield social power. Those who cut back or leave the workplace are socially downgraded and lose marital bargaining power. Working-class single mothers may end up on welfare.

In modern industrialized societies, it is acceptable for the husband's job to take precedence over his family responsibilities, and for the wife's family responsibilities to take precedence over her job. It is not acceptable for the husband who wants to advance in his career to routinely reduce his regular paid work time, his overtime, or his work-based travel because he has family duties. Conversely, the wife who does not cover for her family duties before taking on routine or unusual job responsibilities is considered neglectful, and though she may advance in her career, the micropolitics of the workplace may eventually stigmatize her. The asymmetry of the husband's continued prime responsibility for economic support of the family and the wife's continued prime responsibility for family work leads to gender inequality.

Gender and justice. Although everyone in a society benefits from good parenting, mothers bear an unequal burden. Many Western industrial countries absorb some of the costs of child rearing with child allowances, subsidized day care, free health insurance, and paid parental leave. But even if the workplace is family-friendly and governments or employers provide financial benefits for children, mothers have an extra job. This job does not bring public social rewards or economic success, rather it diminishes both. It is a privatized, disadvantaged status in Western industrialized societies.

Family caretaking is work that takes time, energy, thought, and skill, and that incurs costs and benefits to unpaid caretakers, paid workers, family members, and to the whole social order. All adult men and women are "caring citizens"; women, however, do most of the hands-on family work. To make caring citizenship gender-equal, the adults in a household, men as well as women, have to share family work and be able to balance it with their work time.

Socialist feminism makes it clear that gender equality demands redistribution of responsibilities in the family and degendered access to economic opportunities. Households need to be restructured so that mothers and fathers share work for the family and work for pay. The typing of jobs as "women's work" and "men's work" needs to be eliminated. Women must have the opportunity to go up career ladders, and attain positions of power and authority in professions and in politics.

But the focus on redistribution in the family and in the public sphere is not enough to redress gender inequality. What is also needed is recognition of the devalued and powerless status of women, especially those of disfavored racial ethnic groups. Women are sexually vulnerable and lack control over procreation. They are exploited as sex objects. As long as there are significant social and cultural differences between women and men beyond the biological, economic equality will not translate into full-fledged gender equality.

Nancy Fraser, a feminist political philosopher, has been exploring the tensions between equality and equity, needs and rights, redistribution and recognition since 1989, when she published "Struggle Over Needs: Outline of a Socialist-Feminist Critical Theory of Late Capitalist Political Culture" in *Unruly Practices.* The following excerpt is from her latest exploration; it is part of an exchange with Axel Honneth, a German philosopher. In the first part, she lays out the dimensions of gender as a class and as a status. In the second part, she argues for going beyond economic redistribution in order to affirm the value of women. What is needed, she says, are transformative politics and "cross-redressing" policies that would correct economic maldistribution and at the same time raise devalued social statuses. For example, government-provided quality child care that everyone uses destigmatizes working mothers and defuses class differences.

Redistribution, Recognition, and Cross-Redressing

Nancy Fraser
Professor of Philosophy and Politics, New School University,
New York

Gender, I contend, is a two-dimensional social differentiation. Neither simply a class nor simply a status group, gender is a hybrid category rooted simultaneously in the economic structure and the status order of society. Understanding and redressing gender injustice, therefore, requires attending to both distribution and recognition.

From the distributive perspective, gender serves as a basic organizing principle of the economic structure of capitalist society. On the one hand, it structures the fundamental division between paid "productive" labor and unpaid "reproductive" and domestic labor, assigning women primary responsibility for the latter. On the other hand, gender also structures the division within paid labor between higher-paid, male-dominated manufacturing and professional occupations and lower-paid, female-dominated "pink collar" and domestic service occupations. The result is an economic structure that generates gender-specific forms of distributive injustice, including gender-based exploitation, economic marginalization, and deprivation.

Here, gender appears as a class-like differentiation that is rooted in the economic structure of society. When viewed under this aspect, gender injustice appears as a species of distributive injustice that cries out for redistributive redress. Much like class, gender justice requires transforming the economy so as to eliminate its gender structuring. Eliminating gender-specific maldistribution requires abolishing the gender division of labor—both the gendered division between paid and unpaid labor and the gender divisions within paid labor. The logic of the remedy is akin to the logic with respect to class: it aims to put gender out of business as such. If gender were nothing but a class-like differentiation, in sum, justice would require its abolition.

That, however, is only half the story. In fact, gender is not only a class-like division, but a status differentiation as well. As such, it also encompasses elements more reminiscent of sexuality than class, which bring it squarely within the problematic of recognition. Gender codes pervasive cultural patterns of interpretation and evaluation, which are central to the status order as a whole. As a result, not just women but all low-status groups risk feminization and thus depreciation.

Thus, a major feature of gender injustice is androcentrism: an institutionalized pattern of cultural value that privileges traits associated with masculinity, while devaluing everything coded as "feminine," paradigmatically—but not only—women. Pervasively institutionalized, androcentric value patterns structure broad swaths of social interaction. Expressly codified in many areas of law (including family law and criminal law), they inform legal constructions of privacy, autonomy, self-defense, and equality. They are also entrenched in many areas of government policy (including reproductive, immigration, and asylum policy) and in standard professional practices (including medicine and psychotherapy). Androcentric value patterns also pervade popular culture and everyday interaction. As a result, women suffer gender-specific forms of *status subordination*, including sexual assault and domestic violence; trivializing, objectifying, and demeaning stereotypical depictions in the media; harassment and disparagement in everyday life; exclusion or marginalization in public spheres and deliberative bodies; and denial of the full rights and equal protections of citizenship. These harms are injustices of recognition. They are relatively independent of political economy and are not merely "superstructural." Thus, they cannot be overcome by redistribution alone but require additional, independent remedies of recognition.

Here, gender appears as a status differentiation endowed with sexuality-like characteristics. When viewed under this aspect, gender injustice appears as a species of misrecognition that cries out for redress via recognition. Much like heterosexism, overcoming androcentrism requires changing the gender status order, deinstitutionalizing sexist value patterns and replacing them with patterns that express equal respect for women. Thus, the logic of the remedy here is akin to that concerning sexuality: it aims to dismantle androcentrism by restructuring the relations of recognition.[1]

Gender, in sum, is a two-dimensional social differentiation. It combines a class-like dimension, which brings it within the ambit of redistribution, with a status dimension, which brings it simultaneously within the ambit of recognition. It is an open question whether the two dimensions are of equal weight. But redressing gender injustice, in any case, requires changing both the economic structure and the status order of society.

The two-dimensional character of gender wreaks havoc on the idea of an either/or choice between the paradigm of redistribution and the paradigm of recognition. That construction assumes that the collective subjects of injustice are either classes or status groups, but not both; that the injustice they suffer is either maldistribution or misrecognition, but not both; that the group differences at issue are either unjust differentials or unjustly devalued variations, but not both; that the remedy for injustice is either redistribution or recognition, but not both. Gender, we can now see, explodes this whole series of false antitheses. Here we have a category that is a compound of both status and class. Here difference is constructed from both economic differentials and institutionalized patterns of cultural value. Here both maldistribution and misrecognition are fundamental. Gender injustice can only be remedied, therefore, by an approach that encompasses both a politics of redistribution and a politics of recognition. . . .

Affirmation or transformation?

With this orientation, let us turn now to the issues before us: what institutional reforms can remedy injustices of status and class simultaneously? What political strategy can successfully integrate redistribution and recognition, while also mitigating the mutual interferences that can arise when those two aims are pursued in tandem?

Consider, again, the remedy for injustice, restated now in its most general form: removal of impediments to participatory parity. At first sight, what this means is clear. To remedy maldistribution one must remove economic impediments via redistribution; what is needed, accordingly, is economic restructuring aimed at ensuring the objective conditions for participatory parity. To remedy misrecognition, likewise, one must remove cultural impediments via recognition; what is required here are policies that can supply the intersubjective prerequisites—by deinstitutionalizing patterns of cultural value that impede parity of participation and replacing them with patterns that foster it. Finally, applying this schema to "the third dimension," we could say that to remedy political exclusion or marginalization one must remove political obstacles via democratization, an idea I shall return to later.

The initial appearance of clarity is misleading, however, even for redistribution and recognition. In both those cases, the general formula of removing obstacles to participatory parity is subject to more than one institutional application. As noted earlier, economic restructuring could mean redistributing income and/or wealth; reorganizing the division of labor; changing the rules and entitlements of property ownership; or democratizing the procedures by which decisions are made about how to invest social surpluses. Likewise, as also noted, misrecognition can be redressed in more than one way: by universalizing privileges now reserved for advantaged groups or by eliminating those privileges altogether; by deinstitutionalizing preferences for traits associated with dominant actors or by entrenching norms favoring subordinates alongside them; by privatizing differences or by valorizing them or by deconstructing the oppositions that underlie them. Given this plethora of possible interpretations, the institutional implications are no longer so clear. Which remedies for maldistribution and misrecognition should proponents of justice seek to effect? . . .

Cross-redressing and boundary awareness

. . . What is needed, therefore, is an integrated approach that can redress maldistribution and misrecognition simultaneously.

How might one proceed to develop such an approach? We have already noted the uses of perspectival dualism, which facilitates integration by enabling one to monitor both the distributive implications of recognition reforms and the recognition implications of distributive reforms. Two further postures of thought can be similarly helpful.

The first I call *cross-redressing*. This means using measures associated with one dimension of justice to remedy inequities associated with the other—hence, using distributive measures to redress misrecognition and recognition measures to redress maldistribution.[2] Cross-redressing exploits the imbrication of status and class in order to mitigate both forms of subordination simultaneously. To be sure, it cannot be used wholesale, across the board. Thus, I argued earlier against the reductive economistic view that one can redress all misrecognition by redistribution, while likewise opposing the vulgar culturalist view that one can remedy all maldistribution by recognition. But cross-redressing is perfectly viable on a more limited scale.

Consider, first, some cases in which redistribution can mitigate misrecognition. Theorists of rational choice contend that increased earnings enhance women's exit options from marriage and improve their bargaining position in households; thus, higher wages strengthen women's capacity to avoid the status harms associated with marriage, such as domestic violence and marital rape.[3] Based on this sort of reasoning, some policy analysts claim that the surest way to raise poor women's status in developing countries is to provide them access to paid work.[4] To be sure, such arguments are sometimes over-extended to the point of dismissing the need for recognition reforms altogether; and in such forms they are clearly fallacious. But the point is persuasive when stated more modestly: in some cases, redistribution can mitigate status subordination.

That conclusion is also supported by my previous discussion of transformative redistribution. As we saw, that approach favors universal entitlements to social welfare over targeted aid for the poor; thus, instead of stigmatizing the needy, it fosters social solidarity. In fact, transformative remedies for maldistribution have the potential to reduce misrecognition in ways that are especially useful for combating racism. By enlarging the pie, such policies soften the economic insecurity and zero-sum conflicts that typically exacerbate ethnic antagonisms. And by reducing economic differentials, they create a common material form of life, thereby lessening incentives for maintaining racial boundaries.[5] In such cases, redistributive policies can diminish misrecognition—or, rather, those forms of misrecognition that are closely tied to economic conditions.

Consider, too, some cases in which cross-redressing works in the opposite direction. As we saw, gays and lesbians suffer serious economic disadvantages as a consequence of status subordination. For them, accordingly, measures associated with recognition can mitigate maldistribution. Legalizing gay marriage or domestic partnerships would effectively remove economic penalties currently entrenched in welfare entitlements and in tax and inheritance law; and outlawing heterosexist discrimination in employment and military service would mean higher income and better fringe benefits. The point holds more broadly for despised groups: enhanced respect translates into reduced discrimination—not only in employment, but also in housing and access to credit, hence into improved economic position. In such cases, where maldistribution is tied to status subordination, recognition can help to correct it.

In general, then, cross-redressing represents a useful tactic for integrating redistribution and recognition. Deployed judiciously, as part of a larger coordinated strategy of nonreformist reform, it can help circumvent unpalatable trade-offs.

A second posture that facilitates integration I call *boundary awareness*. By this I mean awareness of the impact of various reforms on group boundaries. As we saw, some efforts to redress injustice serve to differentiate social groups, whereas others serve to de-differentiate them. For example, efforts to redress maldistribution have as their stated aim the abolition or reduction of economic differentials; whether the preferred strategy is affirmative or transformative, the goal is to lessen or abolish class divisions—thus to soften or eliminate boundaries. In contrast, affirmative approaches to recognition aim to valorize group specificity; effectively validating group differentiation, they would affirm existing boundaries. Finally, transformative recognition strategies propose to deconstruct dichotomous classifications; effectively blurring sharp status distinctions, they would destabilize the boundaries between groups.

Efforts to integrate redistribution and recognition must reckon with these varying aims. Absent awareness of boundary dynamics, one can end up pursuing reforms that work at cross-purposes with one another. For example, affirmative efforts to redress racist misrecognition by revaluing "blackness" tend to consolidate racial differentiation; in contrast, transformative efforts to redress racist maldistribution by abolishing the racial division of labor would undermine racial boundaries. Thus, the two sorts of reforms pull in opposite directions; pursued together, they could interfere with, or work against, each other. Boundary awareness can anticipate such contradictions; exposing the self-defeating character of certain combinations of reforms, it can identify more productive alternatives.[6]

The need for boundary-awareness increases, moreover, given the possibility of unintended effects. After all, reforms of every type may fail to achieve their stated aims. We have seen, for example, that affirmative remedies for maldistribution often generate backlash misrecognition, thereby sharpening the very divisions they sought to reduce; thus, while ostensibly seeking to soften group boundaries, they may actually serve to consolidate them. In such cases, too, boundary awareness can anticipate, and help to forestall, perverse effects. Combined with perspectival dualism and cross-redressing, it facilitates efforts to devise an approach that integrates redistribution and recognition.

By themselves, however, these ideas do not add up to a substantive programmatic strategy for integrating redistribution and recognition. Rather, they represent postures of reflection conducive to devising such a strategy. The question remains as to who precisely should use them to that end.

Notes

1. Once again recognition can be accorded in more than one way—for example, by according positive recognition to women's specificity or by deconstructing the binary opposition between masculinity and femininity. In the first case, once again, the logic of the remedy is to valorize the group's "groupness" by recognizing its distinctiveness. In the second case, as before, it is to put the group out of business as a group. . . .

2. The term "cross-redressing" is my own. However, I owe the point to Erik Olin Wright. See "Comments on a General Typology of Emancipatory Projects." Unpublished manuscript, February 1997.

3. Susan Moller Okin, *Justice, Gender and the Family* (New York 1989); Nancy Fraser, "After the Family Wage"; and Barbara Hobson, "No Exit, No Voice: Women's Economic Dependency and the Welfare State," *Acta Sociologica* 33, no. 3 (Fall 1990): 235–250. See also the general argument about exit and voice in Albert O. Hirschman, *Exit, Voice, and Loyalty: Responses to Decline in Firms, Organizations, and States* (Cambridge, MA 1970).

4. Amartya Sen, "Gender and Cooperative Conflicts," in *Persistent Inequalities: Women and World Development*, ed. Irene Tinker (New York 1990).

5. Wright, "Comments."

6. For a detailed comparative assessment of the compatibility of various reform packages with respect to boundary dynamics, see Nancy Fraser, "From Redistribution to Recognition? Dilemmas of Justice in a 'Postsocialist' Age," *New Left Review* 212 (July/August 1995): 68–93; reprinted in Nancy Fraser, *Justice Interruptus: Critical Reflections on the "Postsocialist" Condition* (London & New York 1997).

Critique. Drucilla Cornell, a feminist philosopher, says that in the quest for equality, the question of who is compared with whom is crucial. If disadvantaged women achieve equality with the disadvantaged men of their group, they have not achieved very much. If they outperform them, as has happened for African American and Hispanic American women college and professional school graduates in the United States, then the men in the same groups are seen as endangered. Women may feel they are in a double bind and can't win if they raise themselves as women, leaving their men behind, but they don't want to subordinate themselves to their men, either.

Socialist feminist political action has gone beyond the sources of oppression that are specific to women. Without ignoring sexual exploitation and violence against women, socialist feminism has searched for ways to open access to economic resources, educational opportunities, and political power for all the disadvantaged. The focus is sometimes on gender, but women of different classes may not be interested in political action because their statuses are superior, or because they feel they have too much to lose from changes in the status quo. In some situations, it is necessary to reach out to subordinated men who are similarly oppressed and who want similar changes in the redistribution of resources and recognition of distinct racial ethnic cultures.

Socialist feminism's expansion has turned into a general critique of late capitalist societies on domestic, economic, and political grounds. The feminism is evident in the prominent inclusion of gender, but otherwise the politics of socialist feminism is a struggle for economic and social equality for all the disadvantaged.

Summary

Socialist feminism provides a general theory of inequality that combines the effects of gender, social class, and racial ethnic status. For women, inequality goes beyond their exploitation in the family and workplace. White upper- and upper-middle-class women do not have the same advantages as men of the same status. Men's lack of responsibility for social reproduction of the next generation frees them to pursue careers and political power. Their accumulation of advantages gives them wide-ranging social power and the means to dominate women. Working-class women and women of devalued racial ethnic statuses suffer double and triple oppression compared to the men of the same class and status.

Politically, socialist feminism calls for a redistribution of responsibilities in the family and a redistribution of economic and social power. Equal sharing of family work would give women the opportunity to accumulate the economic and social power now monopolized by men. Also necessary is degendered access to high-paying jobs and positions of power. For all the disadvantaged, socialist feminism has fought for universal entitlements to education, child care, health care, and income support as well as more open access to governmental and non-governmental political power.

Socialist feminism's main contributions have been to lay the groundwork for a structural analysis of the status of women beyond the family and the economy, and to make visible the combined effects of gender, class, and racial ethnic status. They adopted the concept of complex inequality to describe accumulated economic, cultural, and political disadvantages that turn women throughout the world into second-class citizens.

Suggested Readings in Socialist Feminism

Acker, Joan. 1988. "Class, Gender, and the Relations of Distribution." *Signs* 13:473–497.

———. 1989. *Doing Comparable Worth: Gender, Class, and Pay Equity.* Philadelphia: Temple University Press.

———. 1990. "Hierarchies, Jobs, and Bodies: A Theory of Gendered Organizations," *Gender & Society* 4:139–158.

———. 1999. "Rewriting Class, Race, and Gender: Problems in Feminist Rethinking," in *Revisioning Gender,* edited by Myra Marx Ferree, Judith Lorber, and Beth B. Hess. Thousand Oaks, CA: Sage.

Adkins, Lisa. 2001. "Cultural Feminization: 'Money, Sex and Power' for Women." *Signs* 26:669–695.

Armstrong, Chris. 2002. "Complex Equality: Beyond Equality and Difference," *Feminist Theories* 3:67–82.

Britton, Dana M. 2000. "The Epistemology of the Gendered Organization." *Gender & Society* 14:418–434.

Buhle, Mari Jo. 1983. *Women and American Socialism, 1870–1920.* Urbana: University of Illinois Press.

Cornell, Drucilla. 1998. *At the Heart of Freedom: Feminism, Sex and Equality.* Princeton, NJ: Princeton University Press.

Eisenstein, Zillah, ed. 1978. *Capitalist Patriarchy and the Case for Socialist Feminism.* New York: Monthly Review Press.

Ferguson, Kathy E. 1984. *The Feminist Case Against Bureaucracy.* Philadelphia: Temple University Press.

Fraser, Nancy. 1989. *Unruly Practices: Power, Discourse and Gender in Contemporary Social Theory.* Minneapolis: University of Minnesota Press.

———. 1997. *Justice Interruptus: Critical Reflections on the "Postsocialist" Condition.* New York: Routledge.

Fraser, Nancy, and Axel Honneth. 2003. *Redistribution or Recognition? A Political-Philosophical Exchange.* Translated by Joel Golb, James Ingram, and Christiane Wilke. London: Verso.

Glenn, Evelyn Nakano. 1992. "From Servitude to Service Work: Historical Continuities in the Racial Division of Paid Reproductive Labor." *Signs* 18:10–43.

———. 1999. "The Social Construction and Institutionalization of Gender and Race: An Integrative Framework." In *Revisioning Gender,* edited by Myra Marx Ferree, Judith Lorber, and Beth B. Hess. Thousand Oaks, CA: Sage.

Hansen, Karen V., and Ilene J. Phillipson, eds. 1990. *Women, Class and the Feminist Imagination: A Socialist-Feminist Reader.* Philadelphia: Temple University Press.

Hochschild, Arlie Russell. 1983. *The Managed Heart: Commercialization of Human Feeling.* Berkeley: University of California Press.

Holmstrom, Nancy, ed. 2002. *The Socialist Feminist Project: A Contemporary Reader in Theory and Politics.* New York: Monthly Review Press.

Kruks, Sonia, Rayna Rapp, and Marilyn B. Young, eds. 1989. *Promissory Notes: Women in the Transition to Socialism.* New York: Monthly Review Press.

Lister, Ruth. 1997. *Citizenship: Feminist Perspectives.* London: Macmillan.

McCall, Leslie. 2001. *Complex Inequality: Gender, Class, and Race in the New Economy.* New York: Routledge.

Okin, Susan Moller. 1989. *Justice, Gender and the Family.* New York: Basic Books.

Walby, Sylvia. 1997. *Gender Transformations.* New York: Routledge.

Walzer, Michael. 1983. *Spheres of Justice: A Defense of Pluralism and Equality.* New York: Basic Books.

Young, Iris Marion. 1990. *Justice and the Politics of Difference.* Princeton, NJ: Princeton University Press. ✦

Chapter Four

Post-Colonial Feminism

Sources of Gender Inequality

- Undercutting of women's traditional economic base by colonialism.
- Exploitation of women workers in the post-colonial global economy.
- Lack of education for girls.
- Inadequate maternal and child health care.
- Sexual exploitation.
- Patriarchal family structures and cultural practices harmful to women and girls.

Politics

- Protection of women's economic resources in modernization programs.
- Education of girls within an appropriate cultural context.
- Community-based health care, family planning services, and AIDS prevention and treatment.
- Community organizing of mothers.
- National women's movements.

Contributions

- Gender analyses of modernization and economic restructuring programs.
- Data on exploitation of women and children workers.
- Documentation of importance of economic resources to women's social status.
- Laws against transnational sexual traffic and ritual genital cutting.
- Visibility of non-Western feminist perspectives.

Post-colonial feminism applies the socialist feminist analysis of gender, class, and racial ethnic inequality to what has been variously called the third world, the global south, post-colonial and nonindustrial societies, and developing countries. These refer to places like the Caribbean, parts of South America and Africa, India, Bangladesh, Pakistan and other areas of the world with extremes of riches and poverty. Income maldistributions in the developing countries are often made worse by the restructuring policies demanded by Western industrialized states as the price of economic aid and industrial development. Wages are low for most urban women and men. However, women workers in developing countries in Latin America, the Caribbean, and Africa are paid less than men workers, whether they work in factories or do piecework at home.

In rural areas, much of the agriculture is plantation farming for export or at the subsistence level, and there is an extensive "informal" economy of home-based manufacture and production of goods and foodstuffs for local markets. While women are usually significant food providers for their families, working at small farms and home-based businesses, they suffer from illiteracy and deaths in childbirth. Health care is poor, and there is a high rate of mortality in children before the age of five from diarrhea, malaria, infections, and other treatable or preventable illnesses. In both urban and rural areas, devastatingly high rates of rape, sexual exploitation, prostitution, and HIV/AIDS add to women's oppression.

Gender inequality in the global economy. Post-colonial feminism uses theories of colonial underdevelopment and post-colonial development, as well as socialist feminist theories, to analyze the position of women in the global economy, with particular emphasis on newly industrializing countries. *The global economy* links countries whose economies focus on service, information, and finances with manufacturing sites and the sources of raw materials in other countries. Wealth in the form of capital and profits, and legal and undocumented immigrants flow between them.

Men and women workers all over the world supply the labor for the commodities that end up in the stores in your neighborhood. They are not paid according to their skills but according to the going wage, which varies enormously from country to country because it is dependent on the local standard of living. Women workers tend to be paid less than men workers throughout the world, whatever the wage scale, because they are supposedly supporting only themselves. However, in South Korea's economic development zone, many young single women factory workers live in crowded dormitories and eat one meal a day in order to send money home for a brother in college. In Mexico, many older married women's jobs are a significant source of their family's income.

The gendered division of labor in developing countries is the outcome of centuries of European and American colonization. Under colonialism, women's traditional contributions to food production were undermined in favor of exportable crops, such as coffee, and the extraction of raw materials, such as minerals. Men workers were favored in mining and large-scale agriculture, but they were barely paid enough for their own subsistence. Women family members had to provide food for themselves and their children; however, good land was often confiscated for plantations, so women also lived at a bare survival level.

Since becoming independent, many developing nations have sought financial capital and business investments from wealthier European and American countries. The consequent economic restructuring and industrialization disadvantage women. Men workers, considered heads of families, are hired for the better-paying manufacturing jobs. Young single women, although they are working as much for their families as for themselves, are hired for jobs that pay much less than men's jobs. And married women, whose wages frequently go to feed their children, are paid the least of all. For example, in the *maquiladoras*, the Mexican border industries, where 85 to 90 percent of the workers are women, there is a division between the electronics industries, which offer somewhat better working conditions and higher pay but hire only young single women, and the smaller, less modern apparel factories, which employ older women supporting children.

Women's grassroots movements. Feminist research on women's economic and health problems in developing countries has been extensive, but even those who work for government organizations, United Nations agencies, or the World Bank have not had the power to make development or economic restructuring programs more women-friendly. Pooling resources through grassroots organizing, women of different communities have joined together to fight against exploitation and for social services. They do so as mothers, for their children, and so have often been able to accomplish what more obvious political protest cannot, given the entrenchment of wealthy owners of land and factories.

The following excerpt is from a paper originally presented at an international conference, Women and Development: Focus on Latin America and Africa, sponsored by the Institute for Research on Women and the Center for Latin America and the Caribbean, which was held at the State University of New York at Albany in 1989. In it, Edna Acosta-Belén, a Latin American specialist, and Christine Bose, a sociologist, lay out feminist theories dealing with the effects of colonialism, why poor women today are called "the last colony," and strategies of coping by these women.

Gender and Development

Edna Acosta-Belén
Professor of Latin American and Caribbean Studies, and Women's Studies, University at Albany, SUNY

Christine E. Bose
Professor of Sociology and Latin American and Caribbean Studies, and Chair of Women's Studies, University at Albany, SUNY

It is difficult to address gender issues in the developing countries of Latin America and the Caribbean without recognizing that they are inextricably linked to a global capitalist and patriarchal model of accumulation and hence to the history of imperialist expansion and colonialism (Saffioti

1978; Mies et al. 1988). Although it is not always self-evident, both women and colonies have served as the foundations of industrial development of the economically dominant Western nations.

Colonialism, born in the fifteenth century—the gateway to discovery, exploration, and conquest—was to become the mainspring of European industrial development. Since the "discovery" of their existence by European settlers, primarily from Spain, Portugal, Great Britain, France, and the Netherlands, territories in the New World have served as the major sources of precious metals, labor, raw materials, and food products to support the commerce, consumption, and economic development of what are today's industrialized nations. The basis for the ascendancy of capitalism in Europe was the colonial exploitation of its overseas empires. Although the nature of colonization varied from one region of the world to another, the system was based on extracting the wealth of the new lands by using the labor of both the subjugated indigenous populations and that of the displaced and enslaved African populations to support the lavish lives of European aristocracies and the consumption needs of a rising bourgeoisie (Saffioti 1978; Etienne and Leacock 1980). The wealth and natural resources of the colonies were the essence of European mercantilist capitalism and, at a later stage, of its industrial revolution. The manufactured goods produced in European factories with the colonies' raw materials and labor found their way back into colonial markets. With some variations, this cycle has essentially perpetuated itself through the centuries.

In the Americas the United States emerged as a new colonial power to substitute for the Spanish, consolidating itself in the nineteenth century through the pursuit of its Manifest Destiny policies of territorial expansion and the Monroe Doctrine (1823), aimed at reducing European presence and influence in the hemisphere. After its Civil War (1861–65) the United States was determined to become the major economic and geopolitical power in the Americas.

In the twentieth century capitalism entered its new monopoly and multinational stages of development, and the neocolonial relations developed then still link the colonizing and colonized countries into a global economic network. The unequal relationship that has kept Latin American and Caribbean nations dependent helps explain the continuing internal turmoil and clamor for change emanating from most of these nations today.

It is quite evident in the colonial literature that from the beginning of the European monarchies' imperial expansion, the adventurers, missionaries, and officials who came to the New World had little regard for any patterns of communal and egalitarian relationships among the native populations subjugated during the colonial enterprise. In many pre-colonial societies women's position and participation in productive activities was parallel to that of men, rather than subservient (Saffioti 1978; Etienne and Leacock 1980). The imposition of European patriarchal relationships that presupposed the universal subordination of women in many instances deprived indigenous women of property and personal autonomy and restricted the productive functions and any public roles they might have played before colonization (Saffioti 1978; Etienne and Leacock 1980; Nash 1980). These policies continued through the centuries as colonial territories were integrated into the capitalist system of production, and persisted even after those countries gained independence, in part because of the neocolonial relations the industrialized nations still maintain with developing countries. The conditions of *internal colonialism* (Blauner 1972) that later emerged within Western metropolitan centers, wherein immigrant groups and racial minorities are relegated to a structurally marginal position, replicate the patterns of colonial relationships.

Before the work of Ester Boserup (1970), most of the classical development literature tended to ignore women's economic role and contributions. Assuming women were passive dependents, the literature relegated them to reproductive rather than productive roles, confining them to an undervalued domestic sphere isolated from the rest of the social structure. Little attention was paid to differences in productivity between women and men in different developing nations or to women's labor activities in the informal economy. One of Boserup's major contributions was to establish empirically the vital role of women in agricultural economies and to recognize that economic development, with its tendency to encourage labor specialization, was actually depriving women of their original productive functions and on the whole deteriorating their status. . . .

Women as a Last Colony

The conceptualization of women as a last colony, advanced by the work of German feminist scholars Mies, Bennholdt-Thomsen, and Werlhof (1988), has provided a valuable new interpretative model for feminist research on Third World issues. This framework underscores the convergences of race, class, and gender and recognizes one complex but coherent system of oppression. It also allows us to see that the patterns of sexism are compounded by a layer of oppression, shared by Third World men and women, brought about by the colonizing experience.

Werlhof (1988, 25) argues that the relationship of Third World subsistence workers of both genders to First World multinationals in some ways resembles the relationship between men and women worldwide. Women and colonies are both low-wage and nonwage producers, share structural subordination and dependency, and are overwhelmingly poor. Werlhof contends that in response to its accumulation crisis, capitalism is now implicitly acknowledging that the unpaid labor of women in the household goes beyond the reproductive sphere into the production of commodities. Nevertheless, housewives are frequently and explicitly excluded from what is defined as the economy in order to maintain the illusion of the predominance of the male wage worker. The problems with this definition are increasingly obvious, as many Latin American and Caribbean households, using multiple income strategies, rely on women's informal economy activities or subsistence work. . . .

Mies et al. (1988, 7) indicate there are actually three tiers in the capitalist pyramid of exploitation: (1) the holders of capital, (2) wage workers (mostly white men or the traditional proletariat) and nonwage workers (mostly women), and (3) housewives and subsistence producers (men and women) in the colonial countries. Using this model, both Werlhof (1988) and Bennholdt-Thomsen (1988) argue that the new international trend in the division of labor is toward the "housewifization" (*Hausfrauisierung*) of labor, namely, labor that exhibits the major characteristics of housework, and away from the classical proletariat whose labor is now being replaced. Of course, the housewife role entails different things across nations, ranging from cooking, cleaning, washing, and taking care of children and the elderly, to grinding maize, carrying water, or plowing the family plot. The determining factor is always whether or not these tasks are performed for wages. Werlhof (1988, 173) establishes a key link between the undervalued work performed by women and that of Third World populations, which leads her to conclude that the classical proletariat is being replaced by the Third World worker and the housewife as the new "pillars of accumulation." This conclusion also points to the contradiction between any cultural or economic devaluation of women's work and the important role it actually plays.

Following this line of argument, the three authors note that, since the latter part of the nineteenth century, patriarchal capitalist practice and ideology have colonized women by the "housewifization" of their work: by attempting to isolate women in the domestic sphere and devaluing the work they perform there; by ideologically justifying it as a genetic predisposition based on their capacity for motherhood; by regarding any type of income they generate as supplementary or secondary, thus ascribing a lower status to their occupations; and ultimately, by controlling their sexuality. These power relations between men and women are thus comparable to the international division of labor between First and Third World countries. The present-day world economic crisis is not just another cycle of capitalism but rather a new phase of development relying on female forms of labor (i.e., doing any kind of work at any time, unpaid or poorly paid) wherein the industrialized powers try to force Third World nations to "restructure" or adapt their national economies to the needs of the world system for such flexible labor. . . .

Women Organizing for Change

Women are not passive victims in the socioeconomic processes that maintain their lower status. Instead, they are developing creative ways in which to resist the new forms of subordination. Latin American activists expect that changes in sexist practice and ideology can be obtained during economic crises—an experience quite different from that of feminists in the core capitalist countries whose achievements were made in the context of improving material conditions. In Latin America and the Caribbean various types of resistance, solidarity, and collective action are used by women in diverse geographic regions and under different sociopolitical structures, a pattern that is beginning to be recognized in comparative studies of women's movements (Margolis 1993).

Although Latin American women's subsistence activities as peasant producers can be seen as similar to the unpaid housework of women in Europe and the United States, the resultant political strategies are different . . . perhaps because of the class differences between them. In First World countries women have responded to cutbacks in government services to families by entering the paid labor force, especially in the service industry, and by taking over the tasks of eldercare and child care. In Latin America and the Caribbean nations, though some women do create microenterprises, . . . take jobs in export processing zones, or enter the service sector, the vast majority respond to the breakdown of their subsistence economy by organizing collective meals, health cooperatives, mothers' clubs, neighborhood water-rights groups, or their own textile and craft collectives, which produce goods both for street vending and for international markets. Thus, rather than *privatizing* their survival problems, these women *collectivize* them and form social-change groups based on social reproduction concerns. In these new terms, the political discourse and arena of struggle is not worker exploitation and control of the means of production but rather moral persuasion to place demands on the state for rights related to family survival.

Many Latin American women activists contend that their traditional roles as wives and mothers are the basis for these collective actions on behalf of their families. Although most of the groups are composed of poor women, they do not organize either explicitly on a class basis or at the workplace. Instead, they organize at a neighborhood level around a broad list of issues that they redefine as women's concerns, such as running water or transportation for squatter communities. Some feminist scholars argue that this approach constitutes a movement of women but not necessarily a feminist movement; others feel these tactics represent a form of working-class feminism that promotes consciousness of how gender shapes women's lives (Sternback et al. 1992).

References

Bennholdt-Thomsen, Veronika. 1988. " 'Investment of the Poor': An Analysis of World Bank Policy." In *Women: The Last Colony,* ed. Maria Mies, Veronika Bennholdt-Thomsen, and Claudia von Werlhof, pp. 51–63. London: Zed.

Blauner, Robert. 1972. *Racial Oppression in America.* New York: Harper and Row.

Boserup, Ester. 1970. *Women's Role in Economic Development.* New York: St. Martin's Press.

Etienne, Mona, and Eleanor Leacock (eds.). 1980. *Women and Colonization: Anthropological Perspectives.* New York: Praeger.

Margolis, Diane Rothbard. 1993. "Women's Movements Around the World: Cross-Cultural Comparisons." *Gender & Society* 7:379–399.

Mies, Maria, Veronika Bennholdt-Thomsen, and Claudia von Werlhof. 1988. *Women: The Last Colony.* London: Zed.

Nash, June. 1980. "Aztec Women: The Transition from Status to Class in Empire and Colony." In *Women and Colonization: Anthropological Perspectives,* pp. 134–48.

Saffioti, Heleieth I. B. 1978. *Women in Class Society.* New York: Monthly Review.

Sternback, Nancy Saporta, Marysa Navarro-Aranguren, Patricia Chuchryk, and Sonia E. Alvarez. 1992. "Feminisms in Latin America: From Bogot to San Bernardo." *Signs* 17:393–434.

Werlhof, Claudia von. 1988. "Women's Work: The Blind Spot in the Critique of Political Economy." In *Women: The Last Colony,* ed. Maria Mies, Veronika Bennholdt-Thomsen, and Claudia von Werlhof, pp. 13–26. London: Zed.

Women's linked economic and social status. Post-colonial feminism equates women's status with their contribution to their family's economy and their control of economic resources. To be equal with her husband, it is not enough for a married woman to earn money; she has to provide a needed portion of her family's income and also have control over the source of that income and over its distribution as well. In a rural community, that means owning a piece of land, being able to market the harvest from that land, and deciding how the profit from the sale will be spent. In an urban economy, it may mean owning a store or small business, retaining the profit, and deciding what to spend it on or whether to put it back into the business.

There are societies in Africa and elsewhere in the world where women control significant economic resources and so have a high status. In contrast, in societies with patriarchal family structures where anything women produce, including children, belongs to the husband, women and girls have a low value. Post-colonial feminism's theory is that in any society, if the food or income women produce is the main way the family is fed, and women also control the distribution of any surplus they produce, women have power and prestige. If men provide most of the food and distribute the surplus, women's status is low. Whether women or men produce most of the food or bring in most of the family income depends on the society's economy. When a woman is able to own the means of production (land, a store, a business) like a man, she has the chance to be economically independent. If her income is barely above subsistence level because her choices are low-waged work in a factory, piecework in a sweatshop, or sex work as a prostitute, then the fact that she has a job does not give her a very high social status, especially if much of the money she earns is sent back home to her family. Thus, the mode of production and the kinship rules that control the distribution of any surplus are the significant determinants of the relative status of women and men in any society.

Women's rights and cultural traditions. In addition to gendered economic analyses, post-colonial feminism addresses the political issue of women's rights versus national and cultural traditions. At the United Nations Fourth World Conference on Women and the NGO (nongovernmental organizations) Forum held in Beijing in 1995, the popular slogan was "human rights are women's rights and women's rights are human rights." The Platform for Action document that came out of the U.N. Conference condemned particular cultural practices that are oppressive to women—infanticide, dowry, child marriage, and ritual genital cutting. The 187 governments that signed onto the Platform agreed to abolish these practices. However, since they are integral parts of cultural and tribal traditions, giving them up could be seen as kow-towing to Western ideas. The post-colonial feminist perspective, so crit-ical of colonial and cultural imperialism and yet so supportive of women's rights, has found this issue difficult to resolve.

The women's own solution to this dilemma is community organiz-ing around their productive and reproductive roles as mothers—so that what benefits them economically and physically is in the service of their families, not themselves alone. However, this same community organizing and family service can support the continuance of cultural practices that can be harmful to women, such as ritual female genital cutting.

Ritual genital cutting. For more than two thousand years, in a broad belt across the middle of Africa, various forms of female genital cutting have been used to ensure women's virginity until marriage and to inhibit wives' desire for sexual relations after marriage, and also for aesthetic rea-sons. Girls undergo clitorectomies and removal of the outer lips of the vagina to be marriageable and feminine, according to their culture's views of chastity and how women's bodies should look. In many of the same cultural groups, boys undergo removal of the penile foreskin (cir-cumcision) to become a man.

For women, childbirth becomes more dangerous because of tearing and bleeding, and there are risks of infection and urinary problems after the procedures and throughout life. Some anthropologists who have done interviews with African women argue that sexual pleasure after genital cutting is extremely variable. Some ritual genital cutting may increase the transmission of HIV infection for girls and women, but there have been no systematic studies. The data are clearer for boys and men and indicate that circumcision seems to protect against HIV transmission.

When done on children too young to consent, from the viewpoint of the West, female genital cutting seems like the ultimate in child abuse, but from the perspective of the societies where these practices are deeply part of cultural beliefs, not to cut would be a serious breech of parental responsibility. In the parts of the world where these prac-tices are imbued with religious, moral, and esthetic values, ritual geni-tal cutting makes girls into marriageable woman. Change is coming from within, through the influence of Islamic activists, the work of community health educators, and the efforts of educated African women. Western outrage and external efforts to stop female ritual genital cutting often provoke a strong backlash in the countries where these practices are common. This clash of cultural perspectives has led Carla Mahklouf Obermeyer, a German anthropologist, to question whether Western women could ever understand why African women would willingly undergo genital cutting and have it done on their young daughters, any more than African women who have been cut can understand how Western women can live with their ugly genitals. Although Westerners may be reluctant to criticize women's beliefs and practices in cultures not their own, feminist and human rights policies do condemn patriarchal social structures that control and oppress women, as well as practices such as ritual female genital cutting when they are part of women's subordination.

Non-western feminism. Right from the beginning of post-colonial feminism, non-Western feminists have been critical of Western concepts of gender relations and women's oppression. They argue that throughout much of the non-Western world, women are productive workers in their families, not just homemakers and child carers. The nuclear family that is seen as so oppressive by Western feminism is not the typical family structure in non-Western societies—rather, it is the extended family where there are many adults to carry out productive and reproductive work. Non-Western women, like those in Western countries, vary in their social position, depending on the society, economy, and cultural practices; not all are low-status, powerless dependents, nor are all non-Western men patriarchally domineering.

In the mid-1980s, at the beginning of her professional life as a feminist theorist and international activist, Chandra Talpade Mohanty published what became a famous challenge to Western feminists, "Under Western Eyes: Feminist Scholarship and Colonial Discourses." In it, she argued against a simplistic binary formula that ignores racial ethnic, national, and class differences: "Men exploit, women are exploited" (31). She also claimed that Western feminism too often portrayed non-Western women as different from themselves and more oppressed—traditional, religious, family-oriented, legally unsophisticated, illiterate, and embattled in nationalistic revolutions. In her latest book, *Feminism Without Borders,* Talpade Mohanty reprints this essay as the first chapter and rethinks it in the last chapter, "Under Western Eyes Revisited: Feminist Solidarity Through Anticapitalist Struggles." Now she argues that rather than focusing on differences, feminism should mount an anti-globalization struggle against "global economic and political processes [that] have become more brutal, exacerbating economic, racial, and gender inequalities" (230). Feminism's goal should be a solidarity that recognizes local differences, but is without borders, since globalization affects everyone.

Under Western Eyes at the Turn of the Century

Chandra Talpade Mohanty
Professor of Women's Studies, Hamilton College, and Core Faculty, Union Institute and University, Cincinnati, Ohio

I wrote "Under Western Eyes" to discover and articulate a critique of "Western feminist" scholarship on Third World women via the discursive colonization of Third World women's lives and struggles. I also wanted to expose the power-knowledge nexus of feminist cross-cultural scholarship expressed through Eurocentric, falsely universalizing methodologies that serve the narrow self-interest of Western feminism. As well, I thought it crucial to highlight the connection between feminist scholarship and feminist political organizing while drawing attention to the need to examine the "political implications of our analytic strategies and principles." I also wanted to chart the location of feminist scholarship within a global political and economic framework dominated by the "First World."[1]

My most simple goal was to make clear that cross-cultural feminist work must be attentive to the micropolitics of context, subjectivity, and struggle, as well as to the macropolitics of global economic and political systems and processes. I discussed Maria Mies's study of the lacemakers of Narsapur as a demonstration of how to do this kind of multilayered, contextual analysis to reveal how the particular is often universally significant—without using the universal to erase the particular, or positing an unbridgeable gulf between the two terms. Implicit in this analysis was the use of historical materialism as a basic framework, and a definition of material reality in both its local and micro-, as well as global, systemic dimensions. I argued at that time for the definition and recognition of the Third World not just through oppression but in terms of historical complexities and the many struggles to change these oppressions. Thus I argued for grounded, particularized analyses linked with larger, even global, economic and political frameworks. . . .

While my earlier focus was on the distinctions between "Western" and "Third World" feminist practices, and while I downplayed the commonalities between these two positions, my focus now . . . is on what I have chosen to call an anticapitalist transnational feminist practice—and on the possibilities, indeed on the necessities, of cross-national feminist solidarity and organizing against capitalism. While "Under Western Eyes" was located in the context of the critique of Western humanism and Eurocentrism and of white, Western feminism, a similar essay written now would need to be located in the context of the critique of global capitalism (on antiglobalization), the naturalization of the values of capital, and the unacknowledged power of cultural relativism in cross-cultural feminist scholarship and pedagogies.

"Under Western Eyes" sought to make the operations of discursive power visible, to draw attention to what was left out of feminist theorizing, namely, the material complexity, reality, and agency of Third World women's bodies and lives. This is in fact exactly the analytic strategy I now use to draw attention to what is unseen, undertheorized, and left out in the production of knowledge about globalization. While globalization has always been a part of capitalism, and capitalism is not a new phenomenon, at this time I believe the theory, critique, and activism around antiglobalization has to be a key focus for feminists. This does not mean that the patriarchal and racist relations and structures that accompany capitalism are any less problematic at this time, or that antiglobalization is a singular phenomenon. Along with many other scholars and activists, I believe capital as it functions now depends on and exacerbates racist, patriarchal, and heterosexist relations of rule. . . .

Antiglobalization Struggles

Although the context for writing "Under Western Eyes" in the mid-1980s was a visible and activist women's movement, this radical movement no longer exists as such. Instead, I draw inspiration from a more distant, but significant, antiglobalization movement in the United States and around the world. Activists in these movements are often women, although the movement is not gender-focused. So I wish to redefine the project of decolonization, not reject it. It appears more complex to me today, given the newer developments of global capitalism. Given the complex interweaving of cultural forms, people of and from the Third World live not only under

Western eyes but also within them. This shift in my focus from "under Western eyes" to "under and inside" the hegemonic spaces of the One-Third World necessitates recrafting the project of decolonization.

My focus is thus no longer just the colonizing effects of Western feminist scholarship. This does not mean the problems I identified in the earlier essay do not occur now. But the phenomenon I addressed then has been more than adequately engaged by other feminist scholars. While feminists have been involved in the antiglobalization movement from the start, however, this has not been a major organizing locus for women's movements nationally in the West/North. It has, however, always been a locus of struggle for women of the Third World/South because of their location. Again, this contextual specificity should constitute the larger vision. Women of the Two-Thirds World have always organized against the devastations of globalized capital, just as they have always historically organized anticolonial and antiracist movements. In this sense they have always spoken for humanity as a whole.

I have tried to chart feminist sites for engaging globalization, rather than providing a comprehensive review of feminist work in this area. I hope this exploration makes my own political choices and decisions transparent and that it provides readers with a productive and provocative space to think and act creatively for feminist struggle. So today my query is slightly different although much the same as in 1986. I wish to better see the processes of corporate globalization and how and why they recolonize women's bodies and labor. We need to know the real and concrete effects of global restructuring on raced, classed, national, sexual bodies of women in the academy, in workplaces, streets, households, cyberspaces, neighborhoods, prisons, and social movements.

What does it mean to make antiglobalization a key factor for feminist theorizing and struggle? To illustrate my thinking about antiglobalization, let me focus on two specific sites where knowledge about globalization is produced. The first site is a pedagogical one and involves an analysis of the various strategies being used to internationalize (or globalize)[2] the women's studies curriculum in U.S. colleges and universities. I argue that this move to internationalize women's studies curricula and the attendant pedagogies that flow from this is one of the main ways we can track a discourse of global feminism in the United States. Other ways of tracking global feminist discourses include analyzing the documents and discussions flowing out of the Beijing United Nations conference on women, and of course popular television and print media discourses on women around the world. The second site of antiglobalization scholarship I focus on is the emerging, notably ungendered and deracialized discourse on activism against globalization.

Antiglobalization Pedagogies

Let me turn to the struggles over the dissemination of a feminist cross-cultural knowledge base through pedagogical strategies "internationalizing" the women's studies curriculum. The problem of "the (gendered) color line" remains, but is more easily seen today as developments of transnational and global capital. While I choose to focus on women's studies curricula, my arguments hold for curricula in any discipline or academic field that seeks to internationalize or globalize its curriculum. I argue that the challenge for "internationalizing" women's studies is no different from the one involved in "racializing" women's studies in the 1980s, for very similar politics of knowledge come into play here.[3]

So the question I want to foreground is the politics of knowledge in bridging the "local" and the "global" in women's studies. How we teach the "new" scholarship in women's studies is at least as important as the scholarship itself in the struggles over knowledge and citizenship in the U.S. academy. After all, the way we construct curricula and the pedagogies we use to put such curricula into practice tell a story—or tell many stories. It is the way we position historical narratives of experience in relation to each other, the way we theorize relationality as both historical and simultaneously singular and collective that determines how and what we learn when we cross cultural and experiential borders. . . .

The Feminist Solidarity or Comparative Feminist Studies Model. This curricular strategy is based on the premise that the local and the global are not defined in terms of physical geography or territory but exist simultaneously and constitute each other. It is then the links, the relationships, between the local and the global that are foregrounded, and these links are conceptual, material, temporal, contextual, and so on. This framework assumes a comparative focus and analysis of the directionality of power no matter what the subject of the women's studies course is—and it assumes both distance and proximity (specific/universal) as its analytic strategy.

Differences and commonalities thus exist in relation and tension with each other in all contexts. What is emphasized are relations of mutuality, coresponsibility, and common interests, anchoring the idea of feminist solidarity. For example, within this model, one would not teach a U.S. women of color course with additions on Third World/South or white women, but a comparative course that shows the interconnectedness of the histories, experiences, and struggles of U.S. women of color, white women, and women from the Third World/South. By doing this kind of comparative teaching that is attentive to power, each historical experience illuminates the experiences of the others. Thus, the focus is not just on the intersections of race, class, gender, nation, and sexuality in different communities of women but on mutuality and coimplication, which suggests attentiveness to the interweaving of the histories of these communities. In addition the focus is simultaneously on individual and collective experiences of oppression and exploitation and of struggle and resistance.

Students potentially move away from the "add and stir" and the relativist "separate but equal" (or different) perspective to the coimplication/solidarity one. This solidarity perspective requires understanding the historical and experiential specificities and differences of women's lives as well as the historical and experiential connections between women from different national, racial, and cultural communities. Thus it suggests organizing syllabi around social and economic processes and histories of various communities of women in particular substantive areas like sex work, militarization, environmental justice, the prison/industrial complex, and human rights, and looking for points of contact and connection as well as disjunctures. It is important to always foreground not just the connections of domination but those of struggle and resistance as well.

In the feminist solidarity model the One-Third/Two-Thirds paradigm makes sense. Rather than Western/Third World, or North/South, or local/global seen as oppositional and incommensurate categories, the One-Third/Two-Thirds differentiation allows for teaching and learning about points of connection and distance among and between communities of women marginalized and privileged along numerous local and global dimensions. Thus the very notion of inside/outside necessary to the distance between local/global is transformed through the use of a One-Third/Two-Thirds paradigm, as both categories must be understood as containing difference/similarities, inside/outside, and distance/proximity. Thus sex work, militarization, human rights, and so on can be framed in their multiple local and global dimensions using the One-Third/Two-Thirds, social minority/social majority paradigm. I am suggesting then that we look at the women's studies curriculum in its entirety and that we attempt to use a comparative feminist studies model wherever possible.[4]

I refer to this model as the feminist solidarity model because, besides its focus on mutuality and common interests, it requires one to formulate questions about connection and disconnection between activist women's movements around the world. Rather than formulating activism and agency in terms of discrete and disconnected cultures and nations, it allows us to frame agency and resistance across the borders of nation and culture. I think feminist pedagogy should not simply expose students to a particularized academic scholarship but that it should also envision the possibility of activism and struggle outside the academy. Political education through feminist pedagogy should teach active citizenship in such struggles for justice.

My recurring question is how pedagogies can supplement, consolidate, or resist the dominant logic of globalization. How do students learn about the inequities among women and men around the world? For instance, traditional liberal and liberal feminist pedagogies disallow historical and comparative thinking, radical feminist pedagogies often singularize gender, and Marxist pedagogy silences race and gender in its focus on capitalism. I look to create pedagogies that allow students to see the complexities, singularities, and interconnections between communities of women such that power, privilege, agency, and dissent can be made visible and engaged with. . . .

While feminist scholarship is moving in important and useful directions in terms of a critique of global restructuring and the culture of globalization, I want to ask some of the same questions I posed in 1986 once again. In spite of the occasional exception, I think that much of present-day scholarship tends to reproduce particular "globalized" representations of women. Just as there is an Anglo-American masculinity produced in and by discourses of globalization,[5] it is important to ask what the corresponding femininities being produced are. Clearly there is the ubiquitous global teenage girl factory worker, the domestic worker, and the sex worker. There is also the migrant/immigrant serviceworker, the refugee, the victim of war crimes, the woman-of-color prisoner who happens to be a mother and drug user, the consumer-housewife, and so on. There is also the mother-of-the-nation/religious bearer of traditional culture and morality.

Although these representations of women correspond to real people, they also often stand in for the contradictions and complexities of women's lives and roles. Certain images, such as that of the factory or sex worker, are often geographically located in the Third World/South, but many of the representations identified above are dispersed throughout the globe. Most refer to women of the Two-Thirds World, and some to women of the One-Third World. And a woman from the Two-Thirds World can live in the One-Third World. The point I am making here is that women are workers, mothers, or consumers in the global economy, but we are also all those things simultaneously. Singular and monolithic categorizations of women in discourses of globalization circumscribe ideas about experience, agency, and struggle. While there are other, relatively new images of women that also emerge in this discourse—the human rights worker or the NGO advocate, the revolutionary militant and the corporate bureaucrat—there is also a divide between false, overstated images of victimized and empowered womanhood, and they negate each other. We need to further explore how this divide plays itself out in terms of a social majority/minority, One-Third/Two-Thirds World character- ization. The concern here is with whose agency is being colonized and who is privileged in these pedagogies and scholarship. These then are my new que- ries for the twenty-first century. . . .[6]

Notes

1. Here is how I defined "Western feminist" then: "Clearly Western feminist dis- course and political practice is neither singular or homogeneous in its goals, interests, or analyses. However, it is possible to trace a coherence of effects resulting from the implicit assumption of 'the West' (in all its complexities and contradictions) as the primary referent in theory and praxis. My reference to 'Western feminism' is by no means intended to imply that it is a monolith. Rather, I am attempting to draw attention to the similar effects of various textual strategies used by writers which codify Others as non-Western and hence them- selves as (implicitly) Western." I suggested then that while terms such as "First" and "Third World" were problematic in suggesting oversimplified similarities as well as flattening internal differences, I continued to use them because this was the terminology available to us then. I used the terms with full knowledge of their limitations, suggesting a critical and heuristic rather than nonquestioning use of the terms. . . .

2. In what follows I use the terms "global capitalism," "global restructuring," and "globalization" interchangeably to refer to a process of corporate global eco- nomic, ideological, and cultural reorganization across the borders of nation-states.

3. While the initial push for "internationalization" of the curriculum in U.S. higher education came from the federal government's funding of area studies programs during the cold war, in the post–cold war period it is private foundations like the MacArthur, Rockefeller, and Ford foundations that have been instrumental in this endeavor—especially in relation to the women's studies curriculum.

4. A new anthology contains some good examples of what I am referring to as a feminist solidarity or comparative feminist studies model. See Lay, Monk, and Rosenfelt 2002.

5. Discourses of globalization include the proglobalization narratives of neoliberalism and privatization, but they also include antiglobalization dis- courses produced by progressives, feminists, and activists in the antiglobalization movement.

6. There is also an emerging feminist scholarship that complicates these monolithic "globalized" representations of women. See Amy Lind's work on Ecuadorian

women's organizations (2000), Aili Marie Tripp's work on women's social networks in Tanzania (2002), and Kimberly Chang and L. H. M. Ling's (2000) and Aihwa Ong's work on global restructuring in the Asia Pacific regions (1987 and 1991).

References

Chang, Kimberly, and L. H. M. Long. 2000. "Globalization and Its Intimate Other: Filipina Domestic Workers in Hong Kong." In *Gender and Global Restructuring: Sightings, Sites, and Resistances,* edited by Marianne Runyan and Anne Runyan. New York: Routledge.

Lay, Mary M., Janice Monk, and Deborah Silverton Rosenfelt, eds. 2002. *Encompassing Gender: Integrating International Studies and Women's Studies.* New York: Feminist Press of City University of New York.

Lind, Amy. 2000. "Negotiating Boundaries: Women's Organizations and the Politics of Restructuring in Ecuador." In *Gender and Global Restructuring: Sightings, Sites, and Resistances,* edited by Marianne Marchand and Anne Runyan. New York: Routledge.

Ong, Aihwa. 1991. "The Gender and Labor Politics of Postmodernity." *Annual Review of Anthropology* 20: 279–309.

———. 1987. *Spirits of Resistance and Capitalist Discipline: Factory Women in Malaysia.* Albany: State University of New York Press.

Tripp, Aili Marie. 2002. "Combining Intercontinental Parenting and Research: Dilemmas and Strategies for Women." *Signs* 27, no. 3: 793–811.

Critique. Post-colonial feminism has taken marxist and socialist feminist theories and expanded their application to nonindustrial economies and to societies in the process of industrializing. They have found many of the same phenomena that occurred during the nineteenth-century European and American industrial revolution—young, single factory girls exploited as cheap labor, working-class men getting the better-paid factory jobs, and middle- and upper-class men owning the means of production. They also found that the family remains a source of both exploitation and protection for women. Their labor is frequently used as a source of family income, but mothers also form grassroots service and community protest groups. In many post-colonial countries, strong women's movements flourish as part of movements for national liberation.

Post-colonial feminism has developed a split between Western ideas of individualism and human rights and the power and values of local cultures. On the one hand, Western ideas support the rights of girls and women to an education that will allow them to be economically independent. They are also the source of a concept of universal human rights, which can be used to fight subordinating cultural practices. On the other hand, Western ideas undercut communal enterprises and traditional sharing of food production and child care as well as grassroots and national women's movements.

Non-Western post-colonial feminist scholars and activists in their own countries and in Western countries argue that all women cannot be subsumed into a universally oppressed "sisterhood." They show that concepts of individual rights and gender equality are embedded in the history, ideology, and political struggles of Westernized nation-states and cannot be imposed on people with different histories, ideologies, and politics. Post-colonial feminist politics has often split over transnational class and racial hierarchies in what Deborah Mindry, an anthropologist, calls an invidious "politics of virtue"—advantaged urban, White, middle-class women "helping" poor, rural Black women.

Currently, feminists advocate transnational activism, which seeks coalitions that recognize differences but band together over common issues of gender inequality—poverty, education, health care, reproductive rights, sexual exploitation, AIDS, and peace.

Summary

Post-colonial feminism engages the global economy, with its competing state and private economic interests, and the capitalist drive for high production with cheap labor for maximum profits. Gender inequalities and politics are buried deep within class and racial ethnic divides, so that women's interests are intertwined with those of working-class and racially and ethnically disadvantaged men.

Post-colonial feminist research has shown that families all over the world need several workers in order to survive, often including children. Women and girls are doubly vulnerable—as workers and as family members. They are a prime source of low-paid wage workers whose earnings belong first to their families. They also work in family businesses, often unpaid; they make things at home to sell to supplement their family's food supply; they become prostitutes at a young age, often sold as a source of family income. At the same time, women physically maintain households and have babies, and frequently bury them within a year of birth.

There is no doubt that in many parts of the world today, as post-colonial feminism has shown, women are living in dire conditions. To redress their situation, whole economic structures and family and kinship systems need to be overhauled. However, the twentieth-century economic and social revolutions in the Soviet Union and China did not give women equality. Women became full-time workers, but, as in capitalist economies, they earned less than men and did almost all the child care and housework.

Post-colonial feminism makes very evident the political dilemmas of gender reform feminisms. Throughout the world, men own most of the private property, monopolize the better jobs, and make the laws. The outcome of this inequality is men's double exploitation of women in the job market and in the home. Procreative differences are not the cause of women's exploitation, but its justification. Women are subordinate in industrial and developing societies not because they are child bearers or child minders but because economies depend on them as low-paid workers and nonpaid workers for the family. Each form of exploitation of women's work reinforces the other. Women's economic value as waged and low-waged workers and as unpaid workers for the family are the *main* reasons for their subordination in industrialized and nonindustrialized modern societies.

Gender reform feminist politics is correct in pinpointing women's position in the world of paid work as the target for change. The problem is that the entire global economy needs drastic change. If the global economy is not made more equal for everyone, women in general, and poor women in particular, suffer the most. But since the gendered social order as a whole is the source of gender inequality, economic changes alone will not necessarily put women on an equal footing with men. Cultural and ideological recognition of women's worth and the worth of their work as mothers of future generations is the other part of feminist politics.

Suggested Readings in Post-Colonial Feminism

Anzaldúa, Gloria E. 1987. *Borderlands/La Frontera: The New Mestiza*. San Francisco: Spinsters/Aunt Lute.

Basu, Amrita, Inderpal Grewal, Caren Kaplan, and Liisa Malkki, eds. 2001. "Globalization and Gender." Special Issue, *Signs* 26(4): Summer.

Benería, Lourdes. 2003. *Gender, Development, and Globalization: Economics as if All People Mattered*. New York: Routledge.

Bennholdt-Thomsen, Veronika, and Maria Mies. 2000. *The Subsistence Perspective: Beyond the Globalized Economy*. London: Zed.

Bose, Christine E., and Edna Acosta-Belén, eds. 1995. *Women in the Latin American Development Process*. Philadelphia: Temple University Press.

Boserup, Ester. [1970] 1987. *Women's Role in Economic Development*. New York: St. Martin's Press.

Brydon, Lynn, and Sylvia Chant. 1989. *Women in the Third World: Gender Issues in Rural and Urban Areas*. New Brunswick, NJ: Rutgers University Press.

Chow, Esther Ngan-Ling, ed. 2002. *Transforming Gender and Development in East Asia*. New York: Routledge.

———, ed. 2003. "Gender, Globalization and Social Change in the 21st Century." Special Issue, *International Sociology* 18(3): Sept.

Christiansen-Ruffman, Linda, ed. 1998. *The Global Feminist Entitlement: Women and Social Knowledge*. Madrid, Spain: International Sociological Association.

Davis, Kathy. 2002. "Feminist Body/Politics as World Traveler: Translating Our Bodies, Ourselves." *European Journal of Women's Studies* 9:233–247.

Ehrenreich, Barbara, and Arlie Russell Hochschild, eds. 2002. *Global Woman: Nannies, Maids, and Sex Workers in the New Economy*. New York: Henry Holt.

Fernández-Kelly, María Patricia. 1983. *For We Are Sold, I and My People: Women and Industry in Mexico's Frontier*. Albany: State University of New York Press.

Grewal, Inderpal, and Caren Kaplan, eds. 1994. *Scattered Hegemonies: Postmodernity and Transnational Feminist Practice*. Minneapolis: University of Minnesota Press.

Harcourt, Wendy, ed. 1994. *Feminist Perspectives on Sustainable Development*. London: Zed.

Jaquette, Jane, ed. 1989. *The Women's Movement in Latin America: Feminism and the Transition to Democracy*. Winchester, MA: Unwin Hyman.

Kim, Seung-Kyung. 1997. *Class Struggle or Family Struggle? The Lives of Women Factory Workers in South Korea*. Cambridge, UK: Cambridge University Press.

Leacock, Eleanor, and Helen I. Safa, eds. 1986. *Women's Work: Development and the Division of Labor by Gender.* South Hadley, MA: Bergin & Garvey.

Lionnet, Françoise, Obioma Nnaemeka, Susan Perry, and Celeste Schenck, eds. 2004. "Development Cultures: New Environments, New Realities, New Strategies." Special Issue, *Signs* 29(2): Winter.

Marchand, Marianne, and Anne Sisson Runyan, eds. 2000. *Gender and Global Restructuring: Sightings, Sites, and Resistances.* New York: Routledge.

Melhuus, Marit, and Kristi Anne Stolen, eds. 1997. *Machos, Mistresses, Madonnas: Contesting the Power of Latin American Gender Imagery.* London: Verso.

Mies, Maria. 1982. *The Lace Makers of Narsapur: Indian Housewives Produce for the World Market.* London: Zed.

———. 1986. *Patriarchy and Accumulation on a World Scale: Women in the International Division of Labor.* London: Zed.

Mies, Maria, Veronika Bennholdt-Thomsen, and Claudia von Werlhof. 1988. *Women: The Last Colony.* London: Zed.

Mindry, Deborah. 2001. "Nongovernmental Organizations, 'Grassroots,' and the Politics of Virtue," *Signs* 26:1187–1211.

Moghadam, Valentine M., ed. 1994. *Identity Politics and Women: Cultural Reassertions and Feminisms in International Perspective.* Boulder, CO: Westview Press.

———, ed. 1996. *Patriarchy and Development: Women's Positions at the End of the Twentieth Century.* Oxford, UK: Clarendon Press.

Mohanty, Chandra Talpade. 2003. *Feminism Without Borders: Decolonizing Theory, Practicing Solidarity.* Durham, NC: Duke University Press.

Mohanty, Chandra Talpade, Ann Russo, and Lourdes Torres, eds. 1991. *Third World Women and the Politics of Feminism.* Bloomington: Indiana University Press.

Morrissey, Marietta. 1989. *Slave Women in The New World: Gender Stratification in the Caribbean.* Lawrence: University of Kansas Press.

Naples, Nancy A. 1998. *Grassroots Warriors: Activist Mothering, Community Work, and the War on Poverty.* New York: Routledge.

Naples, Nancy A., and Manisha Desai, eds. 2002. *Women's Activism and Globalization: Linking Local Struggles and Transnational Politics.* New York: Routledge.

Narayan, Uma. 1997. *Dislocating Cultures: Identities, Traditions, and Third World Feminism.* New York: Routledge.

Narayan, Uma, and Sandra Harding. 2000. *Decentering the Center: Philosophy for a Multicultural, Postcolonial, and Feminist World.* Bloomington: Indiana University Press.

Nash, June, and María Patricia Fernández-Kelly, eds. 1983. *Women, Men, and the International Division of Labor.* Albany: State University of New York Press.

Newell, Stephanie, ed. 1997. *Writing African Women: Gender, Popular Culture and Literature in West Africa.* London: Zed.

Nfah-Abbenyi, Juliana Makuchi. 1997. *Gender in African Women's Writing: Identity, Sexuality, and Difference.* Bloomington: Indiana University Press.

Nnaemeka, Obioma, ed. 1998. *Sisterhood, Feminism, and Power: From Africa to the Diaspora.* Trenton, NJ: Africa World Press.

Oyěwùmí, Oyèrónkẹ́. 1997. *The Invention of Women: Making an African Sense of Western Gender Discourses.* Minneapolis: University of Minnesota Press.

Peterson, V. Spike. 1992. *Gendered States: Feminist Revisions of International Relations Theory.* Boulder, CO: Lynn Rienner.

Redclift, Nanneke, and M. Thea Stewart, eds. 1991. *Working Women: International Perspectives on Women and Gender Ideology.* New York: Routledge.

Sassen, Saskia. 1998. *Globalization and Its Discontents: Essays on the New Mobility of People and Money.* New York: New Press.

Scheper-Hughes, Nancy. 1992. *Death Without Weeping: The Violence of Everyday Life in Brazil.* Berkeley: University of California Press.

Silliman, Jael, and Ynestra King, eds. 1999. *Dangerous Intersections: Feminist Perspectives on Population, Environment, and Development.* Boston: South End Press.

Sparr, Pam, ed. 1994. *Mortgaging Women's Lives: Feminist Critiques of Structural Adjustment.* London: Zed.

Spivak, Gayatri Chakravorty. 1988. *In Other Worlds: Essays in Cultural Politics.* New York: Routledge.

Tinker, Irene, ed. 1990. *Persistent Inequalities: Women and World Development.* New York: Oxford University Press.

Trinh, T. Minh-ha. 1989. *Woman, Native, Other: Writing Postcoloniality and Feminism.* Bloomington: Indiana University Press.

Visvanathan, Nalini, Lynn Duggan, Laurie Nisonoff, and Nan Wiegersma, eds. 1997. *The Women, Gender and Development Reader.* London: Zed.

Ward, Kathryn, ed. 1990. *Women Workers and Global Restructuring.* Ithaca, NY: ILR Books.

Young, Kate, Carol Wolkowitz, and Roslyn McCullagh, eds. 1981. *Of Marriage and the Market: Women's Subordination in International Perspective.* London: CSE Books.

Yuval-Davis, Nira. 1997. *Gender and Nation.* Thousand Oaks, CA: Sage.

Suggested Readings on Ritual Genital Cutting

Abdalla, Raqiya Haji Dualeh. 1982. *Sisters in Affliction: Circumcision and Infibulation of Women in Africa.* London: Zed.

Abusharaf, Rogata Mustafa. 2001. "Virtuous Cuts: Female Genital Mutilation in an African Ontology." *Differences: A Journal of Feminist Cultural Studies* 12:112–140.

Bashir, L. Miller. 1997. "Female Genital Mutilation: Balancing Intolerance of the Practice with Tolerance of Culture." *Journal of Women's Health* 6:11–14.

Brady, M. 1999. "Female Genital Mutilation: Complications and Risk of HIV Transmission." *AIDS Patient Care and Sexually Transmitted Diseases* 13(12):709–716.

Denniston, George C., Frederick Mansfield Hodges, and Marilyn Fayre Milos, eds. 1999. *Male and Female Circumcision: Medical, Legal, and Ethical Considerations in Pediatric Practice.* New York: Kluwer.

El Dareer, Asma. 1982. *Woman, Why Do You Weep? Circumcision and Its Consequences.* London: Zed.

Ericksen, K. Paige. 1995. "Female Circumcision Among Egyptian Women." *Women's Health: Research on Gender, Behavior, and Policy* 1:309–328.

Gruenbaum, Ellen. 2000. *The Female Circumcision Controversy: An Anthropological Perspective.* Philadelphia: University of Pennsylvania Press.

Hernlund, Ylva, and Bettina Shell-Duncan, eds. 2000. *Female "Circumcision" in Africa: Culture, Controversy, and Change.* Boulder, CO: Lynn Reinner.

James, Stephen A. 1994. "Reconciling Human Rights and Cultural Relativism: The Case of Female Circumcision." *Bioethics* 8(Nov. 1):1–26.

———. 1998. "Shades of Othering: Reflections on Female Circumcision/Genital Mutilation." *Signs* 23:1031–1048.

Koso-Thomas, Olayinka. 1987. *The Circumcision of Women: A Strategy for Eradication.* London: Zed.

Lightfoot-Klein, Hanny. 1989. *Prisoners of Ritual: An Odyssey into Female Circumcision in Africa.* New York: Harrington Park Press.

Leonard, Lori. 2000a. "Interpreting Female Genital Cutting: Moving Beyond the Impasse." *Annual Review of Sex Research* 11:158–191.

———. 2000b. " 'We Did It for Pleasure Only:' Hearing Alternative Tales of Female Circumcision." *Qualitative Inquiry* 6:212–228.

Mackie, Gerry. 1996. "Ending Footbinding and Infibulation: A Convention Account." *American Sociological Review* 61:999–1017.

Njambi, Wairimū Ngaruiya. 2004. "Dualisms and Female Bodies in Representations of African Female Circumcision." *Feminist Theory* 5:281–303. (Responses and reply 305–328).

Obermeyer, Carla Mahklouf. 1999. "Female Genital Surgeries: The Known, the Unknown, and the Unknowable," *Medical Anthropology Quarterly* 13:79–106.

O'Farrell, N., and M. Egger. 2000. "Circumcision in Men and the Prevention of HIV Infection: A 'Meta-analysis' Revisited." *International Journal of Sexually Transmitted Diseases and AIDS* 11:137–42.

Rahman, Anika, and Nahid Toubia. 2000. *Female Genital Mutilation: A Guide to Laws and Policies Worldwide.* London: Zed.

Robertson, Claire. 1996. "Grassroots in Kenya: Women, Genital Mutilation, and Collective Action, 1920–1990." *Signs* 21:615–641.

Shweder, Richard A. 2000. "What About 'Female Genital Mutilation'? And Why Understanding Culture Matters in the First Place." *Daedalus* 129(Fall):209–232.

van der Kwaak, Anke. 1992. "Female Circumcision and Gender Identity: A Questionable Alliance?" *Social Science and Medicine* 35:777–87.

Walker, Alice. 1992. *Possessing the Secret of Joy.* New York: Harcourt Brace Jovanovich.

Weiss, Helen A., Maria A. Quigley, and Richard J. Hayes. 2000. "Male Circumcision and Risk of HIV Infection in Sub-Saharan Africa: A Systematic Review and Meta-Analysis." *AIDS* 14(Oct. 20):2361–2370.

Williams, Lindy, and Teresa Sobieszyzyk. 1997. "Attitudes Surrounding the Continuation of Female Circumcision in the Sudan: Passing the Tradition to the Next Generation." *Journal of Marriage and the Family* 59:966–981.

Winter, Bronwyn. 1994. "Women, The Law, and Cultural Relativism in France: The Case of Excision." *Signs* 19:939–974. ✦

Part III

Gender Resistance Feminisms

In the 1970s, feminist ideas began to make inroads into the public consciousness, and women entered many formerly all-men workplaces and schools. Derogatory remarks about women were no longer acceptable officially, but women became more and more aware of constant putdowns from men they saw every day—bosses and colleagues at work, professors and students in the classroom, fellow organizers in political movements, and worst of all, from boyfriends and husbands at home. These "microinequities" of everyday life—being ignored and interrupted, not getting credit for competence or good performance, being passed over for jobs that involve taking charge—crystallize into a pattern that insidiously wears women down. Mary Rowe, a woman doctor using a pseudonym (because it was too dangerous even in the late 1970s to openly call attention to what men colleagues were doing to women), termed it the "Saturn's Rings Phenomenon" at a Conference on Women's Leadership and Authority in the Health Professions, held in California in 1977. The seemingly trivial sexist incidents, she said, are like the dust particles in the rings around the planet Saturn—separately they are tiny, but when they coalesce, they form a very visible pattern.

The younger women working in the civil rights, anti-Vietnam War, and student new-left movements in the late 1960s had even earlier realized that they were being used as handmaidens, bed partners, and coffee-makers by the men in their protest organizations. Despite the revolutionary rhetoric the young men were flinging in the face of

113

Western civilization in many countries, when it came to women, they might as well have been living in the eighteenth century. Young women activists' realization of their sexual vulnerability to men's physical and emotional demands, to harassment and denigration of their bodies, and especially to rape, battering, and other forms of violence led to new feminisms.

Out of their awareness that sisters had no place in any brotherhood and that their activist brothers could be dangerous to them came the American and European gender resistance feminisms. Their watchword is *patriarchy,* or men's subordination of women. Gender resistance feminisms argue that patriarchy can be found wherever women and men are in contact with each other, in public life, in the family, and in face-to-face encounters. Patriarchy is very hard to eradicate because a sense of superiority to women is deeply embedded in the consciousness and subconsciousness of most men and is built into their privileges in Western society. These privileges have come to be known as the *patriarchal dividend.* It is accompanied by a sense of entitlement to women's bodies and a domination of the cultural and media landscape. Radical feminism argues that patriarchy may best be resisted by forming nonhierarchical, supportive, woman-only organizations, where women can think and act and create freely.

Radical feminism is characterized by small, leaderless, women-only consciousness-raising groups, where the topics of intense discussion come out of the commonalities of women's lives—housework, emotional and sexual service to men, menstruation, childbirth, menopause, the constant sexual innuendoes and come-ons in workplaces and on college campuses, the lack of control over procreation, the fear of physical and sexual abuse. Politically, radical feminism took on the violence in women's oppression—rape and wife beating, the depiction of women as sex objects in the mass media and as pieces of meat in pornography, the global commerce in prostitution. This sexual exploitation of women is the worst effect of patriarchy, according to radical feminism, because its goal is social control of all women. Even if they are not directly attacked, the threat can be enough to keep women fearful and timid.

Lesbian feminism argues that sexual violence and exploitation are the common downside of romantic heterosexual love, which itself is oppressive to women. The lesbian feminist perspective has been an important part of *cultural feminism*—the development of a woman's world perspective in the creation of women's knowledge and culture. Lesbian feminists are active in women-only political activities, such as Take Back the Night marches, and in cultural events, such as women-only festivals, as well as in women-run businesses.

Psychoanalytic feminism provides a psychological theory of why men oppress women. Using Freudian concepts of personality development, psychoanalytic feminism argues that men's fear of castration by their mothers and repression of their primal attachment to her is sublimated in a *phallocentric* (sexually male) culture that symbolically subordinates and controls women. Politically, French feminism counters with cultural productions, particularly literature, that celebrate women's bodies, sexuality, and maternality.

Standpoint feminism brought all these feminist theories and politics together in a research and cultural agenda: Science and social science have to formulate questions and gather data from a *woman's standpoint* and women have to produce their own culture. For standpoint feminists, it has been crucial for women to do research from their own point of view and thus to create new bodies of knowledge in biology, medicine, psychology, economics, sociology, and history. This knowledge starts from premises that put women, not men, at the center. At the same time, standpoint feminists encourage women to make their own culture: literature, arts, theater, classical and popular music, comedy, and crafts.

The important theoretical contribution of gender resistance feminisms has been in showing that women's devaluation and subordination are part of the ideology and values of Western culture, as represented in religion, the mass media, sports, and cultural productions, and are built into the everyday practices of major institutions, such as medicine, the law, science, and social science. They also show how sexual exploitation and violence, especially rape and pornography, are a means of control of women.

Some political remedies—women-only consciousness-raising groups, alternative organizations, and lesbian separatism—are resistant to the gendered social order, but they are not able to transform it, as they stand apart from mainstream social institutions. They are vital in allowing women the "breathing space" to formulate important theories of gender inequality, to develop women's studies programs in colleges and universities, to form communities, and to produce knowledge, culture, ethics, and religions from a woman's point of view. The knowledge and culture produced by resistance feminism has greatly enriched Western societies, but it has sometimes alienated heterosexual White working-class women and women of disadvantaged racial or ethnic groups, who feel that their men are just as oppressed as they are by the dominant society. These women would not desert their brothers for a sisterhood they feel does not always welcome their point of view.

More effective have been the feminist campaigns against sexual harassment, rape, battering, incest, pornography, and prostitution. They have, however, led to head-on confrontations with some men's sense of sexual entitlement and have produced considerable antifeminist backlash. ✦

Chapter Five

Radical Feminism

Sources of Gender Inequality

- Patriarchy—a system of men's oppression of women.
- Men's violence and control of women through rape, battering, murder, and war.
- Legitimation of women's oppression in medicine, religion, science, law, and other social institutions.
- Objectification of women's bodies in advertisements, mass media, and cultural productions.
- Sexual exploitation in pornography and prostitution.
- Sexual harassment at work, in schools, and on the street.

Politics

- Valorizing all kinds of women's bodies, women's sexuality, and maternal qualities.
- Rape crisis centers and battered women's shelters.
- Protection of women from international sex trafficking.
- Sexual harassment guidelines for workplaces and schools.
- Environmental protection movements.
- Antiwar activism.

Contributions

- Theory of patriarchy as a system of sexual, emotional, and physical exploitation of women.
- Recognition of violence against women as a means of direct and indirect control.
- Tracing the global paths of sexual trafficking in women.
- Linkage of sexual exploitation of women with environmental exploitation.
- Identification of rape as a weapon of war.
- Critique of biases against women in biology and medicine.
- Identification of sexual harassment as part of the continuum of violence against women.
- Establishment of accessible rape crisis centers and battered women's shelters.
- Women's studies programs in colleges and universities throughout the world.

The 1970s saw the growth of what has become a major branch of feminism. Originally used as a term for feminists who wanted to do away with the traditional family and motherhood, radical feminism became a perspective that makes motherhood into a valuable way of thinking and behaving. However, it continues to criticize the traditional family as a prime source of patriarchal oppression of women and adds a condemnation of the violent aspects of heterosexuality.

Radical feminism expands the concept of *patriarchy* by defining it as a worldwide system of subordination of women by men through violence and sexual and emotional exploitation. In the radical feminist view, because of Western society's encouragement of aggressiveness in men and sexual display in women, most men are capable of, if not prone to, violence against women, and most women are potential victims. Rape of the enemy's women is a common wartime strategy. Vulnerable young women are sold, forced, and recruited into global sex and pornography work.

Radical feminism sees sexual violence against women as a continuum from sexual murder, rape, and prostitution to sexual harassment and date rape. The constant threat of rape, battering, and murder is a powerful means of keeping women "in their place." Movies, TV, and advertisements in all media sexualize women's bodies. The pervasive sexual objectification encourages men's using women for their own needs. Also, if women are depicted as "sex objects," their intellectual and leadership capabilities disappear from view—they are just so much "meat." Radical ecofeminism equates the objectification, exploitation, and rape of women, animals, and the earth.

For radical feminists, the physical, political, and economic oppression of women reflects a society's inherent violence. In their view, the destruction of the World Trade Center and part of the Pentagon by suicidal plane hijackers on September 11, 2001, and the killing of thousands of people were a prime example of *masculine* violence. Post-September 11, many radical feminists deplored the hypocritical rhetoric of masculine protection that masked the violence of the bombing of Afghanistan and the invasion of Iraq.

Sexual violence. Radical feminism's main political battlefield has been protection of rape victims and battered women and condemnation of pornography, prostitution, and sexual harassment. To some radical feminists, all romantic heterosexual relationships have the potential for sexual violence. They argue that since all men derive power from their dominant social status, any sexual and emotional relationship between women and men takes place in a socially unequal context. Consent by women to heterosexual intercourse is, by this definition, often forced by emotional appeals and threats to end the relationship. When a woman fears that a date or friend or lover or husband will use physical violence if she does not give in, it is *date rape* or *marital rape* and is as abusive as any other kind of rape.

The following excerpt is by Catharine MacKinnon, a feminist lawyer who argues that sexual violence in various forms constitutes a continuum of oppression for women. Her work on rape, pornography, and sexual harassment has become the foundation for radical feminism. This piece was developed for the National Conference on Women and the Law, which met in Boston in 1981.

Sex and Violence

Catharine A. MacKinnon
Professor of Law, University of Michigan

I want to raise some questions about the concept of this panel's title, "Violence Against Women," as a concept that may coopt us as we attempt to formulate our own truths. I want to speak specifically about four issues: rape, sexual harassment, pornography, and battery. I think one of the reasons we say that each of these issues is an example of violence against women is to reunify them. To say that aggression against women has this unity is to criticize the divisions that have been imposed on that aggression by the legal system. What I see to be the danger of the analysis, what makes it potentially cooptive, is formulating it—and it *is* formulated this way—these are issues of violence, *not* sex: rape is a crime of violence, not sexuality; sexual harassment is an abuse of power, not sexuality; pornography is violence against women, it is not erotic. Although battering is not categorized so explicitly, it is usually treated as though there is nothing sexual about a man beating up a woman so long as it is with his fist. I'd like to raise some questions about that as well.

I hear in the formulation that these issues are violence against women, not sex, that we are in the shadow of Freud, intimidated at being called repressive Victorians. We're saying we're *oppressed* and they say we're *repressed*. That is, when we say we're against rape, the immediate response is, "Does that mean you're against sex?" "Are you attempting to impose neo-Victorian prudery on sexual expression?" This comes up with sexual harassment as well. When we say we're against sexual harassment, the first thing people want to know is, "What's the difference between that and ordinary male-to-female sexual initiation?" That's a good question. . . . The same is also true of criticizing pornography. "You can't be against erotica?" It's the latest version of the accusation that feminists are anti-male. To distinguish ourselves from this, and in reaction to it, we call these abuses violence. The attempt is to avoid the critique—we're not against sex—and at the same time retain our criticism of these practices. So we rename as violent those abuses that have been seen to be sexual, without saying that we have a very different perspective on violence and on sexuality and their relationship. I also think a reason we call these experiences violence is to avoid being called lesbians, which for some reason is equated with being against sex. In order to avoid that, yet retain our opposition to sexual violation, we put this neutral, objective, abstract word *violence* on it all.

To me this is an attempt to have our own perspective on these outrages without owning up to having one. To have our point of view but present it as *not* a particular point of view. Our problem has been to label something as rape, as sexual harassment, as pornography in the face of a suspicion that it might be intercourse, it might be ordinary sexual initiation, it might be erotic. To say that these purportedly sexual events violate us, to be against them, we call them not sexual. But the attempt to be objective and neutral avoids owning up to the fact that women do have a specific point of view on these events. It avoids saying that from women's point of view, intercourse, sex roles, and eroticism can be and at times are violent to us as women.

My approach would claim our perspective; we are not attempting to be objective about it, we're attempting to represent the point of view of women. The point of view of men up to this time, called objective, has been to distinguish sharply between rape on the one hand and intercourse on the other; sexual harassment on the one hand and normal, ordinary sexual initiation on the other; pornography or obscenity on the one hand and eroticism on the other. The male point of view defines them by distinction. What women experience does not so clearly distinguish the normal, everyday things from those abuses from which they have been defined by distinction. Not just "Now we're going to take what *you* say is rape and call it violence"; "Now we're going to take what *you* say is sexual harassment and call it violence"; "Now we're going to take what *you* say is pornography and call it violence." We have a deeper critique of what has been done to women's sexuality and who controls access to it. What we are saying is that sexuality in exactly these normal forms often *does* violate us. So long as we say that those things are abuses of violence, not sex, we fail to criticize what has been made of *sex,* what has been done to us *through* sex, because we leave the line between rape and intercourse, sexual harassment and sex roles, pornography and eroticism, right where it is.

I think it is useful to inquire how women and men (I don't use the term *persons,* I guess, because I haven't seen many lately) live through the meaning of their experience with these issues. When we ask whether rape, sexual harassment, and pornography are questions of violence or questions of sexuality, it helps to ask, to whom? What is the perspective of those who are involved, whose experience it is—to rape or to have been raped, to consume pornography or to be consumed through it? As to what these things *mean* socially, it is important whether they are about sexuality to women and men or whether they are instead about "violence"—or whether violence and sexuality can be distinguished in that way, as they are lived out.

The crime of rape—this is a legal and observed, not a subjective, individual, or feminist definition—is defined around penetration. That seems to me a very male point of view on what it means to be sexually violated. And it is exactly what heterosexuality as a social institution is fixated around, the penetration of the penis into the vagina. Rape is defined according to what men think violates women, and that is the same as what they think of as the *sine qua non* of sex. What women experience as degrading and defiling when we are raped includes as much that is distinctive to us as is our experience of sex. Someone once termed penetration a "peculiarly resented aspect" of rape—I don't know whether that meant it was peculiar that it was resented or that it was resented with heightened peculiarity. Women who have been raped often do resent having been penetrated. But that is not all there is to what was intrusive or expropriative of a woman's sexual wholeness.

I do think the crime of rape focuses more centrally on what men define as sexuality than on women's experience of our sexual being, hence its violation. A common experience of rape victims is to be unable to feel good about anything heterosexual thereafter—or anything sexual at all, or men at all. The minute they start to have sexual feelings or feel sexually touched by a man, or even a woman, they start to relive the rape. I had a client who came in with her husband. She was a rape victim, a woman we had represented as a witness. Her husband sat the whole time and sobbed. They couldn't have sex anymore because every time he started to touch her, she would flash to the rape scene and see his face change into the face of the man who had raped her. That, to me, is sexual. When a woman has been raped, and it is sex that she then cannot experience without connecting it to that, it was her sexuality that was violated.

Similarly, men who are in prison for rape think it's the dumbest thing that ever happened. . . . It isn't just a miscarriage of justice; they were put in jail for something very little different from what most men do most of the time and call it sex. The only difference is they got caught. That view is nonremorseful and not rehabilitative. It may also be true. It seems to me we have here a convergence between the rapist's view of what he has done and the victim's perspective on what was done to her. That is, for both, their ordinary experiences of heterosexual intercourse and the act of rape have something in common. Now this gets us into intense trouble, because that's exactly how judges and juries see it who refuse to convict men accused of rape. A rape victim has to prove that it was not intercourse. She has to show that there was force and she resisted, because if there was sex, consent is inferred. Finders of fact look for "more force than usual during the prelimi-naries." Rape is defined by distinction from intercourse—not nonviolence, intercourse. They ask, does this event look more like fucking or like rape? But what is their standard for sex, and is this question asked from the *woman's point of view?* The level of force is not adjudicated at her point of violation; it is adjudicated at the standard of the normal level of force. Who sets this standard?

In the criminal law, we can't put everybody in jail who does an ordinary act, right? Crime is supposed to be deviant, not normal. Women continue not to report rape, and a reason is that they believe, and they are right, that the legal system will not see it from their point of view. We get very low con-viction rates for rape. We also get many women who believe they have never been raped, although a lot of force was involved. They mean that they were not raped in a way that is legally provable. In other words, in all these situa-tions, there was not *enough* violence against them to take it beyond the cat-egory of "sex"; they were not coerced enough. Maybe they were forced-fucked for years and put up with it, maybe they tried to get it over with, maybe they were coerced by something other than battery, something like economics, maybe even something like love.

What I am saying is that unless you make the point that there is much vio-lence in intercourse, as a usual matter, none of that is changed. Also we con-tinue to stigmatize the women who claim rape as having experienced a devi-ant violation and allow the rest of us to go through life feeling violated but thinking we've never been raped, when there were a great many times when we, too, have had sex and didn't want it. What this critique does that is differ-ent from the "violence, not sex" critique is ask a series of questions about nor-mal, heterosexual intercourse and attempt to move the line between hetero-sexuality on the one hand—intercourse—and rape on the other, rather than allow it to stay where it is.

Having done that so extensively with rape, I can consider sexual harass-ment more briefly. The way the analysis of sexual harassment is sometimes expressed now (and it bothers me) is that it is an abuse of power, not sexual-ity. That does not allow us to pursue whether sexuality, as socially con-structed in our society through gender roles, is *itself* a power structure. If you look at sexual harassment as power, not sex, what is power supposed to be? Power is employer/employee, not because courts are marxist but because this is a recognized hierarchy. Among men. Power is teacher/student, because courts recognize a hierarchy there. Power is on one side and sexual-ity on the other. Sexuality is ordinary affection, everyday flirtation. Only when ordinary, everyday affection and flirtation and "I was just trying to be friendly" come into the context of *another* hierarchy is it considered potentially an abuse of power. What is not considered to be a hierarchy is women and men—men on top and women on the bottom. That is not considered to be a question of power or social hierarchy, legally or politically. A feminist perspective suggests that it is.

When we have examples of coequal sexual harassment (within these other hierarchies), worker to worker on the same level, involving women and men, we have a lot of very interesting, difficult questions about sex discrimination, which is supposed to be about gender difference, but does not conceive of gender as a social hierarchy. I think that implicit in race discrimination cases for a brief moment of light was the notion that there is a social hierarchy between Blacks and Whites. So that presumptively it's an exercise of power for a White person to do something egregious to a Black person or for a White institution to do something egregious systematically to many Black people. Situations of coequal power—among coworkers or students or teachers—are difficult to see as examples of sexual harassment unless you have a notion of male power. I think we lie to women when we call it not power when a woman is come onto by a man who is not her employer, not her teacher. What do we labor under, what do we feel, when a man—any man—comes and hits on us? I think we require women to feel fine about turning down male-initiated sex so long as the man doesn't have some *other* form of power over us. Whenever—every and any time—a woman feels conflicted and wonders what's wrong with her that she can't decline although she has no inclination, and she feels open to male accusations, whether they come from women or men, of "why didn't you just tell him to buzz off?" we have sold her out, not named her experience. We are taught that we exist for men. We should be flattered or at least act as if we are—be careful about a man's ego because you never know what he can do to you. To flat out say to him, "You?" or "I don't want to" is not *in* most women's sex-role learning. To say it is, is bravado. And that's because he's a man, not just because you never know what he can do to you because he's your boss (that's two things—he's a man and he's the boss) or your teacher or in some other hierarchy. It seems to me that we haven't talked very much about gender *as* a hierarchy, as a division of power, in the way that's expressed and acted out, primarily I think sexually. And therefore we haven't expanded the definition according to women's experience of sexuality, including our own sexual intimidation, of what things are sexual in this world. So men have also defined what can be called sexual about us. They say, "I was just trying to be affectionate, flirtatious and friendly," and we were just all felt up. We criticize the idea that rape comes down to her word against his—but it really *is* her perspective against his perspective, and the law has been written from his perspective. If he didn't mean it to be sexual, it's not sexual. If he didn't see it as forced, it wasn't forced. Which is to say, only male sexual violations, that is, only male ideas of what sexually violates us as women, are illegal. We buy into this when we say our sexual violations are abuses of power, not sex.

Just as rape is supposed to have nothing against intercourse, just as sexual harassment is supposed to have nothing against normal sexual initiation (men initiate, women consent—that's mutual?), the idea that pornography is violence against women, not sex, seems to distinguish artistic creation on the one hand from what is degrading to women on the other. It is candid and true but not enough to say of pornography, as Justice Stewart said, "I know it when I see it." *He* knows what he thinks it is when he sees it—but is that what *I* know? Is that the same "it"? Is he going to know what I know when I see it? I think pretty much not, given what's on the newsstand, given what is not considered hard-core pornography. Sometimes I think what is obscene is what does *not* turn on the Supreme Court—or what revolts them more. Which is uncommon, since revulsion is eroticized.

We have to admit that pornography turns men on; it is therefore erotic. It is a lie to say that pornography is not erotic. When we say it is violence, not sex, we are saying, there is this degrading to women, over here, and this erotic, over there, without saying to whom. It is overwhelmingly disproportionately men to whom pornography is erotic. It is women, on the whole, to whom it is violent, among other things. And this is not just a matter of perspective, but a matter of reality.

Pornography turns primarily men on. Certainly they are getting something out of it. They pay incredible amounts of money for it; it's one of the largest industries in the country. If women got as much out of it as men do, we would buy it instead of cosmetics. It's a massive industry, cosmetics. We are poor but we have *some* money; we are some market. We spend our money to set ourselves up as the objects that emulate those images that are sold as erotic to men. What pornography says about us is that we enjoy degradation, that we are sexually turned on by being degraded. For me that obliterates the line, as a line at all, between pornography on one hand and erotica on the other, if what turns men on, what men find beautiful, is what degrades women. It is pervasively present in art, also, and advertising. But it is definitely present in eroticism, if that is what it is. It makes me think that women's sexuality as such is a stigma. We also sometimes have an experience of sexuality authentic somehow in all this. We are not allowed to have it; we are not allowed to talk about it; we are not allowed to speak of it or image it as from our own point of view. And, to the extent we try to assert that we are beings equal with men, we have to be either asexual or virgins.

To worry about cooptation is to realize that lies make bad politics. It is ironic that cooptation often results from an attempt to be "credible," to be strategically smart, to be "effective" on existing terms. Sometimes you become what you're fighting. Thinking about issues of sexual violation as issues of violence not sex could, if pursued legally, lead to opposing sexual harassment and pornography through morals legislation and obscenity laws. It is actually interesting that this theoretical stance has been widely embraced but these legal strategies have not been. Perhaps women realize that these legal approaches would not address the subordination of women to men, specifically and substantively. These approaches are legally as abstract as the "violence not sex" critique is politically abstract. They are both not enough and too much of the wrong thing. They deflect us from criticizing everyday behavior that is pervasive and normal and concrete and fuses sexuality with gender in violation and is not amenable to existing legal approaches. I think we need to think more radically in our legal work here.

Battering is called violence, rather than something sex-specific: this is done to women. I also think it is sexually done to women. Not only in where it is done—over half of the incidents are in the bedroom. Or the surrounding events—precipitating sexual jealousy. But when violence against women is eroticized as it is in this culture, it is very difficult to say that there is a major distinction in the level of sex involved between being assaulted by a penis and being assaulted by a fist, especially when the perpetrator is a man. If women as gender female are defined as sexual beings, and violence is eroticized, then men violating women has a sexual component. I think men rape women because they get off on it in a way that fuses dominance with sexuality. . . . I think that when men sexually harass women it expresses male control over sexual access to us. It doesn't mean they all want to fuck us, they just want to hurt us, dominate us, and control us, and that *is* fucking us. They want to be able to have that and to be able to say when they can have it, to *know* that. That is in itself erotic. The idea that opposing battering is about saving the family is, similarly, abstracted, gender-neutral. There are gender-neutral formulations of all these issues: law and order as opposed to derepression, Victorian morality as opposed to permissiveness, obscenity as opposed to art and freedom of expression. Gender-neutral, objective formulations like these avoid asking *whose* expression, from whose point of view? Whose law and whose order? It's not just a question of who is free to express ourselves; it's not just that there is almost no, if any, self-respecting women's eroticism. The fact is that what we do see, what we are allowed to experience, even in our own suffering, even in what we are allowed to complain about, is overwhelmingly constructed from the male point of view. Laws against sexual violation express what men see and do when they engage in sex with women; laws against obscenity center on the display of women's bodies in ways that men are turned on by viewing. To me, it not only makes us cooptable to define such abuses in gender-neutral terms like violence; when we fail to assert that we are fighting for the affirmative definition and control of our own sexuality, of our own lives as women, and that these experiences violate *that*, we have already been bought.

Reprinted from: Catharine A. MacKinnon, "Sex and Violence: A Perspective," 85–92 in *Feminism Unmodified*. Harvard University Press. Copyright © 1987 by Catharine MacKinnon. Reprinted by permission.

Sexual harassment. Sexual harassment is the commonest manifestation of the sexual exploitation of women in Western societies: Unwanted sexual invitations, sexually loaded remarks and jokes, and inappropriate comments on dress or appearance make it difficult for women and girls to do their work (or even to walk down the street unmolested). When the response to a work-related request is "Wow, that sweater really brings out your good points," the not-so-subtle intent is to turn a woman colleague into a "bimbo" and take her out of the running as a serious competitor. More obvious sexual harassment occurs when a boss or teacher threatens the loss of a job or a low grade if a worker or student will not "give a kiss" or if she responds to a grope with a slap. In the military and other hierarchical organizations, women feel that reporting a rape or coerced sex, let alone a pattern of demeaning comments, is useless when the higher-ups have the same sexist attitudes. Women who complain get tainted with a "troublemaker" label, or are harassed by the person they complain to, but their harassers are let off with a mild talking-to. Sexual harassment seems to get attention only when the media report a drunken attack on many women in a public place, or the same situation is found in army base after army base, or a high government official is involved.

When sexual harassment adversely affects a worker's or student's concentration, or contaminates the environment in which they work or study, it becomes a form of discrimination. Radical feminism has made these patterns of sexual harassment and their discriminatory results visible. Its analysis is reflected in the sexual harassment guidelines of many schools and workplaces. In these guidelines, a sexual involvement of any kind between a subordinate and a person in a position of power is considered coercive and is explicitly forbidden. Also actionable is any situation where sexual remarks or uninvited attentions make employees or students so uncomfortable that they are unable to concentrate on work. These guidelines set up formal processes for reports and complaints and rules for actions to be taken in cases of proven sexual harassment.

Valorizing women. Radical feminism is not only critical of men's violence and sexuality, it turns male-dominated culture on its head. It takes all the characteristics that are valued by men in Western societies—objectivity, distance, control, coolness, aggressiveness, and competitiveness—and blames them for wars, poverty, rape, battering, child abuse, and incest. It praises what women do—feed and nurture, cooperate and reciprocate, and attend to bodies, minds, and psyches. The important values, radical feminism argues, are intimacy, persuasion, warmth, caring, and sharing—the characteristics that women develop in their hands-on, everyday experiences with their own and their children's bodies and with the work of daily living. Men could develop these characteristics, too, if they "mothered," but they are much more prevalent in women because women are usually the primary child-carers and nurturers in a family.

The political implications of "maternal thinking" are laid out in the following excerpt by Sara Ruddick, who has written on motherhood, peace, and feminism. She argues that if men "mothered"—intensively cared for children—they would be less prone to the violence, aggression, and militarism radical feminists have deplored.

Maternal Thinking

Sara Ruddick
Professor Emerita, Eugene Lang College,
New School University, New York

Maternal thinking is only one aspect of "womanly" thinking. In articulating and respecting the maternal, I do not underwrite the still current, false, and pernicious identification of womanhood with biological or adoptive mothering of particular children in families. For me, "maternal" is a social category. Although maternal thinking arises out of actual child-caring practices, biological parenting is neither necessary nor sufficient. Many women and some men express maternal thinking in various kinds of working and caring with others. And some biological mothers, especially in misogynistic societies, take a fearful, defensive distance from their own mothering and the maternal lives of any women.

Maternal thought does, I believe, exist for all women in a radically different way than for men. It is because we are *daughters,* nurtured and trained by women, that we early receive maternal love with special attention to its implications for our bodies, our passions, and our ambitions. We are alert to the values and costs of maternal practices whether we are determined to engage in them or avoid them.

It is now argued that the most revolutionary change we can make in the institution of motherhood is to include men equally in every aspect of child care. When men and women live together with children, it seems not only fair but deeply moral that they share in every aspect of child care. To prevent or excuse men from maternal practice is to encourage them to separate public action from private affection, the privilege of parenthood from its cares. Moreover, even when men are absent from the nursery, their dominance in every other public and private room shapes a child's earliest conceptions of power. To familiarize children with "natural" domination at their earliest age in a context of primitive love, assertion, and sexual passion is to prepare them to find equally "natural" and exhaustive the division between exploiter and exploited that pervades the larger world. Although daughter and son alike may internalize "natural" domination, neither typically can live with it easily. Identifying with and imitating exploiters, we are overcome with self-hate; aligning ourselves with the exploited, we are fearful and manipulative. Again and again, family power dramas are repeated in psychic, interpersonal, and professional dramas, while they are institutionalized in economic, political, and international life. Radically recasting the power-gender roles in those dramas just might revolutionize social conscience.

Assimilating men into child care both inside and outside the home would also be conducive to serious social reform. Responsible, equal childcaring would require men to relinquish power and their own favorable position in the division between intellectual/professional and service labor as that division expresses itself domestically. Loss of preferred status at home might make socially privileged men more suspicious of unnecessary divisions of labor and damaging hierarchies in the public world. Moreover, if men were emotionally and practically committed to child care, they would reform the work world in parents' interests. Once no one "else" was minding the child, good day-care centers with flexible hours would be established to which parents could trust their children from infancy on. These day-care centers, like the workweek itself, would be managed flexibly in response to human needs as well as to the demands of productivity, with an eye to growth rather than measurable profit. Such moral reforms of economic life would probably begin with professions and managers servicing themselves. Even in nonsocialist countries, however, their benefits could be unpredictably extensive.

I would not argue that the assimilation of men into child care is the primary social goal for mothers. Rather, we must work to bring a *transformed* maternal thought in the public realm, to make the preservation and growth of *all* children a work of public conscience and legislation. This will not be easy. Mothers are no less corrupted than anyone else by concerns of status and class. Often our misguided efforts on behalf of the success and purity of our children frighten them and everyone else around them. As we increase and enjoy our public effectiveness, we will have less reason to live vicariously through our children. We may then begin to learn to sustain a creative tension between our inevitable and fierce desire to foster our own children and the less compulsive desire that all children grow and flourish.

Nonetheless, it would be foolish to believe that mothers, just because they are mothers, can transcend class interest and implement principles of justice. All feminists must join in articulating a theory of justice shaped by and incorporating maternal thinking. Moreover, the generalization of attentive love to *all* children requires politics. The most enlightened thought is not enough.

Closer to home again, we must refashion our domestic life in the hope that the personal will in fact betoken the political. We must begin by resisting the temptation to construe "home" simplemindedly, as a matter of justice between mothers and fathers. Single parents, lesbian mothers, and coparenting women remind us that many ways to provide children with examples of caring do not incorporate sexual inequalities of power and privilege. Those of us who live with the fathers of our children will eagerly welcome shared parenthood—for overwhelming practical as well as ideological reasons. But in our eagerness, we must not forget that as long as a mother is not effective publicly and self-respecting privately, male presence can be harmful as well as beneficial. It does a woman no good to have the power of the Symbolic Father brought right into the nursery, often despite the deep, affectionate egalitarianism of an individual man. It takes a strong mother and father to resist temptations to domination and subordination for which they have been trained and are socially rewarded. And whatever the hard-won equality and mutual respect an individual couple may achieve, as long as a mother—even if she is no more parent than father—is derogated and subordinate outside the home, children will feel angry, confused, and "wildly unmothered."

Despite these reservations, I look forward to the day when men are willing and able to share equally and actively in transformed maternal practices. When that day comes, will we still identify some thought as maternal rather than merely parental? Might we echo the cry of some feminists—there shall be no more "women"—with our own—there shall be no more "mothers," only people engaging in child care? To keep matters clear I would put the point differently. On that day there will be no more "fathers," no more people of either sex who have power over their children's lives and moral authority in their children's world, though they do not do the work of attentive love. There will be mothers of both sexes who live out a transformed maternal thought in communities that share parental care—practically, emotionally, economically, and socially. Such communities will have learned from their mothers how to value children's lives.

Reprinted from: Sara Ruddick, "Maternal Thinking," in *Rethinking the Family: Some Feminist Questions*, edited by Barrie Thorne, with Marilyn Yalom, 89–91. Copyright © 1982 by The Institute for Research on Women and Gender, Stanford University. Reprinted by permission.

The politics of women's perspectives. Radical feminism's view is that the presence of significant numbers of women can alter values and behavior because their ideas, their outlook, and their experiences are different from those of most men, almost to the point of giving women a different culture. *Ecofeminism* is a movement that applies maternal thinking and radical feminist ideas about the exploitation of women's bodies to protecting the environment and protesting against killing animals for fur and meat. The radical feminist praise of the qualities of women that derive from their nurturance and care of others, especially among those who speak of a woman's culture, has also led to feminist religions and ethics, and to the women's health care movement.

In *religion,* radical feminism argues that while more women clergy and gender-neutral liturgical language are very important in reforming religious practices, they do not make a religion less patriarchal unless there is also a place for women's prayers, rituals, and interpretations of sacred texts. So, at Passover, Jewish feminists hold all-women seders with specially written Haggadahs that tell of the Jews' exodus from Egypt and wanderings in the desert from a woman's point of view. They celebrate Miriam as well as Moses.

Feminist religious scholars have reinterpreted Judeo-Christian history and texts showing the original influence of women spiritual leaders and their gradual exclusion as Judaism became more patriarchal and later, as Christianity became institutionalized. Islamic feminists have found, in their reading of the Qur'an, that Mohammed intended women and men to be equal. Buddhism's many goddesses have been given a more important place in the pantheon by feminists.

As an alternative to teachings of organized religions, Catholic and Protestant feminist ethicists have developed an ethics that puts women's experiences at the center of moral choices. In the United States, they work through an umbrella organization, called Woman-Church, that is composed of feminist groups engaged in reconstructing ethics and sexual morality. One of these groups, the Women's Alliance for Theology, Ethics, and Ritual (WATER), argues for the importance of considering situational contexts in moral judgments. Another group, Catholics for a Free Choice, says that the circumstances of a woman's life and that of her family should determine whether or not an abortion is justified.

Other radical feminists have discarded a traditional religious affiliation altogether and have formed wiccas, or witch's covens. Some feminist spiritual circles have derived their symbols and rituals from the earth and fertility goddesses of pre-Judeo-Christian and pre-Islamic religions. They say that the Virgin Mary is a cultural descendant of a fertility goddess, the Queen of the May, and that three pre-Islamic fertility goddesses were transformed into the daughters of Allah. The Teotihuacán Feathered Serpent of many Mexican cultures originally represented a goddess, and the introduction of Christianity by the Spaniards uprooted the native culture's Corn Mothers. In reviving women-centered religions, radical spiritual feminism is reclaiming women's sexuality, pregnancy and childbirth, menstruation, and menopause from men who have made them into sins or illnesses.

In *medicine,* the women's health care movement resisted medical practices dominated by men; at first, they did so outside of mainstream institutions, but then many of their recommended changes were incorporated into the mainstream. Many women entered medical school in the 1960s and 1970s in the United States and other countries where most of the physicians had been men, but they found it very difficult to change curricula or training. At that time, men's bodies were the norm in textbooks; women's bodies were a deviation because they menstruated and gave birth. Standard medical practice has treated normal pregnancies as illnesses and has used monitors and machines routinely in normal childbirth, distancing women from their own bodies. The new reproductive technologies for infertile couples detach conception from sexual intimacy; for example, in a petri dish, sperm produced by masturbation are mixed with ova that are harvested surgically.

In the 1970s in the United States, the women's health movement tried to take the control of women's bodies out of the hands of the medical system because the care women patients were getting from men doctors took few of their overall needs into consideration and allowed them very little control over their treatment. The solution was women-run clinics for women patients. Nurses and other health care workers taught gynecological self-examination, took a whole-person approach to diagnosis and treatment, and dispensed alternative medicines. The women's health movement did not consider women physicians to be much better than men physicians, since they had been trained in the same medical schools and hospitals. The activists in the women's health movement thought that by educating women patients to be more assertive and knowledgeable health consumers, they would put pressure on the medical system to modify the way men and women physicians are taught to practice.

The women's health movement has encouraged the training and employment of midwives and the experience of family-oriented childbirth at home and in birthing centers separated from hospitals. It has been critical of the new reproductive technologies, breast implants, and cosmetic surgery as violations of women's bodily integrity. The consumer movement in medicine has taken over most of the women's health movement's demands that medicine become more holistic and patient-oriented. Adapting the radical feminist critique and working within mainstream medicine, women physicians in the United States have, in the last few years, promoted research and held conferences on women's medical needs and have published a medical journal devoted to research on women's health. They have pushed for women to be part of all clinical trials for new drugs and have collected statistics on the likelihood of women to contract "men's" illnesses, such as AIDS and heart disease. Female bodies are no longer seen as a deviation from a male norm; rather, the definition of "normal" has been altered.

Critique. Radical feminism is a direct and open confrontation with the gendered social order. Its condemnation of Western society's encouragement of men's violence and aggressive sexuality has led to a critique of the unequal power in heterosexual relationships. It defends the value of mothering over paid work. Thus, it produces a schism among feminists, offending many of those who are in heterosexual relationships, who do not want children, or who are ambitious for careers. The contrast of women's emotional and nurturing capabilities with men's intrusive sexuality and aggressiveness in radical feminism has been seen as *essentialist*—rooted in deep-seated and seemingly intractable differences between two global categories of people.

This concentration on pervasive gender characteristics and oppression has led to accusations that radical feminism neglects racial, ethnic, religious, and social class differences among men and among women, and that it downplays other sources of oppression. However, radical feminism has joined with marxist, socialist, and post-colonial feminisms in political activism to improve the lives of poor and working-class women of disadvantaged racial ethnic groups in industrial and nonindustrial countries.

Another divisive issue has been radical feminism's views on sexuality and pornography's harmfulness. Some feminists do not think pornography is that harmful to women, unlike radical feminists, who are in the forefront of the fights against sexual exploitation, harassment, rape, and battering. Radical feminism's stance against sadomasochism and other forms of "kinky" sex at the 1981 Barnard College conference, "The Scholar and the Feminist IX: Toward a Politics of Sexuality," opened a feminist "sex war" that has not died down to this day.

Yet it was radical feminism's extremism ("radical" means down to the roots) and fury at the throwaway use of women's bodies, sexuality, and emotions that made men and women realize how deeply misogynist our supposedly enlightened social world is. Radical feminism deserves much credit for bringing rape, sexual abuse of children, battering, sexual harassment, and global trafficking in women for prostitution to public attention. Those who try to raise the value of women by praising motherhood have been criticized by feminists who feel this strategy invokes traditional rationales for keeping women out of the public arena. But it does what some radical feminists want—to put women on the social map as different from men but worth just as much, if not more.

Summary

It may seem as if some radical feminists' slogan could be, "Women are not just as good as men, they are *better.*" (Others strongly repudiate such views.) If men are so violent and sexually aggressive, and women are so nurturant and emotionally sensitive, what the world needs is for women, not men, to run things. As leaders, women would be less hierarchical and authoritarian, more cooperative and consensual. They would respect the environment. Ethically, they would look out for others' needs, and spiritually, they would form loving, caring communities that included men.

Despite this utopian vision, radical feminism's practical actions focus on setting up rape crisis centers and battered women's shelters, teaching women karate and other forms of self-defense, developing guidelines against sexual harassment, and educating people about date rape. Radical feminist politics mounts campaigns against prostitution, pornography, and other forms of sex work, as well as against high-tech reproductive technologies, breast implants, cosmetic surgery, and other types of demeaning objectification of women's bodies.

Radical feminism was the theoretical rationale for women's studies programs in colleges and universities. It claims that it is not enough to add women to the curriculum as another social group to be studied; women's ways of thinking have to be brought to the forefront. Women's bodies, sexuality, and emotional relationships are different from men's, and so are women's literature, art, music, crafts, and rituals. If most of what is taught in schools is "men's studies," then what is needed is a separate focus on women's history, knowledge, and culture.

The same argument—that it is not enough to "add women and stir" but that women's experiences produce a radical rethinking—occurs in feminist ethics, religions, and medicine. Women's ethics are based on responsibility to others, not individual rights; women's religious rituals focus on their life cycles, not men's; and women's health care tends to the social as well as physical problems of girls and women.

Organizationally, radical feminists form nonhierarchical, supportive, women-only spaces where women can think and act and create free of constant sexist put-downs, sexual harassment, and the threat of rape and violence. The heady possibilities of creating woman-oriented health care facilities, safe residences for battered women, counseling and legal services for survivors of rape, a woman's culture, and a woman's religion and ethics forge the bonds of sisterhood. Politically, radical feminism's primary mission is fighting for women and against men's social and cultural supremacy.

Radical feminism, by refusing to go along with conventional assumptions, directly confronts the deep-seated denigration and control of women in the gendered social order. It pushes feminism into direct conflict with those in power. The battle cry is no longer "Women deserve equal rights," but "Sisterhood is powerful."

Suggested Readings in Radical Feminism

Theory and Politics

Daly, Mary. 1973. *Beyond God the Father: Toward a Philosophy of Women's Liberation.* Boston: Beacon Press.

———. 1978. *Gyn/Ecology: The Metaethics of Radical Feminism.* Boston: Beacon Press.

———. 1984. *Pure Lust: Elemental Feminist Philosophy.* Boston: Beacon Press.

———. 1998. *Quintessence . . . Realizing the Archaic Future: A Radical Elemental Feminist Manifesto.* Boston: Beacon Press.

Daly, Mary, and Jane Caputi. 1987. *Intergalactic Wickedary of the English Language.* Boston: Beacon Press.

Frye, Marilyn. 1983. *The Politics of Reality: Essays in Feminist Theory.* Trumansburg, NY: The Crossing Press.

Fuss, Diane. 1989. *Essentially Speaking: Feminism, Nature, and Difference.* New York: Routledge.

Gilligan, Carol. 1982. *In a Different Voice: Psychological Theory and Women's Development.* Cambridge, MA: Harvard University Press.

Griffin, Susan. 1978. *Women and Nature: The Roaring Inside Her.* New York: Harper.

MacKinnon, Catharine A. 1979. *Sexual Harassment of Working Women.* New Haven, CT: Yale University Press.

———. 1987. *Feminism Unmodified.* Cambridge, MA: Harvard University Press.

———. 1989. *Toward a Feminist Theory of the State.* Cambridge, MA: Harvard University Press.

Morgan, Robin, ed. 1970. *Sisterhood Is Powerful.* New York: Vintage.

———. 1984. *Sisterhood Is Global: The International Women's Movement Anthology.* New York: Doubleday. Reprint edition, 1996. New York: Feminist Press.

O'Brien, Mary. 1981. *The Politics of Reproduction.* New York: Routledge.

———. 1989. *Reproducing the World: Essays in Feminist Theory.* Boulder, CO: Westview Press.

Pateman, Carole. 1988. *The Sexual Contract.* Stanford, CA: Stanford University Press.

Rothman, Barbara Katz. 1998. *Genetic Maps and Human Imaginations: The Limits of Science in Understanding Who We Are.* New York: W. W. Norton. Reissued as *The Book of Life.* 2001. Boston: Beacon Press.

Bodies

Birke, Lynda. 2000. *Feminism and the Biological Body.* New Brunswick, NJ: Rutgers University Press.

Bordo, Susan R. 1993. *Unbearable Weight: Feminism, Western Culture, and the Body.* Berkeley: University of California Press.

Boston Women's Health Book Collective. [1973] 1998. *Our Bodies, Ourselves.* New York: Simon and Schuster.

Buckley, Thomas, and Alma Gottlieb, eds. 1988. *Blood Magic: The Anthropology of Menstruation.* Berkeley: University of California Press.

Clarke, Adele, and Virginia L. Oleson, eds. 1999. *Revisioning Women, Health, and Healing: Feminist, Cultural, and Technoscience Perspectives.* New York: Routledge.

Davis, Kathy, ed. 1997. *Embodied Practices: Feminist Perspectives on the Body.* London: Sage.

Delaney, Janice, Mary Jane Lupton, and Emily Toth. 1977. *The Curse: A Cultural History of Menstruation.* New York: New American Library.

Donchin, Anne, and Laura Purdy, eds. 1999. *Embodying Bioethics: Recent Feminist Advances.* Savage, MD: Rowman & Littlefield.

Grosz, Elizabeth. 1994. *Volatile Bodies: Toward a Corporeal Feminism.* Bloomington: Indiana University Press.

———. 1996. *Space, Time and Perversion: Essays on the Politics of the Body.* New York: Routledge.

Holmes, Helen Bequaert, and Laura M. Purdy, eds. 1992. *Feminist Perspectives in Medical Ethics.* Bloomington: Indiana University Press.

Hubbard, Ruth, Mary Sue Henifin, and Barbara Fried, eds. 1979. *Women Look at Biology Looking at Women: A Collection of Feminist Critiques.* Cambridge, MA: Schenkman.

Jacobus, Mary, Evelyn Fox Keller, and Sally Shuttleworth, eds. 1990. *Body/Politics: Women and the Discourses of Science.* New York: Routledge.

Knight, Chris. 1991. *Blood Relations: Menstruation and the Origins of Culture.* New Haven, CT: Yale University Press.

Martin, Emily. 1987. *The Woman in the Body: A Cultural Analysis of Reproduction.* Boston: Beacon Press.

Weitz, Rose, ed. 1998. *The Politics of Women's Bodies: Sexuality, Appearance and Behavior.* New York: Oxford University Press.

Zita, Jacqueline N. 1998. *Body Talk: Philosophical Reflections on Sex and Gender.* New York: Columbia University Press.

Disability

Brownworth, Victoria, and Susan Raffo. 1999. *Restricted Access: Lesbians on Disability.* Seattle, WA: Seal Press.

Deegan, Mary Jo, and Nancy A. Brooks, eds. 1985. *Women and Disability: The Double Handicap.* New Brunswick, NJ: Transaction Books.

Fine, Michelle, and Adrienne Asch, eds. 1988. *Women With Disabilities: Essays in Psychology, Culture, and Politics.* Philadelphia: Temple University Press.

Hillyer, Barbara. 1993. *Feminism and Disability.* Norman: University of Oklahoma Press.

Lonsdale, Susan. 1990. *Women and Disability.* New York: St. Martin's Press.

Mairs, Nancy. 1986. *Plaintext.* Tucson: University of Arizona Press.

Wendell, Susan. 1996. *The Rejected Body: Feminist Philosophical Reflections on Disability.* New York: Routledge.

Ecofeminism

Adams, Carol J., ed. 1993. *Ecofeminism and the Sacred.* New York: Continuum.

Adams, Carol J., and Josephine Donovan, eds. 1995. *Animals and Women: Feminist Theoretical Explorations.* Durham, NC: Duke University Press.

Biehl, Janet. 1991. *Finding Our Way: Rethinking Ecofeminist Politics.* New York: Southend Press.

Birke, Lynda. 1994. *Feminism, Animals, Science: The Naming of the Shrew.* Philadelphia: Open University Press.

Diamond, Irene. 1994. *Fertile Ground: Women, Earth, and the Limits of Control.* Boston: Beacon Press.

Diamond, Irene, and Gloria Orenstein, eds. 1990. *Reweaving the World: The Emergence of Ecofeminism.* Berkeley: University of California Press.

Merchant, Carolyn. [1980] 1989. *The Death of Nature: Women, Ecology, and the Scientific Revolution.* New York: Harper & Row.

———. 1992. *Radical Ecology: The Search for a Livable World.* New York: Routledge.

———. 1995. *Earthcare: Women and the Environment.* New York: Routledge.

Mies, Maria, and Vandana Shiva. 1993. *Ecofeminism: Reconnecting a Divided World.* London: Zed.

Ruether, Rosemary Radford. 1992. *Gaia and God: An Ecofeminist Theology of Earth Healing.* San Francisco: HarperSanFrancisco.

———, ed. 1996. *Women Healing Earth: Third World Women on Ecology, Feminism, and Religion.* Maryknoll, NY: Orbis Books.

Shiva, Vandana. 1988. *Staying Alive: Women, Ecology and Survival in India.* New Delhi: Kali for Women.

Warren, Karen, ed. 1994. *Ecofeminism: Multidisciplinary Perspectives.* Bloomington: Indiana University Press.

———, ed. 1997. *Ecofeminism: Women, Culture, Nature.* Bloomington: Indiana University Press.

Ethics

Gatens, Moira. 1996. *Imaginary Bodies: Essays on Corporeality, Power and Ethics.* New York: Routledge.

Held, Virginia. 1993. *Feminist Morality: Transforming Culture, Society and Politics.* Chicago: University of Chicago Press.

———, ed. 1995. *Justice and Care: Essential Readings in Feminist Ethics.* Boulder, CO: Westview Press.

Irigaray, Luce. [1984] 1993. *An Ethics of Sexual Difference.* Translated by Carolyn Burke and Gillian C. Gill. London: Athlone Press.

Noddings, Nel. 2002. *Starting at Home: Caring and Social Policy.* Berkeley: University of California Press.

Sevenhuijsen, Selma. 1998. *Citizenship and the Ethics of Care: Feminist Considerations on Justice, Morality, and Politics.* New York: Routledge.

Tronto, Joan C. 1993. *Moral Boundaries: A Political Argument for an Ethic of Care.* New York: Routledge.

Walker, Margaret Urban. 1998. *Moral Understandings: A Feminist Study in Ethics.* New York: Routledge.

———. 2003. *Moral Contexts.* Lanham, MD: Rowman & Littlefield.

Gendered Global Violence

Enloe, Cynthia. 2000. *Maneuvers: The International Politics of Militarizing Women's Lives.* Berkeley: University of California Press.

————. 2001. *Bananas, Beaches and Bases: Making Feminist Sense of International Politics.* Updated ed. Berkeley: University of California Press.

"Forum: The Events of 11 September 2001 and Beyond." 2002. *International Feminist Journal of Politics* 4:95–113.

Hawthorne, Susan, and Bronwyn Winter, eds. 2002. *September 11, 2001: Feminist Perspectives.* North Melbourne, Australia: Spinifex.

"Roundtable: Gender and September 11." 2002. *Signs* 28:432–479.

"Roundtable: September 11 and Its Aftermath: Voices from Australia, Canada, and Africa." 2004. *Signs* 29:575–617.

Motherhood

Hrdy, Sarah Blaffer. 1999. *Mother Nature: A History of Mothers, Infants, and Natural Selection.* New York: Pantheon.

Rich, Adrienne. 1977. *Of Woman Born: Motherhood As Experience and As Institution.* New York: W. W. Norton.

Rothman, Barbara Katz. 1982. *In Labor: Women and Power in the Birthplace.* New York: W. W. Norton.

————. 1986. *The Tentative Pregnancy: Prenatal Diagnosis and the Future of Motherhood.* New York: Viking.

————. 1989. *Recreating Motherhood: Ideology and Technology in a Patriarchal Society.* New York: W. W. Norton. 2nd ed. New Brunswick, NJ: Rutgers University Press, 2000.

Ruddick, Sara. 1995. *Maternal Thinking: Toward a Politics of Peace.* Boston: Beacon Press.

Trebilcot, Joyce, ed. 1983. *Mothering: Essays in Feminist Theory.* Totowa, NJ: Rowman and Allenheld.

Religion

Ahmed, Leila. 1992. *Women and Gender in Islam.* New Haven, CT: Yale University Press.

Frymer-Kensky, Tikva. 1992. *In the Wake of the Goddesses: Women, Culture and the Biblical Transformation of Pagan Myth.* New York: Fawcett Columbine.

Gimbutas, Marija. 1989. *The Language of the Goddess.* San Francisco: Harper & Row.

————. 1999. *The Living Goddesses.* Edited and supplemented by Miriam Robbins Dexter. Berkeley: University of California Press.

Jayakar, Pupul. 1990. *The Earth Mother: Legends, Ritual Arts, and Goddesses of India.* San Francisco: Harper & Row.

Kien, Jenny. 2000. *Reinstating the Divine Woman in Judaism.* Universal Publishers/uPublish.com.

————. 2003. *The Battle Between the Moon and the Sun: The Separation of Women's Bodies From the Cosmic Dance.* Universal Publishers/uPublish.com.

Mernissi, Fatima. 1987. *Beyond the Veil: Male-Female Dynamics in Modern Muslim Society.* Bloomington: Indiana University Press.

———. 1991. *The Veil and the Male Elite: A Feminist Interpretation of Women's Rights in Islam.* Translated by Mary Jo Lakeland. Cambridge, MA: Perseus Books.

Plaskow, Judith. 1990. *Standing Again at Sinai: Judaism From a Feminist Perspective.* San Francisco: Harper and Row.

Ruether, Rosemary Radford. 1983. *Sexism and God-talk: Toward a Feminist Theology.* Boston: Beacon Press.

Ruether, Rosemary Radford, and Eleanor McLaughlin, eds. 1979. *Women of Spirit: Female Leadership in the Jewish and Christian Traditions.* New York: Simon and Schuster.

Sabbah, Fatna A. 1984. *Woman in the Muslim Unconscious.* Translated by Mary Jo Lakeland. New York: Pergamon.

Starhawk. 1990. *Truth or Dare: Encounters with Power, Authority, and Mystery.* New York: HarperCollins.

———. [1979] 1999. *Spiral Dance: A Rebirth of the Ancient Religion of the Goddess.* 20th Anniversary Edition. New York: HarperCollins.

———. 2001. *The Twelve Wild Swans: A Journey to the Realm of Magic, Healing, and Action.* San Francisco: HarperSanFrancisco.

Wadud, Amina. 1999. *Qur'an and Woman: Rereading the Sacred Text from a Woman's Perspective.* New York: Oxford University Press.

Sexual Violence

Barry, Kathleen. 1979. *Female Sexual Slavery.* Englewood Cliffs, NJ: Prentice-Hall.

———. 1995. *Prostitution of Sexuality: Global Exploitation of Women.* New York: New York University Press.

Bart, Pauline B., and Eileen Geil Moran, eds. 1993. *Violence Against Women: The Bloody Footprints.* Thousand Oaks, CA: Sage.

Brownmiller, Susan. 1975. *Against Our Will: Men, Women and Rape.* New York: Simon and Schuster.

Caputi, Jane. 1987. *The Age of Sex Crime.* Bowling Green, OH: Bowling Green University Popular Press.

Dobash, R. Emerson, and Russell Dobash. 1979. *Violence Against Wives: A Case Against the Patriarchy.* New York: Free Press.

Dworkin, Andrea. 1974. *Woman Hating.* New York: NAL Penguin.

———. 1981. *Pornography: Men Possessing Women.* New York: Perigee (Putnam).

———. 1987. *Intercourse.* New York: Free Press.

Griffin, Susan. 1982. *Pornography and Silence: Culture's Revenge Against Nature.* San Francisco: Harper and Row.

Kazuko, Watanabe. 1994. "Militarism, Colonialism, and the Trafficking of Women: 'Comfort Women' Forced Into Sexual Labor for Japanese Soldiers." *Bulletin of Concerned Asian Scholars* 26: Oct.–Dec.

Lederer, Laura, ed. 1980. *Take Back the Night: Women on Pornography.* New York: Morrow.

Russell, Diana E. H. 1998. *Dangerous Relationships: Pornography, Misogyny, and Rape.* Thousand Oaks, CA: Sage.

Schellstede, Sangmie Choi, ed. 2000. *Comfort Women Speak: Testimony of Sex Slaves of the Japanese Military.* New York: Holmes & Meier.

Yllö, Kersti, and Michele Bograd, eds. 1988. *Feminist Perspectives on Wife Abuse.* Thousand Oaks, CA: Sage. ✦

Chapter Six

Lesbian Feminism

Sources of Gender Inequality

- Oppressive heterosexuality.
- The assumption that everyone is heterosexual (*heteronormativity*).
- Men's domination of women's social spaces.

Politics

- Empowering women-identified women.
- Making lesbian sexuality and relationships visible.
- Fighting dual battles—for women's rights and for homosexual rights.

Contributions

- Critical analysis of heterosexual romantic love and sexual relationships.
- Exploration of women's sexuality.
- Expansion of lesbianism to include community and culture.
- Creating women-only workplaces, cultural events, and political organizations.

Lesbian feminism takes the radical feminist pessimistic view of men to its logical conclusion. If heterosexual relationships are intrinsically exploitative because of men's social, physical, and sexual power over women, why bother with men at all? Women are more loving, nurturant, sharing, and understanding. Men like having women friends to talk to about their problems, but women can only unburden to other women. "Why not go all the way?" asks lesbian feminism. Stop sleeping with the "enemy" and turn to other women for sexual love as well as for intellectual companionship and emotional support.

Women's sexual desire for other women and lesbian relationships, like male homosexuality, had been underground in the United States and other Western countries. Fired by the social protest movements of the 1960s, men's and women's homosexuality became increasingly visible and acceptable. Up to the 1960s, many women professionals and activists, most of whom did not identify themselves as lesbians, were nonetheless able to break the mold of conventional women's roles because of their deeply emotional, supportive friendships with other women, which may or may not have been sexual. Lesbian feminism links sexual desire for other women, women's independent lifestyles, and women's friendships with the idea of women's culture and knowledge, producing a movement of resistance to a gendered social order that expects women to want more than anything else to fall in love with and marry a man.

The pre-Stonewall culture of lesbian resistance became defiantly visible in the years after the gay and lesbian riots in response to a police raid on the famous Greenwich Village nightclub, the Stonewall, on June 28, 1969. With greater openness and acceptance, lesbian resistance shifted from sexual defiance to sexual and gender defiance. Lesbian feminists have argued over identification and community, gendered role behavior, biological motherhood, and now, in the debates over gay marriage, whether marriage is a feminist sell-out, but its core has been sexual desire for women and gender identification as a woman.

Lesbian sexuality. Lesbian feminism's defining stance on sexuality is that heterosexuality is oppressive and therefore women are better off having sexual relationships with women. But there are debates within lesbian feminism over the origin of women's sexual attraction to women—is it inborn and lifelong or can it develop at any time, perhaps beginning with an intense work or political involvement? Another split in lesbian feminism is over sadomasochistic sexual relationships between women, which seem to violate the egalitarian and nonviolent ethos of both feminism and lesbianism.

Bisexuality challenges lesbian feminism behaviorally and politically. Women bisexuals who have sexual relations with both women and men, sometimes simultaneously and sometimes serially, disturb the clear gender and sexual divisions that are the basis for woman-identification and lesbian separatism. Bisexuality may not undercut the identification with women as an oppressed social group, but it undermines the lesbian separatist solution.

The lesbian continuum. Despite popular opinion, most feminists are not lesbians, and many lesbians are not feminists. There is a continuum of relationships, from lifelong friendships among women who identify themselves as heterosexuals and whose sexual partners are men, to women-identified women who are politically active in causes benefiting women and whose sexuality is varied, to women who identify themselves as lesbians and whose sexual and emotional partners are exclusively women.

In the following excerpt, Lillian Faderman, who has written two histories of lesbianism, discusses the changing meaning of women's emotional involvement with other women.

Romantic Friendship and Lesbian Love

Lillian Faderman
Professor of English, California State University, Fresno

Passionate romantic friendship between women was a widely recognized, tolerated social institution before . . . [the twentieth] century. Women were, in fact, expected to seek out kindred spirits and form strong bonds. It was socially acknowledged that while a woman could not trust men outside her family, she could look to another female for emotional sustenance and not fear betrayal. Had a woman of an earlier era *not* behaved with her intimate friend . . . [in an emotional manner], she would have been thought strangely cold. But her relationship to another female went beyond such affectionate exchanges. It was not unusual for a woman to seek in her romantic friendship the center of her life, quite apart from the demands of marriage and family if not in lieu of them. When women's role in society began to change, however—when what women did needed to be taken more seriously because they were achieving some of the powers that would make them adult persons—society's view of romantic friendship changed.

Love between women—relationships which were *emotionally* in no way different from the romantic friendships of earlier eras—became evil or morbid. It was not simply that men now saw the female sexual drive more realistically. Many of the relationships that they condemned had little to do with sexual expression. It was rather that love between women, coupled with their emerging freedom, might conceivably bring about the overthrow of heterosexuality—which has meant not only sex between men and women but patriarchal culture, male dominance, and female subservience. Learning their society's view of love between women, females were compelled to suppress natural emotion; they were taught to see women only as rivals and men as their only possible love objects, or they were compelled to view themselves as "lesbian," which meant "twisted" either morally or emotionally. What was lovely and nurturing in love between women, what women of other centuries clearly understood, became one of the best-guarded secrets of the patriarchy.

In the sophisticated twentieth century women who chose to love women could no longer see themselves as romantic friends, unless they enveloped themselves in a phenomenal amount of naiveté and were oblivious to modern psychology, literature, and dirty jokes. If they persisted in same-sex love past adolescence, they would at least have to take into account what society thought of lesbians, and they would have to decide to what extent they would internalize those social views. If they were unusually strong or had a strong support group, they might escape regarding themselves as sick sinners. For many of them, without models to show that love between women was not intrinsically wrong or unhealthy, the experts' pronouncements about lesbianism worked as a self-fulfilling prophecy. They became as confused and tormented as they were supposed to be. But it was only during this brief era in history that tragedy and sickness were so strongly attributed to (and probably for that reason so frequently found in) love between women.

This changed with the rise of the second wave of feminism. Having made a general challenge to patriarchal culture, many feminists in the last decade began to challenge its taboos on love between women too. They saw it as their job to divest themselves of all the prejudices that had been inculcated in them by their male-dominated society, to reexamine everything regarding women, and finally to reclaim the meaning of love between women. Having learned to question both the social order which made women the second sex and the meaning behind the taboos on love between women, they determined to live their lives through new definitions they would create. They called themselves women-identified-women, or they consciously attempted to lift the stigma from the term "lesbian" and called themselves lesbian-feminists, by which they meant that they would put women first in their lives because men had proven, if not on a personal then on a cultural scale, that they were not to be trusted. Lesbian-feminists see men and women as being at odds in their whole approach to the world: men, as a rule, are authoritarian, violent, and cold, and women are the opposite. Like romantic friends before them, lesbian-feminists choose women, kindred spirits, for their love objects. Unlike most romantic friends, however, they understand through feminist doctrine the sociopolitical meaning of their choice.

Lesbian-feminists differ from romantic friends in a number of ways. Most significantly, the earlier women generally had no hope of actually spending their lives together despite often reiterated fantasies that they might; but also romantic friends did not have an articulated doctrine which would help them explain why they could feel closer to women than to men. And the primary difference which affected their relationship to the world is that romantic friends, unlike lesbian-feminists, seldom had reason to believe that society saw them as outlaws—even when they eloped together. . . . Lesbian-feminists understand, even when they are comfortable within a large support group, that the world outside views them as criminal and reduces their love to a pejorative term. Whatever anger they began with as feminists is multiplied innumerable times as lesbian-feminists as soon as they experience, either in reality or by observation, society's hostility to what is both logical and beautiful to them. Even if they do not suffer personally—if they do not lose their children in court or if they are not fired from their jobs or turned out by their families because of their political-sexual commitments—lesbian-feminists are furious, knowing that such possibilities exist and that many women do suffer for choosing to love other women. Romantic friends never learned to be angry through their love.

There is a good deal on which lesbian-feminists disagree, such as issues concerning class, whether or not to form monogamous relationships, the virtues of communal living, whether separatism is necessary in order to live as a lesbian-feminist, the nature of social action that is efficacious, etc. But they all agree that men have waged constant battle against women, committed atrocities or at best injustices against them, reduced them to grown-up children, and that a feminist ought not to sleep in the enemy camp. They all agree that being a lesbian is, whether consciously or unconsciously perceived, a political act, a refusal to fulfill the male image of womanhood or to bow to male supremacy. Perhaps for romantic friends of other eras their relationship was also a political act, although much more covert: With each other they could escape from many of the externally imposed demands of femininity that were especially stringent throughout much of the eighteenth and nineteenth centuries. They could view themselves as human beings and prime rather than as the second sex. But they did not hope that through their relationship they might change the social structure. Lesbian-feminists do.

They see their lesbian-feminism not just as a personal choice regarding life-style, even though it is certainly a most personal choice. But it is also a political choice which challenges sexism and heterosexism. It is a choice which has been made often in the context of the feminist movement and with an awareness of the ideology behind it. It has seemed the only possible choice for many women who believe that the personal is political, that to reject male supremacy in the abstract but to enter into a heterosexual relationship in which the female is usually subservient makes no sense. Contemporary lesbianism, on the other hand, makes a great deal of sense. It is a combination of the natural love between women, so encouraged in the days of romantic friendships, with the twentieth-century women's freedom that feminism has made possible.

While romantic friends had considerable latitude in their show of physical affection toward each other, it is probable that, in an era when women were not supposed to be sexual, the sexual possibilities of their relationship were seldom entertained. Contemporary women can have no such innocence. But the sexual aspects of their lesbian-feminist relationships generally have less significance than the emotional sustenance and the freedom they have to define themselves. While many lesbian-feminist relationships can and do continue long after the sexual component has worn off, they cannot continue without emotional sustenance and freedom of self-definition. Romantic friends of other eras would probably have felt entirely comfortable in many lesbian-feminist relationships had the contemporary label and stigma been removed.

But many women today continue to be frightened by love between women because the pejorative connotation of the contemporary label and stigma are still very real for them. Such fear is bound to vanish in the future as people continue to reject strict orthodoxy in sexual relationships: Women will be less and less scared off by the idea of same-sex love without examining what it entails beyond "sexual abnormality." The notion of lesbianism will be neutralized. As females are raised to be more independent, they will not assume that heterosexual marriage is necessary for survival and fulfillment; nor will they accept male definitions of womanhood or non-womanhood. They will have no need to repress natural feelings of affection toward other women. Love between women will become as common as romantic friendship was in other eras. The twentieth-century combination of romantic friendship and female independence will continue to yield lesbian-feminism.

In an ideal world lesbian-feminism, which militantly excludes relationships with men, would not exist. And, of course, the romantic friendships such as women were permitted to conduct in other centuries—in which they might be almost everything to each other but in which a male protector was generally needed in order for them to survive—would not exist either. Instead, in a utopia men would not claim supremacy either in social or personal relationships, and women would not feel that they must give up a part of themselves in order to relate to men. Women with ambition and strength and a sense of themselves would have no reason to see men as the enemy out to conquer and subdue them. Nor would there be any attempt to indoctrinate the female with the notion that to be normal she must transfer the early love she felt for her mother first to her father and then to a father substitute—a man who is more than she is in all ways: older, taller, better educated, smarter, stronger. Women as well as men would not select their love objects on the basis of sexual politics, in surrender or in reaction to an arbitrary heterosexual ideology. They would choose to love another only in reference to the individual needs of their own personalities, which ideally had been allowed to develop untrammeled and free of sex-role stereotyping. Potential or actual bisexuality, which is today looked on by lesbian-feminists as a political betrayal and by heterosexuals as an instability, would be normal, both emotionally and statistically. But until men stop giving women cause to see them as the enemy and until there ceases to be coercion to step into prescribed roles without reference to individual needs and desires, lesbian-feminists will continue to view their choice as the only logical one possible for a woman who desires to be her own adult person.

Lesbian identities, lesbian communities. As theory and in politics, lesbian feminism transforms love between women into an identity, a community, and a culture. Lesbian feminism praises women's sexuality and bodies, mother-daughter love, and the culture of women, thus expanding sexual and emotional relationships between women into a wholly engaged life.

Lesbians are not monolithic. In the 1950s, lesbians playing the "fem" role were extremely feminine in their dress, demeanor, and expressions of sexuality, while "butches" were cool, masculine-looking, and assertive. There were also butch-fem role exchangers ("roll overs" or "kikis") who played both parts. More open lifestyles encourage a range of sexual and gender behaviors, and a range of clothing, hairstyles, and cosmetic use. This variety is the surface reflection of a deeper sense of varied identity as a lesbian. As a result, the social and sexual boundaries of lesbian communities have become more fluid.

In the following excerpt, Arlene Stein, a lesbian feminist sociologist, reports on the results of research into the sense of identity and community of feminists who became adults in the 1990s. She contrasts them with an earlier generation of lesbians who came of age in the 1970s.

Questions of Identity Revisited

Arlene Stein
Professor of Sociology, Rutgers University, Livingston, NJ

As a 1980s-influenced researcher looking at the experience of baby boom lesbians, who came of age in the 1970s, I was struck by how salient were their gender and sexual identities. Could the same be said of women coming out today? How, I wondered, do "nineties women"—young lesbians coming of age now—make sense of "seventies questions"? How do they understand their sexual identities, and does this understanding vary significantly from that of their baby boom predecessors? With these broad queries in mind, I interviewed ten lesbian-identified women, ranging in age from 19 to 29, whose median year of birth was 1967, asking many of the same questions I had posed to women of the baby boom.

I imagined that I would find that for these younger women, sexual identifications do not play as central a role as they did for the older cohort. Twenty years of feminism, I surmised, had to some extent normalized lesbianism, making it less stigmatized and therefore less central to their lives. However, with some qualifications, I did not find this to be the case. Though the small number of interviews makes any claims speculative, it appears that among those coming out as lesbians today, as for their predecessors, sexuality is typically a highly salient, central aspect of the self. Becoming a lesbian entails placing oneself outside the dominant heterosexual culture, and all that that implies. Young women in particular, who must construct a sense of personhood as they establish a sexual understanding of themselves, face a complicated and frequently difficult task.

However, while the *salience* of lesbian identification among younger women did not seem significantly different from that of baby boomers at the same age, the *meaning* of this identification did. For example, among baby boomers, talk of "community" embodied the belief that lesbians all shared some basic common ground: a common marginality and a shared project of liberation. They believed that out of the diversity of women's lives and experiences they could construct a collective sense of what it meant to be a lesbian, developing subcultures that could nurture that vision. In contrast, when asked whether they considered themselves members of a "lesbian community," most of the younger women equated the idea of "community" with the imposition of "rules" and with the construction of idealized conceptions of lesbianism with which they could not fully identify.

Speaking of her knowledge of feminist theory and culture, 24-year-old Lucia Hicks told me,

> I went through a period where I identified with "sisterhood is powerful" and all. I learned about it in school. I think that there are some really positive things I can take from that. But as I get older, I think that that whole era was simplistic in a lot of ways. There are a lot of rules. When you read the literature from that period there are a lot of ways of being in the world, and not being in the world. And you fit that picture, or you don't. And that's a little too simplistic for me.

Though criticizing feminism for its alleged simplicity, Lucia is quick to acknowledge that the existence of lesbian feminist culture—books, ideas, music, and simply lesbian visibility—made her own coming out much easier. "I have to attribute my coming out in part to getting a grasp on feminism," she said. While keeping their distance from lesbian feminism, she and other younger women have also been profoundly influenced by it. "My sense is that a lot of younger dykes don't reject lesbian feminism, but they do take it for granted, not in a bad way. They just don't have to particularly announce it," said Lucia. "They just live it." This sensibility is evident in *Go Fish,* a 1994 film about a circle of lesbian friends in Chicago, which enjoyed mass distribution. The story starts from the assumption of an inherent acceptability, and even respectability, of lesbian lives. There are no painful coming out stories, the hallmark of lesbian narratives of the 1970s and 1980s. There are no painstaking justifications for lesbianism. It is the perspective of filmmakers who are in their twenties today, who have come of age two decades after Stonewall.

Nineties women have little hope of constructing a unified, collective sense of what it means to be a lesbian or a feminist. They are leery of attempts to define the "lesbian community," doubting if any one image could possibly represent the complexity of lesbian experiences. Twenty-five-year-old Judy Thomas told me, "What I am is in many ways contradictory. . . . I feel that I'm postfeminist, which isn't to say that I don't think we live in a male-dominated world. I just don't know whether the way to undermine it is to establish new expectations of what we should be. Everything is out there to be sliced and diced and put under the fine microscope." Judy's sense of indeterminacy and contradiction is related to shifts in the relationship between margin and mainstream. To become a lesbian in the 1970s was to stand outside the dominant culture. To affirm and celebrate lesbian lives, feminists were compelled to create an alternative culture. Lesbians of the baby boom went outside the music industry to make a women's music defined against commercial imperatives and "cock rock." They produced films, literature, and theories to make sense of their lives, to make themselves visible. Thanks to these efforts, nineties women have greater access than any previous generation to cultural images, narratives, and other resources that mirror their desires. Today, young women can learn about lesbian lives in women's studies courses, feminist fiction, and, increasingly, in mass-produced popular culture, such as the television show *Roseanne,* or the music of k. d. lang.

Because of these expanded opportunities, women of the postfeminist generation do not feel as strong a sense of loyalty to "feminist" or "women's" culture. They believe that they should be represented in mainstream culture, and they long for that representation. When I asked her what types of music she listened to, 19-year-old Ann Carlson answered, "I like 'cock rock' and women's music. I like both. But I like mainstream women's music the best." Rather than listen to "out" lesbian musicians recording on alternative women's music labels, "I like music that speaks to women but isn't only about women. . . . Tracy Chapman, Melissa Etheridge, Michelle Shocked. They don't use pronouns, proper nouns. To us that's cool. And we notice that men don't listen to that music." Ann subverts the feminist critique of masculinist music by embracing cock rock as a symbol of power *and* women's music as a reminder of her feminist roots. At the same time, however, she prefers "mainstream women's music": women musicians who employ lesbian and feminist imagery but perform for a mass audience. These performers' sexual ambiguity allows for the double appeal of the music—to the subculture, as well as to the mass audience. It permits audience members such as Ann to listen to music they consider to be "lesbian" and know that millions of other people are also listening to it. For her, the ambiguity is part of the appeal.[1] But the pluralization and "mainstreaming" of lesbian images are themselves ambiguous signs of progress: the increasing importance of mass-produced lesbian culture means that while lesbian images are much more plentiful than they ever were before, their production is much more reliant upon the whims of Hollywood and the culture industries, and thus lesbian lives are being commodified.[2] Nonetheless, many younger lesbians welcome this mainstreaming.

Other important differences between the seventies and nineties cohorts concern their views of the sexualization of women's bodies. While the older women claimed power by renouncing lipstick, coquettishness, and sexually explicit representations and by opposing the commercialization of beauty and sex, by 1990 many younger lesbians were asserting their sexual power by reclaiming these practices and withholding access from the conventional male beholder. As the decade wore on, the debates that emerged in bars, in coffee houses, and in the pages of community newspapers often appeared as a generational clash: Were the full-color spreads, in the glossy fashion magazines from *Elle* to *Vanity Fair*, that touted the joys of "lesbian chic" furthering lesbian visibility, or were they creating new, idealized, airbrushed versions of a genteel sapphism? Were younger women, who were pioneering a new roving club scene and unabashedly embracing sexual imagery, the rightful heirs of lesbian feminism or evidence of its demise?

When I first arrived in the Bay Area in 1981, lesbian bars, clubs, and social events were frequented by women who embraced lesbian feminist antistyle—workshirts, jeans, and "sensible shoes." But through the next few years, many lesbians began to dress up. In night clubs and on the street it was not unusual to see younger women flaunt high heels, short skirts, and other trappings of femininity, often consciously evoking the butch-femme codes of the 1950s. Twenty-eight-year-old Jill Dinkins wears her "butch" identity proudly. Whenever she goes out with her girlfriend, they adopt sharply differentiated gender styles. Jill wears leather jackets, short-cropped hair, and men's vests; her girlfriend has long hair and wears makeup and skirts.

As Jill describes these forms of self-presentation, they sound very different from the butch-femme roles practiced by earlier workingclass lesbians. For her, adopting a role is more a matter of play than necessity. "I like to play with power and sexuality. It's all a game." She and other nineties women selectively and self-consciously take on elements of butch-femme style. Some interpret the roles in a essentialized way, as showing their "true" nature and refusing the constraints of straight society, but for many these roles are more ambiguous and less naturalized than in the past. They are an aesthetic practice, a self-reflexive performance.[3]

This commitment to individual choice often also extends to sexual practices. Members of the nineties cohort tend to be much more tolerant of "slippages" of identity in general—of inconsistencies among identity, desires, and sexual practices—than their baby boom predecessors. Judy Thomas, who felt attracted to women and girls at a very early age, and who calls herself a "lesbian virgin" because she has never had a heterosexual experience, told me that she was toying with the idea of sleeping with a man, "just for the experience," and that she did not see this as a threat to her lesbian identity. She related a story about her best friend, a lesbian, who recently told her that she was having an affair with a man, fearing Judy's response. She reassured her friend that this news was not a threat to their friendship. "I was so shocked that she even asked me," she said. If there is a greater tolerance for inconsistencies of identity, this may be related to the greater propensity of younger lesbians to speak openly about their sexual practices.

Certainly, the sexual practices and politics of feminist lesbians were more diverse in private than was publicly admitted. As my interviewees suggested, frank sexual talk was muted in the interest of constructing lesbian solidarity. Recall Cindy Ross's description of lesbian sexuality in the 1970s: "Nobody knew what anyone else was doing." For nineties women, particularly members of urban lesbian subcultures, the gap between theorizing and practicing sexuality has seemingly narrowed. The belief that lesbian sexuality is radically different from and superior to other forms of sexuality, and that sexuality and desire are only peripheral aspects of the lesbian experience, is no longer widely held. As Jill Dinkins told me, "I've heard many conversations about sex recently in social settings. Not necessarily in a loveydovey manner, or in a clinical manner, but in an experimental sense. That's what a lot of young women are going through right now. They're not modeling themselves after older women." Nineties women were more likely to know about different types of sexual practices and to be aware of sexual and relational problems such as "lesbian bed death," the tendency for long-term lovers' sexual interests to wane. They are also far more likely than their baby boom predecessors to consider sexual fringe groups, such as sadomasochists, to be a legitimate part of the lesbian community. Most striking, perhaps, is the tolerance for—and even celebration of—bisexuality.

Women of the baby boom, I have argued, often suppressed their bisexuality in the interest of identifying as lesbian and challenging compulsory heterosexuality. Today, anecdotal evidence suggests that many young women, particularly on college campuses, have come to openly identify as bisexual rather than exclusively lesbian. Twenty-two-year-old Cindy Yerkovich explained that while she is attracted to men, she feels most comfortable with and sexually fulfilled by women. The label that best expresses who she is is "bi-dyke," signifying that her "sexual orientation is bisexual but [her] identity is lesbian." Cindy, who has long hair and a traditionally feminine appearance, said that she fights against the tendency to place her and others "in boxes": "A lot of stuff that has come down on me has been really looksist. People will call me bisexual not knowing whether I've ever slept with a man. Just because I have long hair. It bugs me that people assume I'm bisexual just because I pass. Gay people assume that I'm bisexual, if they don't assume that I'm straight." When I asked my younger interviewees if they were currently friends with or would choose to be friends with a bisexual woman, or how they would feel if a lesbian friend decided to become involved with a man on either a short-term or long-term basis, their responses tended, on the whole, to be quite positive. Some even suggested that lesbians and bisexual women have much in common by virtue of their "queerness."

. . . Individual differences will always exist. We have seen that even among self-identified lesbians, sexualities vary widely. For example, for some women, sexual object choice is open to choice and change. Others experience their sexual desires as relatively fixed. As long as we live in a society in which heterosexuality is normative, women who have early homosexual desires or experiences will develop a more deeply felt sense of difference than those who do not. But this difference is not of paramount significance and should not be used to determine who does and does not belong in our communities. Instead, we need to tolerate ambiguity. We need to question assumptions about who and what constitutes the lesbian community, deliberately courting greater uncertainty rather than seeking closure. This politics is already emerging in practice.

Notes

1. In the early 1990s, a few women were able to "cross over" and achieve mainstream success as out lesbians, integrating their sexuality into their art without allowing it to become either the salient fact or else barely acknowledged. k. d. lang and Melissa Etheridge, who had previously coded their sexuality as "androgyny," came out as lesbians, to great fanfare within lesbian/gay circles and to even greater commercial success. On the phenomenon of the "cross over" artist in popular music, see my "Crossover Dreams: Lesbianism and Popular Music since the 1970s" (Stein 1994).

2. For a more detailed explanation of the political implications of this mainstreaming, see Stein 1994. On the recent commodification of lesbian culture, see Clark 1993.

3. For a longer version of this argument, see Stein 1992.

References

Clark, Danae. 1993. "Commodity Lesbianism." In *The Lesbian and Gay Studies Reader,* edited by Henry Abelove, Michele Barale, and David Halperin. New York: Routledge.

Stein, Arlene. 1992. "All Dressed Up, But No Place to Go? Style Wars and the New Lesbianism." In *The Persistent Desire: A Femme-Butch Reader,* edited by Joan Nestle. Boston: Alyson.

———. 1994. "Crossover Dreams: Lesbians and Popular Music since the 1970s." In *The Good, the Bad and the Gorgeous: Popular Culture's Romance with Lesbianism,* edited by Diane Hamer and Belinda Budge. London: Pandora.

Lesbian identity politics. Politically, lesbian feminists fight on two fronts—for all women's betterment and for the civil rights and social worth of homosexuals. Whether lesbians identify and act politically mostly as homosexuals or mostly as women varies. In the United States, lesbians first identified with homosexual men in their resistance to harassment and discrimination, but after experiencing the same gender discrimination as women in the civil rights and draft-resistance movements, they turned to feminist organizations. There, unhappily, they experienced hostility to their sexuality from heterosexual women. Subsequently, some lesbian feminists developed an oppositional, woman-identified, separatist movement. But many lesbian activist groups welcome heterosexual women in their work for women's issues. Other lesbians have joined with gay men in their battle with the AIDS epidemic, for civil rights, and for legal recognition of committed relationships.

Other potential sources of division among lesbians emerged with the visibility of lesbianism in working-class and racial ethnic communities. Lesbians who once would have left home to live in cities with a lesbian underground or would have closeted their sexuality now confront homophobia *and* antifeminist opposition in some working-class and racial ethnic groups. The politics of identity fragment their sense of self and their activism, as they try to fight for homosexual rights, women's rights, and for their class and racial ethnic group's rights.

Family issues are another potential minefield. Some lesbian women have biological children and raise them with a lesbian partner. Others have been critical of sexual monogamy, with or without children, as imitative of the institution of heterosexual marriage. These lesbians prefer alternative household arrangements of several partners, which may include gay men. Lesbians who would like to have the legal benefits of marriage do not see why they, and not heterosexual feminists, have to give up the goal of legally recognized couple relationships to fight against the subordination of women in the traditional family.

Critique. Lesbian feminism began by claiming that all women can be considered lesbian in their emotional identification with women, even though they may be heterosexual in their sexual relationships. This gender identification was soon submerged by an insistence that lesbian sexual relationships are more feminist than heterosexual relationships, because intimacy with a man undercuts a woman's independence. But feminists who take up with women for political reasons in turn annoy lesbians who feel that sexual orientation is not something you can turn off and on.

A second unresolved argument is over the structure of lesbian relationships. The ideal type of lesbian relationship has been conventionalized as a sexually monogamous, emotionally satisfying bond between two loving women, weakening the critical edge of the lesbian boycott of the conventional family. Even if the structure of lesbian relationships resembles that of heterosexual pairs, lesbians argue that the quality of their relationships is entirely different. Free of male dominance, partners can be fully egalitarian and reciprocal in their behavior toward each other. However, research has shown that just like many heterosexual couples, lesbian couples tend to exaggerate the extent to which they equally share domestic work. The more affluent partner often tends to do less of the work that maintains family life, and the partner in a lower-paid, lower-prestige occupation tends to do more. The partner doing less is likely to claim the division of labor as equal, since she is violating a gendered norm of woman as caretaker as well as the image of the egalitarian lesbian household.

Summary

As an offshoot of radical feminism, lesbian feminism pushes the critique of heterosexuality and conventional family life to its logical extreme. Theoretically, lesbian feminism argues that all heterosexual relationships, especially those that are romantic and sexual, are intrinsically coercive of women. Given men's dominant social position and tendency to oppress women in everyday interaction, it is better to have as little to do with them as possible. Women have to work with men and deal with them in many public arenas, but in their private lives and especially in sexual relationships, lesbian feminists feel that a woman is a far better partner.

Lesbian feminist separatists have created cultural communities, social lives, and political organizations that are for women only. Caring, nurturance, intimacy, and woman-to-woman love of all kinds are the ideals of these women's worlds. In recent years, however, the boundaries between lesbians and heterosexual feminists and between lesbians and gay men are giving way. Lesbians invite heterosexual women into their feminist political activities, and they work with gay men politically. With the advent of men's feminism, lesbian feminism is less wary of even heterosexual men. In many political organizations today, neither gender nor sexual orientation is a significant marker of who sides with whom.

Lesbian feminism at present seems to be going in two directions at once. Some coupled and parenting lesbians are mainstreaming into family-oriented communities, while others are joining gender-defiant queer communities of transgenders. The focus of lesbian feminism of the 1970s—woman-oriented separatism—seems to be fading fast.

Suggested Readings in Lesbian Feminism

Abelove, Henry, Michèle Aina Barale, and David M. Halperin, eds. 1993. *The Lesbian and Gay Studies Reader.* New York: Routledge.

Allen, Jeffner, ed. 1990. *Lesbian Philosophies and Cultures.* Albany: State University of New York Press.

Beemyn, Brett, ed. 1997. *Creating a Place for Ourselves: Lesbian, Gay, and Bisexual Community Histories.* New York: Routledge.

Bernstein, Mary, and Renate Reimann, eds. 2001. *Queer Families, Queer Politics: Challenging Culture and the State.* New York: Columbia University Press.

Bristow, Joseph, and Angelia R. Wilson, eds. 1993. *Activating Theory: Lesbian, Gay, and Bisexual Politics.* London: Lawrence & Wishart.

Carrington, Christopher. 1999. *No Place Like Home: Relationships and Family Life Among Lesbians and Gay Men.* Chicago: University of Chicago Press.

Dalton, Susan E., and Denise D. Bielby. 2000. " 'That's Our Kind of Constellation': Lesbian Mothers Negotiate Institutionalized Understandings of Gender Within the Family." *Gender & Society* 14:36–61.

Faderman, Lillian. 1981. *Surpassing the Love of Men: Romantic Friendship and Love Between Women From the Renaissance to the Present.* New York: William Morrow.

———. 1991. *Odd Girls and Twilight Lovers: A History of Lesbian Life in Twentieth-Century America.* New York: Columbia University Press.

———. 2003. *Naked in the Promised Land: A Memoir.* Boston: Houghton Mifflin.

Feinberg, Leslie. 1993. *Stone Butch Blues.* Ithaca, NY: Firebrand Press.

Dunne, Gillian A. 2000. "Opting Into Motherhood: Lesbians Blurring the Boundaries and Transforming the Meaning of Parenthood and Kinship." *Gender & Society* 14:11–35.

Hoagland, Sarah, and Julia Penelope, eds. 1991. *For Lesbians Only: A Separatist Anthology.* London: Radical Feminist Lesbian Publishers.

Johnston, Jill. 1973. *Lesbian Nation: The Feminist Solution.* New York: Simon and Schuster.

Kennedy, Elizabeth Lapovsky, and Madeline D. Davis. 1993. *Boots of Leather, Slippers of Gold: The History of a Lesbian Community.* New York: Routledge.

Kitzinger, Celia. 1987. *The Social Construction of Lesbianism.* Thousand Oaks, CA: Sage.

Leong, Russell, ed. 1996. *Asian American Sexualities: Dimensions of the Gay and Lesbian Experience.* New York: Routledge.

Lorde, Audre. 1984. *Sister Outsider.* Trumansburg, NY: The Crossing Press.

Phelan, Shane. 1989. *Identity Politics: Lesbian Feminism and the Limits of Community.* Philadelphia: Temple University Press.

———. 1994. *Getting Specific: Postmodern Lesbian Politics.* Minneapolis: University of Minnesota Press.

Ratti, Rakesh, ed. 1993. *A Lotus of Another Color: An Unfolding of the South Asian Gay and Lesbian Experience.* Boston: Alyson Publications.

Rich, Adrienne. 1980. "Compulsory Heterosexuality and Lesbian Existence." *Signs* 5:631–660.

Rust, Paula C. 1995. *Bisexuality and the Challenge to Lesbian Politics: Sex, Loyalty, and Revolution.* New York: New York University Press.

Snitow, Ann, Christine Stansell, and Sharon Thompson, eds. 1983. *Powers of Desire: The Politics of Sexuality.* New York: Monthly Review Press.

Stein, Arlene, ed. 1993. *Sisters, Sexperts, Queers: Beyond the Lesbian Nation.* New York: Plume.

———. 1997. *Sex and Sensibility: Stories of a Lesbian Generation.* Berkeley: University of California Press.

Storr, Merl, ed. 1999. *Bisexuality: A Critical Reader.* New York: Routledge.

Taylor, Verta, and Leila Rupp. 1993. "Women's Culture and Lesbian Feminist Activism: A Reconsideration of Cultural Feminism." *Signs* 19:32–61.

Trujillo, Carla, ed. 1991. *Chicana Lesbians: The Girls Our Mother Warned Us About.* Berkeley, CA: Third Woman.

Valverde, Mariana. 1985. *Sex, Power and Pleasure.* Toronto: Women's Press.

Vance, Carole S., ed. 1984. *Pleasure and Danger: Exploring Female Sexuality.* Boston: Routledge and Kegan Paul.

Walters, Suzanna Danuta. 2001. *All the Rage: The Story of Gay Visibility in America.* Chicago: University of Chicago Press.

Weeks, Jeffrey, Catherine Donovan, and Brian Heaphy. 2001. *Same Sex Intimacies: Families of Choice and Other Life Experiments.* New York: Routledge.

Weston, Kathleen M. 1991. *Families We Choose: Lesbians, Gays, Kinship.* New York: Columbia University Press.

Wittig, Monique. 1992. *The Straight Mind and Other Essays.* Boston: Beacon Press.

Zimmerman, Bonnie, and Toni A. H. McNaron. 1996. *The New Lesbian Studies: Into the Twenty-First Century.* New York: Feminist Press. ✦

Chapter Seven

Psychoanalytic Feminism

Sources of Gender Inequality

- Gendered personality structures—ego-bound men and ego-permeable women.
- Men's sublimated fear of women.
- Cultural domination by men's phallic-oriented ideas, misogyny, and repressed emotions.

Politics

- Correcting the male bias in psychoanalytic theory.
- Producing culture that features women's emotions, sexuality, and connectedness with the body.
- Sharing parenting, so men as well as women parent intensively and children's personalities are degendered.

Contributions

- Analyzing the unconscious sources of masculinity and femininity.
- Producing a feminist psychoanalytic theory of mothering and women's personality development.
- Making evident the dominance of the *phallus* (symbol of masculine power) in Western culture.
- Counteracting with literature written out of women's experiences with their bodies, sexuality, and emotions.

In the 1970s, British, American, and French feminists began to reread and reinterpret Freud. Instead of Freud's primary focus on the personality development of boys, psychoanalytic feminism gives equal attention to the personality development of girls. It locates the origins of Freud's theories in the European patriarchal family structure of the early twentieth century and criticizes the extensive cultural and social effects of men's fear of castration, men's emotional repression, and their ambivalence toward women.

Gendered personalities. Psychoanalytic feminism claims that the source of men's domination of women is men's unconscious ambivalent need for women's emotionality and their simultaneous rejection of women as potential castrators. Women submit to men because of women's unconscious desires for emotional connectedness. These gendered personalities are the outcome of the *Oedipus complex*—the psychological separation from the mother as the child develops a sense of individual identity.

Because the woman is the primary parent, infants bond with her. According to Freudian theory, boys have to separate from their mothers and identify with their fathers in order to establish their masculinity. This identification causes them to develop strong ego boundaries and a capacity for the independent action, objectivity, and rational thinking so valued in Western culture. Women are a threat to their independence and masculine sexuality because they remind men of their dependence on their mothers. However, men need women for the emotional sustenance and intimacy they rarely give each other. Their ambivalence toward women comes out in heterosexual love-hate relationships.

Girls continue to identify with their mothers, and so they grow up with fluid ego boundaries that make them sensitive, empathic, and emotional. It is these qualities that make them potentially good mothers and keep them open to men's emotional needs. But because the men in their lives have developed personalities that are emotionally guarded, women want to have children to bond with. Thus, psychological gendering of children is continually reproduced. To develop nurturing capabilities in men, and to break the cycle of the reproduction of gendered personality structures, psychoanalytic feminism recommends shared parenting—after men are taught how to parent with emotional intimacy.

In an article published in 1976 in a special issue of *Social Problems,* "Feminist Perspectives: The Sociological Challenge," sociologist and psychoanalyst Nancy Chodorow laid out the processes and consequences of the Oedipus complex for women and men. It is a brief summary of the psychoanalytic theories presented in her influential book *The Reproduction of Mothering.*

Oedipal Asymmetries and Heterosexual Knots

Nancy J. Chodorow
Professor of Sociology, University of California, Berkeley

As a result of being parented by a woman, both sexes are looking for a return to this emotional and physical union. A man achieves this directly through the heterosexual bond which replicates for him emotionally the early mother-infant exclusivity which he seeks to recreate. He is supported in this endeavor by women, who, through their own development, have remained open to relational needs, have retained an ongoing inner affective life, and have learned to deny the limitations of masculine lovers for both psychological and practical reasons.

Men, generally, though, both look for and fear exclusivity. Throughout their development, they have tended to repress their affective relational needs and sense of connection, and to develop and be more comfortable with ties based more on categorical and abstract role expectations, particularly in relation to other males. Even when they participate in an intimate heterosexual relationship, it is likely to be with the ambivalence created by an intense relationship which one both wants and fears, demanding from women, then, what they are at the same time afraid of receiving. The relationship to the mother thus builds itself directly into contradictions in masculine heterosexual commitment.

As a result of being parented by a woman and growing up heterosexual, women have different and a more complex set of relational needs, in which exclusive relationship to a man is not enough. This is because women experience themselves as part of a relational triangle in which their father and men are emotionally secondary, or at most equal, in importance to their mother and women. Women, therefore, need primary relationships to women as well as to men. In addition, the relation to the man itself has difficulties. Idealization, growing out of a girl's relation to her father, involves denial of real feelings and to a certain extent an unreal relationship to men.

The contradictions in women's heterosexual relationships, though, do not inhere only in the outcome of early childhood relationships. As I have suggested, men themselves, because of their own development and socialization, grow up rejecting their own and others' needs for love, and, therefore, find it difficult and threatening to meet women's emotional needs. Thus, given the masculine personality which women's mothering produces, the emotional secondariness of men to women, and the social organization of gender and gender roles, a woman's relationship to a man is unlikely to provide satisfaction for the particular relational needs which women's mothering and the concomitant social organization of gender have produced in women.

The two structural principles of the family, then, are in contradiction with each other. The family reproduces itself in form: for the most part people marry, and marry heterosexually; for the most part, people form couples heterosexually. At the same time, it undercuts itself in content: as a result of men and women growing up in families where women mother, these heterosexual relations, married or not, are liable to be strained in the regularized ways I have described.

In an earlier period, father absence was less absolute, production centered in the home, and economic interdependence of the sexes meant that family life and marriage was not and did not have to be a uniquely or fundamentally emotional project. The heterosexual asymmetry which I have been discussing was only one aspect of the total marital enterprise, and, therefore, did not overwhelm it. Women in this earlier period could seek relationships to other women in their daily work and community. With the development of industrial capitalism, however—and the increasingly physically isolated, mobile, and neolocal nuclear family it has produced—other primary relationships are not easy to come by on a routine, daily, ongoing basis. At the same time, the public world of work, consumption, and leisure leaves people increasingly starved for affection, support, and a sense of unique self. The heterosexual relationship itself gains in emotional importance at the very moment when the heterosexual strains which mothering produces are themselves sharpened. In response to these emerging contradictions, divorce rates soar, people flock to multitudes of new therapies, politicians decry and sociologists document the end of the family. And there develops a new feminism.

Reprinted from: Nancy J. Chodorow, "Oedipal Asymmetries and Heterosexual Knots." In *Social Problems,* April 1976, 23(4):454–468. Copyright © 1975 by the Society for the Study of Social Problems, University of California Press. Reprinted by permission.

French psychoanalytic feminism. In France, feminists took on the Freud-ian-oriented cultural critics Jacques Lacan and Jacques Derrida, who say that women cannot create culture because they lack a sense of difference (from the mother) and a phallus (identification with the powerful father). In French feminist psychoanalytic theory, a major part of patriarchal culture reflects the sublimation of men's suppressed infantile desire for the mother and fear of the loss of the phallus, the symbol of masculine difference from powerless women. Women's wish for a phallus and repressed sexual desire for their fathers is sublimated into wanting to give birth to a son; men's repressed sex-ual desire for their mothers and fear of the father's castration of them are sub-limated into cultural creations.

To resist and to counter this phallic centrality with woman-cen-teredness, French feminism calls for women to write from their bio-graphical experiences and their bodies—about menstruation, preg-nancy, childbirth, intimacy with their mothers and their friends, their sexual desires for women as well as for men. Most of all, they need to experience and write about *jouissance,* exultant joy in their sexual bod-ies and emotions.

Luce Irigaray is one of the most influential of the French feminists who developed "psych et po"—psychoanalytically oriented feminist pol-itics based on resistance to phallic thinking and phallic culture. Using what she calls strategic essentialism, Irigaray takes women's valued attributes and through critical imitation (mimesis) turns male-oriented thinking upside-down. Using linguistics, psychoanalysis, and philoso-phy, she recreates language, culture, and sexuality in women's image.

This Sex Which is Not One[1]

Luce Irigaray
Centre National de la Recherche Scientifique, Paris

Female sexuality has always been conceptualized on the basis of mascu-line parameters. Thus the opposition between "masculine" clitoral activ-ity and "feminine" vaginal passivity, an opposition which Freud—and many others—saw as stages, or alternatives, in the development of a sex-ually "normal" woman, seems rather too clearly required by the practice of male sexuality. For the clitoris is conceived as a little penis pleasant to masturbate so long as castration anxiety does not exist (for the boy child), and the vagina is valued for the "lodging" it offers the male organ when the forbidden hand has to find a replacement for pleasure-giving.

In these terms, woman's erogenous zones never amount to anything but a clitoris-sex that is not comparable to the noble phallic organ, or a hole-envelope that serves to sheathe and massage the penis in intercourse: a nonsex, or a masculine organ turned back upon itself, self-embracing.

About woman and her pleasure, this view of the sexual relation has nothing to say. Her lot is that of "lack," "atrophy" (of the sexual organ), and "penis envy," the penis being the only sexual organ of recognized value. Thus she attempts by every means available to appropriate that organ for herself through her somewhat servile love of the father-husband capable of giving her one, through her desire for a child-penis, preferably a boy, through access to the cultural values still reserved by right to males alone and therefore always masculine, and so on. Woman lives her own desire only as the expectation that she may at last come to possess an equivalent of the male organ.

Yet all this appears quite foreign to her own pleasure, unless it remains within the dominant phallic economy. Thus, for example, woman's autoeroticism is very different from man's. In order to touch himself, man needs an instrument: his hand, a woman's body, language . . . And this self-caressing requires at least a minimum of activity. As for woman, she touches herself in and of herself without any need for mediation, and before there is any way to distinguish activity from passivity. Woman "touches herself" all the time, and moreover no one can forbid her to do so, for her genitals are formed of two lips in continuous contact. Thus, within herself, she is already two—but not divisible into one(s)—that caress each other.

This autoeroticism is disrupted by a violent break-in: the brutal separation of the two lips by a violating penis, an intrusion that distracts and deflects the woman from this "self-caressing" she needs if she is not to incur the disappearance of her own pleasure in sexual relations. If the vagina is to serve *also*, but *not only*, to take over for the little boy's hand in order to assure an articulation between autoeroticism and heteroeroticism in intercourse (the encounter with the totally other always signifying death), how, in the classic representation of sexuality, can the perpetuation of autoeroticism for woman be managed? Will woman not be left with the impossible alternative between a defensive virginity, fiercely turned in upon itself, and a body open to penetration that no longer knows, in this "hole" that constitutes its sex, the pleasure of its own touch? The more or less exclusive—and highly anxious—attention paid to erection in Western sexuality proves to what extent the imaginary that governs it is foreign to the feminine. For the most part, this sexuality offers nothing but imperatives dictated by male rivalry: the "strongest" being the one who has the best "hard-on," the longest, the biggest, the stiffest penis, or even the one who "pees the farthest" (as in little boys' contests). Or else one finds imperatives dictated by the enactment of sadomasochistic fantasies, these in turn governed by man's relation to his mother: the desire to force entry, to penetrate, to appropriate for himself the mystery of this womb where he has been conceived, the secret of his begetting, of his "origin." Desire/need, also to make blood flow again in order to revive a very old relationship—intrauterine, to be sure, but also prehistoric—to the maternal.

Woman, in this sexual imaginary, is only a more or less obliging prop for the enactment of man's fantasies. That she may find pleasure there in that role, by proxy, is possible, even certain. But such pleasure is above all a masochistic prostitution of her body to a desire that is not her own, and it leaves her in a familiar state of dependency upon man. Not knowing what she wants, ready for anything, even asking for more, so long as he will "take" her as his "object" when he seeks his own pleasure. Thus she will not say what she herself wants; moreover, she does not know, or no longer knows, what she wants. As Freud admits, the beginnings of the sexual life of a girl child are so "obscure," so "faded with time," that one would have to dig down very deep indeed to discover beneath the traces of this civilization, of this history, the vestiges of a more archaic civilization that might give some clue to woman's sexuality. That extremely ancient civilization would undoubtedly have a different alphabet, a different language . . . Woman's desire would not be expected to speak the same language as man's; woman's desire has doubtless been submerged by the logic that has dominated the West since the time of the Greeks.

Within this logic, the predominance of the visual, and of the discrimination and individualization of form, is particularly foreign to female eroticism. Woman takes pleasure more from touching than from looking, and her entry into a dominant scopic economy signifies, again, her consignment to passivity: she is to be the beautiful object of contemplation. While her body finds itself thus eroticized, and called to a double movement of exhibition and of chaste retreat in order to stimulate the drives of the "subject," her sexual organ represents *the horror of nothing to see.* A defect in this systematics of representation and desire. A "hole" in its scoptophilic lens. It is already evident in Greek statuary that this nothing-to-see has to be excluded, rejected, from such a scene of representation. Woman's genitals are simply absent, masked, sewn back up inside their "crack."

This organ which has nothing to show for itself also lacks a form of its own. And if woman takes pleasure precisely from this incompleteness of form which allows her organ to touch itself over and over again, indefinitely, by itself, that pleasure is denied by a civilization that privileges phallomorphism. The value granted to the only definable form excludes the one that is in play in female autoeroticism. The *one* of form, of the individual, of the (male) sexual organ, of the proper name, of the proper meaning . . . supplants, while separating and dividing, that contact of *at least two* (lips) which keeps woman in touch with herself, but without any possibility of distinguishing what is touching from what is touched.

Whence the mystery that woman represents in a culture claiming to count everything, to number everything by units, to inventory everything as individualities. *She is neither one nor two*. Rigorously speaking, she cannot be identified either as one person, or as two. She resists all adequate definition. Further, she has no "proper" name. And her sexual organ, which is not *one* organ, is counted as *none*. The negative, the underside, the reverse of the only visible and morphologically designatable organ (even if the passage from erection to detumescence does pose some problems): the penis.

But the "thickness" of that "form," the layering of its volume, its expansions and contractions and even the spacing of the moments in which it produces itself as form—all this the feminine keeps secret. Without knowing it. And if woman is asked to sustain, to revive, man's desire, the request neglects to spell out what it implies as to the value of her own desire. A desire of which she is not aware, moreover, at least not explicitly. But one whose force and continuity are capable of nurturing repeatedly and at length all the masquerades of "feminity" that are expected of her.

It is true that she still has the child, in relation to whom her appetite for touch, for contact, has free rein, unless it is already lost, alienated by the taboo against touching of a highly obsessive civilization. Otherwise her pleasure will find, in the child, compensations for and diversions from the frustrations that she too often encounters in sexual relations per se. Thus maternity fills the gaps in a repressed female sexuality. Perhaps man and woman no longer caress each other except through that mediation between them that the child—preferably a boy—represents? Man, identified with his son, rediscovers the pleasure of maternal fondling; woman touches herself again by caressing that part of her body: her baby-penis-clitoris.

What this entails for the amorous trio is well known. But the Oedipal interdiction seems to be a somewhat categorical and factitious law—although it does provide the means for perpetuating the authoritarian discourse of fathers—when it is promulgated in a culture in which sexual relations are impracticable because man's desire and woman's are strangers to each other. And in which the two desires have to try to meet through indirect means, whether the archaic one of a sense-relation to the mother's body, or the present one of active or passive extension of the law of the father. These are regressive emotional behaviors, exchanges of words too detached from the sexual arena not to constitute an exile with respect to it: "mother" and "father" dominate the interactions of the couple, but as social roles. The division of labor prevents them from making love. They produce or reproduce. Without quite knowing how to use their leisure. Such little as they have, such little indeed as they wish to have. For what are they to do with leisure? What substitute for amorous resource are they to invent? Still . . .

Perhaps it is time to return to that repressed entity, the female imaginary. So woman does not have a sex organ? She has at least two of them, but they are not identifiable as ones. Indeed, she has many more. Her sexuality, always at least double, goes even further: it is *plural*. Is this the way culture is seeking to characterize itself now? Is this the way texts write themselves/are written now? Without quite knowing what censorship they are evading? Indeed, woman's pleasure does not have to choose between clitoral activity and vaginal passivity, for example. The pleasure of the vaginal caress does not have to be substituted for that of the clitoral caress. They each contribute, irreplaceably, to woman's pleasure. Among other caresses . . . Fondling the breasts, touching the vulva, spreading the lips, stroking the posterior wall of the vagina, brushing against the mouth of the uterus, and so on. To evoke only a few of the most specifically female pleasures. Pleasures which are somewhat misunderstood in sexual difference as it is imagined—or not imagined, the other sex being only the indispensable complement to the only sex.

But *woman has sex organs more or less everywhere*. She finds pleasure almost anywhere. Even if we refrain from invoking the hystericization of her entire body, the geography of her pleasure is far more diversified, more multiple in its differences, more complex, more subtle, than is commonly imagined—in an imaginary rather too narrowly focused on sameness . . .

However, in order for woman to reach the place where she takes pleasure as woman, a long detour by way of the analysis of the various systems of oppression brought to bear upon her is assuredly necessary. And claiming to fall back on the single solution of pleasure risks making her miss the process of going back through a social practice that *her* enjoyment requires.

For woman is traditionally a use-value for man, an exchange value among men; in other words, a commodity. As such, she remains the guardian of material substance, whose price will be established, in terms of the standard of their work and of their need/desire, by "subjects": workers, merchants, consumers. Women are marked phallicly by their fathers, husbands, procurers. And this branding determines their value in sexual commerce. Woman is never anything but the locus of a more or less competitive exchange between two men, including the competition for the possession of mother earth.

How can this object of transaction claim a right to pleasure without removing her/itself from established commerce? With respect to other merchandise in the marketplace, how could this commodity maintain a relationship other than one of aggressive jealousy? How could material substance enjoy her/itself without provoking the consumer's anxiety over the disappearance of his nurturing ground? How could that exchange—which can in no way be defined in terms "proper" to woman's desire—appear as anything but a pure mirage, mere foolishness, all too readily obscured by a more sensible discourse and by a system of apparently more tangible values?

A woman's development, however radical it may seek to be, would thus not suffice to liberate woman's desire. And to date no political theory or political practice has resolved, or sufficiently taken into consideration, this historical problem, even though Marxism has proclaimed its importance. But women do not constitute, strictly speaking, a class, and their dispersion among several classes makes their political struggle complex, their demands sometimes contradictory.

There remains, however, the condition of underdevelopment arising from women's submission by and to a culture that oppresses them, uses them, makes of them a medium of exchange, with very little profit to them. Except in the quasi monopolies of masochistic pleasure, the domestic labor force, and reproduction. The powers of slaves? Which are not negligible powers, moreover. For where pleasure is concerned, the master is not necessarily well served. Thus to reverse the relation, especially in the economy of sexuality, does not seem a desirable objective.

But if women are to preserve and expand their autoeroticism, their homo-sexuality, might not the renunciation of heterosexual pleasure correspond once again to that disconnection from power that is traditionally theirs? Would it not involve a new prison, a new cloister, built of their own accord? For women to undertake tactical strikes, to keep themselves apart from men long enough to learn to defend their desire, especially through speech, to discover the love of other women while sheltered from men's imperious choices that put them in the position of rival commodities, to forge for themselves a social status that compels recognition, to earn their living in order to escape from the condition of prostitute . . . these are certainly indispensable stages in the escape from their proletarization on the exchange market. But if their aim were simply to reverse the order of things, even supposing this to be possible, history would repeat itself in the long run, would revert to sameness: to phallocratism. It would leave room neither for women's sexuality, nor for women's imaginary, nor for women's language to take (their) place.

Note

1. This text was originally published as "Ce sexe qui n'en est pas un," in *Cahiers du Grif*, no. 5. English translation: "This Sex Which Is Not One," trans. Claudia Reeder, in *New French Feminisms*, ed. Elaine Marks and Isabelle de Courtivron (New York, 1981), 99–106.

The male gaze. A culture's symbol system communicates both obvious and subliminal meanings. Ordinary language reflects gender hierarchies in conscious and deliberate devaluation (as in referring to adult women as "girls") and in careless language that renders women invisible (referring to men and women peers as "the guys"). Symbolic language, however, does not just name in ways that praise and denigrate; symbolic language reflects and creates the culture's "unconscious." Psychoanalytic feminism shows how Western culture represents men's fear of women and dread of emotional involvement in plays, operas, art, movies, rap music, and on MTV.

Phallic cultural productions, according to psychoanalytic feminism, are full of men's aggression, competition between men, men's flight from women or domination of them. The underlying subtext is fear of castration—of becoming women. What women represent in phallic culture is the sexual desire and emotionality men must repress in order to become like their fathers—men who are self-controlled and controlling of others. No matter what role women play in cultural productions, the *male gaze* sees them as potentially castrating mothers or as potentially engulfing objects of desire.

Psychoanalytic feminist analysis has deconstructed the ways art, films, fiction, and the mass media produce the meanings that legitimate men's cultural domination, in particular, their creation of women as the objects of their sexual fantasies. With the male gaze, men simultaneously create and control women either as madonnas (mothers) or whores (sexual objects). Madonnas can castrate, and whores have dangerous vaginas. Women as performers cannot escape the male gaze, and women in the audience see them through men's eyes.

French psychoanalytic feminist Hélène Cixous says that women who take over cultural productions can turn themselves into laughing Medusas who throw their sexuality back at men and turn the power of the male gaze into stone. As a media star, Madonna subverts both symbolic representations of women—as mothers (her name) and as whores (her clothes, gestures, language). Madonna has created an aggressively feminized erotic vocabulary, selling herself sexually while symbolically critiquing conventionally gendered sexuality. She counters the male gaze by making sexy clothing like her pointy-breasted bustiers into symbols of power. In her songs and films, she takes charge. Madonna exaggerates and parodies femininity, turning the male gaze into an instrument of female power. In contrast, Marilyn Monroe, another highly sexualized star, did not distance herself from the male gaze and suffered for it. By taking the male gaze and using it to her own ends, Madonna has made female sexuality into in-your-face resistance.

Critique. Freudian theories of gender and sexuality are based on the bourgeois Western nuclear family, in which the woman is the prime parent and the man is emotionally distant from his children. Feminist psychoanalytic theories are just as narrowly based in a family consisting of two heterosexual parents. There are few tests of Freudian theories of each gender's personality development in single-parent and other types of households. The involvement of fathers in parenting varies enormously in societies throughout the world. Furthermore, it is not only heterosexual women who want the emotional attachment of mothering. Many lesbians who have deep and intense relationships with women also want children.

Psychoanalytic feminism has also been criticized for neglecting racial ethnic differences and colonial histories—not all fathers are powerful. Psychoanalytic feminism's theory of culture is also too generalized—it assumes that all men in Western culture are misogynist and emotionally repressed, and all women are oppressed by being portrayed as madonnas or whores.

By encouraging women to produce woman-centered art and literature, psychoanalytic feminism has opened our eyes to the strengths of female bodies and sexualities. But it can lock women artists, musicians, and writers into a categorically female sensibility and emphasize their difference from men and the dominant culture even more. Women's emotional and erotic power is unleashed and made visible in women's cultural productions, but they are separated from men's culture, which is still dominant.

Summary

In Freudian theory, gendered personality development comes out of the resolution of the Oedipus complex, in which the young boy represses his emotional attachment to his mother and identifies with his more powerful father because he is afraid that otherwise, like her, he will lose his penis. Western culture is the product of men's fear of losing the phallus, the symbol of masculine power. Since women do not have a penis to lose, they do not participate in the creation of culture.

A little girl continues to be emotionally attached to her mother in the development of her feminine identity. When she grows up, she finds that men cannot fill her emotional needs because they are too detached, and the taboo against homosexuality turns her away from sexual relationships with women. The normal woman, in Freudian theory, will want to mother a child. Her attachment to her child, girl or boy, reproduces the cycle of gendered personality development all over again.

Psychoanalytic feminism's solution to these patterns of gendered personalities and phallic cultural productions is twofold. First, men have to be taught how to be emotionally attached parents to their sons and daughters. With a man as an intimate parent to bond with, a boy will not have to detach emotionally to develop a masculine identity, and a girl will be able to develop a strong ego.

Second, women have to create art, music, and literature out of their emotional and sexual experiences and their joy in their female bodies. The dominance of the phallus (symbolic masculinity) in Western culture will thus be undermined by the changes in men's unconscious as well as by women's creativity.

Suggested Readings in Psychoanalytic Feminism

Abel, Elizabeth, Barbara Christian, and Helene Moglen, eds. 1997. *Female Subjects in Black and White.* Berkeley: University of California Press.

Baruch, Elaine Hoffman. 1991. *Women, Love, and Power: Literary and Psychoanalytic Perspectives.* New York: New York University Press.

Benjamin, Jessica. 1988. *The Bonds Of Love: Psychoanalysis, Feminism, and the Problem of Domination.* New York: Pantheon.

Buhle, Mary Jo. 1998. *Feminism and Its Discontents: A Century of Struggle With Psychoanalysis.* Cambridge, MA: Harvard University Press.

Chancer, Lynn S. 1992. *Sadomasochism in Everyday Life: The Dynamics of Power and Powerlessness.* New Brunswick, NJ: Rutgers University Press.

Cheng, Anne Anlin. 2001. *The Melancholy of Race: Psychoanalysis, Assimilation, and Hidden Grief.* New York: Oxford University Press.

Chodorow, Nancy. 1978. *The Reproduction of Mothering.* Berkeley: University of California Press.

———. 1989. *Feminism and Psychoanalytic Theory.* New Haven, CT: Yale University Press.

———. 1994. *Femininities, Masculinities, Sexualities: Freud and Beyond.* Lexington: University Press of Kentucky.

———. 1999. *The Power of Feelings: Personal Meanings in Psychoanalysis, Gender, and Culture.* New Haven, CT: Yale University Press.

Cixous, Hélène. 1976. "The Laugh of the Medusa." Translated by Keith Cohen and Paula Cohen. *Signs* 1:875–893.

Cixous, Hélène, and Catherine Clément. [1975] 1986. *The Newly Born Woman.* Translated by Betsy Wing. Minneapolis: University of Minnesota Press.

Clément, Catherine. [1979] 1988. *Opera, or the Undoing of Women.* Translated by Betsy Wing. Minneapolis: University of Minnesota Press.

Clough, Patricia Ticineto. 2000. *Autoaffection: Unconscious Thought in the Age of Teletechnology.* Minneapolis: University of Minnesota Press.

De Lauretis, Teresa. 1984. *Alice Doesn't: Feminism, Semiotics, Cinema.* Bloomington: Indiana University Press.

———. 1987. *Technologies of Gender.* Bloomington: Indiana University Press.

Dimen, Muriel, and Virginia Goldner, eds. 2002. *Gender in Psychoanalytic Space: Between Clinic and Culture.* New York: Other Press.

Flax, Jane. 1990. *Thinking Fragments: Psychoanalysis, Feminism, and Postmodernism in the Contemporary West.* Berkeley: University of California Press.

Gallop, Jane. 1982. *The Daughter's Seduction: Feminism and Psychoanalysis.* Ithaca, NY: Cornell University Press.

Hochschild, Arlie Russell. 1983. *The Managed Heart: Commercialization of Human Feeling.* Berkeley: University of California Press.

Irigaray, Luce. [1974] 1985. *Speculum of the Other Woman.* Translated by Gillian C. Gill. Ithaca, NY: Cornell University Press.

———. [1977] 1985. *This Sex Which Is Not One.* Translated by Catherine Porter with Carolyn Burke. Ithaca, NY: Cornell University Press.

Marks, Elaine, and Isabelle de Courtivron, eds. 1981. *New French Feminisms.* New York: Schocken.

McClary, Susan. 1991. *Feminine Endings: Music, Gender, and Sexuality.* Minneapolis: University of Minnesota Press.

Mitchell, Juliet. 1975. *Psychoanalysis and Feminism: Freud, Reich, Laing and Women.* New York: Vintage.

Mitchell, Juliet, and Jacqueline Rose, eds. 1985. *Feminine Sexuality: Jacques Lacan and the 'école freudienne'.* New York: W. W. Norton.

Moi, Toril. 1985. *Sexual/Textual Politics: Feminist Literary Theory.* New York: Methuen.

———, ed. 1987. *French Feminist Thought: A Reader.* New York: Basil Blackwell.

Mulvey, Laura. 1989. *Visual and Other Pleasures.* Bloomington: Indiana University Press.

Nair, Rukmini Bhaya. 2002. *Lying on the Postcolonial Couch: The Idea of Indifference.* Minneapolis: University of Minnesota Press.

O'Connor, Noreen, and Joanna Ryan. 1993. *Wild Desires and Mistaken Identity: Lesbianism and Psychoanalysis.* London: Virago.

Schwartz, Adria E. 1998. *Sexual Subjects: Lesbians, Gender, and Psychoanalysis.* New York: Routledge.

Walton, Jean. 2001. *Fair Sex, Savage Dreams: Race, Psychoanalysis, Sexual Difference.* Durham, NC: Duke University Press.

Worell, Judith. 2000. "Feminism in Psychology: Revolution or Evolution?" *Annals of the American Academy of Political and Social Science* 571:183–196. ✦

Chapter Eight

Standpoint Feminism

Sources of Gender Inequality

- The neglect of women's perspective and experiences in the production of knowledge.
- Women's exclusion from the sciences.
- Male bias in social science research.
- Invisibility of women's cultural productions.

Politics

- Making women central to research in the physical and social sciences, as researchers and as subjects.
- Asking research questions from a woman's point of view.
- Listening to women's voices in literature and music, seeing through women's eyes in art and visual media.

Contributions

- Reframing research questions and priorities to include women and other marginalized people.
- Challenging the universality and political neutrality of scientific "facts."
- Creating a feminist paradigm for the production of knowledge and culture that is critical of conventional wisdom and consciously aware of social location.

- Providing showcases and audiences for women's cultural productions.

Radical, lesbian, and psychoanalytic feminist theories of women's oppression converge in standpoint feminism, which argues that knowledge and culture must be produced from a woman's as well as a man's point of view. The main idea among the gender resistance feminisms is that women's experiences and perspectives should be central, not invisible or marginal, in the production of knowledge and culture. This idea is the basis for standpoint feminism. Simply put, standpoint feminism says that women's "voices" are different from men's, and they must be heard.

Standpoint theory. In the twentieth century, philosophers, psychologists, and physicists have argued that the social location, experiences, and point of view of the investigator or "looker," as well as those of the subjects or the "looked at," interact in producing what we know. A complete picture of a school, for instance, has to include the perspectives of the researcher, the teachers, students, their families, the school administrators, the bureaucrats of the department of education, and the politicians who set the school's budget.

The impact of the everyday world in its experiential reality and the structures that limit, shape, organize, and penetrate it are different for people in different social locations—but especially different for women and men because Western society is so gender-divided. Consider the school again—won't viewpoints be different if the teachers and involved parents are mostly women and the school and departmental administrators and politicians mostly men? Is a man or a woman researcher more likely to see the gendered concentration of power and its impact on curriculum and sports programs? Similarly, in a racially or ethnically divided community, it makes a lot of difference in the way research is done when the researcher is a member of the disadvantaged rather than the advantaged community.

Although men could certainly do research on and about women, and women on men, standpoint feminism argues that women are more sensitive to how other women see problems and set priorities and therefore would be better able to design and conduct research from their point of view. It is not enough, however, to just add more women to research teams or even to have them head a team—these women have to have a feminist viewpoint. They have to be critical of mainstream concepts that justify established lines of power, and they should recognize that "facts" often reflect stereotypical values and beliefs about women and men.

In addition to *phenomenology* (the philosophy that says that what we know comes out of our social location and experience), the grounding for standpoint feminism comes from marxist and socialist feminist theory, which applies Marx's concept of class consciousness to women and men, and from psychoanalytic feminist theory, which describes the gendering of the unconscious. Standpoint feminism argues that as physical and social producers of children—out of bodies, emotions, thought, and sheer physical labor—women are grounded in material reality in ways that men are not. Women are responsible for most of the everyday work, even if they are highly educated, while highly educated men concentrate on the abstract and the intellectual. Because they are closely connected to their bodies and their emotions, women's unconscious as well as conscious view of the world is unitary and concrete. If women produced knowledge, it would be much more in touch with the everyday, material world and with the connectedness among people, because that is what women experience.

In the following excerpt, Nancy Hartsock, one of the first standpoint feminists, defines "standpoint" and describes why a woman's labor makes her way of thinking different from a man's.

The Nature of a Standpoint

Nancy C. M. Hartsock
Professor of Political Science, University of Washington, Seattle

A standpoint is not simply an interested position (interpreted as bias) but is interested in the sense of being engaged. It is true that a desire to conceal real social relations can contribute to an obscurantist account, and it is also true that the ruling gender and class have material interests in deception. A standpoint, however, carries with it the contention that there are some perspectives on society from which, however well intentioned one may be, the real relations of humans with each other and with the natural world are not visible. This contention should be sorted into a number of distinct epistemological and political claims: (1) Material life (class position in Marxist theory) not only structures but sets limits on the understanding of social relations. (2) If material life is structured in fundamentally opposing ways for two different groups, one can expect that the vision of each will represent an inversion of the other, and in systems of domination the vision available to the rulers will be both partial and perverse. (3) The vision of the ruling class (or gender) structures the material relations in which all parties are forced to participate, and therefore cannot be dismissed as simply false. (4) In consequence, the vision available to the oppressed group must be struggled for and represents an achievement which requires both science to see beneath the surface of the social relations in which all are forced to participate, and the education which can only grow from struggle to change those relations. (5) As an engaged vision, the understanding of the oppressed, the adoption of a standpoint exposes the real relations among human beings as inhuman, points beyond the present, and carries a historically liberatory role. . . .

The feminist standpoint which emerges through an examination of women's activities is related to the proletarian standpoint, but deeper going. Women and workers inhabit a world in which the emphasis is on change rather than stasis, a world characterized by interaction with natural substances rather than separation from nature, a world in which quality is more important than quantity, a world in which the unification of mind and body is inherent in the activities performed. Yet, there are some important differences, differences marked by the fact that the proletarian (if male) is immersed in this world only during the time his labor power is being used by the capitalist. If, to paraphrase Marx, we follow the worker home from the factory, we can once again perceive a change in the *dramatis personae*. He who before followed behind as the worker, timid and holding back, with nothing to expect but a hiding, now strides in front while a third person, not specifically present in Marx's account of the transaction between capitalist and worker (both of whom are male) follows timidly behind, carrying groceries, baby, and diapers. . . .

Women's activity as institutionalized has a double aspect—their contribution to subsistence, and their contribution to childrearing. Whether or not all of us do both, women as a sex are institutionally responsible for producing both goods and human beings and all women are forced to become the kinds of people who can do both. . . .

Let us trace both the outlines and the consequences of woman's dual contribution to subsistence in capitalism. Women's labor, like that of the male worker, is contact with material necessity. Their contribution to subsistence, like that of the male worker, involves them in a world in which the relation to nature and to concrete human requirements is central, both in the form of interaction with natural substances whose quality, rather than quantity, is important to the production of meals, clothing, etc., and in the form of close attention to the natural changes in these substances. Women's labor both for wages and even more in household production involves a unification of mind and body for the purpose of transforming natural substances into socially defined goods. This too is true of the labor of the male worker.

There are, however, important differences. First, women as a group work more than men.[1] We are all familiar with the phenomenon of the "double day," and with indications that women work many more hours per week than men. Second, a larger proportion of women's labor time is devoted to the production of use values than men's. Only some of the goods women produce are commodities (however much they live in a society structured by commodity production and exchange). Third, women's production is structured by repetition in a different way than men's. While repetition for both the woman and the male worker may take the form of production of the same object, over and over—whether apple pies or brake linings—women's work in housekeeping involves a repetitious cleaning.[2]

Thus, the male worker in the process of production is involved in contact with necessity, and interchange with nature as well as with other human beings, but the process of production or work does not consume his whole life. The activity of a woman in the home as well as the work she does for wages keeps her continually in contact with a world of qualities and change. Her immersion in the world of use—in concrete, many-qualitied, changing material processes—is more complete than his. And if life itself consists of sensuous activity, the vantage point available to women on the basis of their contribution to subsistence represents an intensification and deepening of the materialist world view and consciousness available to the producers of commodities in capitalism, an intensification of class consciousness. The availability of this outlook to even nonworking-class women has been strikingly formulated by Marilyn French in *The Women's Room:*

> Washing the toilet used by three males, and the floor and walls around it, is, Mira thought, coming face to face with necessity. And that is why women were saner than men, did not come up with the mad, absurd

schemes men developed; they were in touch with necessity, they had to wash the toilet bowl and floor.[3]

The focus on women's subsistence activity rather than men's leads to a model in which the capitalist (male) lives a life structured completely by commodity exchange and not at all by production, and at the furthest distance from contact with concrete material life. The male worker marks a way station on the path to the other extreme of the constant contact with material necessity in women's contribution to subsistence. There are, of course important differences along the lines of race and class. For example, working class men seem to do more domestic labor than men higher up in the class structure—car repairs, carpentry, etc. And until very recently, the wage work done by most women of color replicated the housework required by their own households. Still, there are commonalities present in the institutionalized sexual division of labor which make women responsible for both housework and wage work.

The female contribution to subsistence, however, represents only a part of women's labor. Women also produce/reproduce men (and other women) on both a daily and a long-term basis. This aspect of women's "production" exposes the deep inadequacies of the concept of production as a description of women's activity. One does not (cannot) produce another human being in anything like the way one produces an object such as a chair. Much more is involved, activity which cannot easily be dichotomized into play or work. Helping another to develop, the gradual relinquishing of control, the experience of the human limits of one's action—all these are important features of women's activity as mothers. Women as mothers, even more than as workers, are institutionally involved in processes of change and growth and, more than workers, must understand the importance of avoiding excessive control in order to help others grow.[4] The activity involved is far more complex than the instrumental working with others to transform objects. (Interestingly, much of women's wage work—nursing, social work, and some secretarial jobs in particular—requires and depends on the relational and interpersonal skills women learned by being mothered by someone of the same sex.)

This aspect of women's activity too is not without consequences. Indeed, it is in the production of men by women and the appropriation of this labor and women themselves by men that the opposition between feminist and masculinist experience and outlook is rooted, and it is here that features of the proletarian vision are enhanced and modified for the woman and diluted for the man. The female experience in reproduction represents a unity with nature which goes beyond the proletarian experience of interchange with nature. . . .

Notes

1. For a discussion of women's work, see Elise Boulding, "Familial Constraints on Women's Work Roles," in Martha Blaxall and B. Reagan, eds., *Women and the Workplace* (Chicago: University of Chicago Press, 1976), esp. the charts on pp. 111, 113. . . .

2. Simone de Beauvoir holds that repetition has a deeper significance and that women's biological destiny itself is repetition. (See *The Second Sex,* tr. H. M. Parshley [New York: Knopf, 1953,] p. 59.) But see also her discussion of housework in Ibid., pp. 434ff. There her treatment of housework is strikingly negative. For de Beauvoir, transcendence is provided in the historical struggle of self with other and with the natural world. The oppositions she sees are not really stasis vs. change, but rather transcendence, escape from the muddy concreteness of daily life, from the static, biological, concrete repetition of "placid femininity."

3. Marilyn French, *The Women's Room* (New York: Jove, 1978), p. 214.

4. Sara Ruddick, "Maternal Thinking," presents an interesting discussion of these and other aspects of the thought which emerges from the activity of mothering. Although I find it difficult to speak the language of interests and demands she uses, she brings out several valuable points. Her distinction between maternal and scientific thought is very intriguing and potentially useful. (*Feminist Studies* 6: (1980), 350–53)

Feminist science. Standpoint feminism is a critique of mainstream science and social science, a methodology for feminist research, and an analysis of the power that lies in producing knowledge. The sciences and social sciences are supposed to be universal in their application, but they present the world as it is seen through dominant men's eyes. Standpoint feminism argues that this knowledge is not universal because it is shaped by *men's* views of the world. Women see the world from a different angle, and they are still excluded from much of science.

In the social sciences, it is only in the last 25 years that questions have been asked from a woman's point of view. In anthropology, for example, men writing on evolution represented our early primate ancestors as chest-beating, aggressive male gorillas; women in the same field argued that humans were more like the gentler, cooperative male and female chimpanzees.

To create different knowledge takes more than adding women scientists and female subjects of research. It takes choosing research projects that reflect women's needs, and framing research questions that don't assume conventional answers. It takes what Sandra Harding calls strong objectivity—getting beyond taken-for-granted categories and concepts. For example, standard biomedical research on menstruation and menopause treats them as illnesses, with negative physical and emotional symptoms—premenstrual tension, monthly cramps, hot flashes. Feminist researchers found that there was great diversity among women in what they experienced before and during menstruation and menopause and that for many, these body experiences were not negative, but positive. They described premenstrual surges of energy, pride in potential fertility, and postmenopausal wisdom and peace.

Standpoint feminism argues that our social location shapes our view of the world, but the viewpoints of marginalized "others," such as women, transgenders, members of the working-class, people in disadvantaged racial ethnic groups, and people in developing countries, do not enter the production of most knowledge. The European colonial conquests of the past three hundred years not only plundered native resources in North and South America and Africa, but also native agricultural and manufacturing processes, medicines, and maps. These were absorbed into Western science the way Greek, Roman, Chinese, and Islamic discoveries had been earlier, with little acknowledgment of their origin. Local sciences were coopted for European needs; local scientists—farmers, artisans, healers—were denigrated as ignorant and unenlightened. Standpoint feminism claims that many of these local knowledge producers are women, so it is not just women educated in Western science whose work should be fostered, but also the scientific work of women and men who create a body of knowledge in their everyday lives as they grow food, make useful objects, and heal the sick.

The power of social location. Standpoint feminism argues for more than equal representation of all viewpoints. There is a power issue here as well. Setting the agendas for scientific research, constructing educational curriculums, and making cultural representations is a form of power. *Hegemony* is the value base that legitimates a society's unquestioned assumptions. In Western society, the justifications for many of our ideas about women and men come from science. We believe in scientific "facts" and rarely question their objectivity. That is why standpoint feminism puts so much emphasis on demonstrating that scientific knowledge produced mostly by men is not universal and general but partial and particular.

But is all men's and women's experience the same? Is not all knowledge partial? Racial categories, ethnicity, religion, social class, age, and sexual orientation are also social locations. They intersect with gender to produce varied life experiences and outlooks. There may be a common core to women's experiences, perhaps because they share similar bodies, but standpoint feminism cannot ignore the input from social characteristics that are as important as gender. All men may be dominant over the women of their group, but some are certainly subordinate to other men.

As Patricia Hill Collins, one of the major theorists of Black feminism, points out in a critique of standpoint theory, these experiences are not individual but common to the members of a group; thus, they are a vital source of both a worldview and a sense of identity. When a group's experiences frame the production of knowledge and culture and set political agendas, that group has power. Most racial and ethnic groups in a heterogeneous society do not have such power; their experiential life-world views do not become part of the mainstream.

Where's the Power?

Patricia Hill Collins
Professor of Sociology and African American Studies,
University of Cincinnati

First, the notion of a standpoint refers to historically shared, *group*-based experiences. Groups have a degree of permanence over time such that group realities transcend individual experiences. For example, African Americans as a stigmatized racial group existed long before I was born and will probably continue long after I die. While my individual experiences with institutionalized racism will be unique, the types of opportunities and constraints that I encounter on a daily basis will resemble those confronting African Americans as a group. Arguing that Blacks as a group come into being or disappear on the basis of my participation seems narcissistic, egocentric, and archetypally postmodern. In contrast, standpoint theory places less emphasis on individual experiences within socially constructed groups than on the social conditions that construct such groups.

I stress this difference between the individual and the group as units of analysis because using these two constructs as if they were interchangeable clouds understanding of a host of topics, in this case, the very notion of a group-based standpoint. Individualism continues as a taproot in Western theorizing, including feminist versions. Whether bourgeois liberalism positing notions of individual rights or postmodern social theory's celebration of human differences, market-based choice models grounded in individualism argue that freedom exists via the absence of constraints of all sorts, including those of mandatory group membership. Freedom occurs when individuals have rights of mobility in and out of groups, much as we join clubs and other voluntary associations.

But the individual as proxy for the group becomes particularly problematic because standpoint theory's treatment of the group is not synonymous with a "family resemblance" of individual choice expanded to the level of voluntary group association. The notion of standpoint refers to groups having shared histories based on their shared location in relations of power—standpoints arise neither from crowds of individuals nor from groups analytically created by scholars or bureaucrats. Take, for example, the commonality of experiences that emerges from long-standing patterns of racial segregation in the United States. The degree of racial segregation between Blacks and Whites as *groups* is routinely underestimated. Blacks and Whites live in racially segregated neighborhoods, and this basic feature generates distinctive experiences in schools, recreational facilities, shopping areas, health-care systems, and occupational opportunities. Moreover, middle-class Blacks have not been exempt from the effects of diminished opportunities that accompany racial segregation and group discrimination. It is common location within hierarchical power relations that creates groups, not the results of collective decision making of the individuals within the groups. Race, gender, social class, ethnicity, age, and sexuality are not descriptive categories of identity applied to individuals. Instead, these elements of social structure emerge as fundamental devices that foster inequality resulting in groups. . . .

What we now have is increasing sophistication about how to discuss group location, not in the singular social class framework proposed by Marx, nor in the early feminist frameworks arguing the primacy of gender, but within constructs of multiplicity residing in social structures themselves and not in individual women. Fluidity does not mean that groups themselves disappear, to be replaced by an accumulation of decontextualized, unique women whose complexity erases politics. Instead, the fluidity of boundaries operates as a new lens that potentially deepens understanding of how the actual mechanisms of institutional power can change dramatically while continuing to reproduce long-standing inequalities of race, gender, and class that result in group stability. In this sense, group history and location can be seen as points of convergence within hierarchical, multiple, and changing structural power relations.

A second feature of standpoint theory concerns the commonality of experiences and perspectives that emerge for groups differentially arrayed within hierarchical power relations. Keep in mind that if the group has been theorized away, there can be no common experiences or perspectives. Standpoint theory argues that groups who share common placement in hierarchical power relations also share common experiences in such power relations. Such shared angles of vision lead those in similar social locations to be predisposed to interpret these experiences in a comparable fashion. The existence of the group as the unit of analysis means neither that all individuals within the group have the same experiences nor that they interpret them in the same way. Using the group as the focal point provides space for individual agency. While these themes remain meritorious, they simply do not lie at the center of standpoint theory as a theory of group power and the knowledges that group location and power generate.

Unfortunately, the much-deserved attention to issues of individual agency and diversity often overshadow investigating the continued salience of group-based experiences. But group-based experience, especially that of race and/or social class, continues to matter. For example, African American male rates of incarceration in American jails and prisons remain the highest in the world, exceeding even those of South Africa. Transcending social class, region of residence, command of English, ethnic background, or other markers of difference, all Black men must in some way grapple with the actual or potential treatment by the criminal justice system. Moreover, as mothers, daughters, wives, and lovers of Black men, Black women also participate in this common experience. Similarly, children from poor communities and homeless families are unlikely to attend college, not because they lack talent, but because they lack opportunity. Whatever their racial/ethnic classification, poor people as a group confront similar barriers for issues of basic survival. In this sense, standpoint theory seems especially suited to explaining relations of race and/or social class because these systems of power share similar institutional structures. Given the high degree of residential and occupational segregation separating Black and/or working-class groups from White middle-class realities, it becomes plausible to generate arguments about working-class and/or Black culture that emerge from long-standing shared experiences. For both class and race, a much clearer case of a group standpoint can be constructed. Whether individuals from or associated with these groups accept or reject these histories, they recognize the saliency of the notion of group standpoint.

But gender raises different issues, for women are distributed across these other groups. In contrast to standpoints that must learn to accommodate differences within, feminist standpoints must be constructed across differences such as these. Thus, gender represents a distinctly different intellectual and political project within standpoint theory. How effectively can a standpoint theory that was originally developed to explicate the wage exploitation·and subsequent impoverishment of European, working-class populations be applied to the extremely heterogeneous population of women in the contemporary United States, let alone globally? For example, Black women and White women do not live in racially integrated women's communities, separated from men and children by processes such as gender steering into such communities, experience bank redlining that results in refusal to lend money to women's communities, attend inferior schools as a result of men moving to all-male suburban areas, and the like. Instead, Black and White women live in racially segregated communities, and the experiences they garner in such communities reflect the racial politics operating overall. Moreover, proximity in physical space is not necessarily the same as occupying a common location in the space of hierarchical power relations. For example, Black women and women of color routinely share academic office space with middle-class and/or White women academics. It is quite common for women of color to clean the office of the feminist academic writing the latest treatise on standpoint theory. While these women occupy the same physical space—this is why proximity should not be confused with group solidarity—they occupy fundamentally different locations in hierarchical power relations. These women did not just enter this space in a random fashion. An entire arsenal of social institutions collectively created paths in which the individuals assigned to one group received better housing, health care, education, and recreational facilities, while those relegated to the other group did with worse or did without. The accumulation of these different experiences led the two groups of women to that same academic space. The actual individuals matter less than the accumulation of social structures that lead to these outcomes. In this sense, developing a political theory for women involves confronting a different and more complex set of issues than that facing race theories or class-based theories because women's inequality is structured differently.

Cultural feminism. Cultural feminists, applying standpoint theory, say that when women produce culture, they portray women differently than men do. In 1630, an Italian Renaissance artist, Artemisia Gentileschi, made a painting called *Self-portrait as the Allegory of Painting*. She painted herself with an intense and focused look; her body is framed by strong arms holding the brush and palette. It's a confident display of artistic skill by a painter who had been working professionally since girlhood. During her lifetime, Gentileschi had an international career. When she painted familiar subjects, such as Judith cutting off the head of Holofernes, it was with a mixture of masculine and feminine elements, transforming them into heroes with cross-gendered traits. Toward the end of her life, however, she painted more voluptuous heroines, such as Bathsheba, perhaps to sell better.

Frida Kahlo, a twentieth-century Mexican artist, is another woman artist who portrayed defiant strength—in her case, despite great physical pain. She had been in a tram accident as a girl and suffered all her life from the effects of multiple surgeries. She did many bold self-portraits portraying her unflinching stare at the viewer, as if to say, I am a woman and I am here. In other paintings, she used her body as the central figure in allegories of birth, menstruation, and death.

Some Indian women writers have been able to find imagery of strong women in their culture's mythology. The Indian epic *Mahabharata* has many important, active heroines, such as Draupadi, whom the god Krishna clothed when she resisted being shamefully undressed, and whose menstrual blood was a badge of honor. Maxine Hong Kingston modeled herself on Fa Mu Lan, the girl who took her father's place in battle, and other Chinese women warriors.

African American feminists, like Alice Walker, have advocated a *womanist* perspective that is celebratory of women's culture, rather than confrontational. Womanists find their symbolic language in the beauty of everyday objects—quilts, folk songs, wedding dances, food and the dishes to eat it from. Judy Chicago's *The Dinner Party* turns plates decorated with symbolic female genitalia and an elaborately embroidered tablecloth of names into a history of women's accomplishments. In Africa and America, women's music accompanies rituals of birth, puberty, marriage, and death and also everyday activities, like preparing food. These are all part of women's culture.

Cultural feminism thus has a double view of women's culture. It has made women professional artists, writers, musicians, and other culture producers much more visible. Whether or not they have a distinctive woman's voice, as many claim they do not, the high quality of their work deserves an audience. The other aspect of cultural feminism is making visible the cultural productions that grow out of women's domestic lives and ritual events.

Critique. A woman-centered perspective is a needed corrective to a gender-blind neutralism that erases women's experience. But the exclusive focus on "woman" is troublesome. Are women so much alike that they can be expected to always have similar experiences and a unitary perspective? Does standpoint feminism create a universal Woman who is actually middle-class, Western, heterosexual, and White? Does this universal Woman suppress other women's voices? How can they be heard? For that matter, don't men also differ by racial category, ethnicity, religion, social class, and sexual orientation?

Standpoint feminism's answer to the diversity-sameness issue is that what binds all women together is their bodies and their connectedness to people through their work for their families and their nurturing. A strong critique of this view focuses on these claims of essential differences between men and women and the promotion of a separate and distinctive woman's culture rooted in female bodies and nurturing abilities. Many feminists feel that these views are a throwback to biological justifications of women's inferiority.

However, if women's standpoint is not located in the female body but in their caretaking work and in their place in a gendered social order that allows them to be constantly threatened by violence, rape, and sexual harassment, then we can speak of a shared woman's standpoint without reverting to a direct biological cause. Standpoint feminism can legitimately argue that women's bodies are the source of their sexual oppression because of the ways they are used and abused by men, and that their consciousness is shaped by their family role as the primary parent. Women's bodies are not erased but are mediated by social processes.

Similarly, it is not male biology that makes men dominant but their social power, which they get because they have a visible mark of identity that sets them off from women—a penis. Men in diverse social circumstances have something in common—the privileges of dominant status. (Its *symbol* is the *phallus*.) Social locations and experiences, such as growing up a girl or a boy in a poor Black community, create particular women's and men's identities and standpoints. These shared particular identities are like concentric circles within the larger circle of womanhood and manhood. Both the common and the diverse ways of thinking are needed for fully representative knowledge and culture.

Summary

Standpoint feminism claims that what people think is universal, objective knowledge is biased because it does not include the life experiences of those who are not members of the dominant group. It challenges the claim that what is represented as "fact" is applicable to everyone. Phenomenologists and perception psychologists have argued that knowledge is produced out of experience. If that is so, then knowledge produced without women's experiences is not applicable to the universe but only to half of it. In order to balance out the dominance of men's experiences in most knowledge and cultural production, standpoint feminism elevates *women's experience.*

Using marxist, socialist, psychoanalytic, and lesbian feminisms' analyses of how women's lives and work shape their conscious and unconscious thinking, standpoint feminism says that women's distinctive perspectives must be used in producing knowledge and culture.

We think that science is detached from the particulars of everyday life. That is not even true of astronomy and physics, which have a social impact in space travel and nuclear power, but it is especially false when it comes to research on people. When we want to know what makes people think and act the way they do, we are using the data of everyday life. The lives of women and of men of diverse racial categories, ethnicities, religions, social classes, and sexual orientations must be part of these data.

Standpoint feminism challenges the sciences and social sciences to take a more critical view of their basic assumptions, especially about women and men. It criticizes the research on sex/gender differences because women's social and experiential reality are ignored. Modern Western societies today believe in science as an explanation for the way things are; past generations believed life circumstances were God-given. Standpoint feminism claims that when it comes to sex and gender, there is as much faith as fact in men's science.

Women artists, writers, musicians, and other producers of culture have been discovered, nurtured, and celebrated by feminism, not just for their distinctive qualities, but also for their high quality by any critical standard. Cultural feminism, in addition, seeks out the music, art, and poetry of women's everyday lives throughout the world—lullabies and folk songs, dances and work chants, quilts, pottery, and even food.

Standpoint feminism, as the culmination of resistance feminisms, brings women as outsiders into a changed and enriched mainstream.

Suggested Readings in Standpoint Feminism

Art, Literature, Music

Block, Adrienne Fried. 1998. *Amy Beach, Passionate Victorian: The Life and Work of an American Composer, 1867–1944.* New York: Oxford University Press.

Brown, Elsa Barkley. 1989. "African-American Women's Quilting." *Signs* 14:921–929.

Chicago, Judy. 1979. *The Dinner Party: A Symbol of Our Heritage.* New York: Doubleday.

Garrard, Mary D. 1989. *Artemesia Gentileschi: The Image of the Female Hero in Italian Baroque Art.* Princeton, NJ: Princeton University Press.

Gilbert, Sandra M., and Susan Gubar. 1988. *No Man's Land: The Place of the Woman Writer in the Twentieth Century.* 2 vols. New Haven, CT: Yale University Press.

Harris, Anne Sutherland, and Linda Nochlin. 1976. *Women Artists: 1550–1950.* New York: Knopf.

Jackson, Irene V. 1981. "Black Women and Music: A Survey from Africa to the New World." In *The Black Woman Cross-Culturally,* edited by Filomena Chioma Steady. Cambridge, MA: Schenkman.

Jones, Amelia, and Laura Cottingham. 1996. *Sexual Politics: Judy Chicago's Dinner Party in Feminist Art History.* Berkeley: University of California Press.

Kingston, Maxine Hong. 1976. *The Woman Warrior.* New York: Vintage.

Lowe, Sarah M. 1991. *Frida Kahlo.* New York: Universe Books.

Moers, Ellen. 1977. *Literary Women: The Great Writers.* Garden City, NY: Doubleday Anchor.

Marcus, Jane. 1987. *Virginia Woolf and the Languages of Patriarchy.* Bloomington: Indiana University Press.

Nochlin, Linda. 1988. *Women, Art, and Power and Other Essays.* New York: Harper and Row.

Reckitt, Helena, and Peggy Phelan. 2001. *Art and Feminism.* New York: Phaidon Press.

Robinson, Hilary, ed. 1988. *Visibly Female: Feminism and Art Today.* New York: Universe Books.

Solie, Ruth A., ed. 1993. *Musicology and Difference: Gender and Sexuality in Music Scholarship.* Berkeley: University of California Press.

Walker, Alice. 1984. *In Search of Our Mothers' Gardens: Womanist Prose.* New York: Harcourt Brace.

Research and Knowledge

Alcoff, Linda, and Elizabeth Potter, eds. 1993. *Feminist Epistemologies.* New York: Routledge.

Belenkey, Mary Field, Jill Mattuck Tarule, and Nancy Rule Goldberger, eds. 1986. *Women's Ways of Knowing: The Development of Self, Voice, and Mind.* New York: Basic Books.

DeVault, Marjorie. 1999. *Liberating Method: Feminism and Social Research.* Philadelphia: Temple University Press.

Embree, Lester, and Linda Fisher, eds. 1997. *Feminism and Phenomenology.* Boston: Kluwer.

Goldberger, Nancy Rule, and Jill Mattuck Tarule, eds. 1996. *Knowledge, Difference, and Power: Essays Inspired by Women's Ways of Knowing.* New York: Basic Books.

Hartsock, Nancy C. M. 1998. *The Feminist Standpoint Revisited and Other Essays.* Boulder, CO: Westview Press.

Kelly, Joan. 1984. *Women, History, and Theory.* Chicago: University of Chicago Press.

Levesque-Lopman, Louise. 1988. *Claiming Reality: Phenomenology and Women's Experience.* Totowa, NJ: Rowman and Littlefield.

Reinharz, Shulamit. 1992. *Feminist Methods in Social Research.* New York: Oxford University Press.

Smith, Dorothy E. 1987. *The Everyday World as Problematic*. Toronto: University of Toronto Press.

———. 1990. *The Conceptual Practices of Power: A Feminist Sociology of Knowledge*. Toronto: University of Toronto Press.

———. 1990. *Texts, Facts, and Femininity: Exploring the Relations of Ruling*. New York: Routledge.

———. 1999. *Writing the Social: Critique, Theory, Investigations*. Toronto: University of Toronto Press.

Science and Technology

Bleier, Ruth. 1984. *Science and Gender*. New York: Oxford.

Frank Fox, Mary, Deborah Johnson, and Sue V. Rosser, eds. 2005. *Women, Gender, and Technology*. Urbana: University of Illinois Press.

Haraway, Donna. 1989. *Primate Visions*. New York: Routledge.

———. 1991. *Simians, Cyborgs, and Women: The Reinvention of Nature*. New York: Routledge.

———. 1997. *Modest_Witness@Second_Millennium. FemaleMan©_Meets_OncoMouse™: Feminism and Technoscience*. New York: Routledge.

Harding, Sandra. 1986. *The Science Question in Feminism*. Ithaca, NY: Cornell University Press.

———. 1991. *Whose Science? Whose Knowledge? Thinking from Women's Lives*. Ithaca, NY: Cornell University Press.

———. 1998. *Is Science Multicultural? Postcolonialisms, Feminisms, and Epistemologies*. Bloomington: Indiana University Press.

Keller, Evelyn Fox. 1983. *A Feeling for the Organism: The Life and Work of Barbara McClintock*. New York: W. H. Freeman.

———. 1985. *Reflections on Gender and Science*. New Haven, CT: Yale University Press.

Laslett, Barbara, Sally Gregory Kohlstedt, Helen Longino, and Evelyn Hammonds, eds. 1996. *Gender and Scientific Authority*. Chicago: University of Chicago Press.

Laws, Sophie. 1990. *Issues of Blood: The Politics of Menstruation*. London: Macmillan.

Laws, Sophie, Valerie Hey, and Andrea Egan. 1985. *Seeing Red: The Politics of Premenstrual Tension*. London: Hutchinson.

Maddox, Brenda. 2002. *Rosalind Franklin: The Dark Lady of DNA*. New York: HarperCollins.

Parlee, Mary Brown. 1990. "The Social Construction of Premenstrual Syndrome: A Case Study of Scientific Discourse as Cultural Contestation." In *The Good Body: Asceticism in Contemporary Culture*, edited by M. G. Winkler and L. B. Cole. New Haven, CT: Yale University Press.

Roughgarden, Joan. 2004. *Evolution's Rainbow: Diversity, Gender and Sexuality in Nature and People.* Berkeley: University of California Press.

Scheibinger, Londa L. 1989. *The Mind Has No Sex?: Women in the Origins of Modern Science.* Cambridge, MA: Harvard University Press.

———. 1999. *Has Feminism Changed Science?* Cambridge, MA: Harvard University Press.

Sayre, Anne. 1975. *Rosalind Franklin and DNA.* New York: W. W. Norton.

Voda, Anne M., Myra Dinnerstein, and Sheryl R. O'Donnell, eds. 1982. *Changing Perspectives on Menopause.* Austin: University of Texas Press. ✦

Part IV

___

Gender Rebellion Feminisms

Since the late 1980s, gender rebellion feminisms have become major perspectives, challenging the foundations of many areas of knowledge and asking researchers and theorists to seriously address the question of gender. Gender rebellion feminisms critique the limits of gender resistance feminisms, especially the problems of the unity of women, the privileged perspective of women's standpoint, and the sources of identity in identity politics. These feminisms question the unity of the binary gender categories, arguing that they are intersected by other major social statuses and that gender may not always be the most important political issue. Ultimately, gender rebellion feminisms question the stability and necessity of the whole gendered social order.

Gender rebellion feminisms have continued the development of feminist multicultural, multiracial, and multiethnic approaches and initiated feminist studies of men. These perspectives pull apart gender as binary and oppositional. Gender is rather construed as a complex hierarchy of privileged and subordinated men and women. Gender as performance, process, and practice are the mainstays of social construction feminist theories, which recognize both the constraints and the possibilities for change in the social construction of gender. As part of the postmodern questioning of assumptions underlying what we do, think, and believe, postmodern feminism deconstructs how gender is produced and maintained, and emphasizes its malleability and fluidity. Third-wave feminism picks and chooses among the performance aspects of gender, sometimes exaggerating and sometimes ironically parodying them, but always emphasizing people's agency. The politics of gender rebellion feminisms grow out of its claims that gender is above all a human enterprise and so can be shaped, reshaped, and even destroyed by human agency.

Multicultural/multiracial feminism, whose roots are in the history and politics of disadvantaged groups, argues that the major social statuses of a society produce a complex hierarchical stratification system. By teasing out multiple strands of oppression and exploitation, multicultural/multiracial feminism shows that gender, racial categories, and ethnicity are intertwined social structures: How people are gendered differs according to whether they are members of dominant or subordinate racial ethnic groups. Social class is also an especially crucial dimension, given the wide differences between the poor and the rich throughout the world.

Multicultural/multiracial feminism creates theories and politics of gender inequality that interweave gender with the continuum of dominance and subordination of other social statuses. It argues that feminist political activism can no longer be based only on gender but must consider racial identifications, ethnicity, and social class as well. The battle for justice and recognition includes men, but the perspectives, politics, and cultural contributions of women of diverse racial ethnic and cultural groups are its main focus.

Feminist studies of men, drawing on marxist analyses of social class and gay and lesbian critiques of heteronormativity, have described the interlocking structures of power that make one group of men dominant and rank everyone else in a complex hierarchy of privilege and disadvantage. They document the gender practices that both exclude women from competition with men and determine which men are able to attain positions of great power.

The culture of violence in many societies and the way men are drawn to violence in war, terrorism, and even sports is a major part of the theories and politics of feminism studies of men. Like multicultural/multiracial feminism, feminist studies of men use racial categories, ethnicity, religion, social class, and sexual orientation in analyses of men's social statuses, but focus on gender. Men vary in power and privilege, but within each group men have a *patriarchal dividend* of power and privilege, compared to the women of that group.

Social construction feminism comes out of symbolic interaction in social psychology, which shows how people construct multiple meanings and identities in their daily encounters. Social construction feminism analyzes the general processes that create what we perceive to be the differences between women and men. These processes also construct racial and ethnic stereotypes and beliefs about homosexuality as contrasted with heterosexuality. They impose categorical divisions on physiological and behavioral continuums and use visible markers, such as skin color or genitals, as signs of supposedly inborn and essential behavioral characteristics. Because these physiological markers are usually hidden (people do not walk on the streets naked) and varied (some African Americans have pale skin), other identifiers of social status are needed: clothing, jewelry, and hair styles are the most common. In face-to-face encounters, visible cues of gender, class, ethnicity, sexual orientation, and other major social statuses pattern subsequent behavior—they act like team colors. Evident differences within categories of people and similarities between groups are repressed or ignored.

Social construction feminism argues that multiple categories would better reflect the variety in people, but the gendered social order is built on a binary division of labor that uses differentiated categories of women and men for gender-typed roles in the family and the paid workforce. The gendered family and the gendered economy are mainstays of gender as a social institution. As a social institution, gender orders societies and assigns people to legal gender statuses, locking in a binary system that has no room for intersexuals or transgenders.

Postmodern feminism claims that gender and sexuality are performances, and that individuals modify their displays of masculinity and femininity to suit their own purposes. Males can masquerade as women, and females can pass for men. Postmodern feminism argues that, like clothing, sexuality and gender can be put on, taken off, and transformed. Transgenders especially display the fluidities of gender and sexuality, challenging normals to prove that they aren't also making themselves up. Queer theory, the postmodern focus of gay, lesbian, and transgender studies, turns the binaries of sex, sexuality, and gender inside out with "third terms"—intersex, bisexual, transsexual, transvestite.

Third-wave feminism has most recently appeared on the scene to challenge second-wave feminism. Third-wave feminism has young adherents who do not see themselves as oppressed victims, but rather reflect radical feminism in their body orientation and postmodern feminism in their gender displays. They can be outrageous and sexual in their behavior and cultural performances, but they are as serious in their political activism as their feminist foremothers.

Gender rebellion feminisms' theories destabilize what many people think is normal and natural and moral about gender, but they have only begun to develop new practices for work, family life, and intimate relationships. They need to translate multiple categories into everyday living, which could be revolutionary enough. But to fulfill their political potential, these feminisms need to spell out what precisely has to be done in all the gendered institutions and organizations of a society—family, workplace, government, the arts, science, and religion—to break the strangle-hold of oppressive gender practices and ensure equal participation and opportunity for every person in every group. ✦

Chapter Nine

Multicultural/Multiracial Feminism

Sources of Gender Inequality

- The intersection of racial ethnic, social class, and gender discrimination.
- Continued patterns of economic and educational privilege and disadvantage built into the social structure.
- Cultural devaluation of women and men of subordinated racial ethnic groups.

Politics

- Redistribution of privilege—equal access to education, good jobs, and political power.
- Recognition—science and other knowledge production that reflects the subordinate group's perspectives.
- Revaluation of the cultural productions by women and men of varied racial ethnic heritages.

Contributions

- The concept of *intersectionality*—the combined effects of race, ethnicity, class, gender, sexuality, religion, nationality, and other major social statuses in producing a *matrix of domination.*

- A complex politics of identity that includes but does not necessarily foreground gender.
- Making multiple racial ethnic and multicultural viewpoints visible in the production of knowledge and culture through the critical perspective of the *outsider within*.

As part of a long line of critical theory and activist politics, multicultural/multiracial feminism early in the second wave challenged White feminists to address the differences among women. Focusing on the *intersectionality* of gender, racial categories, ethnicity, and social class, multicultural/multiracial feminism argues that you cannot look at one of these social statuses alone, nor can you add them one after another. Their interaction is synergistic: Together they construct a social location. Some locations are more oppressive than others because they are the result of multiple systems of domination.

Matrix of domination. Gender, racial categories, ethnicity, and social class comprise a complex hierarchical stratification system in the United States, in which upper-class White men and women oppress lower-class women and men of disadvantaged racial groups, ethnicities, and religions. In teasing out the multiple strands of oppression and exploitation, multicultural/multiracial feminism has shown that gender is intertwined with and cannot be separated from other social statuses that confer advantage and disadvantage. People are caught in what Patricia Hill Collins, in her influential book *Black Feminist Thought,* calls a *matrix of domination.* The experiences of women and men in different social locations are the ground for their views of the world and their activist politics.

The social location of a man and woman of the same racial ethnic or social class status differs. Men of the subordinate group may be as oppressed as the women but often in different ways. For example, Black men in the United States are rewarded for success in sports, but are punished for violent behavior outside the sports arena; Black women are hired to take care of White children but are stigmatized for having many children of their own. If disadvantaged women achieve equality with the disadvantaged men of their group, they have not achieved very much. If they outperform them, as has happened with African American and Hispanic American women college and professional-school graduates in the United States, then the men in the same groups are seen as endangered.

Multicultural/multiracial feminism thus has to juggle the sometimes competing battles for gender equality and for racial ethnic equality. It has its origins in the 1960s U.S. civil rights and Black power movements and the Chicano, American Indian, and Asian American liberation movements. Out of these multiple groups came coalitions of women who felt that their issues were neglected, but who did not want to abandon entirely the fight against racial ethnic oppression. Today, multicultural/multiracial feminism has a global theoretical, empirical, and political perspective.

Centering the marginal. For both women and men, the dominant group sets the standards for what behavior is valued, what faces and bodies are considered beautiful, what cultural productions represent "everybody." The most advantaged group's values and ideas about the way people should behave usually dominate policies and social agendas. The subordinate group is always less influential unless it can turn the dominant values upside down, as standpoint feminism does when it says women's values and experiences have to be given as much credit as men's.

Multicultural/multiracial feminism takes the standpoint perspective a step further. It is not enough to dissect a social institution or area of social thought from a woman's point of view; the viewpoint has to include the experiences of women of different racial ethnic groups and must also take into consideration social class and local economic conditions. As *outsiders within,* those from disadvantaged groups who have entry into higher education, the arts, and politics can critique and modify conventional knowledge. Multicultural/multiracial feminism's politics focuses on this issue. For example, if the White, middle-class, two-parent family is taken as the norm, then the Black extended family of grandmothers, mothers, aunts, and "othermothers"—all responsible for the children of the household and pooling resources—is a deviant or problem family that needs changing.

Health care is another area where the dominant group's perspective translates into allocation of resources. If psychological stress is defined as resulting from pressure in a high-powered job, then the pressures of living in a ghetto are ignored. Eating disorders are a case in point.

Among young White women, anorexia and bulimia are usually attributed to a desire for a thin, sexually attractive body because there is a culture of thinness in Western societies. For some African American and Hispanic women, however, binge eating and purging are ways of coping with the traumas of their lives—sexual abuse, poverty, racism, and injustice. In all these cases, the underlying cause of the eating disorder is social pressure, but the pressures differ enormously.

The following excerpt by Maxine Baca Zinn and Bonnie Thornton Dill, sociologists who have done extensive research on how gender intertwines with racial ethnic statuses, lays out the theoretical premises of multicultural/multiracial feminism. Because their focus is the United States and its racial stratification system, they call their feminism multiracial.

What Is Multiracial Feminism?

Professor of Sociology, Michigan State University

Bonnie Thornton Dill
Professor of Women's Studies and Sociology,
University of Maryland

A new set of feminist theories have emerged from the challenges put forth by women of color. Multiracial feminism is an evolving body of theory and practice informed by wide-ranging intellectual traditions. This framework does not offer a singular or unified feminism but a body of knowledge situating women and men in multiple systems of domination. U.S. multiracial feminism encompasses several emergent perspectives developed primarily by women of color: African Americans, Latinas, Asian Americans, and Native Americans, women whose analyses are shaped by their unique perspectives as "outsiders within"—marginal intellectuals whose social locations provide them with a particular perspective on self and society. Although U.S. women of color represent many races and ethnic backgrounds—with different histories and cultures—our feminisms cohere in their treatment of race as a basic social division, a structure of power, a focus of political struggle, and hence a fundamental force in shaping women's and men's lives. . . .

We use "multiracial" rather than "multicultural" as a way of underscoring race as a power system that interacts with other structured inequalities to shape genders. Within the U.S. context, race, and the system of meanings and ideologies which accompany it, is a fundamental organizing principle of social relationships. Race affects all women and men, although in different ways. Even cultural and group differences among women are produced through interaction within a racially stratified social order. Therefore, although we do not discount the importance of culture, we caution that cultural analytic frameworks that ignore race tend to view women's differences as the product of group-specific values and practices that often result in the marginalization of cultural groups which are then perceived as exotic expressions of a normative center. Our focus on race stresses the social construction of differently situated social groups and their varying degrees of advantage and power. Additionally, this emphasis on race takes on increasing political importance in an era where discourse about race is governed by color-evasive language and a preference for individual rather than group remedies for social inequalities. Our analyses insist upon the primary and pervasive nature of race in contemporary U.S. society while at the same time acknowledging how race both shapes and is shaped by a variety of other social relations.

In the social sciences, multiracial feminism grew out of socialist feminist thinking. Theories about how political economic forces shape women's lives were influential as we began to uncover the social causes of racial ethnic women's subordination. But socialist feminism's concept of capitalist patriarchy, with its focus on women's unpaid (reproductive) labor in the home, failed to address racial differences in the organization of reproductive labor. As feminists of color have argued, "reproductive labor has divided along racial as well as gender lines, and the specific characteristics have varied regionally and changed over time as capitalism has reorganized" (Glenn 1992). Despite the limitations of socialist feminism, this body of literature has been especially useful in pursuing questions about the interconnections among systems of domination.

Race and ethnic studies was the other major social scientific source of multiracial feminism. It provided a basis for comparative analyses of groups that are socially and legally subordinated and remain culturally distinct within U.S. society. This includes the systematic discrimination of socially constructed racial groups and their distinctive cultural arrangements. Historically, the categories of African American, Latino, Asian American, and Native American were constructed as both racially and culturally distinct. Each group has a distinctive culture, shares a common heritage, and has developed a common identity within a larger society that subordinates them.

We recognize, of course, certain problems inherent in an uncritical use of the multiracial label. First, the perspective can be hampered by a biracial model in which only African Americans and whites are seen as racial categories and all other groups are viewed through the prism of cultural differences. Latinos and Asians have always occupied distinctive places within the racial hierarchy, and current shifts in the composition of the U.S. population are racializing these groups anew.

A second problem lies in treating multiracial feminism as a single analytical framework, and its principle architects, women of color, as an undifferentiated category. The concepts "multiracial feminism," "racial ethnic women," and "women of color" "homogenize quite different experiences and can falsely universalize experiences across race, ethnicity, sexual orientation, and age" (Andersen and Collins 1992, xvi). The feminisms created by women of color exhibit a plurality of intellectual and political positions. We speak in many voices, with inconsistencies that are born of our different social locations. Multiracial feminism embodies this plurality and richness. Our intent is not to falsely universalize women of color. Nor do we wish to promote a new racial essentialism in place of the old gender essentialism. Instead, we use these concepts to examine the structures and experiences produced by intersecting forms of race and gender.

It is also essential to acknowledge that race is a shifting and contested category whose meanings construct definitions of all aspects of social life. In the United States it helped define citizenship by excluding everyone who was not a white, male property owner. It defined labor as slave or free, coolie or contract, and family as available only to those men whose marriages were recognized or whose wives could immigrate with them. Additionally, racial meanings are contested both within groups and between them.

Although definitions of race are at once historically and geographically specific, they are also transnational, encompassing diasporic groups and crossing traditional geographic boundaries. Thus, while U.S. multiracial feminism calls attention to the fundamental importance of race, it must also locate the meaning of race within specific national traditions.

The Distinguishing Features of Multiracial Feminism

By attending to these problems, multiracial feminism offers a set of analytic premises for thinking about and theorizing gender. The following themes distinguish this branch of feminist inquiry.

First, multiracial feminism asserts that gender is constructed by a range of interlocking inequalities, what Patricia Hill Collins calls a "matrix of domination" (1990). The idea of a matrix is that several fundamental systems work with and through each other. People experience race, class, gender, and sexuality differently depending upon their social location in the structures of race, class, gender, and sexuality. For example, people of the same race will experience race differently depending upon their location in the class structure as working class, professional managerial class, or unemployed; in the gender structure as female or male; and in structures of sexuality as heterosexual, homosexual, or bisexual.

Multiracial feminism also examines the simultaneity of systems in shaping women's experience and identity. Race, class, gender, and sexuality are not reducible to individual attributes to be measured and assessed for their separate contribution in explaining given social outcomes, an approach that Elizabeth Spelman calls "popbead metaphysics," where a woman's identity consists of the sum of parts neatly divisible from one another (1988, 136). The matrix of domination seeks to account for the multiple ways that women experience themselves as gendered, raced, classed, and sexualized.

Second, multiracial feminism emphasizes the intersectional nature of hierarchies at all levels of social life. Class, race, gender, and sexuality are components of both social structure and social interaction. Women and men are differently embedded in locations created by these cross-cutting hierarchies. As a result, women and men throughout the social order experience different forms of privilege and subordination, depending on their race, class, gender, and sexuality. In other words, intersecting forms of domination produce *both* oppression *and* opportunity. At the same time that structures of race, class, and gender create disadvantages for women of color, they provide unacknowledged benefits for those who are at the top of these hierarchies—whites, members of the upper classes, and males. Therefore, multiracial feminism applies not only to racial ethnic women but also to women and men of all races, classes, and genders.

Third, multiracial feminism highlights the relational nature of dominance and subordination. Power is the cornerstone of women's differences. This means that women's differences are *connected* in systematic ways. Race is a vital element in the pattern of relations among minority and white women. . . .

Fourth, multiracial feminism explores the interplay of social structure and women's agency. Within the constraints of race, class, and gender oppression, women create viable lives for themselves, their families, and their communities. Women of color have resisted and often undermined the forces of power that control them. From acts of quiet dignity and steadfast determination to involvement in revolt and rebellion, women struggle to shape their own lives. Racial oppression has been a common focus of the "dynamic of oppositional agency" of women of color (Mohanty et al. 1991, 13). . . .

Fifth, multiracial feminism encompasses wide-ranging methodological approaches, and like other branches of feminist thought, relies on varied theoretical tools as well. . . . In the last decade, the opening up of academic feminism has focused attention on social location in the production of knowledge. Most basically, research by and about marginalized women has destabilized what used to be considered as universal categories of gender. Marginalized locations are well suited for grasping social relations that remained obscure from more privileged vantage points. Lived experience, in other words, creates alternative ways of understanding the social world and the experience of different groups of women within it. Racially informed standpoint epistemologies have provided new topics, fresh questions, and new understandings of women and men. . . .

Sixth, multiracial feminism brings together understandings drawn from the lived experiences of diverse and continuously changing groups of women. Among Asian Americans, Native Americans, Latinas, and Blacks are many different national cultural and ethnic groups. Each one is engaged in the process of testing, refining, and reshaping these broader categories in its own image. Such internal differences heighten awareness of and sensitivity to both commonalities and differences, serving as a constant reminder of the importance of comparative study and maintaining a creative tension between diversity and universalization.

References

Andersen, Margaret L., and Patricia Hill Collins, eds. 1992. *Race, Class and Gender: An Anthology.* Belmont, CA: Wadsworth.

Collins, Patricia Hill. 1990.*

Glenn, Evelyn Nakano. 1992. "From Servitude to Service Work: Historical Continuities in the Racial Division of Paid Reproductive Labor." *Signs* 18:1–43.

Mohanty, Chandra Talpade, Ann Russo, and Lourdes Torres, eds. 1991. *Third World Women and the Politics of Feminism.* Bloomington: Indiana University Press.
Spelman, Elizabeth. 1988.*

   * See Suggested Readings.

International multicultural/multiracial feminism. Multicultural/multiracial feminist ideas of intersectionality and outsiders within have been used by global and transnational women's movements. Looking at the stratification systems of developing countries, postcolonial feminism describes their matrices of domination. The concept of outsiders within has a particular cogency in international feminism because feminists in developing countries have cautioned feminists from the United States and other Western countries not to impose their viewpoint on the world. Women's movements in different countries of necessity have to work within their own cultures and make their own international coalitions.

The 2004 winner of the Nobel Peace Prize, Wangari Muta Maathai, is a Kenyan biologist and activist who was head of the National Council of Women of Kenya from 1981 to 1987. In a confrontation with the police, she was knocked unconscious during a women's hunger strike in a city park. Dr. Maathai then engaged in another form of feminism—less confrontational and, in African politics, more successful. She started the Green Belt Movement in 1977. This movement gets tree nurseries throughout Africa to give seedlings to women to plant and pays them a small but useful amount of money if a tree takes root. Tens of millions of trees have been planted in Africa through the Green Belt Movement. By using women who cut brush for cooking fires to replace depleted forests, Dr. Maathai was able to help women and the environment—and also deflect criticism for feminist activism from patriarchal and dictatorial governments. Dr. Maathai was awarded the Nobel Peace Prize for the Green Belt Movement and other environmental activism.

The following excerpt from an article by Obioma Nnaemeka, an African feminist teaching in the United States, lays out the theory and practice of doing feminism Africa's way.

Nego-Feminism

Obioma Nnaemeka
*Professor of French, Women's Studies, and
African/African-Diaspora Studies, Indiana University, Indianapolis*

But what is nego-feminism? First, nego-feminism is the feminism of negotiation; second, nego-feminism stands for "no ego" feminism. In the foundation of shared values in many African cultures are the principles of negotiation, give and take, compromise, and balance. Here, negotiation has the double meaning of "give and take/exchange" and "cope with successfully/go around." African feminism (or feminism as I have seen it practiced in Africa) challenges through negotiations and compromise. It knows when, where, and how to detonate patriarchal land mines; it also knows when, where, and how to go around patriarchal land mines. In other words, it knows when, where, and how to negotiate with or negotiate around patriarchy in different contexts. For African women, feminism is an act that evokes the dynamism and shifts of a process as opposed to the stability and reification of a construct, a framework. My use of space—the third space—provides the terrain for the unfolding of the dynamic process. Furthermore, nego-feminism is structured by cultural imperatives and modulated by ever-shifting local and global exigencies. The theology of nearness grounded in the indigenous installs feminism in Africa as a performance and an altruistic act.[1] African women do feminism; feminism is what they do for themselves and for others.[2] The rest of this section will examine how African women have negotiated disciplinary and pedagogical spaces and also address issues in gender, language, and practice.

The women's studies classroom in the West (in the United States, specifically) functions in a feminized (all/almost-all-female) environment as opposed to the gendered (a healthy mix of women and men) context operative in women's studies classrooms and conferences in Africa.[3] A homogeneous (in terms of sex, at least) classroom that is anesthetized by the comfort of the familiar/"home" needs the "foreignness" that challenges and promotes self-examination; it needs the different, the out of the ordinary, that defamiliarizes as it promotes the multiple perspectives and challenges rooted in heterogeneity. . . .

The negotiations that are made at the level of gender and language are rooted in the indigenous as well: "African patterns of feminism can be seen as having developed within a context that views human life from a total, rather than a dichotomous and exclusive, perspective. For women, the male is not 'the other' but part of the human same. Each gender constitutes the critical half that makes the human whole. Neither sex is totally complete in itself. Each has and needs a complement, despite the possession of unique features of its own" (Steady 1987, 8). African women's willingness and readiness to negotiate with and around men even in difficult circumstances is quite pervasive. As the Cameroonian writer, Calixthe Beyala, puts it at the beginning of her book, *Lettre d' une Africaine à ses soeurs occidentales* (1995), "Soyons clairs: tous les hommes ne sont pas des salauds" (Let's face it, all men are not bastards; 1995, 7). I take that to mean that some men are bastards! But let us stick with Beyala's more benevolent phrasing of the issue. Another example is also by a Francophone African woman writer, Mariama Bâ of Senegal, who dedicated her fine novel, *Une si longue lettre* (1980), to many constituencies including "aux hommes de bonne volonté" (to men of goodwill). This, of course, excludes the bastards among them! By not casting a pall over men as a monolith, African women are more inclined to reach out and work with men in achieving set goals. Sexual politics were huge in Western feminism about two decades ago, but it would be inaccurate to suggest that the politics no longer exist; they are not passé. In my view, Western feminism has turned down the volume on sexual politics, but the residues are still a driving force. The resistance in institutions across the United States (including mine) against changing women's studies programs to gender studies programs is rooted principally in the argument that women's issues will be relegated to the back burner in a gender studies program.[4] I do not see a similar argument flourishing in Africa.[5] The language of feminist engagement in Africa (collaborate, negotiate, compromise) runs counter to the language of Western feminist scholarship and engagement (challenge, disrupt, deconstruct, blow apart, etc.) as exemplified in Amy Allen's excellent book on feminist theory, in which the author states that feminists are interested in "criticizing, challenging, subverting, and ultimately overturning the multiple axes of stratification affecting women" (1999, 2). African feminism challenges through negotiation, accommodation, and compromise. . . .

Border crossing and the chameleon walk

> They have disfigured the legacy of the sixties. . . . What I mean by the sixties legacies in traditional political terms are political activism and engagement on behalf of equality, democracy, tolerance. (Wini Breines 1996, 114)

Nego-feminism in Africa is living those legacies in theory, practice, and policy mat-ters. African women's engagement still nurtures the compromise and hopeful-ness needed to build a harmonious society. As far as theory goes, Barbara Chris-tian (1995) rightly noted that people of color theorize differently. But can feminist theory create the space for the unfolding of "different" theorizing not as an iso-lated engagement outside of feminist theory but as a force that can have a defamiliarizing power on feminist theory? In other words, seeing feminist theoriz-ing through the eyes of the "other," from the "other" place, through the "other" worldview has the capacity to defamiliarize feminist theory as we know it and assist it not only in interrogating, understanding, and explaining the unfa-miliar but also in defamiliarizing and refamiliarizing the familiar in more produc-tive and enriching ways. Thus, the focus will be not on what feminist theory can do in terms of explicating other lives and other places but on how feminist theory is and could be constructed. In this instance, Westerners are led across borders so that they can cross back enriched and defamiliarized and ready to see the familiar anew. How do we deal with the theorizing emanating from other epistemological centers in the so-called third world? How do we come to terms with the multiplicity of centers bound by coherence and decipherment and not disrupted perpetually by endless differences?

In view of the issues about intervention, border crossing, turfism, intersectionality, compromise, and accommodation raised in this article, I will conclude with a piece of advice from my great-uncle. On the eve of my depar-ture for graduate studies in *obodo oyibo* (land of the white people), my great-uncle called me into his *obi* (private quarters) and sounded this note of caution. "My daughter," he said, "when you go to *obodo oyibo,* walk like the chameleon."[6] According to my great-uncle, the chameleon is an interesting animal to watch. As it walks, it keeps its head straight but looks in different directions. It does not deviate from its goal and grows wiser through the knowledge gleaned from the different perspectives it absorbs along the way. If it sees prey, it does not jump on it immediately. First, it throws out its tongue. If nothing happens to its tongue, it moves ahead and grabs the prey. The cha-meleon is cautious. When the chameleon comes into a new environment, it takes the color of the environment without taking over. The chameleon adapts without imposing itself. Whatever we choose to call our feminism is our prerogative. However, in this journey that is feminist engagement, we need to walk like the chameleon—goal-oriented, cautious, accommodating, adaptable, and open to diverse views. Nego-feminists would heed the advice of my great-uncle.

NOTES

1. Take, e.g., the Igbo proverb, *ife kwulu, ife akwudebie* (when something stands, something stands beside it). Sibdou Ouda's action during the "photo-shoot" (i.e., beckoning her children to stand beside her) is a vivid enactment of this proverb.

2. See Nnaemeka 1998a, 5. Also seen . . . where one of the African participants interjected "tell her [Nussbaum] that's not what we came here to do." An African participant made a similar remark when the fight for supremacy erupted among feminists, womanists, and Africana womanists at the first Women in Africa and the African Diaspora (WAAD) conference (see Nnaemeka 1998a, 31, n. 3). [Note: Many African participants concurred with interjections of "go on, my sister," "I agree with you one hundred percent," "speak for us, my dear," "tell her that's not what we came here to do," etc.]

3. At the first international WAAD conference I organized in Nsukka, Nigeria, in 1992, about 30 percent of the participants were male. About the same percentage attended the third WAAD conference in Madagascar. The Women's World conference held in Kampala, Uganda, in 2002 also attracted many male participants/presenters. At the first WAAD conference, some foreign participants complained about the presence of men (see Nnaemeka 1998b, 363–364). I heard the same complaint from the same constituency at the Kampala conference in 2002.

4. Some institutions have negotiated a compromise—women's/gender studies program.

5. One of the most prominent centers in Africa (Cape Town, South Africa) for the study of women assumed the name African Gender Institute, without equivocation.

6. It is important to note that he did not advise me to be like the chameleon but rather to walk like the chameleon. The indeterminacy implicated in being like a chameleon is not lost to my people (Igbo) who denounce chameleonlike behavior in humans—*ifu ocha icha, ifu oji ijie* (when you see white, you turn white; when you see black, you turn black). By advising me to walk like a chameleon, my great-uncle takes the chameleon metaphor in different directions.

REFERENCES

Allen, Amy. 1999. *The Power of Feminist Theory: Domination, Resistance, Solidarity.* Boulder, CO: Westview.

Bâ, Mariama. 1980. *Une si longue lettre.* Dakar: Nouvelles Editions Africaines.

Beyala, Calixthe. 1995. *Lettre d'une Africaine à ses surs occidentales.* Paris: Spengler.

Breines, Wini. 1996. "Sixties Stories' Silences: White Feminism, Black Feminism, Black Power." *National Women's Studies Association Journal* 8(3):101–121.

Christian, Barbara. 1995. "The Race for Theory." In *The Post-colonial Studies Reader,* edited by Bill Ashcroft, Gareth Griffiths, and Helen Tiffin, 457–460. London: Routledge.

Nnaemeka, Obioma. 1998a. "Introduction: Reading the Rainbow." In *Sisterhood, Feminisms, and Power: From Africa to the Diaspora,* edited by Obioma Nnaemeka, 135. Trenton, NJ: Africa World Press.

———. 1998b. "This Women's Studies Business: Beyond Politics and History (Thoughts on the First WAAD Conference)." In *Sisterhood, Feminisms, and Power: From Africa to the Diaspora,* edited by Obioma Nnaemeka, 351–386. Trenton, NJ: Africa World Press.

Steady, Filomina Chioma. 1987. "African Feminism: A Worldwide Perspective." In *Women in Africa and the African Diaspora,* edited by Rosalyn Terborg-Penn, Sharon Harley, and Andrea Benton Rushing, 324. Washington, DC: Howard University Press.

Critique. Some multicultural/multiracial feminist protests are universal, understood by disadvantaged women everywhere, and some are specific to women's different racial and ethnic groups. In the United States, African American women, Latinas, and Asian American women may all encounter racial prejudice in social encounters, but they have markedly different experiences in the job market. A question that is difficult to answer is whether the discrimination these women experience is specific to them as women or whether they share racial ethnic oppression with their men.

If racial ethnic and gender identity are as intertwined as multicultural/multiracial feminism claims, then political unity with men of the same racial ethnic group could severely undermine a consciousness of oppression as women. For example, among African Americans, there has been a controversy over whether Black women's independence and assertiveness threaten their men's ego and sense of masculinity. When this view is adopted by White politicians, it becomes an agenda for family policies that make it extremely difficult for battered women to leave abusive men.

In other countries, issues of gender, social class, and racial ethnic status have entirely different dimensions, but the question of where a woman's loyalty, identification, and politics lie is the same. It may not be with the men of her own racial ethnic group, who may oppress their own women because of a traditional patriarchal culture or because they themselves are oppressed by men at the top of the pyramid. Men's and women's standpoints within the same group may differ considerably, even though they may share a sense of injustice from their mutual racial ethnic status.

A politics based on identity is a complex of interlocking coalitions and oppositional groups. Consciousness of subordination and the forms of struggle may have to be different for women and men. The man who is Other may need to find the voice suppressed by the dominant men; the woman who is Other may need to find the voice suppressed by both dominant *and* subordinate men.

Summary

Throughout the twentieth century, social critics have argued about which aspect of inequality is the most damaging. Feminists have focused on women's oppression, and civil rights activists on raising the status of the members of a particular disadvantaged racial ethnic group. Marxist and socialist men and women have been in the forefront of working-class political struggles. Post-colonial revolutions and nationalism add another focus. Multicultural/multiracial feminism argues that all these aspects of subordination have to be fought at the same time.

The important point made by multicultural/multiracial feminism is that a member of a subordinate group is not disadvantaged just by gender or racial ethnic status or social class, but by a *multiple system or matrix of domination.* Multicultural/multiracial feminism is therefore critical of feminist theories that contrast two global groups—"women" and "men." It argues that in racist societies, no one is just a woman or man; they are, in the United States, for example, a White woman or a Black woman, a White man or a Black man.

The combination of social statuses makes for a particular group standpoint and culture—values, sense of appropriate behavior, and outlook on life (which may be completely distinctive or may overlap with that of other groups). The dominant group's standpoint is the one that prevails in the definition of social problems, in the attribution of their causes, and in allocation of resources to research and to political solutions. Dominant cultures tend to swamp native cultures, as witnessed by the spread of McDonald's, Starbucks, and MTV. Members of disadvantaged racial ethnic and economic groups have fought to have their points of view heard, as have women. In the political arena, however, sometimes women band with other women and sometimes with men of their own social group. The politics of identity, as multicultural/multiracial feminism is so aware, is a complex of shifting sides.

Multicultural/multiracial feminism brings to feminism the tools of racial ethnic and class analysis. It gives us a powerful theory of the intersectionality of the multiple social statuses that shape individual lives and organize local communities and nations. Politically, however, multicultural/multiracial feminism is often caught between the politics of race and ethnicity and that of gender.

Suggested Readings in Multicultural/Multiracial Feminism

Amott, Teresa, and Julie Matthaei. 1991. *Race, Gender, and Work: A Multicultural Economic History of Women in the United States.* Boston: South End Press.

Anzuldúa, Gloria E. [1987] 1999. *Borderlands/La Frontera: The New Mestiza.* San Francisco, CA: Spinsters/Aunt Lute.

———. 1990. *Making Face, Making Soul–Hacienda Caras: Creative and Critical Perspectives by Women of Color.* San Francisco, CA: Spinsters/Aunt Lute.

Anzuldúa, Gloria E., and AnaLouise Keating, eds. 2002. *This Bridge We Call Home: Radical Visions for Transformation.* New York: Routledge.

Breines, Wini. 2002. "What's Love Got to Do with It? White Women, Black Women, and Feminism in the Movement Years." *Signs* 27:1095–1134.

Carby, Hazel. 1987. *Reconstructing Womanhood: The Emergence of the Afro-American Woman Novelist.* Oxford: Oxford University Press.

Cole, Johnnetta, and Beverly Guy-Sheftall. 2003. *Gender Talk: The Struggle for Women's Equality in African American Communities.* New York: Ballantine.

Collins, Patricia Hill. 1990. *Black Feminist Thought: Knowledge, Consciousness, and the Politics of Empowerment.* Boston: Unwin Hyman. (2nd ed., 2000. New York: Routledge.)

———. 1998. *Fighting Words: Black Women and the Search for Justice.* Minneapolis: University of Minnesota Press.

———. 2004. *Black Sexual Politics: African Americans, Gender, and the New Racism.* New York: Routledge.

Combahee River Collective. 1986. *The Combahee River Collective Statement: Black Feminist Organizing in the Seventies and Eighties.* New York: Kitchen Table, Women of Color Press.

Cruz María e Silva, Teresa, and Ari Sitas, eds. 1996. *Gathering Voices: Perspectives on the Social Sciences in Southern Africa.* Proceedings of the International Sociological Association Regional Conference for Southern Africa, Durban, South Africa.

Davis, Angela Y. 1983. *Women, Race and Class.* New York: Vintage.

De la Torre, Adela, and Beatríz M. Pesquera. 1993. *Building With Our Hands: New Directions in Chicana Studies.* Berkeley: University of California Press.

DuBois, Ellen Carol, and Vicki L. Ruiz, eds. 1990. *Unequal Sisters: A Multicultural Reader in U.S. Women's History.* New York: Routledge.

Espiritu, Yen Le. 1997. *Asian American Women and Men.* Thousand Oaks, CA: Sage.

Garcia, Alma, ed. 1997. *Chicana Feminist Thought: The Basic Historical Writings.* New York: Routledge.

Glenn, Evelyn Nakano. 1986. *Issei, Nissei, War Bride.* Philadelphia: Temple University Press.

Gubar, Susan. 1997. *Racechanges: White Skin, Black Face in American Culture.* Oxford: Oxford University Press.

Guy-Sheftall, Beverly, ed. 1995. *Words of Fire: An Anthology of African-American Feminist Thought.* New York: New Press.

hooks, bell. 1981. *Ain't I a Woman: Black Women and Feminism.* Boston: South End Press.

———. 1984. *Feminist Theory: From Margin to Center.* Boston: South End Press (2nd ed., 2000).

———. 1989. *Talking Back: Thinking Feminist, Talking Black.* Boston: South End Press.

———. 1990. *Yearning: Race, Gender, and Cultural Politics* Boston: South End Press.

———. 1994. *Outlaw Culture: Resisting Representations.* New York: Routledge.

———. 1996. *Bone Black: Memories of Girlhood.* New York: Henry Holt.

———. 2000. *Feminism Is for Everybody: Passionate Politics.* Boston: South End Press.

Hull, Gloria T., Patricia Bell Scott, and Barbara Smith, eds. 1982. *All the Women Are White, All the Blacks Are Men, But Some of Us Are Brave: Black Women's Studies.* New York: Feminist Press.

Hurtado, Aída. 1996. *The Color of Privilege: Three Blasphemies on Race and Feminism.* Ann Arbor: University of Michigan Press.

———. 2003. *Voicing Chicana Feminisms: Young Women Speak Out on Sexuality and Identity.* New York: New York University Press.

Jones, Jacqueline. 1986. *Labor of Love, Labor of Sorrow: Black Women, Work, and the Family from Slavery to the Present.* New York: Vintage.

King, Deborah. 1988. "Multiple Jeopardy, Multiple Consciousness: The Context of a Black Feminist Ideology." *Signs* 14:42–72.

Ladner, Joyce A. 1971. *Tomorrow's Tomorrow: The Black Woman.* Garden City, NY: Doubleday.

Landry, Bart, 2000. *Black Working Wives: Pioneers of the American Family Revolution.* Berkeley: University of California Press.

Moraga, Cherríe, and Gloria Anzaldúa, eds. 1981. *This Bridge Called My Back: Writings by Radical Women of Color.* Watertown, MA: Persephone Press.

Morrison, Toni. 2002. *Learning From Experience: Minority Identities, Multicultural Struggles. Berkeley: University of California Press.*

Omolade, Barbara. 1994. *The Rising Song of African American Women.* New York: Routledge.

Nnaemeka, Obioma, ed. 1998. *Sisterhood, Feminisms, and Power: From Africa to the Diaspora.* Trenton, NJ: Africa World Press.

———. 2004. "Nego-Feminism: Theorizing, Practicing, and Pruning Africa's Way." *Signs* 29:357–385.

Radford-Hill, Sheila. 2000. *Further to Fly: Black Women and the Politics of Empowerment.* Minneapolis: University of Minnesota Press.

Romero, Mary, Pierrette Hondagneu-Sotelo, and Vilma Oriz, eds. 1997. *Challenging Fronteras: Structuring Latina and Latino Lives in the U.S.: An Anthology of Readings.* New York: Routledge.

Saldívar-Hull, Sonia. 2000. *Feminism on the Border: Chicana Gender Politics and Literature.* Berkeley: University of California Press.

Sandoval, Chela. 2000. *Methodology of the Oppressed.* Minneapolis: University of Minnesota Press.

Shah, Sonia. 1997. *Dragon Ladies: Asian American Feminists Breathe Fire.* Boston: South End Press.

Smith, Barbara, ed. [1983] 2000. *Home Girls: A Black Feminist Anthology.* New Brunswick, NJ: Rutgers University Press.

Spelman, Elizabeth. 1988. *Inessential Woman: Problems of Exclusion in Feminist Thought.* Boston: Beacon Press.

Stack, Carol B. 1975. *All Our Kin: Strategies for Survival in a Black Community.* San Francisco: Harper and Row.

Thompson, Becky. 1994. *A Hunger So Wide and So Deep: A Multiracial View of Women's Eating Problems.* Minneapolis: University of Minnesota Press.

———. 2001. *A Promise and a Way of Life: White Antiracist Activism.* Minneapolis: University of Minnesota Press.

Thompson, Becky, and Sangeeta Tyagi, eds. 1996. *Names We Call Home: Autobiography on Racial Identity.* New York: Routledge & Kegan Paul.

Trujillo, Carla, ed. 1998. *Living Chicana Theory.* Berkeley, CA: Third Woman.

Wall, Cheryl A., ed. 1989. *Changing Our Own Words: Essays on Criticism, Theory, and Writing by Black Women.* New Brunswick, NJ: Rutgers University Press.

Wallace, Michele. [1978] 1990. *Black Macho and the Myth of the Superwoman.* London: Verso.

Wiegman, Robyn. 1995. *American Anatomies: Theorizing Race and Gender.* Durham, NC: Duke University Press.

Williams, Patricia J. 1991. *The Alchemy of Race and Rights.* Cambridge, MA: Harvard University Press.

———. 1995. *The Rooster's Egg.* Cambridge, MA: Harvard University Press.

———. 1998. *Seeing a Color-Blind Future: The Paradox of Race.* New York: Noonday Press.

Wyatt, Jean. 2004. *Risking Difference: Identification, Race, and Community in Contemporary Fiction and Feminism.* Albany: State University of New York Press.

Yamamoto, Traise. 1999. *Masking Selves, Making Subjects: Japanese American Women, Identity, and the Body.* Berkeley: University of California Press. ✦

Chapter Ten

Feminist Studies of Men

Sources of Gender Inequality

- Dominance of economic and educational resources and political power by one group of men.
- Institutionalized privileges that benefit all men.
- Social values that encourage men's violence and sexual exploitation of women.
- Socialization processes that encourage boys' aggressiveness and unemotionality.

Politics

- Working for greater economic, educational, and political equality.
- Enhancing women's status and also that of disadvantaged men, including homosexuals.
- Making men responsible for controlling their own violent behavior.
- Working for peace.

Contributions

- Analysis of men's gender as part of a set of institutionalized relationships of dominance and subordination.
- Recognition of men's dominance of other men as well as of women.

- Identification of masculinities and their consequences.
- Critiques of war, pornography, rape, and violence in sports as aspects of men's gendering.
- Development of the men's health movement.

Feminist studies of men apply feminist theories to the study of men and masculinity. Feminist studies of men take on the task called for by feminists—to treat men as well as women as a gender and to scrutinize masculinity as carefully as femininity.

Genders—men's and women's—are relational and embedded in the structure of the social order. The original object of analysis in feminist studies of men was masculinity in its oppositional relationship to femininity, since much of masculinity is nonfemininity (and vice versa). What is valued and socially encouraged in men is their difference from women and, most especially, attributes that allow them to be dominant and authoritative—aggressiveness, coolness, physical strength, and willingness to use violence. These masculine attributes are the personality side of the *patriarchal dividend*—men's privileges and advantageous status compared to women. With these privileges comes responsibility for economic support and physical protection.

Later research in feminist studies of men hone in on men's relationships to other men. Masculinity is now masculinities—dominant, subordinate, intersected with the norms of social class, nationalities, religion, racial ethnic cultures, and sexual orientations. Feminist studies of men argue that although a pattern of social dominance over women is prevalent, there are many subordinate men—as studies of working-class men, Black men, and men under colonial domination make very clear.

Today, the focus of feminist studies of men is different men's statuses in social hierarchies, their varying privileges and disadvantages, and cultural, racial ethnic, religious, national, and social class differences in norms and expectations that construct masculinities. The dissection of men as a diverse gender and the calls for changing masculinity and divesting men of their patriarchal privileges are rebellions against the current gender order.

Hegemonic men, hegemonic masculinity. The main theory used in feminist studies of men is that of *hegemony.* It sets out the differences between and within groups of upper-, middle-, and working-class men of different racial ethnic groups and sexual orientations. Hegemonic men are economically successful, from racially and ethnically privileged groups, and visibly heterosexual; they are at the top of the social ladder. In the United States, many are of poor or working-class origins, but most have been educated at good colleges and universities and have professional or managerial careers. Their hegemonic status is produced and legitimated by these valued attributes: Whiteness, wealth, education, social position, heterosexuality. Hegemonic men are both born to these characteristics (e.g., Whiteness) and achieve them (education). Sometimes events propel men of lesser status to a more glorified status. Since September 11, 2001, firefighters in the United States have become the symbol of American strength in the face of adversity. Their valorization as heroes has become international, but their economic and political status in New York City is not quite hegemonic. They are still working-class.

Hegemonic men within a society monopolize privileges, resources, and power. Their hegemony comes from their ability to control politics, set policies, impose their view of what is valuable, virtuous, and moral on the rest of society, and marshal legitimation for their views through the media, education, religion, and law, which they also dominate. Because newly independent countries are still suffering from the effects of colonization, hegemonic men in the Western societies that have been economically and socially dominant for the past 500 years have a double advantage—national and global hegemony. According to R. W. Connell, a major theorist in feminist studies of men, Western masculinity may become the hegemonic worldwide form of masculinity, creating a global gender hierarchy of dominance and subordination that places hegemonic men at the top, coalescing their power.

Jeff Hearn, another major theorist in feminist studies of men, discusses the concept of hegemony in the framework of critical studies of men, which focuses on power. He argues that it is not masculinity that is hegemonic, but men as a gendered social category of people. Hegemonic men's power, he argues, has to be seen as structural—emanating from their social status as the dominant gender—and interactional—resulting from gendered social practices in which they dominate women and subordinate other men. In the following excerpt, based on a talk he gave in 1999 at a Swedish conference, he discusses the theory of men's macro- and micro-power.

The Hegemony of Men

Jeff Hearn
Professor, Huddersfield University and
Swedish School of Economics, Finland

The hegemony of men seeks to address the double complexity that men are both a *social category formed by the gender system* and *dominant collective and individual agents of social practices.*

In this view, there is a greater need to look critically at the ordinary, taken-for-granted accepted dominant constructions, powers and authorities of men—in relation to women, children and other men, both men who are subordinate and those who are superordinate. This involves addressing the formation of the social category of men, and its taken-for-grantedness, as well as men's taken-for-granted domination and control through consent. The deconstruction of the dominant (Hearn 1996a) and the obvious, the social category of men, remains urgent. What indeed would society look like without this category, not through gendercide but through gender transformation?

This perspective on hegemony may take us down a slightly different route to consider not so much the 'matter of pushing and pulling of ready-formed groupings but . . . the formation of these groupings [of men]' (Carrigan et al. 1985: 594) in the first place. Focusing on not just the various forms of *masculinity* (or configurations of gender practice, dominant or otherwise), but rather on that which is taken-for-granted about the categorizations and constructions of *men* (in both senses) is more closely compatible with Gramsci's original concept of hegemony. The task then becomes one of interrogating how hegemony operates through the web of collective political actors—the state, the law, capitalists, intellectuals, and so on; how 'the intellectual, moral and philosophical leadership provided by the class [of men] or alliance of class fractions [of certain men] which is ruling successfully achieves its objective of providing the fundamental outlook of the whole society' (Bocock 1986: 63); and how hegemony involves the active consent of dominated groups (even though that consent is backed by force).

Thus the agenda for the investigation of the hegemony of men in the social world concerns the examination of that which sets the agenda for different ways of being men in relation to women, children and other men, rather than the identification of particular forms of masculinity or hegemonic masculinity. Interestingly, this view of hegemony of men would also likely lead us to ask what are the various dominant ways that there are for governmentally categorizing men—by the state, the law, medical sciences, social sciences, religion, business, and so on—and how these intersect with, complement and contradict each other. These webs of collective political actors are not static; especially important is the way in which various definitions and constructions of the agenda on men are themselves changing. This includes change through globalizing forces, tending to undermine the 'fundamental outlook of a given society'. Contemporary hegemony may involve the absence of a single fundamental outlook on and about men. I return to this point in the concluding discussion.

There would seem to be at least seven major aspects to this agenda and thus associated implications for feminist theory. First, there are the *social processes by which there is a hegemonic acceptance of the category of men.* This would include the unproblematic taken-for-granted categorization of people as 'men' through biological and often medical examination (principally the privileging of the presence or absence of a penis at or shortly after birth); the conduct of state, population and statistical classifications; the practices of organized religion and education; and the mass of other organizational and institutional ways in which particular men are placed within the social category of men. These range from the gender-specific use of toilets to gender-specific practices in entering and within the military. A closely related issue is the relational distinction between 'boys' and 'men'. Religious, educational, military and work institutions represent relevant sites for such hegemonic definitions.

Second, there is the *system of distinctions and categorizations between different forms of men and men's practices* to women, children and other men (and what are now often called masculinities). This comes closest to the current use of the term 'masculinities', though as noted the term has been used in a wide variety of ways in recent years. However, I would suggest a greater attention to the social construction of the *systems* of differentiations of men and men's practices rather than the social construction of particular 'forms' of men, as masculinities.

Third, the question can then be asked *which men and which men's practices—in the media, the state, religion, and so on—are most powerful in setting those agendas of those systems of differentiations.* It is these general ideas and practices that are hegemonic, rather than a particular form of hegemonic masculinity that is hegemonic.

Fourth, we can consider the identification of *the most widespread, repeated forms of men's practices.* In this identification those which are called 'complicit' are likely to take a much more central place in the construction of men and the various ways of being men in relation to women, children and other men. If anything, it is the complicit that is most hegemonic.

Fifth, we may consider *the description and analysis of men's various and variable everyday, 'natural(ized)', 'ordinary', 'normal' and most taken-for-granted practices* to women, children and other men and their contradictory, even paradoxical, meanings—rather than the depiction of the most culturally valued ideal or the most exaggerated or over-conforming forms of men's practices.

Sixth, there is the question of *how women may differentially support certain practices of men,* and subordinate other practices of men or ways of being men.[1] This brings us to the place of women's 'consent' with the hegemony of men.

Seventh, there are various interrelations between these six elements above. Perhaps of most interest is *the relationship between 'men's' formation within a hegemonic gender order, that also forms 'women', other genders and boys, and men's activity in different ways in forming and reforming hegemonic differentiations among men.*

This overall approach involves placing biology and biological difference firmly in a cultural frame. Contemporary 'western' systems of construction of men and men's practices are cultural systems, just as much as those which embody third sexes and third genders, and other seemingly more complex patterns still (for example, Herdt 1994; Lorber 1994). Hegemony is not so much, or at least not only, a matter of the social contestation and reproduction of particular forms of *hegemonic masculinities* as the contestation and reproduction of the *hegemony of men* in a particular society or combination of globalizing societies (Hearn 1996a), both as a social category and in men's practices. This may indeed offer possibilities of a rapprochement between transgender and queer studies, on the one hand, and materialist, embodied and gender class studies, on the other.[2]

As Mark Surman (1994) puts it: "Hegemony is taking one way of seeing things, and convincing people that this way of seeing things is natural, that it is 'just the way things are.' " This sense of 'naturalness,' including 'naturalness' about men and the way men are, may itself be becoming increasingly subject to globalizing social forces and processes (Connell 1998).

Having said that, there are a number of areas of difficulty in working on this kind of revision of hegemony in relation to men. The parallels and the differences with class-based versions need to be noted. Men are, or more precisely can be understood as, both a ruling class and not a ruling class. 'Men' are both *formed in* men's hegemony (or a hegemonic gender order), and *form* that hegemony. 'Men' are formed in a hegemonic gender order that also forms 'women', but men are also active in different ways in forming and re-forming hegemonic differentiations among men . . .

Another contemporary complication is that there appear to be social changes in the constructions and interrelations of social divisions. It seems increasingly difficult to discuss gender or any other social division in isolation from others. Though this may have always been so historically, it does not seem to have been noticed so much until recently. Societal changes such as towards virtualities and information societies may contribute to the increasing elaboration of intersectionalities between social divisions. The very formation of 'people' as persons, bodies, individuals may be in the process of profound historical change. Rather than people being formed primarily as fixed embodied *members* of given collectivities, defined by single social divisions, people may increasingly appear to exist and be formed in social relations, spaces and practices *between* multiple power differentials. Persons and bodies no longer appear so easily as equivalents (Hearn 2004: 207). At the same time, these intersectionalities, however, may be treated with caution, as these may also be part of contemporary hegemonic ways of obscuring gender, men and men's powers.

There is also a difficulty of operationalization. If hegemony is such an embedded and pervasive social process, how do (diversely gendered) 'we' study 'it', especially as we are part of it? Key substantive elements in hegemony include the reliance on forces other than force, and the configuration of fractions rather than a single dominating power. More specifically, what is the relation of men's domination with and through force and men's domination without force? Men's domination with force can be formally organized (for example, with corporate violence, military violence) or individualized and interpersonal (for example, with men's violence to known women and children in the home). Men's domination without force can also be formally organized (for example, men's supposedly 'peaceful' domination of managerial positions) or individualized and interpersonal (for example, with men's social status as fathers, husbands). The configurations and interrelations of these various forms of organized or interpersonal domination, with or without force, are a key empirical task . . .

Notes

1. I am grateful to Marie Nordberg for raising this sixth point. This is also taken up in Bourdieu (2001).
2. At this point, one might consider reformulating gender system hegemony in terms of 'masculine domination' (Bourdieu 2001). Though that analysis may be relevant here, it brings ambiguities around the linguistic/symbolic and embodied/social meaning of 'the masculine', and may have sociological difficulties coping with the social complexities of men and men's relations to power and hegemony in different societies. This is in addition to its nonengagement with feminist theory, recent CSM and its own gendered positioning.

References

Bocock, R. 1986. *Hegemony*. London: Tavistock.

Bourdieu, P. 2001. *Masculine Domination*. Stanford: Stanford University Press.

Carrigan, T., R. W. Connell and J. Lee. 1985. "Towards a New Sociology of Masculinity." *Theory and Society* 14(5): 551–604.

Connell, R. W. 1998. "Men in the World: Masculinities and Globalization." *Men and Masculinities* 1(1): 3–23.

Gramsci, A. 1971. *Selections From the Prison Notebook*. London: Lawrence and Wishart.

Hearn, J. 1996. "Deconstructing the Dominant: Making the One(s) the Other(s)." *Organization* 3(4): 611–626.

———. 2004. "Information Societies are Still Societies," 205–208 in T. Heiskanen and J. Hearn (eds.), *Information Society and the Workplace: Spaces Boundaries, and Agency*. London: Routledge.

Endangered and dangerous men. Not all men are privileged and powerful. In many countries, young working-class urban men's impoverished environment and "taste for risk" have made them an endangered species. They put their bodies on the line in confronting seeming slurs on their manhood, and they incur physical traumas in their work, in recreation, and especially when they become professional athletes.

Men and boys in any social strata engage in gang rape as a way of showing off their sexual prowess to their friends. Feminist studies of men blame sports, the military, fraternities, and other arenas of male bonding for encouraging physical and sexual violence and misogyny. They deplore the social pressure on men to identify with but not be emotionally close to their fathers, and to be "cool" and unfeeling toward the women in their lives and distant from their own children.

Although feminist studies of men use psychoanalytic theories of the need to detach from the mother to explain men's emotional repression, they are critical of men's movements that foster a search for the inner primitive, or "wild man." They also regard religiously oriented men's organizations, such as Promise Keepers, as dangerous to women's autonomy because they link responsibility to family with patriarchal concepts of manhood. Feminist studies of men argue that these movements seek to change individual attitudes and do not address the structural conditions of gender inequality or the power differences between men and women and among men.

These power differences emerge from different men's places in gender regimes, and they change as the regimes change. Successful religious revolutions in Islamic countries have downgraded college-educated, middle-class men and upgraded religious mullahs and martyrs. High birth rates and slow economic development have provided few well-paid jobs for college-educated men. An alternative route to valued masculinity is to die heroically as a martyr. Many terrorists have been college-educated men who became embittered by being locked out of middle-class careers. Michael Kimmel, author of a history of masculinity in America and many other works in feminist studies of men, compared the terrorists of September 11 to the American White supremacist Timothy McVeigh, who bombed a federal building in Oklahoma in 1995, killing 168 people. In the following article, Kimmel describes the terrorists' and White supremacists' path from loss of middle-class male privilege, to anger and resentment at those more successful, to a violent restoration of masculine pride.

Gender, Class, and Terrorism

Michael S. Kimmel
Professor of Sociology, State University of New York, Stony Brook

The events of September 11 [2001] have sent scholars and pundits alike scrambling to make sense of those seemingly senseless acts. While most analyses have focused on the political economy of globalization or the perversion of Islamic teachings by Al Qaeda, several commentators have raised gender issues.

Some have reminded us that in our haste to lionize the heroes of the World Trade Center collapse, we ignored the many women firefighters, police officers, and rescue workers who also risked their lives. We've been asked to remember the Taliban's vicious policies toward women; indeed, even Laura Bush seems to be championing women's emancipation.

A few have asked us to consider the other side of the gender coin: men. Some have rehearsed the rather tired old formulae about masculine bloodlust or the drive for domination and conquest, with no reference to the magnificent humanity displayed by so many on September 11. In an article in *Slate,* the Rutgers anthropologist Lionel Tiger trotted out his old male-bonding thesis but offered no understanding of why Al Qaeda might appeal to some men and not others. Only the journalist Barbara Ehrenreich suggests that there may be a link between the misogyny of the Taliban and the masculinity of the terrorists.

As for myself, I've been thinking lately about a letter to the editor of a small, upstate–New York newspaper, written in 1992 by an American GI after his return from service in the Gulf War. He complained that the legacy of the American middle class had been stolen by an indifferent government. The American dream, he wrote, has all but disappeared; instead, most people are struggling just to buy next week's groceries.

That letter writer was Timothy McVeigh from Lockport, N.Y. Two years later, he blew up the Murrah federal building in Oklahoma City in what is now the second-worst act of terrorism ever committed on American soil.

What's startling to me are the ways that McVeigh's complaints were echoed in some of the fragmentary evidence that we have seen about the terrorists of September 11, and especially in the portrait of Mohammed Atta, the suspected mastermind of the operation and the pilot of the first plane to hit the World Trade Center.

Looking at these two men through the lens of gender may shed some light on both the method and the madness of the tragedies they wrought.

McVeigh was representative of the small legion of white supremacists—from older organizations like the John Birch Society, the Ku Klux Klan, and the American Nazi Party, to newer neo-Nazi, racist skinhead, white-power groups like Posse Comitatus and the White Aryan Resistance, to radical militias.

These white supremacists are mostly younger (in their early 20s), lower-middle-class men, educated at least through high school and often beyond. They are the sons of skilled workers in industries like textiles and tobacco, the sons of the owners of small farms, shops, and grocery stores. Buffeted by global political and economic forces, the sons have inherited little of their fathers' legacies. The family farms have been lost to foreclosure, the small shops squeezed out by Wal-Marts and malls. These young men face a spiral of downward mobility and economic uncertainty. They complain that they are squeezed between the omnivorous jaws of global capital concentration and a federal bureaucracy that is at best indifferent to their plight and at worst complicit in their demise.

As one issue of *The Truth at Last,* a white-supremacist magazine, put it:

> Immigrants are flooding into our nation willing to work for the minimum wage (or less). Superrich corporate executives are flying all over the world in search of cheaper and cheaper labor so that they can lay off their American employees.

> . . . Many young White families have no future! They are not going to receive any appreciable wage increases due to job competition from immigrants.

What they want, says one member, is to "take back what is rightfully ours."

Their anger often fixes on "others"—women, members of minority groups, immigrants, gay men, and lesbians—in part because those are the people with whom they compete for entry-level, minimum-wage jobs. Above them all, enjoying the view, hovers the international Jewish conspiracy.

What holds together these "paranoid politics"—antigovernment, antiglobal capital but pro-small capitalist, racist, sexist, anti-Semitic, homophobic—is a rhetoric of masculinity. These men feel emasculated by big money and big government—they call the government "the Nanny State"—and they claim that "others" have been handed the birthright of native-born white men.

In the eyes of such downwardly mobile white men, most white American males collude in their own emasculation. They've grown soft, feminized, weak. White supremacists' Web sites abound with complaints about the "whimpering collapse of the blond male"; the "legions of sissies and weaklings, of flabby, limp-wristed, nonaggressive, nonphysical, indecisive, slack-jawed, fearful males who, while still heterosexual in theory and practice, have not even a vestige of the old macho spirit."

American white supremacists thus offer American men the restoration of their masculinity—a manhood in which individual white men control the fruits of their own labor and are not subject to emasculation by Jewish-owned finance capital or a black- and feminist-controlled welfare state. Theirs is the militarized manhood of the heroic John Rambo, a manhood that celebrates their God-sanctioned right to band together in armed militias if anyone, or any government agency, tries to take it away from them. If the state and the economy emasculate them, and if the masculinity of the "others" is problematic, then only "real" white men can rescue America from a feminized, multicultural, androgynous melting pot.

Sound familiar? For the most part, the terrorists of September 11 come from the same class, and recite the same complaints, as American white supremacists.

Virtually all were under 25, educated, lower middle class or middle class, downwardly mobile. The journalist Nasra Hassan interviewed families of Middle Eastern suicide bombers (as well as some failed bombers themselves) and found that none of them had the standard motivations ascribed to people who commit suicide, such as depression.

Although several of the leaders of Al Qaeda are wealthy—Osama bin Laden is a multimilionaire, and Ayman al-Zawahiri, the 50-year-old doctor thought to be bin Laden's closest adviser, is from a fashionable suburb of Cairo—many of the hijackers were engineering students for whom job opportunities had been dwindling dramatically. (Judging from the minimal information I have found, about one-fourth of the hijackers had studied engineering.) Zacarias Moussaoui, who did not hijack one of the planes but is the first man to be formally charged in the United States for crimes related to September 11, earned a degree at London's South Bank University. Marwan al-Shehhi, the chubby, bespectacled 23-year-old from the United Arab Emirates who flew the second plane into the World Trade Center, was an engineering student, while Ziad Jarrah, the 26-year-old Lebanese who flew the plane that crashed in Pennsylvania, had studied aircraft design.

Politically, these terrorists opposed globalization and the spread of Western values; they opposed what they perceived as corrupt regimes in several Arab states (notably Saudi Arabia and Egypt), which they claimed were merely puppets of American domination. "The resulting anger is naturally directed first against their rulers," writes the historian Bernard Lewis, "and then against those whom they see as keeping those rulers in power for selfish reasons."

Central to their political ideology is the recovery of manhood from the emasculating politics of globalization. The Taliban saw the Soviet invasion and westernization of Afghanistan as humiliations. Bin Laden's October 7 videotape describes the "humiliation and disgrace" that Islam has suffered "for more than 80 years." And over and over, Nasra Hassan writes, she heard the refrain: "The Israelis humiliate us. They occupy our land, and deny our history."

Terrorism is fueled by a fatal brew of antiglobalization politics, convoluted Islamic theology, and virulent misogyny. According to Ehrenreich, while these formerly employed or self-employed males "have lost their traditional status as farmers and breadwinners, women have been entering the market economy and gaining the marginal independence conferred by even a paltry wage." As a result, "the man who can no longer make a living, who has to depend on his wife's earnings, can watch Hollywood sexpots on pirated videos and begin to think the world has been turned upside down."

The Taliban's policies thus had two purposes: to remasculinize men and to refeminize women. Another journalist, Peter Marsden, has observed that those policies "could be seen as a desperate attempt to keep out that other world, and to protect Afghan women from influences that could weaken the society from within." The Taliban prohibited women from appearing in public unescorted by men, from revealing any part of their body, and from going to school or holding a job. Men were required to grow their beards, in accordance with religious images of Muhammad, yes; but also, perhaps, because wearing beards has always been associated with men's response to women's increased equality in the public sphere, since beards symbolically reaffirm biological differences between men and women, while gender equality tends to blur those differences.

The Taliban's policies removed women as competitors and also shored up masculinity, since they enabled men to triumph over the humiliations of globalization and their own savage, predatory, and violently sexual urges that might be unleashed in the presence of uncovered women.

All of these issues converged in the life of Mohammed Atta, the terrorist about whom the most has been written and conjectured. Currently, for example, there is much speculation about Atta's sexuality. Was he gay? Was he a repressed homosexual, too ashamed of his sexuality to come out? Such innuendoes are based on no more than a few circumstantial tidbits about his life. He was slim, sweet-faced, neat, meticulous, a snazzy dresser. The youngest child of an ambitious lawyer father and a pampering mother, Atta grew up shy and polite, a mama's boy. "He was so gentle," his father said. "I used to tell him, 'Toughen up, boy!' "

When such revelations are offered, storytellers seem to expect a reaction like "Aha! So that explains it!" (Indeed, in a new biography of Adolf Hitler, *The Hidden Hitler,* Lothar Machtan offers exactly that sort of explanation. He argues that many of Hitler's policies—such as the killing of longtime colleague and avowed homosexual Ernst Rohm, or even the systematic persecution and execution of gay men in concentration camps—were, in fact, prompted by a desire to conceal his own homosexuality.)

But what do such accusations actually explain? Do revelations about Hitler's or Atta's possible gay propensities raise troubling connections between homosexuality and mass murder? If so, then one would also have to conclude that the discovery of Shakespeare's "gay" sonnet explains the Bard's genius at explicating Hamlet's existential anguish, or that Michelangelo's sexuality is the decisive factor in his painting of God's touch in the Sistine Chapel.

Such revelations tell us little about the Holocaust or September 11. They do, however, address the consequences of homophobia—both official and informal—on young men who are exploring their sexual identities. What's relevant is not the possible fact of Hitler's or Atta's gayness, but the shame and fear that surround homosexuality in societies that refuse to acknowledge sexual diversity.

Even more troubling is what such speculation leaves out. What unites Atta, McVeigh, and Hitler is not their repressed sexual orientation but gender—their masculinity, their sense of masculine entitlement, and their thwarted ambitions. They accepted cultural definitions of masculinity, and needed someone to blame when they felt that they failed to measure up. (After all, being called a mama's boy, a sissy, and told to toughen up are demands for gender conformity, not matters of sexual desire.) Gender is the issue, not sexuality.

All three failed at their chosen professions. Hitler was a failed artist—indeed, he failed at just about every job he ever tried except dictator. McVeigh, a business-college dropout, found his calling in the military during the Gulf War, where his exemplary service earned him commendations; but he washed out of Green Beret training—his dream job—after only two days. And Atta was the odd man out in his family. His two sisters both became doctors—one a physician and one a university professor. His father constantly reminded him that he wanted "to hear the word 'doctor' in front of his name.

We told him, your sisters are doctors and their husbands are doctors and you are the man of the family."

Atta decided to become an engineer, but his degree meant little in a country where thousands of college graduates were unable to find good jobs. After he failed to find employment in Egypt, he went to Hamburg, Germany, to study architecture. He was "meticulous, disciplined, and highly intelligent, an ordinary student, a quiet, friendly guy who was totally focused on his studies," according to another student in Hamburg.

But his ambitions were constantly undone. His only hope for a good job in Egypt was to be hired by an international firm. He applied and was continually rejected. He found work as a draftsman—highly humiliating for someone with engineering and architectural credentials and an imperious and demanding father—for a German firm involved with razing low-income Cairo neighborhoods to provide more scenic vistas for luxury tourist hotels.

Defeated, humiliated, emasculated, a disappointment to his father and a failed rival to his sisters, Atta retreated into increasingly militant Islamic theology. By the time he assumed the controls of American Airlines Flight 11, he evinced a hysteria about women. In the message he left in his abandoned rental car, he made clear what mattered to him in the end. "I don't want pregnant women or a person who is not clean to come and say good-bye to me," he wrote. "I don't want women to go to my funeral or later to my grave." Of course, Atta's body was instantly incinerated, and no burial would be likely.

The terrors of emasculation experienced by lower-middle-class men all over the world will no doubt continue, as they struggle to make a place for themselves in shrinking economies and inevitably shifting cultures. They may continue to feel a seething resentment against women, whom they perceive as stealing their rightful place at the head of the table, and against the governments that displace them. Globalization feels to them like a game of musical chairs, in which, when the music stops, all the seats are handed to others by nursemaid governments.

The events of September 11, as well as of April 19, 1995 (the Oklahoma City bombing), resulted from an increasingly common combination of factors—the massive male displacement that accompanies globalization, the spread of American consumerism, and the perceived corruption of local political elites—fused with a masculine sense of entitlement. Someone else—some "other"—had to be held responsible for the terrorists' downward mobility and failures, and the failure of their fathers to deliver their promised inheritance. The terrorists didn't just get mad. They got even.

Such themes were not lost on the disparate bands of young, white supremacists. American Aryans admired the terrorists' courage and chastised their own compatriots. "It's a disgrace that in a population of at least 150 million White/Aryan Americans, we provide so few that are willing to do the same [as the terrorists]," bemoaned Rocky Suhayda, the chairman of the American Nazi Party. "A bunch of towel heads and niggers put our great White Movement to shame."

It is from such gendered shame that mass murderers are made.

Vicarious masculinity. Feminist studies of men have described another part of the masculine stratification system—homophobia and homosexuality. Prominent men of all racial and ethnic groups in politics, sports, and the mass media must appear heterosexual, which sometimes leads to constant womanizing. Feminist studies of men also criticize the jockeying for leading positions in whatever arena men find themselves. It is not an accident that so much of the language of competition is the language of sports, because organized sports not only are an immediate site for demonstrations of masculinity but also are a source for vicarious competitiveness and for the creation of icons of masculine strength and beauty. Unfortunately, some athletes who have attained icon status feel free to use physical and sexual violence against women.

Feminist studies of men say that office-bound men's identification with the bruisers on football and soccer fields allows them to feel masculine and yet above such gross displays of physicality. White middle-class men who participate vicariously in the violent professional sports played by mostly Black and Hispanic men from economically disadvantaged backgrounds (but now very rich) admire their masculine physical prowess, extravagant wealth, and flaunted sexuality, but they also maintain their own racial and class superiority. White middle-class men who are themselves involved in professional sports are most of the owners, lawyers, agents, financial managers, journalists, and advertisers who make the athletes' careers. As a significant source of the social construction of masculinities in Western society, sport stratifies men.

Sexual stratification. Feminist studies of men overlap with gay studies in analyzing the social dimensions of male homosexuality. Examining homosexuality from a gender perspective shows that homosexual men are *men,* not a third gender, and partake of the privileges (or lack of them) and lifestyle of men of the same racial ethnic group and social class. Nonetheless, because homosexual men do not have sexual relationships with women—an important marker of manhood in Western society—they are considered not-quite-men. Thus, like other men who do not have the marks of dominant status (being White, economically successful, heterosexual), homosexual men are lower on the scale of privilege and power in Western society. Homosexual men, however, do not subvert the gender order, because they retain some of the "patriarchal dividend" of men's status.

Critique. Feminist studies of men provide a needed corrective in bringing men into gender research as a specific subject of study, but except for the concept of masculine hegemony they do not offer a new theoretical perspective. Rather, feminist studies of men use elements of marxist, psychoanalytic, multicultural, social construction, and gay studies. Women feminists have also written about masculinity, men's roles at work and in the family, and how men are changing, however slowly. The question, then, is whether feminist studies of men bring a different view on men's status because men themselves are writing about it critically.

Feminist men's politics include educating young men about date rape and fraternity gang rape. Feminist men who were athletes have written and lectured about the violent values in sport. Black and Hispanic men feminists have analyzed the dangers of risk taking and machismo. Gay men have analyzed and documented the recent history of homosexuality, and its path from the headiness of the Greenwich Village Stonewall riot to the tragedies of AIDS. A thriving men's health movement is developing a body of knowledge about how men's risky lifestyle causes illness.

There is a comprehensive body of knowledge in feminist studies of men, but politically, the men's movement has been taken over by the Iron Johns and the Promise Keepers, who offer versions of masculinity that are not much different from the conventional beliefs in men's intrinsic "wildness" or need to be the "head of the house."

Another strand in the nonfeminist politics of masculinity is the argument that says that men's power is a myth because so many men's roles are dangerous. They, and not women, are exploited—fighting wars, fires, criminals, and terrorists. Women feminists, not men, have countered this argument with studies of women in the military, the police, and other occupations where formerly only men showed they had the "right stuff." (Women could not enter such occupations until fairly recently.) A woman feminist has documented men's rapid rise up the "glass escalator" to the top positions in *women's* occupations. Both types of data—that women can do the dangerous work men do and that men doing women's work have the advantage of their dominant gender status—are analyses that came from women, not men, writing about men.

If feminist studies of men are to add the dimension of the insider's view, men have to turn the gender lens on themselves in all the arenas where they still dominate—fundamentalist religions, science, politics, the higher echelons of finance, and the capitalist markets of the global economy.

Summary

Feminist studies of men focus on men and masculinity, with overlaps in research on the body, sexuality, violence, personality development, health, and family relationships. These overlaps make feminist studies of men an increasingly valuable part of feminist studies.

Feminist studies of men have brought attention to the fact that men as well as women have a gender status. Men's gender status is dominant in most societies, although there is a hierarchy of hegemonic and subordinate men. Even though disadvantaged men may be lower on the status scale than hegemonic men, they are usually dominant over the women of their own group, giving them what has been called a patriarchal dividend. Men's hegemonic status in the structure of privilege, as well as the sexist practices and violent behavior that maintain all men's dominance over women in their group, have been dissected and deplored by feminist studies of men.

Another important focus of feminist studies of men is the analysis of violence in men in war and terrorism. Even in sports, racial and economic stratification and a culture of violence take a high toll on the players and on aspiring teenagers. A few professional athletes have careers that are rewarding financially and in popularity, but for the most part, the money in sport is made by White, middle-class men. In the health field, the high death rate of young men from poor urban centers and the short life expectancy of older men have been attributed to gendered, racial, ethnic, and economic pressures.

Feminist studies of men should be distinguished from the men's movements that focus on individual change. Bonding with symbolic brothers and fathers and dancing to drums in the woods may make men more emotionally expressive, but it does nothing about the structural sources of gender inequality. Feminist studies of men also criticize movements that offer men a rightful place as heads of their families in exchange for the promise of taking responsibility for the welfare of their wives and children. Feminist men would rather see men and women sharing family work and economic support as equal partners. Feminist men have also undertaken an active program of anti-rape and anti-battering education.

In its perspectives on men and masculinities as part of the gendered social order and the processes that reproduce and maintain it, feminist studies of men have offered a challenge to their perpetuation. Feminist men's calls for redistribution of hegemonic men's advantages and their questioning men's control over politics, the media, education, law, religions, and cultural productions, undercut men's superiority. Without the patriarchal dividend men of all groups still have, the gender order would be close to collapsing.

Suggested Readings in Feminist Studies of Men

Abalos, David T. 2001. *The Latino Male: A Radical Redefinition.* Boulder, CO: Lynne Rienner.

Adams, Rachel, and David Savran, eds. 2002. *The Masculinity Studies Reader.* Malden, MA: Blackwell.

Bordo, Susan. 1999. *The Male Body: A New Look at Men in Public and in Private.* New York: Farrar, Straus and Giroux.

Bowker, Lee H., ed. 1997. *Masculinities and Violence.* Thousand Oaks, CA: Sage.

Braudy, Leo. 2003. *From Chivalry to Terrorism: War and the Changing Nature of Masculinity.* New York: Knopf.

Breines, Ingeborg, R. W. Connell, and Ingrid Eide, eds. 2000. *Male Roles, Masculinities and Violence: A Culture of Peace Perspective.* Paris: UNESCO.

Brownell, Susan, and Jeffrey N. Wasserstrom, eds. 2002. *Chinese Femininities/Chinese Masculinities: A Reader.* Berkeley: University of California Press.

Brod, Harry, and Michael Kaufman, eds. 1994. *Theorizing Masculinities.* Thousand Oaks, CA: Sage.

Byrd, Rudolph, and Beverly Guy-Sheftall, eds. 2001. *Traps: African American Men on Gender and Sexuality.* Bloomington: Indiana University Press.

Carby, Hazel V. 2000. *Race Men.* Cambridge, MA: Harvard University Press.

Cleaver, Frances, ed. 2002. *Masculinities Matter! Men, Gender and Development.* London: Zed.

Cockburn, Cynthia. 1983. *Brothers: Male Dominance and Technological Change.* London: Pluto Press.

Collinson, David L., and Jeff Hearn, eds. 1996. *Men as Managers, Managers as Men: Critical Perspectives on Men, Masculinities and Managements.* London: Sage.

Connell, R. W. 1990. "The State, Gender and Sexual Politics." *Theory and Society* 19:507–544.

———. 1995. *Masculinities.* Berkeley: University of California Press.

———. 2000. *The Men and The Boys.* Berkeley: University of California Press.

Cornwall, Andrea, and Nancy Lindisfarne, eds. 1994. *Dislocating Masculinity: Comparative Ethnographies.* New York: Routledge.

Digby, Tom, ed. 1998. *Men Doing Feminism.* New York: Routledge.

Dudink, Stefan, Josh Tosh, and Karen Hagemann, eds. 2004. *Masculinities in Politics and War: Gendering Modern History.* Manchester, UK: Manchester University Press.

Ehrenreich, Barbara. 1983. *Hearts of Men: American Dreams and the Flight From Commitment.* New York: Anchor Doubleday.

Eng, David L. 2001. *Racial Castration: Managing Masculinity in Asian America.* Durham, NC: Duke University Press.

Ferguson, Ann Arnett. 2000. *Bad Boys: Public Schools in the Making of Black Masculinity.* Lansing: University of Michigan Press.

Gardiner, Judith Kegan, ed. 2002. *Masculinity Studies and Feminist Theory.* New York: Columbia University Press.

Gerson, Kathleen. 1993. *No Man's Land: Men's Changing Commitments to Family and Work.* New York: Basic Books.

Ghoussoub, Mai, and Emma Sinclair-Webb, eds. 2000. *Imagined Masculinities: Male Identity and Culture in the Modern Middle East.* London: Saqi Books.

Gibson, J. William. 1994. *Warrior Dreams: Paramilitary Culture in Post-Vietnam America*. New York: Hill and Wang.

Gutmann, Matthew C. 1996. *The Meanings of Macho: Being a Man in Mexico City*. Berkeley: University of California Press.

Haywood, Chris, and Máirtín Mac an Ghaill. 2003. *Men and Masculinities: Theory, Research and Social Practice*. Milton Keynes, UK: Open University Press.

Hearn, Jeff. 1987. *The Gender of Oppression: Men, Masculinity and the Critique of Marxism*. New York: St. Martin's Press.

———. 1992. *Men in the Public Eye: The Construction and Deconstruction of Public Men and Public Patriarchies*. London: Routledge.

Hearn, Jeff, and David Morgan, eds. 1990. *Men, Masculinities and Social Theory*. London: Unwin Hyman.

Herdt, Gilbert. 1981. *Guardians of the Flutes: Idioms of Masculinity*. New York: McGraw-Hill.

Higate, Paul, ed. 2003. *Military Masculinities: Identity and the State*. Westport, CT: Praeger.

Hobson, Barbara, ed. 2002. *Making Men Into Fathers: Men, Masculinities and the Social Politics of Fatherhood*. Cambridge, UK: Cambridge University Press.

hooks, bell. 2003. *We Real Cool: Black Men and Masculinity* (new ed.). New York: Routledge.

Kaplan, Danny. 2003. *Brothers and Others in Arms: The Making of Love and War in Israeli Combat Units*. New York: Harrington Press.

Kimmel, Michael S., ed. 1991. *Men Confront Pornography*. New York: Meridian.

———. 1996. *Manhood in America: A Cultural History*. New York: Free Press.

———. 2003. "Globalization and its Mal(e)contents: The Gendered Moral and Political Economy of Terrorism." *International Sociology* 18: 603–620.

Kimmel, Michael S., and Amy Aronson, eds. 2004. *Men and Masculinities: A Social, Cultural, and Historical Encyclopedia*. Santa Barbara: ABC-Clio.

Kimmel, Michael S., Jeff Hearn, and R. W. Connell, eds. 2004. *Handbook of Studies on Men and Masculinities*. Thousand Oaks, CA: Sage.

Kimmel, Michael S., and Michael A. Messner, eds. 2004. *Men's Lives*, 6th ed. Boston: Allyn and Bacon.

Klein, Alan. 1993. *Little Big Men: Body-Building Subculture and Gender Construction*. Albany: State University of New York Press.

Lefkowitz, Bernard. 1997. *Our Guys: The Glen Ridge Rape and the Secret Life of the Perfect Suburb*. Berkeley: University of California Press.

Mac an Ghaill, Máirtín, ed. 1996. *Understanding Masculinities: Social Relations and Cultural Arenas*. Milton Keynes, UK: Open University Press.

Majors, Richard, and Janet Mancini Billson. 1992. *Cool Pose: The Dilemmas of Black Manhood in America*. New York: Lexington Books.

McKay, Jim, Michael A. Messner, and Donald Sabo, eds. 2000. *Masculinities, Gender Relations, and Sport.* Thousand Oaks, CA: Sage.

Messner, Michael A. 1992. *Power at Play: Sports and the Problem of Masculinity.* Boston: Beacon Press.

———. 1997. *Politics of Masculinities: Men in Movements.* Newbury Park, CA: Sage.

Messner, Michael A., and Donald F. Sabo, eds. 1990. *Sport, Men, and the Gender Order: Critical Feminist Perspectives.* Champaign, IL: Human Kinetics.

Messerschmidt, James W. 1993. *Masculinities and Crime: Critique and Reconceptualization of Theory.* Lanham, MD: Rowman & Littlefield.

Mirande, Alfredo. 1997. *Hombres y Machos: Masculinity and Latino Culture.* Boulder, CO: Westview.

Nardi, Peter M., ed. 1992. *Men's Friendships.* Thousand Oaks, CA: Sage.

———. 2000. *Gay Masculinities.* Thousand Oaks, CA: Sage.

Oudshoorn, Nelly. 2003. *The Male Pill: A Biography of a Technology in the Making.* Durham, NC: Duke University Press.

Pease, Bob. 2000. *Recreating Men: Postmodern Masculinity Politics.* London: Sage.

Pease, Bob, and Keith Pringle, eds. 2002. *A Man's World? Changing Men's Practices in a Globalized World.* London: Zed.

Petersen, Alan 1998. *Unmasking the Masculine: 'Men' and 'Identity' in a Sceptical Age.* London: Sage.

Pope, Harrison G., Jr., Katharine A. Phillips, and Roberto Olivardia. 2000. *The Adonis Complex: The Secret Crisis of Male Body Obsession.* New York: Free Press.

Putnam, Michael. 2001. *Private I's: Investigating Men's Experiences of Pornographies.* Ph.D. dissertation, Graduate School, City University of New York.

Riska, Elianne. 2004. *Masculinity and Men's Health: Coronary Heart Disease in Medical and Public Discourse.* Lanham, MD: Rowman & Littlefield.

Sabo, Don, and David Frederick Gordon, eds. 1995. *Men's Health and Illness: Gender, Power and the Body.* Thousand Oaks, CA: Sage.

Sabo, Donald F., Terry A. Kupers, and Willie London, eds. 2001. *Prison Masculinities.* Philadelphia, PA: Temple University Press.

Sanday, Peggy Reeves. 1990. *Fraternity Gang Rape: Sex, Brotherhood, and Privilege on Campus.* New York: New York University Press.

Schacht, Steven P., and Doris Ewing, eds. 1998. *Feminism and Men: Reconstructing Gender Relations.* New York: New York University Press.

Schwalbe, Michael. 1996. *Unlocking the Iron Cage: The Men's Movement, Gender Politics, and American Culture.* New York: Oxford University Press.

Scully, Diana. 1990. *Understanding Sexual Violence: A Study of Convicted Rapists.* Boston: Unwin Hyman.

Segal, Lynne. 1990. *Slow Motion: Changing Masculinities, Changing Men.* New Brunswick, NJ: Rutgers University Press.

———. 1994. *Unreasonable Men: Masculinity and Social Theory.* New York: Routledge.

Srivastava, Sanjay, ed. 2004. *Sexual Sites, Seminal Attitudes: Sexualities, Masculinities and Culture in South Asia.* Thousand Oaks, CA: Sage.

Stoltenberg, John. 1990. *Refusing to Be a Man: Essays on Sex and Justice.* New York: Meridian.

———. 1993. *The End of Manhood: A Book for Men of Conscience.* New York: Plume.

Wacquant, Loïc. 2003. *Body and Soul: Notebooks of an Apprentice Boxer.* New York: Oxford University Press.

Whitehead, Stephen M. 2002. *Men and Masculinities: Key Themes and New Directions.* Cambridge, UK: Polity Press.

Williams, Christine L. 1995. *Still a Man's World: Men Who Do Women's Work.* Berkeley: University of California Press. ✦

Chapter Eleven

Social Construction Feminism

Sources of Gender Inequality

- Practices and processes of gendering in everyday life.
- Gendered work organizations.
- Reproduction of gender by the division of labor in the family.
- Scientific search for sex differences that downplays similarities between women and men.
- Legal power of gender as a social institution.

Politics

- Making the processes of gender construction visible.
- Recognizing and counteracting the power of gender norms at work and in the family.
- Questioning gender boundaries in everyday life.
- Breaking down the binaries of sex, sexuality, and gender.
- Challenging the assumptions of science and legal gender categories.

Contributions

- A theory of gender that connects face-to-face interaction with institutional structures.
- Evidence of the ways supposedly natural sex differences are socially constructed.

- Analysis of the social construction of sexuality and its social control.
- Documentation of how the gendered social order can be changed by changing gendered practices and organizing processes.

While multicultural/multiracial feminism focuses on how women suffer from the effects of a system of racial ethnic disadvantage, and feminist studies of men focus on the hierarchical relationships of men to other men and to women, social construction feminism looks at the structure of the gendered social order as a whole and at the processes that construct and maintain it. Social construction feminism sees gender as a society-wide institution because it is built into all the major social organizations. As a social institution, gender determines the distribution of power, privileges, and economic resources. Other major social statuses combine with gender to produce an overall stratification system, but gender privileges men over women in most social groups.

Through parenting, the schools, and the mass media, gendered norms and expectations get built into boys' and girls' sense of self as a certain kind of human being. Other social statuses, such as racial ethnic identification and religion, are similarly socially constructed and reproduced, but gender is so deeply embedded that it is rarely examined or rebelled against. By the time people get to be adults, alternative ways of acting as women and men and arranging work and family life are literally unthinkable.

Doing gender, doing power. The social construction of gender not only produces the differences between men's and women's characteristics and behavior, it also produces gender inequality by building dominance and subordination into gendered relationships. Yet we cannot stop "doing gender" because it is part of our basic identity. In a social order based on gender divisions, everyone always "does gender" almost all the time. That was the insight in "Doing Gender," by Candace West and Don Zimmerman that has become a classic of social construction feminism. It lays out the interconnections between "doing gender" in the course of everyday life and the build-up of both gendered self-identity and gendered social structures.

In the following excerpt, Patricia Yancey Martin, a sociologist who has studied women and men in work organizations, describes how people do gender without even thinking about it and what the consequences are in discriminatory practices that demean and marginalize women. Her stories illuminate the main theoretical principle of social construction feminism—the reproduction of gender and gender inequality through everyday practices.

Seeing and Doing Gender at Work

Patricia Yancey Martin
Professor of Sociology, Florida State University

In this section, I report three stories—two from a telecommunications company and one from an engineering company. The first one, about Tom and Betsy, had acquired apocryphal status by the time I interviewed employees in their company. Everyone knew and had opinions about the events it reports. I think this event may have stimulated an aggressive policy of promoting more women into senior positions, although no official acknowledged that point to me. The third story, about Valerie, an engineer, shows men collectively mobilizing masculinities (defined below) in ways that she experienced as harmful. All three stories offer clues to past and future dynamics; as Czarniawska (1998, 20) noted, "Organizational narratives [or stories] are inscriptions of past performances and scripts and staging instructions for future performances."

Tom, Betsy, and the Telephone

Tom and Betsy, both vice-presidents in a Fortune 100 company, stood talking in a hallway after a meeting. Along the hallway were offices but none was theirs. A phone started to ring in one office and after three or so rings, Tom said to Betsy, "Why don't you get that?" Betsy was surprised by Tom's request but answered the phone anyway and Tom returned to his office. Afterwards, Betsy found Tom to ask if he realized what he had done. She told him: "I'm a vice-president too, Tom, and you treated me like a secretary. What were you thinking?" Betsy's reaction surprised Tom. He did not mean anything by his action, he said, commenting: "I did not even think about it." Tom apologized to Betsy. She told Tom his behavior was "typical of how men in High Tech Corporation [a pseudonym] treat women. You're patronizing and [you] don't treat us as equals." Tom was again surprised and decided to ask other women if they agreed with Betsy. (Field notes, *Fortune 100* telecommunications company 1994)

After this occurrence, Tom talked to Betsy and an additional 18 women about their experiences at High Tech. Some women talked for hours, and some cried over the hurtfulness of their experiences. Hardly any said life at High Tech was "just fine" for themselves or women generally. Several women (and some men) told me they would not want their daughters to work there because High Tech was not "woman friendly." This experience inspired Tom to start a "gender group" of 18 men and 18 women that, ultimately, met periodically over two years. Betsy helped start the group but was transferred to another location before it ended. Tom kept the group going until he reached age 55, at which time High Tech encouraged him to accept a golden parachute and retire.

According to everyone who knew this story (and most people at the director and vice president ranks knew it), Betsy became angry with Tom for asking and with herself for answering the telephone. Tom and Betsy were both familiar with and skilled in gender practices; thus, they simply "hopped into the [gender] river and swam" (see discussion on swimming below). They did not reflect. They did not analyze the situation; they were "practiced" in gender; they practiced gender. The gender institution holds women accountable to pleasing men; it tells men/boys they have a (gender) right to be assisted by women/girls; Tom and Betsy knew this. Tom's request and Betsy's behavior are thus unsurprising. Without stopping to reflect, Tom practiced a kind of masculinity that the gender institution makes available to him, which is to request practical help from women; Betsy responded in kind by complying with his request.

These practices existed before Tom and Betsy's encounter, as do many parallel practices at home, for example, "fix my dinner," "wash my clothes," "clean my home," "cook my food," or "raise my kids." Such requests, while operative, are rarely articulated; they are simply understood. They would not have been needed in this case if Betsy had been a secretary. When she articulates what was jarring for her in the interaction, she did so in the language of institutionalized positions that are gendered over time and across situations, that is, "like a secretary," which means both "like a subordinate" and "like a woman." She did not dispute the assumptions or practices made available to Tom by the gender institution (about women as helpers of men) that allowed him to make a demand that was bureaucratically inappropriate from one vice president to another. After her initial compliance, she then enacted an alternative norm to challenge a gendered practice of treating women as subordinates and "did gender" in a way that was not merely nonconforming, as it would have been if she refused to answer the phone, but actively resistant. She practiced gender in and through resistance, making her a "different kind of woman" in her eyes, and in Tom's, than a woman who would just "take that kind of treatment." Betsy thus gained Tom's respect.

Most of the time, women are in structural positions that make active assertions of the gender order unnecessary (e.g., good secretaries need not be told to answer the phone, and women are still far more likely to be secretaries than vice presidents), or they are willing to do gender in expected ways (e.g., accept being inappropriately told to answer the phone) because disrupting the gender order is seen as "rocking the boat," as upsetting to the social structure and coordinated actions that are premised in gendered expectations. But without rocking the boat, the gender institution cannot be changed. Betsy took a risk in how she did gender and won the gamble by making Tom aware of the nature of gendered practices in the firm.

Betsy, equally as well schooled in gender as Tom, knew the practices of femininity/femininities that entail taking care of men. She knew that women are expected to help/serve men and to do routine/repetitive labor for men, described by Dorothy Smith (1987) as the everyday/every night material labor that keeps the body whole and social systems functioning, for example, the family, the school, the workplace. Betsy acted unreflexively in answering the phone. What was her intention? We do not know; she may not know. She simply acted, engaging in a gender practice that unreflexively complied with the femininity rule that tells women to help men (see Simmons 2002 on femininity rules). After she acted and reflected on her actions, and on Tom's, she became angry, questioning the triumph of the gender order over the bureaucratic workplace and coming to the conclusion that Tom treated her not as a colleague but as "woman to his man."

In Judith Butler's (1993, 12–16) terms, Tom's and Betsy's actions were citational of the gender order. They showed awareness of and skill in reinstituting the gender institution within which they live—as man, as woman. Their normative enactments were made possible by the gender institution, and their reiteration of normative gender practices kept/keeps the gender institution going. They required no reflexivity. Tom's request made perfect gender sense to both. Viewed from Robert Connell's (1995) framework, Tom enacted a masculinity/masculinities practice associated with being a man who, due to his superior gender status, could expect help from a woman. He enacted a form of masculinity that is hegemonic in western societies, including inside formal, for-profit corporations, that allows men to call on women for practical, as well as emotional, support (Fletcher 1999; Pierce 1995; Yancey Martin 2001).

If Betsy had said on the spot, "Why should I answer the phone? Why don't you?" she would have challenged the gender system and its norms then and there, but, as noted above, she would have been viewed as "uppity" and overly sensitive. In failing to reflect before acting on how the workplace and situation were gendered, she acted "like a woman" more than like a vice president. She had enough awareness of the inappropriateness of the gendered behavior she and Tom fell into to confront Tom about it, however, and for him to respond by making the gender order problematic. The result of this quite minor incident was a shift in the normativity of the gender order in that workplace, at least to a degree for a period of time.

Tom and Dining Alone With "a Woman"

This same Tom told a story about a personal policy he had followed for 30 years. Tom traveled often on his job and, when he traveled, met his "host" at the other end for a dinner to make plans for the upcoming day. He was "a Christian married man," he said, and did not want anyone to think he was doing anything improper. Thus, if his host at the other end was a woman, he would not have dinner with her.

> Many years ago . . . when I first started working, uh, I made a rule to myself that I would never have dinner with a woman alone, just the two of us. And, to be quite honest, I said I never want to be in a position where either I would be tempted or anyone could come in and see [us] and develop a wrong impression. So, I have breakfast with them [women], and I would have lunch, but I would never have dinner alone with a woman. Just a rule . . . that Tom [referring to himself] put into effect when he probably just had gotten married. And, suddenly, in this process [the "gender group" process, described earlier], I got an insight . . . that if you go into a new town that rule might, if you fly into [city X], and the director of personnel is a woman, if that director of personnel was a man and you had two days to spend, you would kind of meet with that man the night before over dinner, a long dinner, and get set for the next couple of days to really understand what was going on. . . . In other

words, you would create an informal network with that man. (Field notes, *Fortune 100* company corporate headquarters 1994)

He continued, "I realize now that this discriminates. . . . It meant I never got to know the women as well; that maybe it hurt them in some way." At the end of our interview, I asked Tom if his realization made him change his policy. "Well," he said, "no. I still will not have dinner with a woman; I do not want to start rumors or give the wrong impression."

Tom's policy of not eating dinner alone with a woman coworker frames women as sexual beings, as signs of sexuality, as a temptation to engage in sex. His belief that others might perceive him as sexually interested in another (nonwife) woman prevented him, for 30 years, from having dinner alone with a woman work associate, even once. This story illustrates both gender practices and Tom's practicing of a particular kind of masculinity. Within the gender institution, Tom framed himself as risking temptation by having dinner alone with a strange woman, thereby framing women as temptresses and men as easily tempted. He framed anyone who might see him with a woman companion as apt to assume he was unfaithful to his wife in violation of the standards of a "Christian married man." He held himself accountable to the gender institution, as he understood and had experienced it. Tom assumed that strange women are sexual temptresses, but he did not assume that two men having dinner together would sexually tempt him or be negatively perceived; two men eating dinner alone would not suggest a homosexual relationship, in Tom's view.

Tom's actions showed agency. He followed a policy for 30 years that reflected his personal views on sexuality, women, and femininity. His policy was defensive in preventing him from breaking the norms of marital fidelity, protecting him from temptation, and protecting him from gossip and a bad reputation. It had unintended consequences for women, however, that he was unaware of until he participated in the gender group. His 30-year policy was accountable to certain features of the gender institution rather than the corporation that paid his salary. If Tom had been faithful to bureaucratic ideals, he would have ignored the gender practices that led him to treat women colleagues as women more than as colleagues.

The gender sensitivity group that Tom established could not fundamentally change the gender order in High Tech Corporation. Even as someone now reflexively aware of his gendered practices and their unintended negative effects on women, Tom did not change his policy and practices. For Tom, the gendered practices of the institutions of family and religion were stronger than those of the bureaucratic workplace that ideally rejects gender as a basis for making policies and decisions.

Valerie the Engineer: "Not Gregarious Enough"

Valerie Parks, a 32-year-old engineer, had worked for a scientific research company for three years. With seven years' experience in an architectural firm and degrees in engineering and architecture, she liked doing research. Compared to men at her career stage, she felt she wasn't "going anywhere" and was trying to understand why. Her boss told her she was "not gregarious enough," which she interpreted as insufficiently aggressive about promoting herself. Besides feeling uncomfortable about "getting in the face" of senior researchers to "tell them how great I am," Valerie did not want to stay after hours to make up time spent "visiting" during the day. Although her male peers had less experience and no degree in architecture, they received more research assignments.

> They're younger than me too. . . . I have more experience so I feel I should be doing at least as well as they are, probably better. But I'm not. They're getting all kinds of assignments that I'm not getting. . . . I'm thinking I'm in the wrong line of work. [Why not change companies?] Well, there aren't many companies that do research and I really like research. I think it would be boring to do regular engineering projects.

Valerie's annual performance evaluation showed she complained, as she had done the year before, that her supervisor was not giving her good assignments or enough responsibility.

> He [her boss] said to me, "You're not gregarious enough." [What does that mean?] I'm not aggressive, I guess. I see some of these people [men at the company], they spend half the day going around talking to people. I'm trying to change my views on that; I try to see it as important. I just want to come in and get my work done and go home. I guess I see sitting around talking as a waste of time. . . . They [men] apparently don't see it as wasted time. But it's just not me to do that; I can't go tell people how wonderful I am or get in their face. But that's what my boss tells me I've got to do. He said, "*I'll never think of you* [emphasis mine] when there's a project. I'm not going to assign you. *You* have to do it." [What does that mean?] I don't know. But it's discouraging. . . . I just have a bachelor's degree but so do lots of others. And the guys with bachelors [degrees] are getting lots more responsibility than I am. [How

is that happening?] I don't know; I guess they are just more aggressive. (Field notes, *Fortune 100* company 1995)

When I entered the field to study gender dynamics, a pattern I soon discovered was women's minimal concern about individual men's practicing of masculinity/masculinities but deep discouragement over men's collective mobilizing of masculinity/masculinities (Yancey Martin 2001). Indeed, women seemed reconciled to the inevitability and even normalcy of individual men's doings of masculinity/masculinities. But men's collective practicing of masculinities affected women negatively even when they believed that men intended them no harm. I use the term *mobilizing masculinities* for "practices wherein two or more men jointly bring to bear, or bring into play, masculinity/ies" (Yancey Martin 2001, 588).[1] When women see and/or experience groups of men mobilize(ing) masculinities in ways women cannot frame as working, they often perceive men as acting like men, instead of like vice presidents, chemists, or engineers. When this occurs, they experience a range of negative feelings—for example, feeling exhausted, different, excluded, unsure of themselves, and, as Valerie said, as if they are "in the wrong line of work" (Yancey Martin 2001).

Valerie, who saw junior men "visiting" in the afternoons to tell senior (men) engineers "how great they are," concluded that men collaborate with each other this way as men instead of seeking/obtaining work assignments in an orderly, rational-technical way. She experienced their behavior as gendered, irrespective of what the men may have viewed themselves as doing. She was dispirited by her experiences because she lacked the inclination or ability to act this way and because she felt she should not have to "sell herself" or stay after work to do her job. While Valerie may be framed as making mountains out of molehills, her reactions to the men's practices caused her to doubt her competence and choice of engineering as a profession. . . .

To counteract hidden and subtle but widespread and invidious forms of gender discrimination, the twin dynamics of gendering practices and practicing of gender at work must be made visible in organizational analyses. Practices that often are conflated with work relations and work dynamics have gendered consequences in perpetuating men's advantage and women's disadvantage. Theories and research that ignore gendering practices and the practicing of gender at work mischaracterize workplaces and workers' experiences, leaving their presence and effects unchallenged. . . .

Notes

1. As noted in Yancey Martin (2001), I define masculinities as practices that are represented or interpreted by an actor and/or observer as masculine within a system of gender relations that gives them meaning as gendered "masculine." Behavior can be represented, perceived, or interpreted as masculine because of (1) who does it and/or how, (2) the social and/or cultural contexts in which it is done, or (3) how those in power represent it.

References

Butler, Judith. 1993. *Bodies That Matter: On the Discursive Limits of "Sex."* New York: Routledge.

Connell, R. W. 1995. *Masculinities.* Berkeley: University of California Press.

———. 2000. *The Men and the Boys.* Berkeley: University of California Press.

Czarniawska, Barbara. 1998. *A Narrative Approach to Organization Studies.* Thousand Oaks, CA: Sage.

Fletcher, Joyce. 1999. *Disappearing Acts: Gender, Power, and Relational Practice at Work.* Cambridge, MA: MIT Press.

Martin. Patricia Yancey. 2001. " 'Mobilizing Masculinities': Women's Experiences of Men at Work." *Organization* 8 (November): 587–618.

Pierce, Jennifer. 1995. *Gender Trials: Emotional Lives in Contemporary Law Firms.* Berkeley: University of California Press.

Simmons, Rachel. 2002. *Odd Girl Out: The Hidden Culture of Aggression in Girls.* New York: Harcourt.

Smith, Dorothy E. 1987. *The Everyday World as Problematic: A Feminist Sociology.* Boston: Northeastern University Press.

Reprinted from: Patricia Yancey Martin, " 'Said and Done' versus 'Saying and Doing': Gendering Practices, Practicing Gender at Work," *Gender & Society* 17: 345–350, 361. Copyright © 2003 by Sociologists for Women in Society. Reprinted by permission of Sage Publications, Inc.

From these stories, it is easy to see how authority gets gendered. Although there have been women heads of state, the very concept of the boss, manager, and commander-in-chief are masculine, so that women in the top positions of authority often become "honorary men." Women who are not so high on the power scale do not have the "status shield" of women presidents, prime ministers, and cabinet members. As Yancey Martin's stories show, they have a harder time maintaining their authority.

People's behavior in face-to-face interaction constantly constructs and reinforces these gendered beliefs about leadership ability. When people are evaluated highly, the others in their social situation take what they have to say seriously, follow their suggestions, and defer to their judgment. Those who have low status in the eyes of the others are not listened to, their advice is ignored, and their bids for leadership are simply not acknowledged. Status superiors are granted the benefit of the doubt if they make a mistake; status inferiors have to prove their competence over and over again. In order to be an effective leader, people have to follow you. Men are much more likely to have followers than women. That is how gender inequality gets built into the social production of prestige and power.

The family as a producer of gender. Like work organizations, the family is another prime site for the maintenance of gender differences. In dual-earner families, women do more housework than the men they live with even if they work longer hours or make more money. In most households, women do most of the daily cooking, cleaning, and laundry. Men's primary family role is earning enough money to support the family economically. Married women may earn as much or even more than their husbands, but to be a good woman, they need to physically and emotionally care for family members. Work for the family not only maintains the household, it also reinforces gender distinctions.

The organization of work reflects these gendered assumptions. The "worker" in a factory or in a bureaucracy is supposed to be a man—someone who does not have daily responsibility for the maintenance of a home or care of children. The structure of work—hours, overtime, travel—as well as pay scales and promotion ladders reflect the assumption that the ideal worker is a man and not a woman. Countries with paid parental leave, such as Sweden and Norway, have had to deliberately allocate "daddy days" that the father must take or they are forfeited in order to ensure that at least some of the parental responsibility is undertaken by men and that men will not be penalized by their employers for taking time off to be with their children.

The social construction of gendered bodies. In social construction feminism, bodies as well as behavior are gendered. Bodies have a material reality but their meaning, value, and uses are social and cultural.

Social construction feminism asks, Which women's and men's bodies are beautiful? How are the physical capacities of human men and women enhanced in physical labor and sports? What physical aspects of women and men are valued in different societies? Social construction feminism focuses on the practices that exaggerate and minimize differences and similarities among people and examines the ways that masculine and feminine bodies are literally made through physical labor, exercise, sports, and cosmetic surgery.

Social construction feminism singles out gender as one of the most significant factors in the transformation of physical bodies into social bodies. In Western culture, dieting, breast enhancement, and face-lifts are ways that women have changed their appearance to fit ideals of feminine beauty. Men lift weights, take muscle-building drugs, get hair transplants, and undergo cosmetic surgery to mold their bodies and faces to a masculine ideal. These practices may lead to illnesses, such as eating disorders, and to life-long physical damage. To social construction feminists, the larger damage is to young people's self-confidence caused by these culturally idealized views of how women's and men's bodies should look.

The physiology and anatomy of female and male bodies do not determine the ways women's and men's bodies look and are used. According to social construction feminist theory, the "ideal types" of bodies are the product of a society's gender ideology, practices, and stratification system. Western societies expect men to be aggressive initiators of action and protectors of women and children; therefore, their bodies should be muscular and physically strong. Women are expected to be nurturant and emotionally giving, willing to subordinate their own desires to please men and their own interests to take care of children. Therefore, women's bodies should be yielding and sexually appealing to men when they are young and plump and maternal when they are older.

The ideas and practices that shape bodies do not just produce visible differences between women and men (one major reason for them); they also reproduce the gender stratification system, in which men's bodies are viewed as superior to women's bodies. Sports is a prime cultural arena for the social construction of men's and women's bodies. In sports, men's bodies have an extremely high value, paying off in prestige and income. Women's sports do not pay off as well, even though the bodies of women athletes have physical capabilities most ordinary men and women could not emulate.

Another area in which gender norms affect bodies is health and illness. Here, men are more disadvantaged. Young men put themselves at risk for accidents, homicides, and drug and alcohol abuse, which cut down their life span. Young women with eating disorders also put themselves at risk, but the death rates are not so high. When it comes to risk of HIV/AIDS, young women are becoming even more vulnerable than young men. Both women and men are disadvantaged by physical disability, but gender norms affect them in somewhat different ways.

As social construction feminism points out, there cannot be a gender-neutral or androgynous or "unisex" body in deeply gendered societies, because bodies (and the way they are dressed and adorned) signal a major identity. People want to to know quickly and precisely where to place others they encounter for the first time or in short, face-to-face interactions. Parents of intersexed children are urged to have their genitalia surgically altered to look "normal" at an early age. Children can be dressed in gender-neutral clothes, but parents are warned that they will be mocked and ostracized if other children see their ambiguous genitalia. Social identity is a gendered identity, and is documented throughout life by identity papers and bureaucratic records. We'll never know how much of this gendering is biology and how much is social construction unless we have a degendered society, one that doesn't produce or exaggerate differences through markedly different treatment and expectations of boys and girls.

Gendering children. One of the reasons that gender differences are so deep-seated is that infants are gendered from a very early age. Experimental studies have shown that adults respond differently to an infant depending on whether they are told it is a "girl" or a "boy" (regardless of the actual sex). They offer the child what they think are gender-appropriate toys and are more gentle with "girls" and more likely to rough-house with "boys." Although elementary school teachers today are attuned to the dangers of treating boys and girls differently, they still separate them in class teams and do not encourage their playing together in games or sports. Children who behave in gender-appropriate ways are considered normal; anything else (girls insulting, threatening, and physically fighting boys and other girls; boys who do not like sports and who cry a lot) is considered "gender deviance."

At the end of her extensively researched book on gendered behavior in schools, Barrie Thorne, a sociologist, has a chapter on how adults can deliberately minimize the social construction of gender differences in the classroom and on the playground. This excerpt is taken from that chapter.

Gender Lessons for Adults

Barrie Thorne
Professor of Sociology and Women's Studies,
University of California, Berkley

One of the most hopeful lessons I have drawn from research on schooling is that gender-related patterns, such as boys participating more actively and receiving more teacher attention than girls in classroom settings, are, at the most, a matter of statistical difference. There is wide individual variation in patterns like readiness to talk in class, and classrooms vary in patterns of teacher-student interaction. Comparing kids' gender relations in different kindergartens, Goodenough found that informal interactions in some classrooms were far less male dominated than in others.[1] *Understanding that gender relations are not fixed and invariant but vary by context can help teachers and aides reflect on their practices and extend those that seem to promote equitable interactions.*

Only one of the teachers whose practices I observed was explicitly concerned about sexism. Mrs. Smith, the Ashton kindergarten teacher, told me that several years before when she was teaching at another school, she had students line up by gender because it was "convenient," but the other kindergarten teacher told her she should discontinue the practice because of Title IX. Soon after, Mrs. Smith attended a Title IX workshop and gave more thought to grouping practices. She shifted to having students form single lines or sort themselves according to criteria like what they liked to eat or the color of their shoes, which, she observed, was a useful way to teach classification. Mrs. Smith occasionally talked to her colleagues about their practices. For example, as they were preparing for the opening of school, she noticed that another teacher was making pink name tags for girls and blue name tags for boys. "That's sexist," she told her colleague, who reflected on it and then shifted to yellow for everyone.[2] Mrs. Johnson, the Ashton second-grade teacher, was unconcerned about and somewhat dismissive of gender issues. "They're just kids," she said when I first met her and she learned of my interest in gender. But her practices were far from neutral. The graphics on her walls were quite stereotyped, and she verbally separated girls and boys with repeated admonitions like "you girls should get busy." On the other hand, although I doubt this was her intent, some of Mrs. Johnson's practices did lessen the salience of gender. For example, she organized permanent classroom seating according to principles like "hearing, sight, height" and thereby increased communication between girls and boys. In contrast, Miss Bailey, the Oceanside fourth-fifth-grade teacher, let her students choose their own seating, which resulted in almost total gender separation. And she ratified the gender divide by pitting boys against girls in math and spelling contests. But when she formed reading groups based on ability and organized lines according to the principle of "hot lunch versus cold lunch," her practices drew girls and boys together.

By setting up contests that pitted boys against girls, Miss Bailey tried to harness gender rivalry as a motivation for learning. The resulting group antagonism sometimes spilled beyond the academic purposes at hand. When kids defined "the girls" and "the boys" as separate and antagonistic groups, primarily in the lunchrooms and on the playgrounds where they were freer to shape the grounds of interaction, they created pockets of trouble for adults intent on maintaining order. In both schools a few noontime aides were responsible for a large number of students. These were part-time, working-class women employees, some of them mothers or aunts of the students. Students called the aides by their first names and were more familiar and informal with them than with most teachers. The aides often had to respond to the combustible, angry feelings and the yelling, taunting, and complaining that accompanied scenes of cross-gender chasing and invasion. Several Ashton aides tried to solve problems of cross-gender hassling by keeping boys and girls totally apart from one another, for example, by banning boys to the grassy playing fields and telling girls to stay near the building. Ironically, efforts to maintain order by separating girls and boys perpetuate the very polarization, the sense of being opposite and antagonistic sides, that sets spirals of hostility into motion in the first place. After a particularly difficult lunch period when a small number of boys continually raised a ruckus, Betty, an Ashton aide, told all the second-grade boys that for the rest of the week they had to sit at a separate table so she could "keep an eye on" them. Talking above the noisy eaters, Betty loudly said to me, "This is my boys' table. I made them sit here. They're wild, but I love every one." When I went over to the girls' table, formed by default when the aide pulled out all the boys, one of the girls volunteered, "The boys have to sit over there; they're naughty." "Yeah, boys are naughty," echoed several other girls with self-righteous tones.

Separating all boys from all girls perpetuates an image of dichotomous difference (all boys as "naughty" and "wild"; all girls as better behaved) and encourages psychological splitting. Pressed by cultural ideals to display themselves as "good" and "nice," girls may displace anger and conflict onto boys, defining them as "naughty." Boys, in turn, may project forbidden feelings of vulnerability and dependence when they taunt girls as "crybabies" and "tattletales."[3] More cross-gender interaction, of the relaxed rather than borderworking kind, would undermine these cycles of projection. When girls and boys are separated, it is easier to objectify and stereotype the other gender.

A few researchers have examined the gender-related practices, and thinking, of teachers, aides, and principals, including the ways in which they think about interactions among gender, race/ethnicity, social class, and age.[4] Clearly the same individual may engage in contradictory actions, and beliefs and actual practices do not always coincide. Within one school, as at Ashton and Oceanside, there will no doubt be an array of beliefs and practices.[5] For example, compared with staff who work mostly in classrooms, playground aides may deal with a different sort of gender imagery, with more emphasis on the physical, such as connections between sports and dominant forms of masculinity. Overall, however, school staff may be less likely to engage in practices that polarize boys and girls if they question the notion of "natural" and dichotomized gender differences (the empirical evidence overwhelmingly counters that notion) and become aware of alternative ways of grouping and interacting with students.

Notes

1. Wilkinson and Marrett, eds., *Gender Influences in Classroom Interaction*; Klein, ed., *Handbook for Achieving Sex Equity Through Education*; and Goodenough, "Small Group Culture and the Emergence of Sexist Behavior."
2. This incident raises a topic that needs more extensive research: how teachers and staff influence one another's gender practices. Feminist teachers report collegial experiences ranging from acceptance to hostility. See Sara Delamont, *Sex Roles and the School*; R. W. Connell, *Teachers' Work*; and Kathleen Weiler, *Women Teaching for Change: Gender, Class, and Power.*
3. Drawing on research in schools in England, Walkerdine (*Schoolgirl Fictions*) describes this process. She also observed that teachers tended to adulate boys more than girls, "reading" boys as independent, intelligent, and rational as well

as, and through displays of, "naughty." In contrast, she found that teachers downplayed the good performance of girls by calling them "hardworking," "boring," and "not brilliant."

4. In *Women Teaching for Change,* Weiler provides a detailed account of the backgrounds, experiences, and daily practices of feminist teachers in public high schools, including the contradictions they face, for example, as White middle-class women teaching Black working-class boys. Also see Connell, *Teachers' Work,* and Delamont, *Sex Roles and the School.*

5. Patricia S. Griffin compares the techniques of three teachers of physical education in the same middle school. Two used practices that assumed that boys and girls are groups with separate and nonoverlapping interests, talents, and physical characteristics. For example, these teachers had all girls use nerf or rubber footballs, while all boys used regular footballs, and they instituted a rule that "a girl must touch the ball before a shot on goal is taken." Some girls, in fact, were bigger and played better than some boys. The third teacher, who had attended a gender equity workshop, used inclusive language (e.g., changing "defenseman" to "defense person"), grouped students by ability or randomly rather than by gender, deliberately chose both girls and boys for leadership positions, and interrupted sexist student interactions. See Griffin, "Teachers' Perceptions of and Responses to Sex Equity Problems in a Middle School Physical Education Program."

References

Delamont, Sara. 1990. *Sex Roles and the School.* 2nd ed. New York: Routledge.

Goodenough, Ruth G. 1987. "Small Group Culture and the Emergence of Sexist Behavior: A Comparative Study of Four Children's Groups." In *Interpretive Ethnography of Communication,* edited by George Spindler and Louise Spindler, 409–445. Hillsdale, NJ: Lawrence Erlbaum.

Griffin, Patricia S. 1985. "Teachers' Perceptions of and Responses to Sex Equity Problems in a Middle School Physical Education Program." *Research Quarterly for Exercise and Sport* 56:103–110.

Klein, Susan S., ed. 1985. *Handbook for Achieving Sex Equity through Education.* Baltimore: Johns Hopkins University Press.

Walkerdine, Valerie. 1990. *Schoolgirl Fictions.* London: Verso.

Weiler, Kathleen. 1988. *Women Teaching for Change: Gender, Class, and Power.* South Hadley, MA: Bergin and Garvey.

Wilkinson, Louise Cherry, and Cora B. Marrett, eds. 1985. *Gender Influences in Classroom Interaction.* New York: Academic Press.

Gendering sexuality. Social construction feminism has paid as much attention to how society shapes sexuality as it has to how society creates gendered bodies and patterns of behavior. As with bodies and behavior, social construction feminism analyzes how sexuality is gendered. Sexual "scripts" differ for women and for men whether they are heterosexual, homosexual, bisexual, transsexual, or transvestite. Linking the experience of physical sex and gendered social prescriptions for sexual feelings, fantasies, and actions are individual bodies, desires, and patterns of sexual behavior, which coalesce into gendered sexual identities. These identities, however various and individualized, are categorized and patterned into socially recognized gendered sexual statuses—heterosexual man, heterosexual woman, homosexual man, lesbian woman, bisexual man, bisexual woman. The relationships and sexual practices expected of women and men in each sexual category differ. Transgendered men (female-to-male) and transgendered women (male-to-female) are supposed to have heterosexual desires, although some are bisexual.

In the social construction perspective, the reaction to deviations from established norms of gender and sexuality are manifestations of power and social control. Religion, the law, and medicine reinforce the boundary lines between women and men. Gender rebellion is sinful, illegal, and abnormal. However, most people voluntarily go along with their society's prescriptions because the norms and expectations get built into their individual sense of worth and identity. Even transgenders want to live as "normal" women or men—they pass over to the other gender. The power of social construction is evident not only in the gendering of the bodies and appearance of transgenders, but in what happens to them in work and family roles. Male-to-female transgenders find that the jobs they are hired for as women pay less than those they had as men. Female-to-male transgenders benefit from the patriarchal dividend—men's superior social status. Permanent transgenders have to change all of their identity papers, from birth certificates to passports, to be legally recognized in their new gender. If they are married, they usually have to get divorced. Changing gender is changing one's basic social status.

The social construction of sex differences. In social construction feminist theory, inequality is the core of gender itself: Women and men are socially differentiated in order to justify treating them unequally. Thus, although gender is intertwined with other unequal statuses, remedying the gendered part of these structures of inequality may be the most difficult, because gendering is so pervasive. Indeed, it is this pervasiveness that leads so many people to believe that gendering is biological, and therefore "natural." In this belief, there are two and only two genders, and bodies, sexualities, and personalities are lined up on one side or the other. Intersexes and transgenders are supposed to have a "true gender" buried in ambiguously sexed bodies or cross-gender identities. The belief in categorically binary genders has been legitimated by the constant search for sex differences in the body and brain. Much of the research on the biological sources of gendered behavior compares genetically identified females and males (sex differences) to explain social behavior (gender differences). In biology, the hypothesized source of sex differences has been XX and XY chromosomes, then testosterone and estrogen, and now it is the prenatal "hardwiring" of the brain through genetic and/or hormonal input. Thus, a girl's choice of a career in elementary school teaching and a boy's selection of engineering is attributed to genes, chromosomes, hormones, brain organization, or prehistoric human evolution. Socialization, family and peer pressure, the advice of school counselors, and the gender-typing of jobs are omitted from the picture.

Even though there has been experimental evidence since the 1930s that the so-called male and female hormones are equally important to the development of both sexes, and we know from sex testing at sports competitions that people with XY chromosomes can have female anatomy and physiology, all of the research efforts in the twentieth century were geared to finding clear male-female differences, preferably with an easily identifiable physiological source. Before the intensive criticism of feminist scientists and social scientists, there was very little effort to document how the biases in science both reflect and construct stereotypes of masculinity and femininity in Western societies.

The social construction perspective on sex differences is that genes and hormones have a loop-back effect with physical environments and individual life experiences. There is agency and intention in how we shape our bodies, whether we conform to, resist, or rebel against conventional models of how female and male bodies should look and function, and how men and women should behave.

Critique. Social construction feminism is faced with a political dilemma. Getting people to understand the constrictions of gender norms and expectations and encouraging rebellion against them in daily life will not necessarily change social structures. Couples who have set up egalitarian households and who scrupulously share parenting run into work-scheduling problems. Men are still supposed to put work before family, and women, family before work. Conversely, getting work organizations to hire men for women's jobs and women for men's jobs has not changed gender norms. Women bosses are criticized for being too assertive, while men teachers, social workers, and nurses are quickly pushed ahead into administration.

The dilemma of structure and action is built into the theory of social construction. Socially patterned individual actions and institutional structures construct and reinforce each other. People constantly re-create and maintain the gender norms and expectations and patterns of behavior that are built into work and family structures. They may rebel, but the main patterns of the gendered social order are very slow to change.

In addition to challenging the ideological underpinnings of gender divisions and gendered behavior as natural, long-lasting change of the deeply gendered social order would have to mean a conscious reordering of the gendered division of labor in the family and at work, and at the same time, the assumptions about the capabilities of women and men that justify the status quo have to be challenged. Such change is unlikely to come about unless the pervasiveness of the social institution of gender and its social construction are openly confronted. Since the processes of gendering end up making them invisible, where are we to start? With individual awareness and attitude change, or with restructuring social institutions and behavioral change? Certainly, both individuals and institutions need to be altered to achieve gender equality, but it may be impossible to do both at once.

Summary

Social construction feminism focuses on the processes that both create gender differences and render the construction of gender invisible. The common social processes that encourage us to see gender differences and to ignore overlaps are the gendered division of labor in the home that allocates child care and housework to women; the consensus that only the man is the breadwinner of a family; gender segregation and gender typing of occupations so that women and men do not do the same kind of work; regendering (as when an occupation goes from men's work to women's work and is justified both ways by "natural" masculine and feminine characteristics); selective comparisons that ignore similarities; and containment, suppression, and erasure of gender-inappropriate behaviors and appearances. Deviations from what is considered normal for boys and girls are subject to disapproval and punishment by parents, teachers, and peers. In adults, attempts at gender rebellion are controlled by laws, religions, and psychiatry. The beliefs about gender norms are legitimated by the constant scientific search for sex differences. This search replicates gender divisions by downplaying overlaps and similarities between male and female physiology and men's and women's behavior.

For the most part, people act in approved ways because the whole gendered social order is set up for men and women to feel different and act differently. Even when social institutions change, as when girls are admitted to an all-boys' school or men are hired for a "woman's" job, such as nurse, gender boundaries are not erased. Ways are found for the girls to be distinguishable from the boys (skirts, longer hair), and for the men to do more masculine work (nursing men patients, becoming administrators).

The gendered social order constructs not only differences but gender inequality. Appropriately gendered behavior builds up masculine dominance and feminine subordination. The gendered structure of family work puts more of the burden of housework and child care on the wife, even if she is a high earner in a prestigious career. The gendered division of the labor market reserves better paying jobs and positions of authority for men. All this has been well documented by earlier feminisms. What social construction feminism reveals is how we all collude in maintaining the unequal gendered social order, most of the time without even realizing we are "doing gender." In addition, social construction feminism has analyzed the multiple ways that gender is built into the social structure of all the institutions in a society. In this feminist theory, gender itself is a social institution.

Suggested Readings in Social Construction Feminism

Acker, Joan. 1990. "Hierarchies, Jobs, and Bodies: A Theory of Gendered Organizations." *Gender & Society* 4:139–158.

Berk, Sarah Fenstermaker. 1985. *The Gender Factory: The Apportionment of Work in American Households.* New York: Plenum.

DeVault, Marjorie L. 1991. *Feeding the Family: The Social Organization of Caring as Gender Work.* Chicago: University of Chicago Press.

Fausto-Sterling, Anne. 1985. *Myths of Gender: Biological Theories About Women and Men.* New York: Basic Books.

———. 2000. *Sexing the Body: Gender Politics and the Construction of Sexuality.* New York: Basic Books.

Fineman, Martha Albertson. 1995. *The Neutered Mother, the Sexual Family and Other Twentieth Century Tragedies.* New York: Routledge.

Foucault, Michel. 1978. *The History of Sexuality: An Introduction.* Translated by Robert Hurley. New York: Pantheon.

Gagnon, John, and William Simon. 1973. *Sexual Conduct: The Social Sources of Human Sexuality.* Chicago: Aldine.

Goffman, Erving. 1976. *Gender Advertisements.* New York: Harper Colophon.

Greenberg, David F. 1988. *The Construction of Homosexuality.* Chicago: University of Chicago Press.

Hearn, Jeff R., and Wendy Parkin. 2002. *Gender, Sexuality and Violence in Organizations: The Unspoken Forces of Organization Violations.* Thousand Oaks, CA: Sage.

Kessler, Suzanne J., and Wendy McKenna. 1978. *Gender: An Ethnomethodological Approach.* Chicago: University of Chicago Press.

Kitzinger, Celia. 1987. *The Social Construction of Lesbianism.* Thousand Oaks, CA: Sage.

Laqueur, Thomas W. 1990. *Making Sex: Body and Gender from the Greeks to Freud.* Cambridge, MA: Harvard University Press.

———. 2003. *Solitary Sex: A Cultural History of Masturbation.* New York: Zone Books.

Laws, Judith Long, and Pepper Schwartz. 1977. *Sexual Scripts: The Social Construction of Female Sexuality.* New York: Holt, Rinehart and Winston.

Lorber, Judith. 1994. *Paradoxes of Gender.* New Haven, CT: Yale University Press.

———. 2005. *Breaking the Bowls: Degendering and Feminist Change.* New York: W. W. Norton.

Martin, Patricia Yancey. 2004. "Gender as Social Institution." *Social Forces* 82:1249–1275.

———. 2003. " 'Said and Done' versus 'Saying and Doing': Gendering Practices, Practicing Gender at Work," *Gender & Society* 17:342–366.

Ortner, Sherry B., and Harriet Whitehead, eds. 1981. *Sexual Meanings: The Cultural Construction of Gender and Sexuality.* Cambridge, UK: Cambridge University Press.

Oudshoorn, Nelly. 1994. *Beyond the Natural Body: An Archeology of Sex Hormones.* New York: Routledge.

Ridgeway, Celia. 1997. "Interaction and the Conservation of Gender Inequality: Considering Employment." *American Sociological Review* 62:218–235.

Risman, Barbara. 1997. *Gender Vertigo: Toward a Post-Gender Family.* New Haven, CT: Yale University Press.

Rubin, Gayle. 1975. "The Traffic in Women: Notes on the Political Economy of Sex." In *Toward an Anthropology of Women,* edited by Rayna R. [Rapp] Reiter, 157–210. New York: Monthly Review Press.

———. 1984. "Thinking Sex: Notes for a Radical Theory of the Politics of Sexuality." In *Pleasure and Danger: Exploring Female Sexuality,* edited by Carole S. Vance, 267–319. Boston: Routledge & Kegan Paul.

Thorne, Barrie. 1993. *Gender Play: Girls and Boys at School.* New Brunswick, NJ: Rutgers University Press.

van den Wijngaard, Marianne. 1997. *Reinventing the Sexes: The Biomedical Construction of Femininity and Masculinity.* Bloomington: Indiana University Press.

West, Candace, and Sarah Fenstermaker. 1995. "Doing Difference," *Gender & Society* 9:8–37.

West, Candace, and Don Zimmerman. 1987. "Doing Gender," *Gender & Society* 1:125–151. ✦

Chapter Twelve

Postmodern Feminism

Sources of Gender Inequality

- The belief that gender is fixed and inevitable.
- Heteronormativity—the assumption that everyone is heterosexual.
- Cultural and individual replication of normative gender behavior.

Politics

- Constantly questioning what is supposedly normal about gender and sexuality.
- Demonstrating the fluidity of gender and sexual boundaries.
- Queering—subverting binary gender and sexual categories through deliberate mixtures of clothing, makeup, jewelry, hair styles, behavior, names, and pronouns (he and she).

Contributions

- The concept of performativity—gender does not exist without doing gender identity and display.

- Deconstruction—making visible the gender and sexual symbolism in cultural productions that support beliefs about what is normal and natural.
- Queer theory—challenging the gender, sex, and sexual binaries with bisexuality, intersex, and transgendering.

Postmodern feminism goes the furthest in challenging gender categories as dual, oppositional, and fixed. It argues that sex, sexuality, and gender are shifting, fluid, multiple categories, and that they do not exist without doing identity and display. Postmodern feminism criticizes feminist politics based on a universal category, Woman, and presents instead a more subversive view that undermines the solidity of a social order built on two sexes, two sexualities, and two genders. The introduction of third terms—intersex, bisexuality, and transgender—immediately call into question the opposition of one to the other that the binaries imply. Additional challenges come from queer theory, which claims that three is hardly the limit to sex, sexuality, and gender categories. Ambiguities and border shifts undermine the foundations of biological, sexual, and gender difference. Equality will come when there are so many recognized sexes, sexualities, and genders that one cannot be played against the other.

Postmodernism and feminism. Postmodernism undermines foundational categories by insisting that bodies, identities, and statuses are contingent—time-bound, situational, and culturally shaped. Feminism has been a movement for and about women. If woman and man, male and female, heterosexuality and homosexuality are not clear oppositional categories, then how can we have feminist research and politics? Where will the data that show inequality come from? How will activists fight for the rights of the oppressed if the oppressed are constantly shape-shifting? Some feminists have rejected postmodernism, claiming it undermines the whole feminist enterprise. Others have called for using postmodern ideas to advance feminism's project of challenging the gender order.

Postmodern feminists argue that because it insists that everything is a cultural construction, postmodernism can free feminism from the constraints of gender norms, body ideals, and heteronormativity. Using postmodern methods of deconstructing the ways that cultures produce symbolic social worlds of images and values, postmodern feminism shows how gender, sexuality, and bodies are produced and reproduced.

But gender, sexuality, and bodies are also personal productions. Judith Butler's concept of *performativity* encompasses the process of making gendered selves that reproduce social norms of femaleness and maleness, femininity and masculinity, heterosexuality and homosexuality. This process also produces gendered selves, bodies, and sexual identities. In this concept, you cannot separate the doer of gender from the doing, just the way you cannot separate the dancer from the dance. Self and social are one and the same; one does not precede the other. And there lies the possibility for "gender trouble." Gendering has to be done over and over, almost ritualistically, to reproduce the social norms. But different ways of gendering produce differently gendered people. So, with deliberation, one might create oneself differently gendered, and indeed, transgenders do just that. The question is whether anyone can transgender, degender, undo gender.

The concept of performativity comes from Judith Butler's *Gender Trouble*. First published in 1990, when her ideas were almost incomprehensible, *Gender Trouble* has become the classic of postmodern feminism. Butler ends *Gender Trouble* by arguing for the subversive political possibilities inherent in gender performativity. In the preface to the tenth anniversary edition, she says that she was somewhat too elated about these possibilities, forgetting normative gender's deep tentacles into our psyches. By 1993, she was rethinking other aspects of gender performativity. In *Bodies That Matter*, she takes up the materiality or bodiedness of gender performativity and discusses how doing gender is doing sex and sexuality as well.

Gender, Sex, and Sexual Performativity

Judith Butler
*Professor of Rhetoric and Comparative Literature,
University of California, Berkeley*

If gender is a construction, must there be an "I" or a "we" who enacts or performs that construction? How can there be an activity, a constructing, without presupposing an agent who precedes and performs that activity?

How would we account for the motivation and direction of construction without such a subject? As a rejoinder, I would suggest that it takes a certain suspicion toward grammar to reconceive the matter in a different light. For if gender is constructed, it is not necessarily constructed by an "I" or a "we" who stands before that construction in any spatial or temporal sense of "before." Indeed, it is unclear that there can be an "I" or a "we" who has not been submitted, subjected to gender, where gendering is, among other things, the differentiating relations by which speaking subjects come into being. Subjected to gender, but subjectivated by gender, the "I" neither precedes nor follows the process of this gendering, but emerges only within and as the matrix of gender relations themselves.

This then returns us to the second objection, the one which claims that constructivism forecloses agency, preempts the agency of the subject, and finds itself presupposing the subject that it calls into question. To claim that the subject is itself produced in and as a gendered matrix of relations is not to do away with the subject, but only to ask after the conditions of its emergence and operation. The "activity" of this gendering cannot, strictly speaking, be a human act or expression, a willful appropriation, and it is certainly *not* a question of taking on a mask; it is the matrix through which all willing first becomes possible, its enabling cultural condition. In this sense, the matrix of gender relations is prior to the emergence of the "human." Consider the medical interpellation which (the recent emergence of the sonogram notwithstanding) shifts an infant from an "it" to a "she" or a "he," and in that naming, the girl is "girled," brought into the domain of language and kinship through the interpellation of gender. But that "girling" of the girl does not end there; on the contrary, that founding interpellation is reiterated by various authorities and throughout various intervals of time to reenforce or contest this naturalized effect. The naming is at once the setting of a boundary, and also the repeated inculcation of a norm.

Such attributions or interpellations contribute to that field of discourse and power that orchestrates, delimits, and sustains that which qualifies as "the human." We see this most clearly in the examples of those abjected beings who do not appear properly gendered; it is their very humanness that comes into question. Indeed, the construction of gender operates through *exclusionary* means, such that the human is not only produced over and against the inhuman, but through a set of foreclosures, radical erasures, which are, strictly speaking, refused the possibility of cultural articulation. Hence, it is not enough to claim that human subjects are constructed, for the construction of the human is a differential operation that produces the more and the less "human," the inhuman, the humanly unthinkable. These excluded sites come to bound the "human" as its constitutive outside, and to haunt those boundaries as the persistent possibility of their disruption and rearticulation.[1]

As a result of this reformulation of performativity, (a) gender performativity cannot be theorized apart from the forcible and reiterative practice of regulatory sexual regimes; (b) the account of agency conditioned by those very regimes of discourse/power cannot be conflated with voluntarism or individualism, much less with consumerism, and in no way presupposes a choosing subject; (c) the regime of heterosexuality operates to circumscribe and contour the "materiality" of sex, and that "materiality" is formed and sustained through and as a materialization of regulatory norms that are in part those of heterosexual hegemony; (d) the materialization of norms requires those identificatory processes by which norms are assumed or appropriated, and these identifications precede and enable the formation of a subject, but are not, strictly speaking, performed by a subject; and (e) the limits of constructivism are exposed at those boundaries of bodily life where abjected or delegitimated bodies fail to count as "bodies." If the materiality of sex is demarcated in discourse, then this demarcation will produce a domain of excluded and delegitimated "sex." Hence, it will be as important to think about how and to what end bodies are constructed as it will be to think about how and to what end bodies are *not* constructed and, further, to ask after how bodies which fail to materialize provide the necessary "outside," if not the necessary support, for the bodies which, in materializing the norm, qualify as bodies that matter.

How, then, can one think through the matter of bodies as a kind of materialization governed by regulatory norms in order to ascertain the workings of heterosexual hegemony in the formation of what qualifies as a viable body? How does that materialization of the norm in bodily formation produce a domain of abjected bodies, a field of deformation, which, in failing to qualify as the fully human, fortifies those regulatory norms? What challenge does that excluded and abjected realm produce to a symbolic hegemony that might force a radical rearticulation of what qualifies as bodies that matter, ways of living that count as "life," lives worth protecting, lives worth saving, lives worth grieving? . . .

Notes

1. For different but related approaches to this problematic of exclusion, abjection, and the creation of "the human," see Julia Kristeva, *Powers of Horror: An Essay*

on Abjection, tr. Leon Roudiez (New York: Columbia University Press, 1982); John Fletcher and Andrew Benjamin, eds., *Abjection, Melancholia and Lover: The Work of Julia Kristeva* (New York and London: Routledge, 1990); Jean-Francois Lyotard, *The Inhuman: Reflections on Time,* tr. Geoffrey Bennington and Rachel Bowlby (Stanford: Stanford University Press, 1991).

Deconstruction. Postmodern feminism examines the ways societies create beliefs about gender at any time (now and in the past) with *discourses* embedded in cultural representations or *texts*. Not just art, literature, and the mass media, but anything produced by a social group, including newspapers, political pronouncements, and religious liturgy, is a *text*. A text's *discourse* is what it says, does not say, and hints at (sometimes called a *subtext*). The historical and social context and the material conditions under which a text is produced become part of the text's discourse. If a movie or newspaper is produced in a time of conservative values or under a repressive political regime, its discourse is going to be different from what is produced during times of openness or social change. Who provides the money, who does the creative work, and who oversees the managerial side all influence what a text conveys to its audience. The projected audience also shapes any text, although the actual audience may read quite different meanings from those intended by the producers. *Deconstruction* is the process of teasing out all these aspects of a text.

The concepts of deconstruction and texts derived from cultural studies may sound quite esoteric, but we are all familiar with these processes. The coverage of Princess Diana's death and funeral created discourses about her—as wife, mother, divorcée, and benefactor. The days before the funeral were full of discourses on the meaning of royalty. Her funeral became a public ritual with a subtext on the proper expression of grief. As spectators, we read ourselves into the text of her life, using parallels with our own lives or fantasies about how we would like to live.

Soap operas and romance novels are "read" by women the way Diana's life was; action films and war novels are the stuff of men's spectatorship. Postmodern feminism deconstructs cultural representations of gender, as seen in movies, videos, TV, popular music, advertising—whether aimed at adults, teenagers, or children—as well as paintings, operas, theater productions, and ballet. All these media have discourses that overtly and subliminally tell us something about female and male bodies, sexual desire, and gender roles. A romantic song about the man who got away glorifies heterosexuality; a tragedy deploring the death of a salesman tells us that men's hard work should pay off. These discourses influence the way we think about our world, without questioning the underlying assumptions about gender and sexuality. They encourage approved-of choices about work, marriage, and having children by showing them as normal and rewarding and by showing what is disapproved of as leading to a "bad end." By unpacking the covert as well as more obvious meanings of texts, postmodern deconstruction reveals their messages. We can then accept or reject them, or use them for our own purposes.

Queer theory. Queer theory goes beyond cultural productions to examine the discourses of gender, sex, and sexuality in everyday life. In queer theory, doing gender, body, or sexuality can be subversively nonconforming. What we wear and how we use our bodies are signs of gender and sexual orientation. These can be parodied, flaunted, played with, and mixed up any way we want. Recently, seated in the audience at an academic lecture was a young man with a conventional haircut but with orange hair, one long earring, dark red lipstick, blue nail polish on fingers and toes, a unisex black T-shirt, a yellow sarong skirt of the kind worn by men and women in tropical resorts, and clunky, open-toed sandals. Queer theorists claim such mixed gender displays create a freer social space for gender rebels and transgenders.

Cross-dressing for drag performances, costume parties, Mardi Gras, and gay pride parades are displays of queerness, deliberately playing with gender and sexuality. Drag, in the sense that it openly and deliberately confronts and plays with gender, can be subversive. In the following excerpt, Leila Rupp, a historian, and Verta Taylor, a sociologist, discuss the ways that drag performances can be part of a social movement to subvert the gendered social order. Their conclusions are based on three years of research at the 801 Cabaret in Key West, Florida. They interviewed dozens of drag queens, attended performances, and were photographed in female drag. They suggest three criteria that make a cultural performance like a drag show oppositional and political.

Thinking About Drag as Social Protest

Leila J. Rupp
Professor of Women's Studies, University of California, Santa Barbara

Verta Taylor
Professor of Sociology, University of California, Santa Barbara

[W]e argue that the drag queens are performing protest, are part of the gay and lesbian movement's efforts to make the world a better place for those of us with same-sex desires. Through their dress, gestures, routines, dancing, talk, comedy, and interaction with the audience, they make understandable the concept that people and desires and sexual acts and emotions cannot always be simply categorized into one of two or three possibilities. In making this argument, we are suggesting that cultural forms such as drag performances are political, and that the fact that they are cast as entertainment may make them especially effective in reaching people and changing the ways they think.

Finally, we see the consequences of the drag queens' performance of protest. In a very complicated way, they affirm gay/lesbian/bisexual/transgender identities in contrast to heterosexual ones; but they also break down those differences and assert the common interests of all people. That they do indeed make people think and that they do indeed have the potential to change minds, if not immediately the world, are confirmed by what audience members take away from the shows.

What happens at an evening at the 801 is, we think, a story about more than one particular bar. That is partly because of the sharing of drag queen repertoires across the county, including through such major national events as Wigstock, the annual New York drag extravaganza that ended a seventeen-year run in 2001, and the multitude of local and regional drag queen contests and competitions.[1] The 801 Girls even announced one year a plan to sponsor "Drag Queen University" in Key West. An article in *Celebrate!* describes familiar scenes at Diva's, where Inga and Gugi went to perform:

> It is a place where gender blurs and reality is relative. . . . Straight men clamor to press dollar bills into Inga's cleavage or rush to the stage to offer homage to Vogue, whose flawless rendition of Tina Turner's stage moves makes your heart pound. Lesbian ladies find themselves all fired up by Gugi Gomez's spicy Latina Sensuality and straight women ignore

their dates to steal a kiss and run their hands along Colby's taunt [sic] thighs. Somehow, the talents of these performers take the audience outside of themselves. At Diva's, you can be anyone you want to be.[2]

You can be anyone you want to be—and you are challenged to think differently about what you thought you were.

This is more than the story of the 801 Cabaret in yet another sense . . . we think that what happens onstage has implications for the larger question of what makes certain types of cultural expressions political. Drag shows are entertaining, as we have seen. They attract a whole slew of people who might never venture out to watch, much less join, a gay pride celebration or a demonstration. Yet they elicit strong emotions, even sexual responses, which are likely to have a powerful impact on people. Such visceral moments make change possible. We suggest that what makes drag shows—as well as other cultural performances—political is that they subvert the traditional (in this case, gender and sexual) order, that the performers intend them to have these consequences, and that they build and affirm a gay/lesbian collective identity and also broaden the meaning of community by linking diverse audience members to the performers and to each other. Drag shows help us to see how social movements have an effect, how social movements matter.

Notes

1. See *www.wigstock.nu/*.
2. Kate Reynolds, "The Naked Eye Review: Diva's: A Divine Diversion," *Celebrate!*, April 13, 2001, 2.

Is the circus, night club, or theater the only place gender can be defied? Queer theory argues that we can be gender rebels by queering gender, sexuality, and sex in everyday life. To do this, we have to subvert gender norms for behavior as well as dress. Transgenders, bisexuals, and intersex people who are open about their ambiguous bodies and sexuality are queering the belief that there are only two sexes, sexualities, and genders, and that they line up neatly on each side of the binary divide. These "third terms" disrupt conventional binaries, but queer theory goes further, and suggests that there can be many sexes, sexualities, and genders, and that they will be fluid and constantly "in play."

Critique. If social construction feminism puts too much emphasis on institutions and structures and not enough on individual actions or agency, postmodern feminism has just the opposite problem. Its emphasis is on agency, impression management, and presentation of the self in the guise and costume most likely to produce or parody conformity. Postmodern feminism is mainly concerned with deconstructing cultural productions, neglecting the more iron-bound and controlling discourses embedded in organizational, legal, religious, and political texts.

Social construction feminism's analyses of the institutional and organizational practices that maintain the gender order could be combined with postmodern feminist analyses of gender performance and deconstruction of how high- and pop-culture representations of women and men produce gender and sexual "normality." Social construction feminism argues that the gendered social order is constantly restabilized by individual action, but postmodern feminism has shown how individuals can consciously and purposefully create disorder and gender instability, opening the way to social change.

However, the underlying gendered social order is stubbornly persistent. For example, elaborate traditional weddings are cultural displays that reinforce romantic heterosexuality. When gay men and lesbians have similarly elaborate weddings, do they subvert or replicate their "hetero-gendered" symbolism? When a male transgender wants to be "read" as a woman, she wears a demure dress, stockings, and high-heeled shoes, and often passes successfully. Nonconformers are much more problematic. Someone whose looks are unconventionally gendered, whose body has ambiguous sex markers, and whose sexuality is fluid belongs nowhere in our constantly gendered social world. The big woman who dresses androgynously is kicked out of women's bathrooms. The transgender cannot get appropriate health care. The lady with a beard is stared at openly on the street and can find work only in a circus.

Summary

Postmodern feminism questions all the conventional assumptions about gender, sex, and sexuality, arguing that the categories of "man," "woman," "heterosexual," "homosexual," "male," "female" are performances and displays. Like social construction feminism, postmodern feminism claims that gender is created in the doing—the way we dress, use our bodies, talk, behave. But postmodern feminists do not focus on the social structures that are built up out of repeated gender performances. They argue that gender, sex, and sexuality are always in flux, never fixed. There are no permanent identities, making identity politics questionable.

Politically, postmodern feminists deconstruct the messages we get about gender, bodies, and sexuality in the mass media, popular culture, and the arts. These messages or texts are subliminal sermons on how to be a man or a woman, how male and female bodies should look, and how to be heterosexually sexy. If we can see through these messages, we can rebel against them.

Queer theory goes even further in destabilizing gender, sex, and sexuality. In queer theory, a body can be female and male at the same time, as when a transgender uses hormones to grow breasts but does not have surgery to remove the penis. Bisexuality upsets the heterosexual-homosexual division. Drag queens and kings parody femininity and masculinity. Queering the way you look in everyday life can play with gendered bodies, sexualities, and identities. Queer politics turns what we think is normal and natural inside out by showing how genders, bodies, and sexualities are created for conformity, and how they could be different.

Postmodern feminism is playful but has the serious intent of making us think about what we take for granted—that men and women, homosexuals and heterosexuals, males and females are totally different creatures, and that we can't make and remake ourselves. Politically, its watchword is gender rebellion. Genders, sexes, and sexualities can be as numerous and varied as the imagination can dream up.

Suggested Readings in Postmodern Feminism

Postmodern Feminist Theory

Benhabib, Seyla. 1992. *Situating the Self: Gender, Community and Postmodernism in Contemporary Ethics.* Cambridge: Polity Press.

Butler, Judith. 1990. *Gender Trouble: Feminism and the Subversion of Identity.* New York: Routledge. (Tenth anniversary edition, 1999).

————. 1993. *Bodies That Matter: On the Discursive Limits of "Sex."* New York: Routledge.

————. 2004. *Undoing Gender.* New York: Routledge.

Epstein, Julia. 1990. "Either/Or—Neither/Both: Sexual Ambiguity and the Ideology of Gender." *Genders* 7:100–142.

Garber, Marjorie. 1992. *Vested Interests: Cross-Dressing and Cultural Anxiety.* New York: Routledge.

————. 1995. *Vice Versa: Bisexuality and the Eroticism of Everyday Life.* New York: Simon and Schuster.

————. 1998. *Symptoms of Culture.* New York: Routledge.

Herdt, Gilbert, ed. 1994. *Third Sex, Third Gender: Beyond Sexual Dimorphism in Culture and History.* New York: Zone Books.

Hird, Myra J. 2000. "Gender's Nature: Intersexuals, Transsexuals, and the 'Sex'/'Gender' Binary." *Feminist Theory* 1:347–364.

Ingraham, Chrys. 1999. *White Weddings: Romancing Heterosexuality in Popular Culture.* New York: Routledge.

Jacobs, Sue Ellen, and Jason Cromwell. 1992. "Visions and Revisions of Reality: Reflections of Sex, Sexuality, Gender, and Gender Variance." *Journal of Homosexuality* 23:43–69.

Lorber, Judith. 2001. "It's the 21st Century—Do You Know What Gender You Are?" In *An International Feminist Challenge to Theory, Advances in Gender Research,* Vol.5, edited by Marcia Texler Segal and Vasilikie Demos. Greenwich, CT: JAI Press.

Lucal, Betsy. 1999. "What It Means to Be Gendered Me: Life on the Boundaries of a Dichotomous Gender System." *Gender & Society* 13:781–797.

Mann, Patricia S. 1994. *Micro-Politics: Agency in a Post-Feminist Era.* Minneapolis: University of Minnesota Press.

Nicholson, Linda J., ed. 1990. *Feminism/Postmodernism.* New York: Routledge.

Richardson, Diane, ed. 1996. *Theorizing Heterosexuality: Telling It Straight* Buckingham, UK: Open University Press.

Rubin, Gayle. 1992. "Of Catamites and Kings: Reflections on Butch, Gender and Boundaries." In *The Persistent Desire: A Femme-Butch Reader,* edited by Gayle Rubin. Boston: Alyson Publications.

Walters, Suzanna Danuta. 1995. *Material Girls: Making Sense of Feminist Cultural Theory.* Berkeley: University of California Press.

Wilchins, Ricky Anne. 1997. *Read My Lips: Sexual Subversion and the End of Gender.* New York: Firebrand Books.

Queer Theory

Atkins, Dawn, ed. 1998. *Looking Queer: Image and Identity in Lesbian, Bisexual, Gay and Transgendered Communities.* Binghamton, NY: Haworth.

Beemyn, Brett, and Mickey Eliason, eds. 1996. *Queer Studies: A Lesbian, Gay, Bisexual and Transgender Anthology.* New York: New York University Press.

Jagose, Annamarie. 1996. *Queer Theory (Interpretations).* Melbourne, Aus.: Melbourne University Press.

Namaste, Ki. 1994. "The Politics of Inside/Out: Queer Theory, Poststructuralism, and a Sociological Approach to Sexuality." *Sociological Theory* 12:220–231.

Sedgwick, Eve Kosofsky. 1990. *Epistemology of the Closet.* Berkeley: University of California Press.

———. 1993. *Tendencies.* Durham, NC: Duke University Press.

———, ed. 1997. *Novel Gazing: Queer Readings in Fiction.* Durham, NC: Duke University Press.

Seidman, Steven. 1997. *Difference Troubles: Queering Social Theory and Sexual Politics.* Cambridge, UK: Cambridge University Press.

Stein, Arlene and Ken Plummer. 1994. " 'I Can't Even Think Straight.' 'Queer' Theory and the Missing Sexual Revolution in Sociology." *Sociological Theory* 12:178–187.

Thomas, Calvin, ed. 2000. *Straight With a Twist: Queer Theory and the Subject of Heterosexuality.* Urbana: University of Illinois Press.

Warner, Michael, ed. 1993. *Fear of a Queer Planet: Queer Politics and Social Theory.* Ann Arbor: University of Michigan Press.

Weed, Elizabeth, and Naomi Senor, eds. 1997. *Feminism Meets Queer Theory.* Bloomington: Indiana University Press.

Whisman, Vera. 1996. *Queer by Choice: Lesbians, Gay Men and the Politics of Difference.* New York: Routledge.

Drag

Newton, Esther. 1979. *Mother Camp: Female Impersonators in America.* Chicago: University of Chicago Press.

Rupp, Leila J., and Verta Taylor. 2003. *Drag Queens at the 801 Cabaret.* Chicago: University of Chicago Press.

Schacht, Steven. 2000. "Paris is Burning: How Society's Stratification Systems Makes Drag Queens of Us All." *Race, Gender & Class* 7:147–166.

Schacht, Steven, with Lisa Underwood, eds. 2004. *The Drag Queen Anthology: The Absolutely Fabulous and Flawlessly Customary World of Female Impersonators.* New York: Haworth Press.

Troka, Donna Jean, Kathleen LeBesco, and Jean Bobby Noble, eds. 2002. *The Drag King Anthology,* New York: Haworth Press.

Volcano, del La Grace, and Judith Halberstam. 1999. *The Drag King Book*. London: Serpent's Tail.

Intersex

Chase, Cheryl. 1998. "Hermaphrodites With Attitude: Mapping the Emergence of Intersex Political Activism." *GLQ: A Journal of Lesbian and Gay Studies* 4:189–211.

Dreger, Alice Domurat. 1998. *Hermaphrodites and the Medical Invention of Sex*. Cambridge, MA: Harvard University Press.

———, ed. 1999. *Intersexuality in the Age of Ethics*. Hagerstown, MD: University Publishing Group.

Eugenides, Jeffrey. 2002. *Middlesex*. New York: Farrar, Strauss & Giroux.

Hird, Myra J. 2003. "Considerations for a Psychoanalytic Theory of Gender Identity and Sexual Desire: The Case of Intersex." *Signs* 28:1067–1092.

Kessler, Suzanne J. 1998. *Lessons From the Intersexed*. New Brunswick, NJ: Rutgers University Press.

Preves, Sharon E. 2003. *Intersex and Identity: The Contested Self*. New Brunswick, NJ: Rutgers University Press.

Transgender

Bornstein, Kate. 1994. *Gender Outlaw: On Men, Women, and the Rest of Us*. New York: Vintage.

Bullough, Bonnie, Vern Bullough, and James Elias, eds. 1997. *Gender Blending*. Amherst, NY: Prometheus.

Califia, Pat. 1997. *Sex Changes: The Politics of Transgenderism*. San Francisco, CA: Cleis Press.

Cromwell, Jason. 1999. *Transmen and FTMs: Identities, Bodies, Genders, and Sexualities*. Chicago: University of Chicago Press.

Denny, Dallas, ed. 1997. *Current Concepts in Transgender Identity*. New York: Garland Publishing.

Devor, Holly. 1989. *Gender Blending: Confronting the Limits of Duality*. Bloomington: Indiana University Press.

———. 1997. *FTM: Female-to-Male Transsexuals in Society*. Bloomington: Indiana University Press.

Ekins, Richard. 1997. *Male Femaling: A Grounded Theory Approach to Cross-Dressing and Sex-Changing*. New York: Routledge.

Ekins, Richard, and Dave King, eds. 1996. *Blending Genders: Social Aspects of Cross-Dressing and Sex-Changing*. New York: Routledge.

Epstein, Julia, and Kristina Straub, eds. 1991. *Body Guards: The Cultural Politics of Gender Ambiguity*. New York: Routledge.

Feinberg, Leslie. 1996. *Transgender Warriors: Making History From Joan of Arc to Dennis Rodman.* Boston: Beacon Press.

Gagné, Patricia, and Richard Tewksbury. 1998. "Rethinking Binary Conceptions and Social Constructions: Transgender Experiences of Gender and Sexuality." In *Advances in Gender Research,* Vol.3, edited by Marcia Texler Segal and Vasilikie Demos. Greenwich, CT: JAI.

———. 1999. "Knowledge and Power, Body and Self: An Analysis of Knowledge Systems and the Transgendered Self." *Sociological Quarterly* 40:59–83.

Gagné, Patricia, Richard Tewksbury, and Deanna McGaughey. 1997. "Coming Out and Crossing Over: Identity Formation and Proclamation in a Transgender Community." *Gender & Society* 11:478–508.

Halberstam, Judith. 1998. *Female Masculinity.* Durham, NC: Duke University Press.

Heyes, Cressida J. 2003. "Feminist Solidarity After Queer Theory: The Case of Transgender." *Signs* 28:1093–1120.

Jacobs, Sue-Ellen, Wesley Thomas, and Sabine Lang. 1997. *Two-Spirit People: Native American Gender Identity, Sexuality, and Spirituality.* Urbana: University of Illinois Press.

Kates, Gary. 1995. *Monsieur d'Eon Is a Woman: A Tale of Political Intrigue and Sexual Masquerade.* New York: Basic Books.

Kulick, Don. 1998. *Travesti: Sex, Gender, and Culture Among Brazilian Transgendered Prostitutes.* Chicago: University of Chicago Press.

Meyerowitz, Joan. 2002. *How Sex Changed: A History of Transsexuality in the United States.* Cambridge, MA: Harvard University Press.

Middlebrook, Diane Wood. 1998. *Suits Me: The Double Life of Billy Tipton.* Boston: Houghton Mifflin.

Namaste, Viviane. 2000. *Invisible Lives: The Erasure of Transsexual and Transgendered People.* Chicago: The University of Chicago Press.

Roen, Katrina. 2002. " 'Either/Or' and 'Both/Neither': Discursive Tensions in Transgender Politics." *Signs* 27:501–522.

Rust, Paula, ed. 2000. *Bisexuality in the United States.* New York: Columbia University Press.

Tucker, Naomi, ed. 1995. *Bisexual Politics: Theories, Queries, and Visions.* Binghamton, NY: Harrington Park Press.

Wickman, Jan. 2001. *Transgender Politics: The Construction and Deconstruction of Binary Gender in the Finnish Transgender Community.* Åbo, Finland: Åbo Akademi University Press.

Woodhouse, Annie. 1989. *Fantastic Women: Sex, Gender, and Transvestism.* New Brunswick, NJ: Rutgers University Press.

Woolf, Virginia. [1928] 1956. *Orlando: A Biography.* New York: Harcourt Brace. ✦

Chapter Thirteen

Third-Wave Feminism

Second Wave: Mothers of Feminism	Third Wave: Daughters of Feminism
• Women are oppressed victims.	• Women have agency.
• Activism is hard and bitter work.	• Stick to the big fights: reproductive rights, AIDS, economic inequality, racism.
• Sisterhood is power.	• "Grrrls" are power.
• Identities are collective.	• Identities are individual and complex.
• Heterosexual sex is dangerous.	• Any kind of sex is fun.
• Femininity degrades women.	• "Girlie" culture is empowering.
• Women's rights are the political focus.	• Human rights are the political focus.

Third-wave feminism is an emerging theoretical perspective that is both a continuation of and a break with second-wave feminisms. Third-wave feminism plays with sex, sexuality, and gender: In that sense, it is similar to postmodern feminism. It is inclusive of multiple cultures and men, and so continues multicultural/multiracial feminism and feminist studies of men. But it is rebellious when it comes to radical feminism. It rejects the sense of women as oppressed victims and heterosexual sex as dangerous. It does not valorize mothers or the womanly qualities of nurturance, empathy, and caretaking. Instead, third-wave feminism valorizes women's agency and female sexuality as forms of power.

Third-wave feminist daughters and granddaughters of feminism (often literally, as several are daughters of famous feminists) don't see themselves simply as "women" but as "sexy girls," "strongblackwomen," and "queer dykes." They want to choose how they look. They do not see heterosexuality as a threat to their autonomy, and they experiment with bisexuality. They do not seek feminist sisters but form fluid groups of "riot grrrls" and "guerrilla grrrls"—hip-hop bands and art producers. The "grrr" is a playful parody of a confrontational snarl.

Racial ethnic, sexual, and gender identities are complex and individual—biracial, bisexual, transgendered. No one claims to speak for a like-minded group. In activist politics, third-wave feminists are as apt to make a stand with men as with other women. Lesbians are no longer separatists, but join with gay men in fighting homophobia and AIDS. Black "brothas" join their fight against racism, even as third-wave sisters, daughters, and partners fight with them about sexism.

Third-wave feminism's brief history. In 1991, in the Anita Hill–Clarence Thomas Supreme Court appointment hearings, a Black woman and man were pitted against each other in a bitter and very public fight over sexual harassment. In 1992, in what Astrid Henry argues was a response to this event, Rebecca Walker, Alice Walker's daughter, wrote a piece for *Ms. Magazine* entitled "Becoming the Third Wave." Black women's third wave is a call to claim feminism in the name of their African American foremothers, both those who publicly identified and wrote as feminists, and those who struggled against racial oppression and raised children on their own but did not call themselves feminists.

Subsequently, young White feminists declared their separation from second-wave feminism. They argued that they did not have to choose feminism as a special identity. They grew up with feminist parents and the visibility of women's public accomplishments. They are familiar with feminist theory and research from women's studies courses. Feminism is there for the taking, if they want it, but they do not want their mother's feminism.

White third-wave feminists feel they have to forge separate identities from their feminist mothers and foremothers and find their own political goals. Some of the identities they choose are for fun—"girlie" clothes—and some are to shock their feminist mothers—punk clothes, piercings, bizarrely cut and dyed hair. Heterosexuality is not a threat, and they have bisexual relationships and sex friends. Lesbians often identify as queer and find companions in the gay as well as young lesbian community. "Girlie culture" revels in outrageous sexual openness.

White and Black third-wavers shrug off the remnants of sexism, sexual harassment, and patriarchal privilege. Their battles are against restrictions on reproductive choice, AIDS, racism, homophobia, and economic inequalities. They adapt popular culture, especially hip-hop and rock music, to express their rebellious identities.

Revolt of the daughters. To the White daughters of third-wave feminism, second-wave feminism is a dowdy, outmoded, puritanical mother. Much of their third-wave opposition to second-wave feminism's "vanilla" sexuality and rejection of heterosexuality exaggerates these stances to provide a foil for third-wave opposition. Yet the thrust for independence from critical mothers who created modern feminism is a way of creating a feminism of their own. Without the space to make a new mark, third-wave feminists feel they can only be lesser imitations of feminist icons they grew up with.

In the following excerpt from *Not My Mother's Sister,* Astrid Henry, a young feminist scholar, lays out the daughters' perspectives. She ends with a wry comment on how quickly the younger generation becomes in turn the older one.

Sisters vs. Daughters

Astrid Henry
Professor of English and Women's Studies,
St. Mary's College, Indiana

Handed to us at birth, feminism no longer requires the active identification that it once did.[1] We often don't need to get to feminism through some means—whether consciousness-raising, activism, or reevaluating our personal relationships—because feminism is already there for us.[2] As Barbara Findlen writes in *Listen Up,* "My feminism wasn't shaped by antiwar or civil rights activism; I was not a victim of the problem that had no name.[3] We don't need to create feminism, it already exists. We don't need to become feminists, we already are. Because women of my generation often do not experience feminism as a process—that is, as something we actively choose or help to create—we have a much more ambivalent identification with it. Even for those of us who see ourselves as aligned with second-wave feminism, our sense of owning feminism can still feel tenuous. We own feminism in the sense that it is our birthright, yet in other ways it is not ours. It belongs to another generation, another group of women: second-wave feminists. They were the ones who went through the heady experience of *creating* feminism; we just get to reap the benefits.

In order to get a sense of how different feminism felt for second-wave feminists, one need only look at Gloria Steinem's introduction to Walker's anthology, *To Be Real*. In it, she writes, "Because I entered when feminism had to be chosen and even reinvented, I experienced almost everything about it as an unmitigated and joyful freedom—and I still do."[4] When one compares Steinem's "unmitigated and joyful freedom" with the depressing sense of confinement and curbed independence found in some third-wave texts, it is clear that there has been a definite generational shift in the way that women experience feminism. Perhaps the third-wave complaint that feminism feels constricting—as opposed to feeling like "unmitigated freedom"—should be read as a lament for what we missed out on: entering feminism when it had to be chosen and reinvented.[5]

The tendency within much third-wave writing toward making a clean break with the past, rather than maintaining a sense of connection, may be inevitable given the language used to describe the third wave's relationship to feminism. Conceiving of feminism as a birthright passed from mother to daughter undoubtedly influences the third wave's understanding of and relationship to feminism. It may be that something inherited from one's mother is likely to be rejected, no matter what it is. It may be that a birthright, bound up as it is with one's mother, is unable to produce individuality. Defining what she terms "matrophobia," Adrienne Rich writes of "the womanly splitting of the self, in the desire to become purged once and for all of our mother's bondage, to become individuated and free."[6] Given this matrophobia, identifying with one's mother and with her feminism may ultimately incite rebellion, a desire "to move away," as Denfeld calls for.[7]

In fact, I would argue that the excessive focus on individualism by many third-wavers reveals more than just a preference for liberal feminism. In their descriptions of what this individuality is set in opposition to, one gets the sense that individuality provides a means of resisting the group identity implied by the terms "feminists" and "women." Beyond simply disidentifying with these two identity categories, this resistance might also suggest a desire to break away from their mothers, both real and figurative. In *Fire with Fire*, for example, Wolf describes power feminism, the feminism she advocates, as that which "[e]ncourages a woman to claim her individual voice rather than merging her voice in a collective identity."[8] Wolf gives us a clue about what individuality represents for many third-wave feminists: it is the antithesis of "merging her voice in a collective identity." What is to be resisted is staying (sub)merged in collectivity. Wolf's description suggests that in order to retain—or even to gain—one's identity and autonomy, one must unmerge, move away, break free. . . .

In the third wave's relationship to the second wave, I believe we see signs of the difficulty that individuation poses for women, particularly in the face of a powerful mother figure: in this case, feminism. As one third-wave writer notes, "A daughter fears that she will somehow be co-opted by her mother's desires, drives, and idiosyncrasies and will become the mother at the expense of the self."[9] In both their retaining of the identity "feminist" and in the rare moments when they champion second-wave feminism, third-wavers maintain a connection to their mothers' generation—and often to their real mothers. Like the shared gender identity between mother and daughter, they are not easily able to extricate themselves from the shared identity of feminist. In their frequent attempts to radically break free from the feminism of the past, however, their desire for autonomy and their own individual identity is revealed. They want a shared connection through feminism, but they want their freedom and individuality too.[10]

In her introduction to *To Be Real*, Walker describes a new generation of feminists that seeks to challenge many of the second wave's perceived orthodoxies; she argues for a feminism that includes contradictions and an ability to go beyond political correctness. As she describes the feminism of the previous generation: "For many of us it seems that to be a feminist in the way that we have seen or understood feminism is to conform to an identity and way of living that doesn't allow for individuality, complexity, or less than perfect personal histories."[11] Challenging the perceived dogmatism of second-wave feminism, third-wavers have steered clear of prescribing a particular feminist agenda and instead have chosen to stress individuality and individual definitions of feminism.[12] As Heywood and Drake note, "[T]he ideology of individualism is still a major motivating force in many third wave lives."[13] Individualism as a shared ideology makes for a political paradox, of course, since historically women's liberation movements, like other civil rights movements, have required some sense of collectivity to pursue political goals. Yet this collectivity—or what a previous generation may have termed "sisterhood"—no longer seems available or even desirable. "The same rights and freedoms feminists won for us have allowed us to develop into a very diverse generation of women, and we value our individuality," writes Denfeld. "While linked through common concerns, notions of sister-hood seldom appeal to women of my generation."[14]

Third-wave feminists' preference for defining feminism in their own terms—that is, for each individual feminist to define feminism *for herself individually*—can be seen in the original declaration of the third wave, Rebecca Walker's 1992 statement "*I am* the Third Wave." In calling for a new wave, Walker does not speak in a collective voice. There is no "we" in this statement, just an "I."[15] An early expression of what was to become a common theme within third-wave discourse, Walker's essay does not attempt to speak in the name of other women. Rather, she writes about her own, individual desire to devote her life to feminism.[16]

The third wave's "ideology of individualism" has found its perfect form in the autobiographical essay, the preferred writing genre of third-wavers and one that shares little with the group manifestos of a previous generation. The majority of third-wave anthologies published since the mid-1990s have been structured around such personal essays and, correspondingly, personal definitions of feminism. Such essays can be seen as the first step in the con-sciousness-raising process developed from the earlier women's liberation movement. That is, they provide a means by which to express individual experiences and to analyze those experiences in larger social and political terms. Where the third wave has often appeared stuck, however, is in mov-ing from this beginning consciousness-raising stage of self-expression to developing a larger analysis of the relationship between individual and col-lective experience, culminating in theory and political action. [17]

The third wave's individualistic form of feminism also has an interesting relationship to another second-wave concept: identity politics. As it was conceived by second-wave feminists, as well as other groups from the period, identity politics posits a relationship between one's gender, racial, and class experience and one's political interests. While these identity cate-gories are also routinely stressed in third-wave texts, there is little sense that they can provide a coalescing structure to bring people together, nor are claims in the name of any one group, such as "women," likely to be found in these texts. . . .

In its attention to speaking from an embodied and particular position, one that is always inflected by race, class, sexuality, religion, and educational status, this litany of identity categories reveals the influence of second-wave feminism. Yet unlike the second wave, the third wave does not move beyond these individual assertions of identity to a larger, collective political identity. The Asian bisexual can only speak for herself, not for other Asians nor other bisexuals. For the third wave, identity politics is limited to the expression of individual identity.

Within this "ideology of individualism," feminism has frequently been reduced to one issue: choice. In its most watered-down version, this form of third-wave feminism is appealing to many since it rarely represents political and social issues in ways that suggest the need for collective action or change other than on the individual level. As Elspeth Probyn has noted, it is a "choice freed of the necessity of thinking about the political and social ramifications of the act of choosing."[18] Feminism thus becomes an ideology of individual empowerment to make choices, no matter what those choices are. . . .[19]

Generations

One of the great ironies of writing about generations—particularly when the topic is so contemporary—is that one inevitably finds one's own generation being replaced. In the years it has taken me to finish this project, I have watched the "new" generation of which I am a part become eclipsed by something even more current: the next generation of American youth, variably called Generation Y or the Millennial Generation.[20] Within feminism, a similar replacement may soon be occurring. As one of my students recently reported back from the Feminist Majority's "Feminist Expo," there is now talk of a "fourth wave" of feminism among women in their late teens and early twenties. While admittedly isolated, pronouncements of a feminist "fourth wave" make me recall Rosi Braidotti's comment that "[i]t's strange how quickly one ages within feminism." As she continues, "[H]ere I am: barely 40, still sexually active but having to represent the 'older generation'—how did this happen?"[21]

The inevitability of such generational replacement should be a caution. The mother-daughter trope is an impoverished model of generational relations, one that allows for only two possible points of identification: mother or daughter. Within the familial structure used to describe feminist generations, it is inevitable, then, that those who are now feminism's daughters will, over time, become its mothers—and given the negative image associated with such mothers, who would want such a fate?

While feminism's familial language is, in fact, figurative, the metaphors we use to describe feminism have real effects in the world and in the ways that feminists develop intergenerational relationships and participate in intergenerational dialogue. What does it mean, for example, for "younger" feminists to view "older" feminists—whether they are their friends, lovers, teachers, colleagues, or adversaries—as mothers? When we remain stuck in feminism's imagined family, we lose sight of the myriad relations feminists have with one another as well as the possibility of cross-generational identification and similarities. As Susan Fraiman argues, there "is a difference less between seventies and nineties feminists than between seventies and nineties *feminisms*—a difference that finds mothers and daughters alike more apt in the nineties to boot up than sit in and that calls for ideological rather than oedipal diagnosis."[22] The focus on generational differences has also limited our ability to recognize the various ideological and political differences among and between feminists and feminisms, reducing such differences to the singular difference of age and generation. "Attributing our differences to generation rather than to politics," writes Lisa Marie Hogeland, "sets us firmly into psychologized thinking, and into versions of mother/daughter relations—somehow, we are never sisters who might have things to teach each other across our differences and despite our rivalries."[23]

In arguing against the dominant matrophor used to describe "the persistent nature of maternal metaphors in feminism," some feminists have maintained that we should return to the language of sisterhood as "an alternative to the divisive mother-daughter model."[24] While itself quite reductive, the sororal metaphor at least allows for a language of collectivity, something not seen in much of the "daughter" discourse examined here. Yet while I sympathize with the desire to break out of the mother-daughter dyad, I am not so optimistic that a return to sisterhood will solve the problem. This trope has its own troubled history, the least of which is its inability to recognize differences among women. While the mother-daughter dyad seems hopelessly fixated on the notion of difference—"I'm not like you"—the sisterhood trope seems to offer us the opposite problem—"We're the same."

As feminism has been made into a mother, the qualities that have been attributed to this maternal figure are disturbing, to say the least. While "younger" feminists may wish to depict feminists of the past as "dated and dowdy" in order to represent themselves as new and cutting-edge, such representations of "mother feminism" invariably conform to a conservative image of motherhood: one where mothers are moralistic, asexual prudes. For younger feminists who may not be mothers themselves, representing the maternal in these terms may seem an effective way to make feminism the repository of all that is to be rebelled against.[25] Ultimately, however, this representation only serves to maintain a conservative and ideologically suspect view of motherhood, one we should resist.

Finally, and potentially most troubling, the ubiquitous focus in recent feminist discourse on generational differences between women has ensured that much energy has gone into internal conflicts within feminism rather than external battles against sexism, racism, and homophobia, among other pressing concerns. As such, the focus on feminism's mother-daughter duo has meant that the father, as it were, has dropped out of the picture altogether.[26] As Judith Roof writes:

> Seeing relationships among feminists as generational means adopting the metaphor of the patriarchal family in the throes of its illusory battle against mortality. Our enticement by this model with its chimera of order and all-too-real Oedipal drama focuses blame, energies, and even the dilemma of women's relationships in the wrong place: among women themselves.[27]

Conflict within feminism, even when posited as generational, should not be avoided. Some of feminism's current struggles may very well be among women themselves and thus vitally necessary for feminists to examine in more detail. Unlike Roof, then, I do not think the solution to our current generational impasse is to sidestep the problem of generations in order to move on. Rather, we must continue to examine our generational differences and alliances in order to understand their psychological power for feminists.[28] Where I am in agreement with Roof, however, is that the attention on generational differences has dramatically shifted feminism's focus from external enemies to internal ones. If feminism is indeed like a family, it would be wise of us not to forget its absent father.

Notes

1. As Rose Glickman has noted, "To be a feminist is one among many options for [women in their twenties and early thirties], because they do not recognize it as a process, as a perspective that informs other choices. They interpret the word as an end in itself." Glickman, *Daughters of Feminists* (New York: St. Martin's Press, 1993), 5.

2. On the generational difference regarding consciousness-raising, Denfeld writes: "While CR might have been helpful for women raised in eras where women didn't talk about their experiences with sexism—let alone talk about sex—my generation often finds it redundant. Unlike our mothers, we grew up in a world where issues such as sex discrimination, sexual harassment, abortion, birth control, homosexuality, and relationships are openly discussed. My friends and I have the kind of explicit talk about our sex lives and personal experiences that would give Jerry Falwell a heart attack. . . . Yet my mother tells me such a thing would have been unthinkable in her day." Denfeld, *The New Victorians*, 204–205.*

3. Findlen, "Introduction," xii. See also Laurie Ouellette, who writes, "I am a member of the first generation of women to benefit from the gains of the 1970s'

women's movement without having participated in its struggles." Ouellette, "Building the Third Wave," *On the Issues* 14 (Fall 1992).

4. Steinem, "Foreward," in *To Be Real*, xxvi.*

5. For more on this process of reinvention, see Orr, "Charting the Current of the Third Wave," *Hypatia* 12 (Summer 1997): 32–33.

6. Adrienne Rich, *Of Woman Born: Motherhood as Experience and Institution* (New York: W. W. Norton & Company, 1976), 236.

7. Rene Denfeld, "Feminism 2000: What Does It Really Mean (to You)?" *Sassy* 9 (May 1996): 60.

8. Wolf, *Fire With Fire*, 137.*

9. Madelyn Detloff, "Mean Spirits: The Politics of Contempt Between Feminist Generations," *Hypatia* 12 (Summer 1997): 92.

10. While the writers who are my focus here clearly see feminism as limiting their individuality—feminism as Big Sister or, more accurately, Big Mother—other third-wave writers offer a different understanding of what feminism has meant to them. For these writers, such as several featured in *Listen Up* and *To Be Real,* feminism is described as something which enables them to *acquire* individuality. In other words, feminism is depicted as an empowering force in their lives, allowing them to question society's rules about how they should be in the world. I would argue that this identification with feminism is much more like the descriptions offered by early second-wave writers who describe the process of becoming feminists in positive terms, emphasizing, in Steinem's words, "the joyful freedom" found in coming into feminism. It is interesting, however, that even this more positive third-wave understanding of what feminism has to offer seems inextricably linked to the mother-daughter relationship. See, for example, Sharon Lennon's essay in *Listen Up:* "My mother, who had allowed and encouraged me to be who I was through most of my youth, viewed [my interest in feminism] as a major point of contention between us. . . . In my quest for individuality through feminism, there were a lot of screaming matches between my mother and me." Lennon, "What Is Mine," in Findlen, ed., *Listen Up*, 127.*

11 Walker, "To Be Real," xxxiii.*

12. Adds Paula Kamen, "The vast majority of people of my generation have little patience for anything that seems too ideological, dogmatic, or revolutionary. It smacks of extremist, shortsighted rhetoric from the late sixties. We mistrust such either-or, black-or-white thinking that renders us inflexible to changing conditions." Kamen, "My 'Bourgeois' Brand of Feminism," in *Next: Young American Writers on the New Generation*, ed. Eric Liu (New York: W. W. Norton & Company, 1994), 87.

13. Heywood and Drake, "Introduction," 11.*

14. Denfeld, *The New Victorians*, 263.* Karen Lehrman adds, "the idea of a rigid political sisterhood—of a 'women's movement' with a distinct ideological

agenda—has become not only anachronistic but counterproductive." Lehrman, *The Lipstick Proviso: Women, Sex and Power in the Real World* (New York: Anchor Books, 1997), 179.

15. Representing third-wave feminism as something individual feminists can define individually for themselves is also a key theme in and guiding structure of the documentary *Gloria Steinem, the Spice Girls, and Me: Defining the Third Wave of Feminism*, dir. Krista Longtin, 2002.

16. Walker, "Becoming the Third Wave," *Ms.* (Jan-Feb 1992): 39–41.

17. An exception can be found in *Catching a Wave,* where editors Dicker and Piepmeier explicitly describe their anthology's format as following the second-wave principle of consciousness-raising in order to move the reader from personal experience to theory and action. See Dicker and Piepmeier, "Introduction."*

18. Elspeth Probyn, "New Traditionalism and Post-Feminism: TV Does the Home," *Screen* 31 (Summer 1990): 156.

19. In this regard, I find it interesting that the next books published by Denfeld, Roiphe, and Wolf moved away from policy or academic issues to more personal topics. Denfeld's *Kill the Body, the Head Will Fall: A Closer Look at Women and Aggression* (New York: Warner Books, 1997) addresses her experience training as a boxer; Roiphe's *Last Night in Paradise: Sex and Morals at the Century's End* (Boston: Little, Brown and Company, 1997) addresses HIV, AIDS, and sexual morality from a personal rather than policy perspective; and Wolf's *Promiscuities: The Secret Struggle for Womanhood* (New York: Random House, 1997) addresses the sexual-coming-of-age stories of Wolf and friends. For reviews of these books, see Michiko Kakutani, "Feminism Lite: She Is Woman, Hear Her Mate," *New York Times*, June 10, 1997, B6 (review of *Promiscuities*); and Courtney Weaver, "Growing Up Sexual," *New York Times Book Review*, June 8, 1997, 12 (review of *Promiscuities* and *Last Night in Paradise*). See also Naomi Wolf, *Misconceptions: Truth, Lies, and the Unexpected Journey to Motherhood* (New York: Doubleday, 2001).

20. It's worth noting that the Millennial Generation, or Generation Y, is a substantially bigger demographic group than Generation X and is thus more like the Baby Boom generation in its population size.

21. Rosi Braidotti, "Generations of Feminists, or, Is There Life after Post-Modernism?" *Found Object* 16 (1995): 55. This point is echoed by Jacquelyn Zita in her introduction to the *Hypatia* special issue on third-wave feminisms, where she writes, "Strangely, I have become an 'old timer' as I look back now on more than a quarter century of feminist theory and politics." Zita, "Third Wave Feminisms: An Introduction," *Hypatia*, 12 (Summer 1997): 1.

22. Susan Fraiman, "Feminism Today: Mothers, Daughters, Emerging Sisters," *American Literary History* 11, no. 3 (Fall 1999): 532, emphasis in original.

23. Lisa Marie Hogeland, "Against Generational Thinking, or, Some Things that 'Third Wave' Feminism Isn't," *Women's Studies in Communication* 24, no. 1 (Spring 2001): 118.

24. Rebecca Dakin Quinn, "An Open Letter to Institutional Mothers," in *Generations: Academic Feminists in Dialogue*, ed. Devoney Looser and Ann Kaplan (Minneapolis: University of Minnesota Press, 1997), 179; Louise D'Arcens, "Mothers, Daughters, Sisters," in *Talking Up: Young Women's Take on Feminism*, ed. Rosamund Else-Mitchell and Naomi Flutter (North Melbourne, Australia: Spinifex Press, 1998), 114. Susan Fraiman makes a similar call to return to sisterhood in her praise of *Third Wave Agenda* for "usefully direct[ing] our attention away from mother-daughter tensions and back to sisterly ties. Fraiman, "Feminism Today," 543.*

25. For more positive images of motherhood, see recent texts by third-wave mothers, such as Spike Gillespie's "Sex and the Single Mom," in *Sex and Single Girls: Straight and Queer Women on Sexuality*, ed. Lee Damsky (Seattle: Seal Press, 2000), 357–367. See also editors Ariel Gore and Bee Lavender's anthology, *Breeder: Real-Life Stories from the New Generation of Mothers* (Seattle: Seal Press, 2001).

26. For more on the "father" within feminist familial discourse, see Helena Michie, "Not One of the Family: The Repression of the Other Woman in Feminist Theory," in *Discontented Discourses: Feminism, Textual Intervention, Psychoanalysis,* ed. Marleen S. Barr and Richard Feldstein (Urbana: University of Illinois Press, 1989), 15–28.

27. Judith Roof, "Generational Difficulties; or, the Fear of a Barren History," in Looser and Kaplan, eds., *Generations*, 85.*

28. Here I am echoing Devoney Looser's point in *Generations: Academic Feminists in Dialogue,* where she writes, "we should continue to examine what are already quite entrenched and *perceived* feminist generational differences and alliances. These deserve to be further theorized now, even if they are ultimately cast out of our critical vocabulary." Looser, "Introduction 2," in Looser and Kaplan, eds., *Generations*, 33, emphasis in original.*

* See Suggested Readings.

Strongblackwomen. African American women were an intrinsic part of third-wave feminism from its inception by Rebecca Walker. But rather than rejecting their feminist foremothers, African American third-wave feminists want to be like them—strong, active, political, and confrontational. Second-wave Black feminism was critical of sexist, domineering, heterosexual men, but tended not to reject them, so a return to heterosexuality is not a major part of Black third-wave feminism. More important is to claim an independent political and cultural space.

In the following excerpt from an article in *Signs*, Kimberly Springer, a teacher, writer, editor, and independent radio producer, explores the politics of Black third-wave feminism.

Third Wave Black Feminism?

Kimberly Springer
Professor of American Studies, King's College, London

The term *third wave feminism* as we now know it signals a new generation of feminists. It came to public consciousness, or at least leftist consciousness, in the form of Rebecca Walker's founding of the Third Wave Foundation in 1992, which initially conducted a Freedom Summer-styled voter registration campaign that same year.[1] This generation of third wave feminism credits previous generations for women-centered social and political advances. This acknowledgment, however, took the form of seeming ungratefulness and historical amnesia in Walker's anthology, *To Be Real* (Steinem 1995; Walker 1995). Some contributors voiced a sense of feeling stifled by the previous generation's organizing style and seemed to reduce the third wave's argument to a gripe about feminism as lifestyle dogma. Yet, more recent writings about third wave feminism—particularly Jennifer Baumgardner and Amy Richards's recent book *Manifesta: Young Women, Feminism, and the Future* (2000)—attempt to define third wave politics and mend the generational rift that arose between some older and younger white feminists. Moreover, *Manifesta* at least gives lip service to the role of women of color, lesbians, and, to a lesser degree, poor women in the third wave women's movement.[2]

The wave model perpetuates the exclusion of women of color from women's movement history and feminist theorizing. Still, as it is so deeply embedded in how we examine the history and future of the women's movement, it remains useful for internal critique. As it is used historically and today, it is too static. To serve a wide range of women's needs, it is imperative that the wave model includes women of color's resistance to gender violence.

What to do with our mothers' gardens?

If we proceed with this idea of third wave feminism in its most obvious form, that of denoting generations of feminism, what is the relationship between Black feminists of differing generations? Does a generational rift exist between them? One aspect of the generational tensions between feminists in general is the frustration that older feminists feel at watching younger women reinvent the wheels of social change. Michele Wallace, in retrospect, recognized the irritation of her mother and other women of her mother's generation. In her essay "To Hell and Back," Wallace writes of the late 1960s: "My thesis had been that I and my generation were reinventing youth, danger, sex, love, blackness, and fun. But there had always been just beneath the surface a persistent counter-melody, . . . what I might also call my mother's line, a deep suspicion that I was reinventing nothing, but rather making a fool of myself in precisely the manner that untold generations of young women before me had done" (1997, 11). Other than this autobiographical insight by Wallace, few sources speak of conflicts or distinctions between Black feminists of different generations. . . .

As young white feminists are seeking to step outside of what they consider rigid lifestyle instructions of their feminist foremothers (e.g., stylistic and political), young Black women are attempting to stretch beyond the awe-inspiring legendary work of women like Fannie Lou Hamer, Coretta Scott King, Ruby Doris Smith Robinson, Barbara Smith, bell hooks, and Angela Davis. Their work cannot be matched. When Jones poses the question, "Do you know who speaks through you?" (1994, 26), she poses a rhetorical question that recognizes the significance of history in giving current struggles meaning. . . .

Another aspect of Black women's relationships is how Black women relate to one another. Young Black women writers both highlight the support they feel from other Black women and bear witness to the misguided power that Black women, sharing similar experiences around racism and sexism, exert over one another to wound in unfathomable ways. Competition, vying for status, and degraded self-worth can be Black women's worst interpersonal enemies. Morgan, Chambers, and Jones heed Audre Lorde's call in her essay "Eye to Eye" (1984) for Black women to face how we treat one another and what that says about how we feel about ourselves.

Chambers recalls encounters with other Black girls that, while not unusual, emphasize the ways that African-American women try to hold one another back, from calling Chambers a "sellout" to accusing her of "talking white" because she takes her education seriously. Morgan, in her chapter entitled "Chickenhead Envy," cogently calls out the behavior of said Chickenheads (Morgan 1999, 185–186).[3] To her credit, she is also self-reflective, exploring what so-called Chickenheads reflect back to Black women who are independent and ambitious. Morgan is initiating much-needed dialogue about Black women's culpability in our own oppression and how we oppress one another, especially in the areas of class, color, and sexual orientation. Morgan and Chambers, in fact, disrupt the notion that there is a unified Black sisterhood. While that may be the ideal, these authors point out how Black sisterhood is sometimes far from the reality of our relationships.

For all the emphasis on truth telling and exploring the totality of Black women's lives, the writers explored here are noticeably silent on issues of heterosexism, homophobia in the Black community, and Black women's sexuality in general. Jones and Morgan cogently delve into the history of stereotyping Black women as hypersexual and animalistic, yet there is no discussion of what a positive Black female sexuality would look like. Instead, Black women's (hetero)sexuality is alluded to in their musing on "fine brothers" and dating mores. Black women's sexuality is something to be repressed, except on a surface level of relationships with Black men.

Chambers's only mention of her own sexuality, for example, discusses her fear of an unwanted pregnancy derailing her educational and career goals. This deprioritizing of teen sexuality sheds light on her mother's understated reaction to Veronica's first menstrual cycle. Rather than celebrating her step into young womanhood, her mother makes sure Veronica knows how not to get pregnant. In her later potentially sexual encounters with young men, Chambers can only call on the experiences of friends raised by single mothers, as she was, and friends who were single mothers. Of flirting and potential intimate involvements, Chambers says, "No guy ever said a word to me that didn't sound like a lie. The answer [to sex] was always no" (Chambers 1996, 70–71). While access to her sexuality is by no means dependent on engaging in sexual relations with anyone, blanket denials of her sexual self vis-à-vis young men also deny Chambers access to her own sexual agency. Even an avocation of abstinence would be an exertion of sexual agency.

Given the abundance of writing by African-American lesbians and their influence on Black feminist theory, the lack of attention to heterosexism is a step backward in moving a Black feminist agenda forward. In her chapter on "The F-Word," Morgan declares her allegiance to feminism because she feels feminism claimed her. The most she says about lesbians or heterosexism is a toned-down rebuttal to a man who said she must just need the right man, "as if I'd consider being mistaken for a lesbian an insult instead of an inaccuracy" (Morgan 1999, 42). Yet, in the context of these three texts, examining heterosexuality as a construct is ignored. Instead, within the texts it is a given that they are "straight girls."

The absence of frank discussions about sexuality is an odd repression that barely even acknowledges the authors' own sexuality, much less the variability of human sexuality. This is a noticeable elision given their attentive focus on the complexity of Black women's identities. This omission, or tentative dance, around Black women's sexuality leaves one to conclude that sexual stereotypes have been so debilitating that refuting them only results in the negation of a fuller spectrum for Black female sexual expression. When Black women, for example Alice Walker, Michele Wallace, and Rebecca Walker, frankly discuss their own and Black women's sexuality—be they heterosexual, lesbian, bisexual, or transgender—they run a constant threat of censure inside and outside the Black community through the deployment of degrading, historically rooted stereotypes of licentious Black female sexuality. . . .

In "Toward a Genealogy of Black Female Sexuality," Evelyn Hammonds makes critical note of Black feminist theorizing on Black women's sexuality. In particular, she observes that "historically, Black women have reacted to the repressive force of the hegemonic discourse on race and sex and this image [Black women as empty space] with silence, secrecy, and a partially self-chosen invisibility" (Hammonds 1997, 171). Hammonds later calls not only for intervention that disrupts negative stereotypes about Black women's sexuality but also for critical engagement between Black heterosexual women and Black lesbians to develop a fuller Black feminist praxis around sexuality.

In light of the historical, strategic use of silence around Black women's sexuality by nineteenth-century reformers and the contemporary maligning of Black women such as Anita Hill and Lani Guinier, it is not surprising that Morgan, Jones, and Chambers skirt the issue of Black women's sexuality. The challenge that comes from analyzing their work is, as Hammonds (1997) suggests, the disruption of stereotypes but also the frank discussion of Black women's relationship to their sexual lives through consciousness-raising at all age levels. . . .

Keepin' it real: Old school analysis and new school music

There is no guarantee that the work of Chambers, Morgan, or Jones will reach those young people who need it the most—young people who will not be exposed to Black feminist theory and thought in college classrooms. Though their writing appears in free publications in major cities, what guarantees that a young Black woman on her way to work or school in Manhattan will stop and pick up the *Village Voice* and find Black feminism within its pages? Moreover, these writers' regional focus—they all live and work in New York City—also raises questions about the reach of young Black feminist theorizing geographically.

Ideally, by even daring to write about gender and the Black community, these writers give organizers and educators a springboard. Certain modes of resistance have lost their power; for example, Washington, D.C., marches have become more of a C-SPAN spectacle than the powerful form of radical agitation that the March on Washington was in 1963. Moreover, as we see with some protests against globalization, the state apparatus has become quite adept at shutting down direct action before it even starts. One reason that young people focus on writing and music as forms of protest—not that these are new—is because we need fresh modes for developing collective consciousness.

It is up to those of us with resources and commitment to take these writings and synthesize them into programs that appeal to the next generation, which needs them the most. I propose a project fusing music and intellectualism in much the same way that Public Enemy and Boogie Down Productions did with the resurgence of Black cultural nationalism in the early 1990s. Music is one of the most accessible educational tools left untapped.

How might educators and those who work closely with young people use a compact disc containing hip-hop, R&B, and rap songs along with an educator's guide to readings and discussion questions about gender and African Americans? How many more people would Black feminism reach if, instead of defending against what Black feminism is not, we offered Black feminist visions for the future? . . .

Young Black feminists are not uniform in political thought, so it would be dishonest to assert that Black women still feel the need to apologize for engaging feminist politics. Yet, in linking with the work of feminist foremothers, contemporary, young Black feminist writers continue to explain feminism's relevance to Black communities. Far from reinventing the feminist wheel, young Black feminists are building on the legacy left by nineteenth-century abolitionists, antilynching crusaders, club women, Civil Rights organizers, Black Nationalist revolutionaries, and 1970s Black feminists. They are not inserting themselves into the third wave paradigm as much as they are continuing the work of a history of Black race women concerned with gender issues. . . .

Notes

1. Today, the Third Wave Foundation focuses on inspiring and cultivating feminist activism among women ages fifteen to thirty, who are considered within the demographic of the third wave. Defining the waves of feminism according to generation also raises the question of where women who are older than thirty,

but were children during the height of second wave activism, fall in this generational schemata.

2. Disability as an issue for women is wholly absent from this text, as well as the texts by young Black feminists examined here.

3. A "chickenhead" is a woman who is a materialist, dresses in barely there outfits ("skankwear"), and, according to Morgan, is adept at stroking the male ego (185). She is also calculating, cunning, and savvy when it comes to getting what she wants—all acceptable traits for men in white, capitalist patriarchy but wholly unacceptable for Black women.

References

Baumgardner, Jennifer, and Amy Richards. 2000. "Thou Shalt Not Become Thy Mother." In their *Manifesta: Young Women, Feminism and the Future,* 219–234.*

Chambers, Veronica. 1996. *Mama's Girl.**

Davis, Angela. (1971) 1995. "Reflections on the Black Woman's Role in the Community of Slaves." In *Words of Fire: An Anthology of African-American Feminist Thought,* ed. Beverly Guy-Sheftall, 200–218. New York: New Press.

Hammonds, Evelyn. 1997. "Toward a Genealogy of Black Female Sexuality: The Problematic of Silence." In *Feminist Genealogies, Colonial Legacies, Democratic Futures,* eds. M. Jacqui Alexander and Chandra Talpade Mohanty, 170–181. New York: Routledge.

Jones, Lisa. 1994. *Bulletproof Diva.**

Lorde, Audre. 1984. "Eye to Eye: Black Women, Hatred and Anger." In her *Sister Outsider,* 145–175. Trumansburg, NY: Crossing.

Morgan, Joan. 1999. *When Chickenheads Come Home to Roost.**

Steinem, Gloria. 1995. "Foreword." In Walker 1995, xiii–xxviii.

Walker, Rebecca. 1995. *To Be Real.**

Wallace, Michele. 1997. *To Hell and Back: On the Road With Black Feminism.* Pamphlet. Brooklyn, NY: Olympia X.

* See Suggested Readings.

Reprinted from: Kimberly Springer, "Third Wave Black Feminism?" *Signs* 27, 2002, 1063–1064, 1068, 1072–1074, 1077–1079. Copyright © 2002 by the University of Chicago. Reprinted by permission.

Critique. In a special issue of *Hypatia* on third-wave feminism published in 1997, Rita Alfonso of the University of Memphis and Jo Trigilio from the University of Oregon recorded their email dialogue, "Surfing the

Third Wave: A Dialogue Between Two Third-Wave Feminists." Their interchange showed considerable disagreement over what third-wave feminism is or could be. Trigilio argued that "one must be a post-modernist to be a third waver." Alfonso countered that "the two positions—postmodernism and third wave feminism—are not equitable." On politics, Trigilio said, "No large, distinctive activist feminist movement seems to be occurring out of which a third wave of feminism is rising." Alfonso felt that the critiques of women of color in the United States and also grassroots AIDS activism were examples of third-wave politics.

They both agreed on the disruptiveness of third-wave "sexy sexuality." Trigilio said,

> I went to a dyke punk show the other night. . . . Their antics most likely would have seemed offensive and male-identified to feminists twenty years ago. Two members of the band were hard-core butches, one is a sexy femme complete with low-cut shirt, and the lead singer performed bare-breasted and with a big black dildo hanging out of her pants zipper. She cut it off with a giant knife and flung it into the audience.

But she also noted that there aren't coherent political strategies to evaluate the production of new sexualities.

Alfonso discussed groups like the Riot Grrrls, who go back to the early 1990s. She says they were similar to the Redstockings, radical feminists of the 1970s who disrupted beauty pageants. The Redstockings had much more of a political impact in their critique of heterosexuality, femininity, and stereotypical beauty. They wanted a new view of beauty and femininity valorizing diverse looks and women's intellectual accomplishments. The Riot Grrrls, in contrast, parodied the glorification of "girlishness" revealing it to be a form of "sluttiness." Alfonso says,

> Unlike the Redstockings, who protested by throwing items used in the oppression of women into the "freedom trashcan" at the 1968 Miss America Beauty Pageant, the Riot Grrrls donned and reclaimed, in a perverse manner, the accoutrements of femininity. They made a display of the power that these accoutrements brought to them, and simultaneously mocked this power through parody.

But is this political? Does it have an impact outside of youth culture?

Summary

Third-wave feminism is a young feminists' movement that began in the early 1990s. For Black feminists, who began the movement, it is a search to shape a feminism beyond "our mother's gardens." Black third-wave feminists want to take feminism out of the academy and away from an ideology of women as victims and men as oppressors. While not ignoring Black men's sexism, Black third-wave feminists bring them along in the fight against racism, AIDS, and poverty. They see themselves as continuing the tradition of their strong and resistant foremothers, who were embodiments of women's struggles to survive and raise children in conditions of economic and racial ethnic disadvantage. These foremothers did not call themselves feminists, but to their real and spiritual daughters, they were the true feminists. Young Black women claim these foremothers and name their own continuing battles for economic, racial ethnic, and gender equality third-wave feminism. Moving forward, they adapt Black hip-hop and rock culture for girls as a way of engaging them in feminism.

White third-wave feminists position themselves against and beyond second-wave feminism. They are critical of their actual feminist mothers and foremothers, claiming they are puritanical about sexuality, reject heterosexual relationships, and are reluctant to give up portraying women as victims of men and patriarchy. They grew up with feminism "in the air" and know the canonical feminist texts from women's studies courses. Their own brand of feminism is sexually assertive, bisexual, and transgendered in identities and relationships. They are more likely to call themselves queer than postmodern. Like Black third-wave feminists, they embrace confrontational popular culture, making it into "girlie culture." Music, art, dress, and cosmetics are all turned into elements of "girl power."

Many Black and White third-wave feminists march along with their mothers (and fathers and brothers) for reproductive rights, peace, and global economic equality, but their lifestyle and political views are complexities of racial ethnic, sexual, and gender identities.

Suggested Readings in Third-Wave Feminism

Alfonso, Rita, and Jo Trigilio. 1997. "Surfing the Third Wave: A Dialogue Between Two Third-Wave Feminists." Special Issue, "Third-Wave Feminisms." *Hypatia: A Journal of Feminist Philosophy* 12:7–16.

Bailey, Cathryn. 2002. "Unpacking the Mother/Daughter Baggage: Reassessing Second- and Third-Wave Tensions." *Women's Studies Quarterly* 30:136–154.

Baumgardner, Jennifer, and Amy Richards. 2000. *Manifesta: Young Women, Feminism, and the Future.* New York: Farrar, Straus, and Giroux.

Bhavnani, Kum-Kum, Kathryn R. Kent, and France Winddance Twine, eds. 1998. Special Issue: "Feminisms and Youth Cultures." *Signs* 23(3): Spring.

Bondoc, Anna, and Meg Daly, eds. 1999. *Letters of Intent: Women Cross the Generations to Talk about Family, Work, Sex, Love and the Future of Feminism.* New York: Simon and Schuster.

Braidotti, Rosi. 1995. "Generations of Feminists, or, Is There Life After Post-modernism?" *Found Object* 16:55–62.

Carlip, Hillary. 1995. *Girlpower: Young Women Speak Out!* New York: Warner Books.

Chambers, Veronica. 1996. *Mama's Girl.* New York: Riverhead.

Corral, Jill, and Lisa Miya-Jervis, eds. 2001. *Young Wives' Tales: New Adventures in Love and Partnership.* Seattle, WA: Seal Press.

Damsky, Lee, ed. 2000. *Sex and Single Girls: Straight and Queer Women on Sexuality.* Seattle, WA: Seal Press.

Denfield, Rene. 1995. *The New Victorians: A Young Woman's Challenge to the Old Feminist Order.* New York: Warner Books.

Dicker, Rory, and Alison Piepmeier, eds. 2003. *Catching a Wave: Reclaiming Feminism for the 21st Century.* Boston: Northeastern University Press.

Edut, Ophira, ed. 1998. *Adiós Barbie: Young Women Write About Image and Sexuality.* Seattle, WA: Seal Press.

Else-Mitchell, Rosalind, and Flutter, Naomi, eds. 1998. *Talking Up: Young Women's Take on Feminism.* Melbourne: Spinifex.

Findlen, Barbara, ed. 2001. *Listen Up: Voices From the Next Feminist Generation,* 2nd ed. Seattle, WA: Seal Press.

Fraiman, Susan. 1999. "Feminism Today: Mothers, Daughters, Emerging Sisters." *American Literary History* 11:525–544.

Garrison, Ednie Kaeh. 2000. "U.S. Feminism-Grrrl Style! Young (Sub)Cultures and the Technologies of the Third Wave." *Feminist Studies* 26:141–170.

Gillis, Stacy, and Rebecca Munford. 2003. Special Issue, "Harvesting Our Strengths, Third Wave Feminism and Women's Studies." *Journal of International Women's Studies* 4(2), April.

Gillis, Stacy, Gillian Howie, and Rebecca Munford, eds. 2004. *Third Wave Feminism: A Critical Exploration.* London: Palgrave Macmillan.

Glickman, Rose L. 1993. *Daughters of Feminists.* New York: St. Martin's Press.

Gore, Ariel, and Bee Lavender, eds. 2001. *Breeder: Real-Life Stories From the New Generation of Mothers.* Seattle, WA: Seal Press.

Henry, Astrid. 2004. *Not My Mother's Sister: Generational Conflict and Third-Wave Feminism.* Bloomington: Indiana University Press.

Hernández, Daisy, and Bushra Rehman. 2002. *Colonize This! Young Women of Color on Today's Feminism.* Seattle, WA: Seal Press.

Heywood, Leslie, and Drake, Jennifer, eds. 1997. *Third Wave Agenda: Being Feminist, Doing Feminism.* Minneapolis: University of Minnesota Press.

Johnson, Merri Lisa, ed. 2002. *Jane Sexes It Up: True Confessions of Feminist Desire.* New York: Four Walls Eight Windows.

Jones, Lisa. 1994. *Bulletproof Diva: Tales of Race, Sex, and Hair.* New York: Doubleday.

Kamen, Paula. 1991. *Feminist Fatale: Voices from the "Twentysomething" Generation Explore the Future of the "Women's Movement."* New York: Donald I. Fine.

———. 2000. *Her Way: Young Women Remake the Sexual Revolution.* New York: New York University Press.

Karp, Marcelle, and Debbie Stoller, eds. 1999. *The Bust Guide to the New Girl Order.* New York: Penguin.

Kitwana, Bakari. 2002. *The Hip Hop Generation: Young Blacks and the Crisis in African-American Culture.* New York: Basic Civitas Books.

Lay, Mary M., Janice Monk, and Deborah S. Rosenfelt, eds. 2002. *Encompassing Gender: Integrating International Studies and Women's Studies.* New York: Feminist Press.

Lehrman, Karen. 1997. *The Lipstick Proviso: Women, Sex and Power in the Real World.* New York: Anchor Books.

Looser, Devoney, and Ann Kaplan, eds. 1997. *Generations: Academic Feminists in Dialogue.* Minneapolis: University of Minnesota Press.

Maglin, Nan Bauer, and Donna Perry, eds. 1996. *"Bad Girls"/"Good Girls": Women, Sex, and Power in the Nineties.* New Brunswick, NJ: Rutgers University Press.

Minnich, Elizabeth Kamarch. 1998. "Feminist Attacks on Feminisms: Patriarchy's Prodigal Daughters." *Feminist Studies* 24:159–175.

Mitchell, Allyson, Lisa Bryn Rundle, and Lara Karaian, eds. 2001. *Turbo Chicks: Talking Young Feminisms.* Toronto: Sumach Press.

Morgan, Joan. 1999. *When Chickenheads Come Home to Roost: My Life as a Hip-Hop Feminist.* New York: Simon & Schuster.

O'Barr, Jean, and Mary Wyer, eds. 1992. *Engaging Feminisms: Students Speak Up and Speak Out.* Charlottesville: University Press of Virginia.

O'Reilly, Andrea, and Sharon Abbey, eds. 2000. *Mothers and Daughters: Connection, Empowerment, and Transformation.* Boston: Rowman and Littlefield.

Purvis, Jennifer. 2004. "Grrls and Women Together in the Third Wave: Embracing the Challenges of Intergenerational Feminism(s)." *NWSA Journal* 16:93–123.

Queen, Carol. 1997. *Real Live Nude Girl: Chronicles of a Sex-Positive Culture.* San Francisco: Cleis Press.

Queen, Carol, and Lawrence Schimel, eds. 1997. *PoMoSexuals: Challenging Assumptions About Gender and Sexuality.* San Francisco: Cleis Press.

Rasmusson, Sarah L. 2003. "Third Wave Feminism: History of a Social Movement," In *Encyclopedia of American Social Movements,* edited by Immanuel Ness. Armonk, NY: M.E. Sharpe.

Roiphe, Katie. 1993. *The Morning After: Sex, Fear, and Feminism on Campus.* Boston: Little, Brown.

———. 1997. *Last Night in Paradise: Sex and Morals at the Century's End.* Boston: Little, Brown.

Rosenberg, Jessica, and Gitana Garofalo. 1998. "Riot Grrrl: Revolutions From Within." *Signs* 23:809–841.

Taormino, Tristan, and Karen Green, eds. 1997. *A Girl's Guide to Taking Over the World: Writings From the Girl Zine Revolution.* New York: St. Martin's Press.

Trioli, Virginia. 1996. *Generation f: Sex, Power, and the Young Feminist.* Melbourne, Aus.: Minerva.

Walker, Rebecca. 1992. "Becoming the Third Wave." *Ms.,* January-February, 39–41.

———, ed. 1995. *To Be Real: Telling the Truth and Changing the Face of Feminism.* New York: Anchor.

Walter, Natasha. 1998. *The New Feminism.* Boston: Little, Brown.

———, ed. 1999. *On the Move: Feminism for a New Generation.* London: Virago.

Weir, Sara, and Constance Faulkner. 2004. *Voices of a New Generation: A Feminist Anthology.* Boston: Allyn & Bacon.

Wolf, Naomi. 1993. *Fire With Fire: The New Female Power and How It Will Change the 21st Century.* New York: Random House.

———. 1997. *Promiscuities: The Secret Struggle for Womanhood.* New York: Random House.

———. 2001. *Misconceptions: Truth, Lies, and the Unexpected Journey to Motherhood.* New York: Doubleday.

Zita, Jacquelyn N., ed. 1997. Special Issue, "Third-Wave Feminisms." *Hypatia: A Journal of Feminist Philosophy* 12(3) Summer. ✦

Part V

Do We Need a New Feminism?

Feminism has been proclaimed dead, irrelevant, a movement whose goal of equality for women has been achieved, a Western middle-class movement that doesn't address the needs of poor women and women in developing countries, and a movement that should address all the ills of the modern world. In my view, feminism is alive and percolating in many political activities, even when it is not named. As Mary Hawkesworth said in her criticism of the "burial" of feminism:

> Within the official institutions of state in Africa, Asia, Australia, Europe, Latin America, and North America, feminist projects are ongoing through gender mainstreaming and the creation of "national machinery" for women, such as ministries for women, women's bureaus, and gender equality commissions. The feminist arm of the United Nations, the United Nations Development Fund for Women (UNIFEM), is working with indigenous women's organizations on all continents to safeguard women's lives and livelihoods and to secure their economic, political, and civil rights. Several states, such as Sweden and the Netherlands, have included gender equity efforts among their major foreign policy initiatives. Femocrats work within public agencies in all but one or two nations to structure policy initiatives that address women's needs, concerns, and interests, however contested these concepts may be (Eisenstein 1991). In the aftermath of four UN-sponsored world conferences on women, 162 nations have ratified the Convention to Eliminate All Forms of Discrimination against Women (CEDAW), and women's rights activists in all those nations are working to pressure their governments to change constitutions, laws, and customary practices in accordance with CEDAW provisions. A near universal consensus among nations

supports the Beijing Platform for Action, and feminist activists work locally as well as through the UN monitoring processes to press for implementation of the Beijing Platform.

Feminist NGOs have proliferated, creating a vibrant feminist civil society. Web sites such as "Electrapages" and "Euronet" provide information about tens of thousands of organizations around the globe created by and for women that seek to develop women's political agendas, conduct gender audits and gender impact analyses of government policies, build progressive coalitions among women, deepen the meaning of democracy and democratization, deliver much-needed services to women, and pressure public and private sectors to include more women and respond better to women's concerns. The substantive scope of such feminist work includes subsistence struggles; the politics of food, fuel, and firewood; women's health and reproductive freedom; education for women and girls; employment opportunity, equal pay, safe working conditions, and protection against sexual harassment; rape and domestic violence; sexual trafficking; women's rights as human rights; militarization; peace making; environmentalism; sustainable development; democratization; welfare rights; AIDS; parity in public office; women's e-news; feminist journals and presses; and curriculum revision, feminist pedagogy, and feminist scholarship. (2004, 961–962)[1]

Feminist theories are still being debated and refined. They have changed as the limitations of one set of ideas were critiqued and addressed by what was felt to be a better explanation about why women and men were so unequal in status and power. It has not been a clear progression by any means, because many of the debates went on simultaneously, and are still going on. All of the feminisms have insight into the problems of gender inequality, and all have come up with good strategies for remedying these problems, so their politics are still very much with us.

As there have been from the beginning of the second wave of feminism, there are continuities and convergences, as well as sharp debates, among the different feminisms on how to conceptualize the focus of research and politics. Feminists want a social order in which gender does not privilege men as a category nor give them power over women as a category. As with feminists of the past, feminists today are faced with the dilemma of opting for gender-neutral *equality* or gender-marked *equity*. Feminists who argue for gender equality claim that women and men are more alike than different in their capabilities, so they should be treated the same. Feminists who take the perspective of gender equity focus on the physiological and procreative sex differences between females and males and look for ways to make them socially equivalent. These two perspectives have produced a debate over whether to talk about *gender* or *women*.

Gender Feminism and Difference Feminism

At the beginning of the second wave of feminism, the use of *gender* in place of sex by English speakers was a deliberate strategy to counter prevailing ideas about the universality and immutability of sex differences. What we now call gender was originally conceptualized as *sex roles*—the social and cultural overlay that exaggerates and builds on the biological differences between males and females, with procreative functions the most obvious and universal. Sex roles are the appropriate behavior and attitudes boys and girls learn in growing up that are then applied to adult work and family situations.

As the concept of gender has developed in the social sciences, it has moved from an attribute of individuals that produces effects in the phenomenon under study (e.g., women and men have different crime rates, voting patterns, labor force participation) to a major building block in the social order and an integral element in every aspect of social life (e.g., how crime is conceptualized and categorized is gendered, political processes are gendered, the economy and the labor force are gender-segregated and gender-stratified).

As a concept, gender includes men as well as women. Gendering describes the practices and processes that shape the way organizations are run and people interact with each other. Gender status is one's place in a complex hierarchy of power and privilege. Gender intersects with other major statuses—racial ethnic group, social class, religion, nationality, education, occupation, sexual orientation, age, and physical ability—to produce the social advantages and disadvantages in people's lives. The increasing use of the concept of gender in place of women by feminists has been contested by those who feel it erodes feminist politics focused on the oppression of women (Foster 1999).

Gender feminists contend that sex, sexuality, and gender are constructed in everyday interaction within the constraints of social norms.

The intertwining of sex, sexuality, and gender with each other and with other socially produced categories, such as social class, racial groups, and ethnicity, results in multiple and fluid social identities. These identities place people in the social order and give them the privileges or disadvantages that help or hinder them throughout life. Gender feminists in addition contend that the social order itself is gendered—work organizations slot women and men into different jobs, men's jobs pay better and are valued more, women have much less political power and cultural clout.

Difference feminists argue that the experience of female bodies and sexuality produces a common and stable identity—woman. In this perspective, women's procreative potential enhances their nurturing capacities; their emotional openness makes them good mothers and bonds them to other women. Their sexuality, however, makes them vulnerable to violence and exploitation. Conversely, the social encouragement of male aggression and their patriarchal entitlement encourages the violent potentialities of men's control of women's bodies, sexuality, and emotions.

Gender reform and *gender rebellion feminists* tend to be comfortable with the concept of gender as a social status that is produced and maintained through social processes. *Gender resistance feminists* are uncomfortable with a concept that downplays the distinctive qualities of women—their relationship to their bodies and sexuality, their emotional and nurturing capabilities, their special viewpoint in male-dominated societies and cultures.

These two perspectives in feminism have polarized because difference feminists have contended that a focus on gender erases the category "woman" on which so much of feminist theory, research, and politics is based. However, non-White, non-European feminists have already critiqued the global conceptualization of "woman" and insisted on racial, ethnic, and cultural multiplicities. Feminists writing about men have described the differences among them—bodily, sexual, racial, ethnic, and social class. In addition, a large body of theory and research from gay, lesbian, and transgender studies has provided extensive data on the variety in gendered sexualities.

These perspectives are not as far apart as they may seem. A gender perspective locates the source of women's oppression in the organization of the social world, so that biology and sexuality are socially constructed as gendered. Therefore, biological and sexual sources of oppression are symptoms of the underlying pathology—the gendered social order. Menstruation, menopause, hormonal fluctuations, pregnancy, eating disorders, and propensities to different illnesses are biological phenomena that are mediated by social experiences. Feminists who would not be considered gender feminists have described the social constraints on childbirth and motherhood. Others have laid out the politics of the social formation and control of sexual practices. They all argue that bodies do matter and the way they matter is a social phenomenon. Gender theory adds another layer, claiming that the body is always gendered, therefore female and male bodies are made feminine or masculine by family and peer approval, through mass media representations, and through sports and other physical activity.

Gender feminism and difference feminism both argue that emotions are gendered as well. Empathy and ability to nurture emerge from responsibility for care of others, so men as well as women who do intensive parenting become good at it. Rape, battering, and other forms of sexual aggression are encouraged and discouraged in different situations. Gang rape, for instance, has occurred at fraternity parties where there is heavy drinking and sexual showing off.

Gender feminism and difference feminism merge in analyses of how psyches get structured in girls and boys. *Psychoanalytic feminism* links the division of parenting in the heterogendered Western nuclear family to emotional repression in men and emotional openness and nurturance in women. Both emerge from the primacy of women in parenting. Boys' separation from their mothers and identification with their fathers leads to becoming part of the dominant world of men but also necessitates continuous repression of their emotional longings for their mother and fear of castration by their father. Girls' continued identification with their mothers makes them available for intimacy, but the men they fall in love with have been taught to repress their emotions. So women put their emotions into their children, which reproduces the family structure from which gendered psyches emerge. Difference feminists focus on the divergent emotions of women and men, gender feminists on the family structure that makes them so at odds with each other.

Ideas about patriarchy and the dominance of men over women have become more nuanced. Difference feminists have used the concept of *patriarchy* as a shorthand way of referring to men's control of economic resources, entitlement to sexual services, domination of political processes and positions of authority, and sense of superiority. *Multicultural* and *post-colonial feminists* claim that systems of dominance and subordination are complex—some men are subordinate to other men, and to some women as well. All men may have a "patriarchal dividend" of privilege and entitlement to women's labor, sexuality, and emotions, but some men additionally have the privileges of whiteness, education, and property ownership. A gender analysis sees gender hierarchies as inextricable from other hierarchies, such as economic class, racial categorization, and educational achievement.

In all these ways, *difference* has been expanded from men versus women to the multiplicities of sameness and difference among women and among men and within individuals as well, differences that arise from similar and different social locations. Thus, both equality and equity are needed for a complete feminist politics. It sounds paradoxical, but people have to be treated under the law as equals, and at the same time, the advantages and disadvantages that come from the different social positions of groups and individuals have to be attended to as well. To make them equitable, they may need to be treated differently. These seemingly contradictory goals of feminist politics may result in conflicting strategies of action, but the long-term goal of all the feminisms is a social world where gender means interesting diversities rather than discrimination and disadvantage.

New Directions in Feminist Research

Feminist research now looks at men and women of many different social groups, not just women. It is sensitive to multicultural perspectives and tries not to impose Western values on data analysis. Feminist researchers have developed an awareness of the conflict between analysis and activism. They maintain a critical distance while doing research, although what is studied and the way questions are framed, as in any other form of research, are influenced by a gender politics whose goal is equality for all.

By recognizing the multiplicity of genders, sexes, and sexualities, feminist research is able to go beyond the conventional binaries. The problem is that we need categories for comparison, even while we are critically deconstructing them. We know that the content and dividing lines for genders, sexes, and sexualities are fluid, intertwined, and cross-cut by other major social statuses. How, then, do we do research without reifying the conventional categories?

What we consider inevitable opposing categories are actually variable cultural and temporal constructions of "opposites." Michael Kimmel (2002) told the following anecdote that illustrates the problem of "opposites" very well. When his son was three years old, they played a game called "opposites"—he would tell Zachary a word and Zachary would tell him its opposite. Once, when Zachary's grandmother was visiting, she played the game with him. She asked, "Zachary, what's the opposite of boy?" Zachary took a few seconds to think. "Man," he said.

What are the "opposites" in feminist research? In the past, most feminist research designs assumed that each person has one sex, one sexuality, and one gender, which are congruent with each other and fixed for life. Research variables were "sex," polarized as "females" and "males;" "sexuality," polarized as "homosexuals" and "heterosexuals;" and "gender," polarized as "women" and "men." But these vary, and for accurate data, we need the variations. How do we include intersexuals, transsexuals, cross-dressers and their partners in sexual relationships, masculine women, feminine men, bisexual women and men? We also need to compare women and men across different racial ethnic groups, social classes, religions, nationalities, residencies, occupations. In some research, we need to compare the women and men within these groups.

The main questions are, Who is being compared to whom? Why? What do we want to find out? The goal of our research design needs to be clear before we can decide on our comparison categories. The choice of categories is a feminist political issue because using the conventional categories without question implies that the "normal" (e.g., heterosexuality, boys' masculinity) does not have to be explained as the result of processes of socialization and social control, but is a "natural" phenomenon.

Deconstructing sex, sexuality, and gender reveals many possible categories embedded in social experiences and social practices, as does the deconstruction of race and class. Multiple categories disturb the neat polarity of familiar opposites that assume one dominant and one subordinate group, one normal and one deviant identity, one hegemonic status and one "other." As Barrie Thorne comments in her work on children,

> The literature moves in a circle, carting in cultural assumptions about the nature of masculinity (bonded, hierarchical, competitive, "tough"), then highlighting behavior that fits those parameters and obscuring the varied styles and range of interactions among boys as a whole. (1993, 100)

Multiplying the conventional categories. Multiplying research categories uses several strategies. One strategy is to recognize that sexual and gender statuses combined with other major statuses produce many identities in one individual. Another is to acknowledge that individuals belong to many groups. Therefore, it is extremely important to figure out what you want to know before choosing the variables and subjects for comparison. Samples have to be heterogeneous enough to allow for multiple categories of comparison.

The common practice of comparing women and men frequently produces data that is so mixed that it takes another level of analysis to sort out meaningful categories for comparison. It would be better to start with categories derived from data analysis of all subjects and see the extent to which they attach to the conventional global categories of sex, sexuality, and gender, or better yet, to one or more of the components. However, in order to do this second level of analysis, the sample groups have to be heterogeneous in the first place.

The differentiating variables are likely to break up and recombine the familiar categories in new ways that go beyond the conventional dichotomies. As Linda Nicholson says in "Interpreting *Gender,*"

> Thus I am advocating that we think about the meaning of *woman* as illustrating a map of intersecting similarities and differences. Within such a map the body does not disappear but rather becomes a historically specific variable whose meaning and import are recognized as potentially different in different historical contexts. Such a suggestion . . . [assumes] that meaning is found rather than presupposed. (1994, 101–102)

Developing a critical point of view. There are revolutionary possibilities inherent in rethinking the categories of gender, sexuality, and physiological sex. Feminist data that challenges conventional knowledge by reframing the questions could provide legitimacy for new ways of thinking. When one term or category is defined only by its opposite, resistance reaffirms the polarity. The margin and the center, the insider and the outsider, the conformist and the deviant are two sides of the same concept. Introducing even one more term, such as bisexuality, forces a rethinking of the oppositeness of heterosexuality and homosexuality. "A critical sexual politics, in other words, struggles to move beyond the confines of an inside/outside model" (Namaste 1994, 230).

Data that undermines the supposed natural dichotomies on which the social orders of most modern societies are still based could radically alter political discourses that valorize biological causes, essential heterosexuality, and traditional gender roles in families and workplaces. Research using a variety of gendered sexual statuses has already challenged long-accepted theories. For example, lesbian and homosexual parenting, as well as single-parent households, call into question ideas about parenting and gendered personality development based on heterogendered nuclear families. In psychoanalytic theory, having a woman as a primary parent allows girls to maintain their close bonding and identification with women, but forces boys to differentiate and separate in order to establish their masculinity. The open personality structure of adult women supposedly makes them good mothers, and they want children as substitutes for emotionally distant men. Then how do we explain lesbians who want a child with an emotionally close woman partner?

Not all full-time mothering is emotionally intense, nor is all intensive mothering done by women. Barbara Risman (1998), in her study of fifty-five men who became single fathers because of their wives' death, desertion, or giving up custody, found that their relationships with their children were as intimate as those of single mothers and mothers in traditional marriages.

In work organizations, position in the hierarchy does and does not override a worker's gender. The behavior of men and women doctors sometimes reflects their professional status and sometimes their gender, and it is important to look at both aspects to understand their relationships with patients (Lorber 1984). The men workers in women's occupations and the women workers in men's occupations cannot be lumped in a minority category. The women come up against the glass ceiling that blocks their upward mobility, whereas the men are on what Christine Williams (1992) has called a "glass escalator"—they are encouraged to compete for managerial and administrative positions.

As Lynn Chancer (1992) shows in *Sadomasochism in Everyday Life: The Dynamics of Power and Powerlessness,* only in a strict and unchanging hierarchy are dominants always dominant and submissives always submissive. Using the concept of *sadomasochism,* Chancer analyzes the psychological "chains of command" emerging from work organizations' hierarchies. Since in so many workplaces, the higher positions are held by men, she argues that many women workers experience a sense of psychological masochism and dependency toward their bosses, who in turn are likely to be conscious or unconscious sadists in their enactments of power. However, the superior in any hierarchical relationship, whether a woman or a man, is likely to feel and act the same toward inferiors of either gender. The psychological aspects come from the situation, not the person, because the same person can be sadistic toward inferiors and masochistic toward superiors. It depends on their social location, or *standpoint.*

The View From Somewhere

The concept of *standpoint,* or perspective from one's social location, is an important one in feminist research. Standpoint theory in feminism argues that women's viewpoint must be privileged in order to counteract the dominance of men's perspectives. Whoever sets the agendas for scientific research, shapes the content of higher education, chooses the symbols that permeate cultural productions, and decides political priorities has hegemonic power. Standpoint feminism therefore insists that women's perspective, women's ways of seeing the world, be privileged in the production of knowledge and culture, in setting political agendas, and in doing research.

But is all women's experience the same? Donna Haraway claims that all knowledge is partial, dependent on social location, situated somewhere. She says,

> Situated knowledges are about communities, not isolated individuals. The only way to find a larger vision is to be somewhere in particular. The science question in feminism is about objectivity as positioned rationality. Its images are not the products of escape and transcendence of limits (the view from above) but the joining of partial views and halting voices into a collective subject position that promises a vision of the means of ongoing finite embodiment, of living within limits and contradictions—of views from somewhere. (1988, 600)

Sandra Harding, who did the groundbreaking work on bringing women's standpoint into science, raised the question of fractured standpoints in 1986 and now argues for the multicultural aspects of science. In post-colonial feminist science studies, Harding (1998) notes that where Western feminists critique the exploitative and dominating concepts and practices of technologically based science, non-Western feminists look at the work of African, Chicana, Asian, Indian, Native American, Aboriginal, Maori, and other women and deplore the loss of their knowledge and technology.

Western science should be multicultural. Patricia Hill Collins (1999) is critical of studies of Western women in science that ignore their other social characteristics. She says, "If the absence of women is critical in the production of scientific knowledge, then the absence of racial, ethnic, and social class diversity among women who critique science certainly must have an impact on the knowledge produced. Whether intentional or not, feminist scholarship on scientific knowledge seems wedded to the experiences of White, Western, and economically privileged women" (267). What is needed, she says, is *intersectional analyses.* "This approach means choosing a concrete topic that is already the subject of investigation and trying to find the combined effects of race, class, gender, sexuality, and nation, where before only one or two interpretive categories were used" (278).

Problems of perspective. Standpoint theory argues for presenting the woman's point of view; intersectionality argues for a multidimensional approach. How are we to do both? With an insider point of view? How many insides can we have? With a *verstahen* point of view—putting yourself in the shoes of the subject? That's a lot of different shoes!

In much activist research, the researcher engages in social interaction with the people being studied with a dual goal: data that accurately reflects their lives and information for political action to benefit them. Such research is often conducted by participant observation, where the researcher becomes a member of the group being researched, or by in-depth interviewing, which sometimes involves a sharing of experiences. The advantages are well-known—insightful understanding of the perspectives, experiences, and meaning of others, and a basis for action that will make a difference in their lives. The problems are perhaps less well known.

First, there is the problem of the *insider* and the *outsider*. If you are a member of the group, you don't have to study it—just relate your own experiences. And for some feminists, that is what feminist research should be.

But what group are you a member of? Everyone knows that people differ by social class (past and present), where you live, where you were born, what language you speak, what culture you are comfortable with, what religion and politics you practice, what your sexual orientation and sexual experiences have been, and how your body functions, so your membership in any one group is affected by your simultaneous membership in other groups. Reliance on insider knowledge can get severely shaken if it is assumed that women understand all other women because they are all women.

If you are not a member of the group, but an outsider, there is the problem of trust and betrayal. Even if you were honest and above board about your role as a researcher, and you are careful to preserve anonymity, people may be hurt when you publish your findings—especially if you are critical. In asking whether one can be a reflexive participant observer and a true feminist, Judith Stacey honestly appraised the advantages and disadvantages of ethnography and her own use and response to intensive interviewing and involvement with her respondents' lives. She discussed the "delusion of alliance" and the "delusion of separateness." She says:

[E]thnographic method appears to (and often does) place the research and her informants in a collaborative, reciprocal quest for understanding, but the research product is ultimately that of the researcher, however modified or influenced by informants. With very rare exceptions, it is the researcher who narrates, who "authors" the ethnography. In the last instance an ethnography is a written document structured primarily by a researcher's purposes, offering a researcher's interpretations, registered in a researcher's voice. (1988, 23)

I think it would be an unfortunate irony if feminists, in an attempt to shrug off the role of the male-oriented Other, felt comfortable only researching women like themselves, and only with methods that put them in their subject's shoes. To do any kind of research—sociology or anthropology or history or literary or art criticism—the scholar has to maintain some distance, has to closely examine the contradictions in data because they are likely to be crucially informative, and has to be able to challenge respondents' voices with voices from other worlds (Koskoff 1993). Sometimes you have to be able to look at the familiar world as if you came from another planet. As Dorothy Smith says, we cannot take the everyday world for granted but must see it "as problematic, where the everyday world is taken to be various and differentiated matrices of experience—the place from which the consciousness of the knower begins" (1990, 173).

When researchers construct the patterns of social reality from everyday experiences of subjects, they do it from the standpoint of their own social realities. Even if the researcher and the subject are the same gender, they are not likely to come from the same social location. And even if they did, the social researcher still needs a bifurcated consciousness which can bring to bear a somewhat abstracted larger social reality (the social relations of capitalism, for instance) on the patterns and experience of the everyday world.

Feminist Politics and Multiple Identities[2]

The problem of standpoint in feminist research is mirrored by the problem of standpoint in feminist politics. Feminism has been a movement that is by, for, and about women. The unity of this identity—*woman*—has been challenged by recent feminist theory, research, and politics. Socialist, multicultural, and post-colonial feminists have shown how women are divided by ethnic allegiances and social class differences. Postmodern critiques have destabilized concepts of permanent identity and sense of collectivity. Degendering and mainstreaming focuses on men as well as women.

Theories aside, the lived reality of people's experiences is that they belong to many different groups and have multiple identities. Being a woman may be a major social identity, but it may not be a rallying point for everyone for political activity. Iris Marion Young (1994) argues that gender, racial category, and class are *series*—comparatively passive collectives grouped by their similar social conditioning. These locations in social structures may or may not become significant sources of self-identification or political action.

The shift in focus from women in the unitary sense to women as multicultural creates a tension between *gender visibility*—attention to the ways in which societies, cultures, groups, and individuals are gendered and how this process comes about and is maintained through the practices of institutions, cultures, groups, and individuals—and *gender diversity*—attention to the ways in which women and men, boys and girls are not homogeneous groups but intersected by cultures, religions, ethnicities, social class, sexualities, bodies, and so on.

The effect of focusing on gender visibility is to foreground women's experiences, as standpoint feminism has urged. The effect of focusing on gender diversity is to incorporate diverse women's experiences, as multicultural feminism has urged. Diverse and intersecting perspectives can be both a source of knowledge and a source of political activism.

Can we recognize gender diversity and also continue to rally around the flag of womanhood? Judith Butler says, "Surely, it must be possible both to use the term, to use it tactically . . . and also to subject the term to a critique which interrogates the exclusionary operations and differential power-relations that construct and delimit feminist invocations of 'women' " (1993, 29). Is it possible to conceptualize Woman as a stable category and to use the experiences of women with varying other important identities at the same time? There may be a common core to women's experiences, but feminist politics cannot ignore the input from social statuses that may be as important as gender. Therefore, it is not enough to take political action using only a woman's point of view;

feminist politics has to include the experiences of women of different social classes, educational levels, racial, ethnic, and religious groups, marital and parental statuses, sexual orientations, ages, and degrees of able bodiedness. These intersecting group memberships and multiple identities are not a weakness in the feminist movement, but a strength. If they become a basis for national and international coalitions, cross-cutting group memberships and multiple statuses can be a powerful feminist weapon.

Feminist identity politics. Feminists throughout the world are confronted by many cleavages, which have created conflicts over coalitions and political strategies. The boundaries of who belongs with whom shift depending on what identity you are talking about and what the political issue is. And since many of these identities emerge from life experiences, the identities themselves shift over time, and people may have different combinations of identities at different times in their lives. Which identity is most salient may depend on their own situation or on the politics of their countries, their political affiliation, their communities. So how can we have a feminist politics?

Some feminist politics are universal, understood by women everywhere, and some are specific to women of different racial and ethnic groups. In the United States, African American women, Latinas, and Asian American women all experience racial prejudice in social encounters, but they have markedly different experiences in schools and in the job market, and so their strategies for action have to be different.

Another problematic issue for gender politics is that sometimes the discrimination disadvantaged women experience is specific to them as women, and at other times they share class, racial, and ethnic oppression with their men. Since class, racial, ethnic, and gender identity are intertwined, political unity with the men of the same group can severely undermine a consciousness of their oppression as women. Where, then, do a woman's loyalty, identification, and politics lie? It may not be with the men of their own racial or ethnic group, who may be oppressive to their own women because of a traditional patriarchal culture or because they themselves are oppressed by men at the top of the pyramid. Men's and women's standpoints within the same group may differ considerably, even though they may share a sense of injustice from their mutual racial or ethnic status.

Feminist multidimensional political action goes beyond the sources of oppression that are specific to women. Without giving up the fight against sexual exploitation and violence against women, feminists have had to search for ways to open access to economic resources, educational opportunities, and political power. We have focused on gender when it is necessary, but we have also had to recognize that women of different classes may not be interested in political action because their statuses are superior, or because they feel they have too much lose from changes in the status quo. In some situations, it may be necessary to reach out to subordinated men who are similarly oppressed and who want similar changes in the redistribution of resources and recognition of distinct cultures.

Politics of identification. Rather than identity politics, where membership in a particular social category is required for activism, Susan Hekman argues for a "politics of identification" (2000, 304–305). She advocates identification with political causes and activism for political goals without regard to personal status. But this kind of inclusion requires not only that "outsiders" see others' causes as important to fight for, but that the "insiders" accept them as legitimate political actors. Sylvia Walby says,

> Working with those who are 'different' is hard if the political form employed is based on empathy rather than debate, friendship rather than alliances, community rather than association, consensual agreement rather than majority voting. Political differences in this context can become highly emotive, fragmenting friendships, communities and the political project itself. (2000, 198)

She continues,

> Politics across difference demands . . . the acceptance of greater difference within the organization, collegiality rather than friendship, respect rather than empathy, voting rather than consensus. That is, a politics based on appeal to principles rather than to identity. It is this which facilitates transformation, rather than an embrace of existing identity. (2000, 199)

This thought was stated more bluntly by Dale Bauer and Priscilla Wald in the millennial issue of *Signs*:

> Coalition politics does not offer a united front of feminism. . . . The differences are always in view and always potentially disruptive. . . . So when we coalesce—come together—we have to give up any secure sense of self. We merge, and we change. And we cannot count on a supportive environment. A coalition comes together to get some work done, not to nurture. (2000, 1300)

The structure of feminist politics. There is a structure to feminist politics that takes us from identity politics at the grass roots level to coalitions of people of diverse identities in nongovernmental organizations. NGOs have the potential to work with feminists coming from different political groups who enter state, national, and international governments and bureaucracies.

At the grassroots level, political action centering in primary identities makes particular injustices visible and also forms a basis for organizing around those identities. Thus, poor women mobilize around their traditional roles as wives and mothers to fight for better living and working conditions and improved health care for their families. As Christine Bose and Edna Acosta-Belén note, in Latin America and the Caribbean, women organize

> collective meals, health cooperatives, mothers' clubs, neighborhood water-rights groups, or their own textile and craft collectives. . . . Thus, rather than *privatizing* their survival problems, these women *collectivize* them and form social-change groups based on social reproduction concerns. In these new terms, the political discourse and arena of struggle is . . . moral persuasion to place demands on the state for rights related to family survival. (1995, 28)

In the process, they define their needs not as family or gender issues, but as citizenship claims on states.

At this level, identities are primary, problems and solutions are localized. But since social problems of subsistence, shelter, and work opportunities in the face of economic restructuring are global, the collective solutions can become the basis for transcommunity and transnational organizing, and for a global redefinition of what it means to be a citizen.

At the next level, NGOs are formed to sustain the grassroots collective political action and problem-solving tactics, to bring in people with varied skills, and to raise money. The central identities of gender or racial/ethnic group or class may blur as middle-class administrators and credentialed professionals join. The central focus shifts from identity politics to specific political issues, such as legal protections and rights or to specific social problems, such as battering, rape, or prostitution. A focus might be the needs of women in a particular area growing out of historic events, such as the Network of East West Women, a coalition of women in East European former Soviet republics and women in the United States. Within the geographic area, they have focused on legal issues, reproductive rights, and transnational prostitution. Women Living Under Muslim Laws is an international informational and support network of women living in diverse Muslim communities. Through this network, women share knowledge of differing interpretations and applications of *shari'ah,* Islamic rules of conduct and personal status laws. The goals are exchange of knowledge and links to other women in similar situations in common projects as well as a base for political action (Shaheed 1994).

NGOs encourage data collection by feminist researchers and use feminist academics' theories and structural analyses. There is often reciprocal feedback between members of NGOs and feminist academics and researchers, with activism and the search for viable solutions to problems suggesting research designs and correcting theories and analyses.

At the next level, feminists start infiltrating governments and governmental agencies—local, state, national, and international—where they can showcase feminist issues and pressure for equal representation of women. A positive outcome of feminists within a government is South Africa's gender-egalitarian constitution (Seidman 1999).

When feminists work within established governments and bureaucracies, the thrust of their feminism will necessarily be diluted in the course of trying to gain allies to pass laws and promulgate policies. Any critique of the establishment has to be moderated, since they are now part of it. The searchlight on practices and problems that need changing floats as events reorder priorities, as happened after September 11 in the United States. Feminists within governments may not be as radical or critical as feminists at the grassroots or NGO levels, but they come in with a different perspective, and they can be reached by feminists on the outside (Eisenstein 1996).

In my view, the most productive international feminist work is done at the NGO level, where problem solving and political action can be focused, but not so narrowly as to preclude useful coalitions. Simultaneous memberships in groups can bring those groups together in what Nira Yuval-Davis (1997) calls *transversal politics,* where borders are crossed and boundaries are redrawn to create coalitions and bridge divides. Members of NGOs can work with members of grassroots collectives and government organizations as bridges to each and between them.

Some of the most powerful NGOs have been what Valentine Moghadam (2000) calls *transnational feminist networks*—"organizations linking women in developing and developed regions and addressing social, economic and foreign policy issues in supra-national terms" (59). They are, she says, "a new organizational and a new form of collective action in an era of globalization" (58). Some of the networks she discusses in her article in *International Sociology* are DAWN (Development Alternatives with Women for a New Era), which has branches in the Caribbean, Latin America, and South America; WIDE (Women in Development in Europe), based in Brussels; and WLUML (Women Living Under Muslim Laws), whose members live in Muslim countries or practice Islam in non-Muslim countries.

It is here that multiple identities become so valuable. Multiple identities encourage cross-fertilization of ideas and tactics. Multiple standpoints recognize differences but work with commonalities.

In short, what seems like fragmentation becomes, with the pressure of coalition politics, a multi-voiced, multi-branched, intertwined, and dense feminist political movement growing in force. So how can we live with diversity and still do feminist political action? We can reach out to people who are similarly oppressed and who want similar changes, enlist subordinated and sympathetic men in feminist political action, and attack the whole matrix of domination, not just women's part of it.

A New Feminism

I raised the question earlier of whether we need a new feminism for the twenty-first century. It is clear from the trends of the last twenty years that new dimensions of feminist theory and research have already emerged, and that a new feminism is already here. It is in the diverse perspectives of situated knowledges. It is in the multiplicities of research categories of sex, sexuality, and gender. It is in the politics of shifting identities and global coalitions.

The future strength of the feminist movement lies in the variety and density of multiple identities—not just Woman. The primary identity of feminists may be gender, racial ethnic group, religion, social class, or sexual orientation in some combination. The focus of feminist work may be peace, sexual violence, political parity, economic opportunity, or one of many proliferating causes. The beneficiaries may be one specific oppressed group or many. Feminist identity may be way down the list, implicit, or even masked, but as long as the perspective is critical and the goal is political, economic, and cultural equality for all, then it is feminism.

Notes

1. The Web address for the Electra pages directory is *http://www.electrapages.com.* The Web address for Euronet, a database of women's organizations around the globe, is *http://www.distel.ca/womlist/womlist.html.*

2. Adapted from Lorber 2005.

References

Bauer, Dale M., and Priscilla Wald. 2000. "Complaining, Conversing, Coalescing." *Signs* 25:1299–1303.

Bose, Christine E., and Edna Acosta-Belén. 1995. "Colonialism, Structural Subordination, and Empowerment: Women in the Development Process in Latin America and the Caribbean." In *Women in the Latin American Development Process.* Philadelphia: Temple University Press.

Butler, Judith. 1993. *Bodies That Matter: On the Discursive Limits of "Sex."* New York: Routledge.

Chancer, Lynn. 1992. *Sadomasochism in Everyday Life: The Dynamics of Power and Powerlessness.* New Brunswick, NJ: Rutgers University Press.

Collins, Patricia Hill. 1999. "Moving Beyond Gender: Intersectionality and Scientific Knowledge." In *Revisioning Gender,* edited by Myra Marx Ferree, Judith Lorber, and Beth B. Hess. Thousand Oaks, CA: Sage.

Eisenstein, Hester. 1991. *Gender Shock: Practicing Feminism on Two Continents.* Boston: Beacon.

————. 1996. *Inside Agitators: Australian Femocrats and the State.* Philadelphia: Temple University Press.

Foster, Johanna. 1999. "An Invitation to Dialogue: Clarifying the Position of Feminist Gender Theory in Relation to Sexual Difference Theory." *Gender & Society* 13:431–456.

Haraway, Donna. 1988. "Situated Knowledges: The Science Question in Feminism and the Privilege of Partial Perspective." *Feminist Studies* 14:575–599.

Harding, Sandra. 1998. *Is Science Multicultural? Postcolonialisms, Feminisms, and Epistemologies.* Bloomington: Indiana University Press.

Hawkesworth, Mary. 2004. "The Semiotics of Premature Burial: Feminism in a Postfeminist Age." *Signs* 29:961–985.

Hekman, Susan. 2000. "Beyond Identity: Feminism, Identity and Identity Politics." *Feminist Theory* 1:289–308.

Kimmel, Michael. 2002. Personal communication, Sept. 10.

Lorber, Judith. 1984. *Women Physicians: Careers, Status, and Power.* New York: Tavistock.

————. 2005. *Breaking the Bowls: Degendering and Feminist Change.* New York: W. W. Norton.

Moghadam, Valentine M. 2000. "Transnational Feminist Networks: Collective Action in an Era of Globalization." *International Sociology* 15:57–85.

Namaste, Ki. 1994. "The Politics of Inside/Out: Queer Theory, Poststructuralism, and a Sociological Approach to Sexuality." *Sociological Theory* 12:220–231.

Nicholson, Linda J. 1994. "Interpreting *Gender.*" *Signs* 20:79–105.

Risman, Barbara J. 1998. *Gender Vertigo: American Families in Transition.* New Haven, CT: Yale University Press.

Seidman, Gay W. 1999. "Gendered Citizenship: South Africa's Democratic Transition and the Construction of a Gendered State." *Gender & Society* 13:287–307.

Shaheed, Farida. 1994. "Controlled or Autonomous: Identity and the Experience of the Network, Women Living Under Muslim Laws." *Signs* 19:997–1019.

Smith, Dorothy E. 1990. *Texts, Facts, and Femininity: Exploring the Relations of Ruling.* New York: Routledge.

Stacey, Judith. 1988. "Can There Be a Feminist Ethnography?" *Women's Studies International Forum* 11:21–27.

Thorne, Barrie. 1993. *Gender Play: Boys and Girls in School.* New Brunswick, NJ: Rutgers University Press.

Walby, Sylvia. 2000. "Beyond the Politics of Location: The Power of Argument in a Global Era." *Feminist Theory* 1:189–206.

Williams, Christine L. 1992. "The Glass Escalator: Hidden Advantages for Men in the 'Female' Professions." *Social Problems* 39:253–267.

Young, Iris Marion. 1994. "Gender as Seriality: Thinking About Women as a Social Collective." *Signs* 19:713–738.

Yuval-Davis, Nira. 1997. *Gender & Nation.* Thousand Oaks, CA: Sage. ✦

Glossary

Affirmative action bringing women into occupations and professions dominated by men and promoting them to positions of authority.

Complex inequality the result of the accumulation of advantages that gives people wider social power and the means to dominate those with fewer advantages.

Consciousness-raising groups small-group meetings where the topics of intense discussion come out of the commonalities of women's lives.

Cultural feminism development of a woman's worlds perspective in the creation of women's knowledge and culture.

Deconstruction making visible the gender and sexual symbolism in cultural productions that support beliefs about what is normal and natural.

Difference feminists take the perspective that the experience of female bodies and sexuality produces a common and stable identity among women.

Discourse cultural, social, and symbolic meanings embedded in texts and subtexts.

Dual systems theory marxist feminism's analysis of patriarchy and capitalism as twin systems of men's domination of women.

Flextime workplace policy that offers employees a choice of what hours and what days of the week to work.

Gender a social status, a legal designation, and a personal identity.

Gender balance attaining equality or parity in numbers of women and men throughout society, in their domestic responsibilities, and in their access to work and business opportunities, positions of authority, political power, education, and health care.

Gender diversity attention to the ways that women and men, boys and girls are not homogenous groups but cross-cut by cultures, religions, ethnicities, social class, sexualities, bodies, and other major statuses.

Gender equality treating women and men as legally the same.

Gender equity treating women and men differently but legally equivalent.

Gender feminists take the perspective that sex, sexuality, and gender are constructed in everyday interaction within the constraints of social norms.

Gender ideology the values and beliefs that justify the gendered social order.

Gender visibility attention to the ways in which societies, cultures, groups, and individuals are gendered and how this process comes about and is maintained through the practices of institutions, cultures, groups, and individuals.

Girlie culture in third-wave feminism, sexuality and female empowerment.

Glass ceiling women's restricted entry into top positions, even where most of the workers are women.

Glass escalator rapid promotion of men in women-dominated occupations.

Global economy links countries whose economies focus on service, information, and finances with manufacturing sites and the sources of raw materials in other countries; workers and capital flow between them.

Hegemony social, cultural, and political domination.

Heteronormativity the assumption that everyone is heterosexual.

Intersectionality the combined effects of race, class, gender, sexuality, religion, nationality and other major social statuses in producing systematic advantages and disadvantages.

Job queues the best jobs are kept for men of the dominant racial ethnic group; as jobs lose their prestige and income level, they become open for women and disadvantaged men.

Jouissance women's exultant joy in their sexual bodies.

Kanter hypothesis predicted that as workplaces became more gender-balanced, men would become more accepting of women colleagues.

Mainstreaming gender ensuring that government or organizational policies address women's needs.

Male gaze cultural creation of women as the objects of men's sexual fantasies.

Matrix of domination the combined effects of discrimination by gender, race and ethnicity, social class, religion, nationality, and other disadvantaged statuses.

Mentoring coaching by a senior person about the norms and expectations of workplaces and professional organizations.

Microinequities denigration of women in face-to-face encounters at work, in school, in political and other organizations.

Networking finding out about job and promotion opportunities through word-of-mouth and being recommended by someone already there.

Occupational gender segregation division of jobs into women's work and men's work; men work with men and women work with women.

Occupational gender stratification men dominate the best positions in organizational hierarchies.

Outsider within viewpoint of the disadvantaged in critiquing and changing hegemonic knowledge and culture.

Patriarchy men's systematic and pervasive domination of women as built into the social order; men's control of economic resources, entitlement to sexual services, domination of political processes and positions of authority.

Patriarchal dividend men's privilege and entitlement to women's labor, sexuality, and emotions.

Performativity gender does not exist without doing gender identity and display.

Phallocentric culturally male-centered.

Queer theory challenging the gender and sexual binaries with bisexuality and transgendering.

Queering subverting binary gender and sexual categories through deliberate mixtures of clothing, makeup, jewelry, hair styles, behavior, names, and use of language.

Reserve army of labor married women who primarily work in the home but are hired when the economy needs workers, fired when it does not.

Second shift women's continued responsibility for the maintenance of the household and husband and children even when they have full-time paid jobs.

Sex a complex interplay of genes, hormones, environment, and behavior, with loop-back effects between bodies and society.

Sex roles behavior and attitudes appropriate to women and men that are learned in growing up and applied to adult work and family situations.

Sexuality lustful desire, emotional involvement, and fantasy, as enacted in a variety of long- and short-term intimate relationships.

Social reproduction the work women do in raising children to be future members of society.

Standpoint the view of the world from where you are located physically, mentally, emotionally, and socially.

Subtext hidden meaning in a text, sometimes emerging from what is not in it.

Texts art, literature, the mass media, newspapers, political pronouncements, religious liturgy, and any other social production.

Transgendering living in a gender that is different from that assigned at birth.

Transsexuality surgical and hormonal transformation of bodies to change genders.

Transnational feminist networks organizations that link women in developing and developed regions and address social, economic, and foreign policy issues in supranational terms.

Transversal politics crossing national borders and redrawing political boundaries to create coalitions and bridge divides. ✦

Internet Sources for Research on Women, Men, Feminism, and Gender

Lists of Links

http://globetrotter.berkeley.edu/GlobalGender/index.html

http://libr.org/wss/WSSLinks/index.html

http://research.umbc.edu/~korenman/wmst/

http://www.library.wisc.edu/libraries/WomensStudies/

http://www.mith2.umd.edu/WomensStudies/index.html

http://www.umlib.um.edu.my/olis/women.htm

http://www-unix.umbc.edu/~korenman/wmst/links.html

http://www.york.ac.uk/services/library/subjects/womenint.htm

Women's Studies List (WMST-L) File Collection, listed alphabetically and in topical sub-sections—*http://www.umbc.edu/wmst/wmsttoc.html*

Women- and gender-related email lists— *http://www.umbc.edu/wmst/forums.html*

Archives

Alternative Press Index—*http://www.altpress.org/*

International Information Centre and Archives for the Women's Movement—*http://www.iiav.nl/eng/iiav/index.html*

Jewish Women's Archive—*http://www.jwa.org/index.html*

Lesbian and gay archives— *http://www.archivists.org/saagroups/lagar/guide/guide.htm*

Lesbian Herstory Archives—*http://www.lesbianherstoryarchives.org/*

UN—"Engendering the Global Agenda: The Story of Women and the United Nations"—*http://www.unsystem.org/ngls/documents/publications.en/develop.dossier/dd.06/contents.htm*

Underground Press Collection, 1963–1985—
 http://www.il.proquest.com/research/pd-product-Underground-Press-Collections-51 2.shtml

Women's history—*http://www2.h-net.msu.edu/~women/* and *http://www.cwluherstory.com/*

Women's Liberation Movement—*http://scriptorium.lib.duke.edu/wlm*

Women's studies—
 http://www.library.wisc.edu/libraries/WomensStudies/progs.htm

General Resources

AAUW (Association of American University Women) Research Reports—*http://www.aauw.org*

Convention on the Elimination of Discrimination Against Women (CEDAW)—
 http://www.un.org/womenwatch/daw/cedaw/

Disabled women—*http://www.disabilityhistory.org*

Feminism—*http://www.wwwomen.com/category/femini1.html*

Feminist Academic Press Column—*http://www.litwomen.org/fapc/fapc.html*

Feminist Majority Foundation (FMF) Education Equity program—
 http://www.feminist.org/education

Feminist periodicals—*http://library.wisc.edu/libraries/WomensStudies*

Feminist theory—*http://www.cddc.vt.edu/feminism*

Gender At Work—knowledge network for gender equality and institutional change—*http://www.genderatwork.org*

Gender and society—*http://www.trinity.edu/~mkearl/gender.html*

Institute for Research on Women and Gender—
 http://www.umich.edu/~irwg/index.html

Murray Research Center—*http://www.radcliffe.harvard.edu/murray/*

National Coalition of Anti-Violence Programs (NCAVP)—*http://www.avp.org*

National Council for Research on Women—*http://www.ncrw.org*

NOEMA: The Collaborative Bibliography of Women in Philosophy—
 http://billyboy.ius.indiana.edu/WomeninPhilosophy/WomeninPhilo.html

National Women's Law Center—*http://www.nwlc.org/*

Sociologists for Women in Society—*http://newmedia.colorado.edu/~socwomen/*

Sophia Smith Collection—*http://www.smith.edu/libraries/libs/ssc*

Status of women in U.S. (by states)—*http://www.iwpr.org/states/index.html*

Stop Violence Against Women—*http://www.stopvaw.org/*

Syllabi on the Web for Women- and Gender-Related Courses— *http://www.umbc.edu/cwit/syllabi.html*

UN Division for the Advancement of Women—*http://www.un.org/womenwatch/*

UN Chronicle—United Nations efforts in the advancement of women— *http://www.un.org/Pubs/chronicle/index.html*

UNICEF—Facts and Figures on Women and Girls— *http://www.unicef.org/gender/index_factsandfigures.html*

Understanding Prejudice and Discrimination— *http://www.understandingprejudice.org/*

Violence against women (Amnesty International)— *http://web.amnesty.org/library/index/ENGACT770362004*

Women of achievement and history—*http://www.undelete.org*

Women's athletics—*http://webpages.charter.net/womeninsport/*

Women's Audiovisuals in English (WAVE)— *http://digital.library.wisc.edu/1711.dl/WAVE*

Women of color—*http://www.hsph.harvard.edu/grhf/WoC*

Women's literature—*http://www.litwomen.org*

Women Living Under Muslim Laws international solidarity network— *http://www.wluml.org* (Email: *wluml@wluml.org*)

Women Make Movies—*http://www.wmm.com*

Women Nobel Peace Laureates— *http://www.nobel.se/peace/articles/heroines/index.html#anchor50216*

Women's rights—*http://www.socialrights.org*

Women's Studies Section of the Association of College and Research Libraries— *http://libr.org/wss/*

Women in Print—*http://www.litwomen.org/WIP/index.html*

World's Children 2004: Girls, Education and Development— *http://www.unicef.org/sowc04/*

Health and Reproduction

BioMed Central Open Access journals on women's health— *http://www.biomedcentral.com*

Canadian Women's Health Network—*http://www.cwhn.ca*

Female Genital Mutilation Education and Networking Project— *http://www.fgmnetwork.org/html/index.php*

Gender and Aids—(email) *gender-aids@eforums.healthdev.org*

Global Reproductive Health Forum at Harvard—*http://www.hsph.harvard.edu/grhf*

National Women's Health Information Center—*http://www.4woman.gov*

Planned Parenthood Federation of Canada (PPFC)—sexual and reproductive health and HIV/AIDS—*http://www.ppfc.ca/ppfc/HIV/e/welcome_e.html*

Population Council—*http://www.popcouncil.org*

Pregnancy and Childbirth—
http://www.biomedcentral.com/bmcpregnancychildbirth/

Society for Women's Health Research—*http://www.womenshealthresearch.org*

UNAIDS: World AIDS Campaign 2004—"Women, Girls, HIV and AIDS"—
http://www.unaids.org/wac2004/index_en.htm

Women's Health—*http://womenshealth.medscape.com*

World Health Organization: Fact Sheet on Gender and Disasters—
http://www.who.int/gender/other_health/en/genderdisasters.pdf

Women of Color Health Data Book—
http://www4.od.nih.gov/orwh/wocEnglish2002.pdf

International

Caribbean Association for Feminist Research and Activism (CAFRA)—
http://www.cafra.org

Circular Crossings: Area Studies and Women's Studies—
http://www.womencrossing.org

European women's issues—*http://women-www.uia.ac.be/women*

Global activism—*http://www.womenswire.net*

International Research and Training Institute for the Advancement of Women (INSTRAW)—*http://www.un-instraw.org/*

Women Living Under Muslim Laws (WMUL)—
http://www.wluml.org/english/index.shtml

Women's Edge—*http://www.womensedge.org/index.jsp*

Women's Environment and Development Organization (WEDO)—
http://www.wedo.org

Women and International Development—*http://www.isp.msu.edu/WID*

Women's International Studies Europe (WISE)—
http://www.uia.ac.be/women/wise/

Women Watch: UN Internet Gateway on the Advancement and Empowerment of Women—*http://www.un.org/womenwatch*

Lesbian, Gay, Transgender, Intersex

Gay and Lesbian Atlas—*http://www.urban.org/pubs/gayatlas/*

Gender and Sexuality Studies—*http://vos.ucsb.edu/browse.asp?id=2711*

Guide to Gay and Lesbian Resources—
http://www.lib.uchicago.edu/e/su/gaylesb/glguide.html

Human Rights Campaign (gay marriage vs. civil unions)—*http://www.hrc.org/*

International Homo/Lesbian Information Center and Archive (IHLIA)—
http://www.ihlia.nl

Intersex Society of North America—*http://www.isna.org/drupal/*

Lesbigay scholars directory—*http://newark.rutgers.edu/~lcrew/lbg_edir.html*

Lesbian Battering and Sexual Violence Bibliography—
http://www.loribgirshick.com/bibliography.html

Lesbian, Gay, Bisexual and Transgender Domestic Violence—
http://www.vawnet.org/externallinks/vaworganizations/#lgbti

Minnesota Center Against Violence and Abuse—
http://www.mincava.umn.edu/documents/bibs/samesex/samesex.html

Transgender and feminism—*http://www.transfeminism.org*

Transgender issues—*http://www.ifge.org*

Transgender links—*http://www.gender.org/resources/links.html*

Television programs—*http://www.fau.edu/~jdennis/gaytv/gaytvindex.htm*

Men's Issues

Men's bibliography: A comprehensive bibliography of writing on men,
masculinities, gender, and sexualities—*http://www.xyonline.net/mensbiblio/*

Men Can Stop Rape—*http://www.mencanstoprape.org/*

Men's health—*http://menshealthnetwork.org*

NOMAS: National Organization for Men Against Sexism—
http://www.nomas.org/sys-tmpl/html/

Toolkit for Working With Men and Boys to Prevent Gender-Based Violence—
http://www.endabuse.org/toolkit

White Ribbon Campaign (Men against violence against women)—
http://www.whiteribbon.ca

Science and Technology

Center for the Study of Women, Science, and Technology—
http://www.wst.gatech.edu
Information society technologies and women—*http://www.sigis-ist.org*

Online Journals

AVIVA—*http://www.aviva.org*
Feminism and Nonviolence Studies—*http://www.fnsa.org*
Femspec (feminist science fiction)—*http://csuohio.edu/femspec*
Fierce—*http://www.fiercemag.com/home.html*
Genders—*http://www.genders.org*
Thirdspace—*http://www.thirdspace.ca*
Women's eNews—*http://www.womensenews.org* ✦

Index